entrepreneurship

A SMALL BUSINESS APPROACH

Charles E. Bamford
Queens University of Charlotte

Garry D. Bruton
Texas Christian University

McGraw Hill

Connect
Learn
Succeed™

ENTREPRENEURSHIP: A SMALL BUSINESS APPROACH
Published by McGraw-Hill, a business unit of The McGraw-Hill Companies, Inc., 1221 Avenue of the Americas, New York, NY, 10020. Copyright © 2011 by The McGraw-Hill Companies, Inc.

Some ancillaries, including electronic and print components, may not be available to customers outside the United States.

This book is printed on acid-free paper.

1 2 3 4 5 6 7 8 9 0 DOW/DOW 1 0 9 8 7 6 5 4 3 2 1 0

ISBN 978-0-07-340311-3
MHID 0-07-340311-3

Vice president/Editor in chief: *Elizabeth Haefele*
Vice president/Director of marketing: *John E. Biernat*
Sponsoring editor: *Alice Harra*
Developmental editor: *Kristin Bradley*
Editorial coordinator: *Vincent Bradshaw*
Marketing manager: *Keari Green*
Lead media producer: *Damian Moshak*
Digital developmental editor: *Kevin White*
Director, Editing/Design/Production: *Jess Ann Kosic*
Lead project manager: *Kathryn W. Mikulic*
Senior production supervisor: *Janean A. Utley*
Senior Designer: *Marianna Kinigakis*
Senior photo research coordinator: *Jeremy Cheshareck*
Photo researcher: *David Tietz, Editorial Image, LLC*
Media project manager: *Cathy L. Tepper*
Cover design: *Daniel Krueger*

Typeface: *11/13 Minion*
Compositor: *Laserwords Private Limited*
Printer: *R. R. Donnelley*
Cover image: © *James W. Porter/Corbis*

Library of Congress Cataloging-in-Publication Data

Bamford, Charles E.
    Entrepreneurship : a small business approach / Charles E. Bamford, Garry D. Bruton. — 1st ed.
        p. cm.
    Includes index.
    ISBN-13: 978-0-07-340311-3 (alk. paper)
    ISBN-10: 0-07-340311-3 (alk. paper)
    1. New business enterprises. 2. Small business. 3. Success in business. I. Bruton, Garry D. II. Title.
HD62.5.B36 2011
658.1′1—dc22

                                        2009046143

The Internet addresses listed in the text were accurate at the time of publication. The inclusion of a Web site does not indicate an endorsement by the authors or McGraw-Hill, and McGraw-Hill does not guarantee the accuracy of the information presented at these sites.

www.mhhe.com

To Yvonne: The book is done, let's go to Vegas!
To our team at McGraw-Hill: Thank you so much. This process was
a pleasure and the credit for this effort goes to you.

Charles E. Bamford

To my parents, John C. and Ruth W. Bruton, who empowered me
with their love, encouragement, and support.

Garry Bruton

Dr. Charles E. Bamford   Dr. Chuck Bamford is a Professor and the Dennis Thompson Chair of Entrepreneurial Leadership at the McColl School of Business at Queens University of Charlotte. He earned his AS degree at Northern Virginia Community College, a BS degree at the University of Virginia (McIntire School of Business), an MBA at Virginia Tech, and a Ph.D. in Strategy & Entrepreneurship at the University of Tennessee. During a twelve-year span prior to pursuing his Ph.D., he held positions managing Business Analysis (Mergers & Acquisitions, Dispositions, and Small Business Consulting) for Dominion Bankshares Corporation (now Wells Fargo Corporation). Other positions during his business career included Director of Corporate Training, Systems Analyst, COBOL programmer, and full-time instructor in the early 1980s at Virginia Western Community College..

His research has been published *in the Strategic Management Journal, Journal of Business Venturing, Entrepreneurship Theory & Practice, Journal of Business Research, Journal of Business Strategies, Journal of Technology Transfer, and Journal of Small Business Management.*

Chuck has taught courses in Strategic Management and Entrepreneurship at the undergraduate, graduate, and executive levels. His teaching experience includes courses taught at universities in Scotland, Hungary, and the Czech Republic. Prior to joining Queens University he held positions as an Associate Professor at Texas Christian University and at the University of Richmond. He has taught Executive MBA courses at TCU, The University of Notre Dame, Tulane University, and at Queens University of Charlotte.

Dr. Bamford is an active consultant whose clients have included numerous small business start-ups, as well as large regional and international businesses.

Chuck has won fifteen individual teaching excellence awards during his career, including seven Executive MBA Teacher of the Year Awards. He is also a Noble Foundation Fellow in Teaching Excellence.

Dr. Garry D. Bruton

Dr. Garry Bruton is aProfessor of Entrepreneurship and Strategy at the M. J. Neeley School of Business at Texas Christian University in Forth Worth, Texas where he holds the Fehmi Zeko Faculty Fellowship and serves as Academic Director of the Neeley Entrepreneurship Program. He received his Ph.D. in 1989 from Oklahoma State University. Prior to that time he had received his MBA from George Washington University, and his BA with Honors from the University of Oklahoma. He worked as a bank economist for one of the leading commercial banks in the Southwest United States prior to pursuing his doctorate.

Professor Bruton has published over 75 academic articles in some of the leading academic publications for small business and entrepreneurship, including the *Academy of Management Journal, Strategic Management Journal, Journal of International Business, Journal of Business Venturing,* and *Entrepreneurship Theory & Practice.* Garry currently serves as editor of the *Academy of Management Perspectives* and is President of the Asia Academy of Management. He serves on six additional editoral boards. His research interests focus on entrepreneurship in emerging economies.

Dr. Bruton's publications have been used in some of the leading MBA programs around the world and writings have appeared in the Wall Street Journal. He was selected as the first holder of the Kathryn and Craig Hall Distinguished Chair in Entrepreneurship in 2005, sponsored by the Fulbright Program.

Professor Bruton has taught around the world including courses in Russia at the Moscow Institute of Electronics Technology; at Wirtschaftsuniversitat-Wein, Vienna, Austria; and at Chinese University of Hong Kong. The courses he has taught at the graduate and undergraduate levels have included small business management, entrepreneurship, venture capital, international strategy, strategy, and international management.

He has won a variety of teaching and research awards at each of the schools with which he has been associated. In addition, he has advised a number of MBA teams that have participated and placed in regional and national competitions for business plans and case analysis.

(brief) table of contents

table of (contents)

PART 2: Due Diligence on the Business Idea
chapter 4

EXTERNAL ANALYSIS   62

Defining Your Industry   64

Defining Your Customers   66

Developing the Information for the External Analysis of Competitors   68

Developing a Competitive Map   70

Additional Issues for External Analysis   73

Competitive Advantage   75

chapter 5

BUSINESS MISSION AND STRATEGY   82

Mission Statements   84

Sustainable Competitive Advantage   91

Step 1: Develop a List of Your Business's Assets and Capabilities   92

Step 2: Split the List into Standard and Extraordinary Assets   92

Step 3: Evaluate Competitiveness of Extraordinary Resources/ Capabilities   94

Strategy   95

chapter 14

FRANCHISING AND PURCHASING AN EXISTING BUSINESS   288

Have you ever thought about the strip mall closest to your house? It probably has the most convenient place to pick up an emergency gallon of milk or drop off your dry cleaning. If it is like many strip malls, it has that empty storefront that changes about once a year and has been everything from a pet store to a takeout pizza parlor. Why have some businesses been in that strip mall as long as you can remember while others change with the seasons?

Success or failure as an entrepreneur is not a mystery. It is, however, a potent mix of hard work, thoughtful planning, skilled decision making, and a little bit of luck. Understanding this formula, and ultimately succeeding in small business, is the key learning outcome for *Entrepreneurship: A Small Business Approach*. The target audience is as varied as the small business model itself. This text strives to make the core concepts of business as applicable to a student taking a few required business courses as it is to students with a long-term small business goal.

Entrepreneurship Is Not a Scary Word

If you are taking this course, it is likely that you fall into one of two categories:

Category 1: You want to be your own boss one day. You have a long-range plan to start (and succeed) at your own business venture, and you see this course as groundwork for that plan.

Category 2: You have to take a business course as a requirement. You don't want own your own business; you just want to graduate, and you need this course to do it.

The good news is that regardless of which category you fall into, this course has something for you. If you consider yourself a member of Category 1, you know why you're here. This text will outline the key components involved in starting your own business, along with explaining core business concepts that apply to all businesses.

For those of you who are in Category 2, there are real, applicable reasons to take this course. Since 50 percent of all U.S. employees work for small businesses, the odds are at some point in your career you will work for a small business. Small businesses are everywhere and encompass doctors' offices, law firms, construction companies, hospitals, and the makers and sellers of a myriad of other goods and services that impact our daily lives. Understanding the components of success and failure for your future employer makes you a better employee.

Chapter Outline

To develop the understanding necessary to design, start, and manage a small business, we have organized the material into 14 chapters. These chapters are in turn organized into five major sections. The first section sets the groundwork needed prior to developing a new business idea.

Many individuals have considered starting a new business when an opportunity was presented to them or they were frustrated by their current positions. However, prior to this step there are several areas that demand examination. The potential entrepreneur(s) should carefully examine her personal propensities or willingness to take on risk. Chapter 1 provides you with an understanding of the impact of small business in society. Chapter 2 develops the constructs necessary to evaluate individual needs/desires, as well as the group dynamics so common in the start-up of a new venture. Chapter 3 focuses on how to generate ideas for a small business.

The next section of the text is entitled "Due Diligence." **Due Diligence** is a process/terminology that arises out of mergers & acquisitions (M&A). In the process of an acquisition, each firm examines the other business's books, strategies, people, environment, etc., in order to determine a fair price. Chapter 4 launches the first step in the due diligence process by establishing a set of methods for examining the environment in which the new business might operate. Chapter 5 develops the crucial steps necessary for the development of a strategy, including the firm's mission. Chapter 6 is a detailed examination of the tools to help the small business person conduct the initial financial evaluation of the small business the individual is planning.

Section 3 is designed to put some action to all the analysis completed thus far. The difference between people with good ideas and those that are entrepreneurs is the *action* of establishing and running a business. Chapter 7 reviews the legal frameworks for a new small business, regulations that impact the operation of any business, and the basics of developing and executing contracts. Chapter 8 begins the examination of the actual business operations of the small business. Finally, establishing the accounting and financial framework crucial for a business is discussed in Chapter 9.

The fourth section examines operational issues as the firm begins to expand. The topics included are the establishment of the human resources (Chapter 10), marketing (Chapter 11), and tracking/monitoring (Chapter 12), which includes obtaining financing for the firm. Each of these topics is uniquely important in the early growth of a new small business.

The last section examines two other issues critical to a small business. Chapter 13 examines a wide variety of ways for exiting a business. Chapter 14 looks at two means to buy into a business rather than starting it from scratch. They are buying an existing business and franchising.

Key Text Features

Each chapter includes key features that help illuminate important ideas in interesting and applied ways.

Chapter Opening Vignettes

Every chapter begins with a profile of a real small business. These realistic portraits provide an overview of both the everyday successes and the failures associated with small business ownership.

Philo Asian Grille

This running case looks at chapter topics within the context of a small business. Each chapter provides a new aspect of small business to consider, ultimately giving you a fully realized look at a small business.

Rodriquez Family Auto Repair

This running case examines many of the same elements as the Philo Asian Grille Case, but adds the secondary considerations involved with running a family business.

Ethical Challenges Boxes

These dilemma-based questions look at ethical realities within the successful creation of a small business and challenge students to examine the moral complexities of small businesses.

End-of-Chapter Cases

These longer cases look at real businesses within the context of chapter subjects. They examine a real entrepreneur and how that owner approached the small business and the struggles associated with success. They offer practical, real-world examples of core concepts within the chapter.

Supplementary Materials

Test Bank: Every chapter provides a series of test questions, available in our Test Bank. Questions are organized by Learning Outcome and Bloom's Taxonomy. A Test Table aligns questions with the content and makes it easy for you to determine the questions you want to include on tests and quizzes.

Instructor's Manual: The IM outlines course materials, additional in-class activities, and support for classroom use of the text. It has been organized by Learning Outcome to both give instructors a basic outline of the chapter and assist in all facets of instruction. For every question posed in the text, the IM provides a viable answer. Ultimately, this will be to an instructor's greatest advantage in using all materials to reach all learners.

PowerPoints: PowerPoint slides include important chapter content and teaching notes tied directly to Learning Outcomes. They are de-signed to engage students in classroom discussions about the text.

Asset Map: We know that instructors' time is valuable. To help you prepare, we have created an Asset Map. The Asset Map identifies the chapter, Learning Outcome, page number, and exactly which supplements are available for you to use.

***Everyday Edisons* Videos:** Series videos from the popular, Emmy award winning PBS series *Everyday Edisons* use inventors as a platform to discuss entrepreneurship. Each video explains the business logistics of the creative process and is accompanied by a teaching note in the Instructor's Manual.

Business Videos: A combination of small business profiles and scripted business obstacles provide an added framework for learning entrpreneurship principles. These videos will also have applied teaching notes in the Instructor's Manual.

Outcomes

Our ultimate goal is that students will leave this class not only with a much greater appreciation for what it takes to start a small business, but with the foundations necessary to actually start that business. The small businesses that surround you every day did not come into operation or stay in operation by chance. Instead, it took tremendous effort and work for these businesses to exist and succeed.

We expect that some of you will be able to take what we present here as a foundation for your own business. Small business entrepreneurs are the economic backbone of this nation and the central hope for its future.

entrepreneurship

A SMALL BUSINESS APPROACH

Introduction

learning outcomes

After studying this chapter, you will be able to:

1.1 Explain the rationale behind starting a small business.

1.2 Discuss the history of entrepreneurship in the United States.

1.3 Identify the type of people who are small business owners.

1.4 Describe the impact of small business on society.

1.5 Relate the worldwide scope of small businesses.

1.6 Define small business.

Stoner, Inc.

Successful small business requires a small group of people to run the multiple dimensions of business very well. Large firms have many employees to handle the myriad of business issues that need to be addressed. However, the small firm has fewer people and fewer excess resources, so if it does a task poorly, the consequences can be more serious.

Stoner, Inc. is located in Lancaster County, Pennsylvania, and manufactures specialized cleaners, lubricants, and coatings for business and consumers. The firm was founded by Paul Stoner 60 years ago. The firm today is headed by his grandson, Robert Ecklin, Jr. The firm is the smallest firm ever to have won the Malcolm Baldrige National Quality Award. This award is given to those firms in the United States which represent the best quality practices in the country.

The senior management at Stoner typically have numerous years' experience at the firm. Thus, there is strong consistency in the firm. In part, this consistency comes from the fact that the firm provides a performance-based bonus system that allows workers to share in the success of the company. One key value of the firm is exceeding customers' expectations. As a result, the firm has a customer retention rate of over 90 percent.

The firm relies on direct mail, catalogs, magazine advertising, and telephone selling. The catalogs developed by the firm have been recognized by the judges at *Catalog Age* as among the best in the nation.

Source: www.stonersolutions.com.

LO 1.1 Why Start a Business?

Small business is the growth engine of the U.S. economy. To illustrate this, consider the following statistics from the **United States Small Business Administration (SBA)**[1]:

1. Approximately 22.9 million small businesses were in existence in the United States in 2002.
2. Approximately 75 percent of all net new jobs are added by small businesses.
3. Small businesses represent 99.7 percent of all employers.
4. They employ 50 percent of the private work force.
5. They represent 97 percent of all U.S. exporters.
6. They pay 45 percent of all U.S. private payroll.

Beyond the statistics, there are countless stories of small business success in every community around the world. Some of these firms ultimately grow to be very large. For example, Google was formed in 1998 by two students, Sergey Brin and Larry Page. These two did not set out to establish a firm that would come to dominate the search engines on the Internet; instead, they simply sought to establish a small business to meet their needs and those of their friends. In the past 10 years, Google has come to lead the industry, and the company has annual sales of over $10 billion. While Google's growth was amazingly fast, this story is not unique. Recall from history that entrepreneurs like Henry Ford (Ford Motor Company), Steve Jobs (Apple computers), Frank Perdue (Perdue Farms chicken), Ray Kroc (McDonald's), H. Ross Perot (Electronic Data Systems or EDS), Muhammad Yunus (Grameen Bank microfinance group), Ralph Lauren (fashion), Sam Walton (Walmart), Estee Lauder (cosmetics), Oprah Winfrey (media), and Richard Branson (Virgin) all started out as small business owners. Every business that you can name today started out as a small business. Each one was the brainchild of a single individual or a small group of people. This does not mean that every small business will ultimately grow to dominate some aspect of world business. What it does mean is that small business is the foundation for all businesses. Some grow large; some do not. Regardless, they all initially go through a process much like the one you will study in this book, and that process of business development is quite different from those followed by established businesses. We suggest that the process of developing, initiating, and running a new business is its own unique area of study.

Contrast the success of small business in the United States with the facts that **Fortune 500** companies employ fewer total employees today than they did 10 years ago, and that 10 years ago, that figure was smaller than it was 20 years ago. There is a consistent pattern of decline in employment by large firms in this nation's economy. The decline in large firms has been offset by a growth in small business.

The success of small businesses is derived in part because they are simply more efficient in many ways than their large corporate counterparts. On average, small firms produce 13 to 14 more patents per

United States Small Business Administration (SBA)

The agency officially organized in 1953 as a part of the Small Business Act of July 30, 1953, to "aid, counsel, assist and protect, insofar as is possible, the interests of small business concerns." It is a wealth of information and assistance at all levels of organizational development and management. See also www.sba.gov.

Frank Perdue is an excellent example of a small business owner with a vision that exceeded expectations. Can you think of other examples of small businesses that grew into major corporations?

Fortune 500

The list published annually by Fortune Magazine of the 500 largest corporations (by sales) in the United States.

employee than do large firms, and those patents (legal protection for an innovation) are historically among the 1 percent most utilized.[2] There is also evidence that this research impact is increasing as the percentage of firms with high impact is increasingly coming from small firms.[3]

Large firms have the ability to obtain **economies of scale** in some industries. In other words, large firms can do some things more efficiently due to their ability to operate on a large scale.[4] For example, advertising is typically much cheaper per unit if purchased in large volume. Thus, a large firm like Walmart can buy its advertising much cheaper on a per unit basis than can a small retailer. Similarly, in manufacturing it is often much cheaper to produce large volumes of a product than to produce small volumes. This is the reason that small car manufacturers must charge an extraordinarily high price to cover their costs.

Years ago those apparent efficiencies led some economists to predict that small business would be largely replaced by a much smaller number of large businesses. Instead, the ability of small business to respond more quickly and to operate more effectively has led to a growth in small business rather than a decline. Even in a mature, established industry like banking, each year there are almost 200 new, independent banks born in the United States.[5] So the growth of small business occurs not only in new, expanding industries but also in mature industries.

This text develops the methods, applications, and processes that lead to the idea generation, investigation, start-up, and successful management of a new small business. We firmly believe that the development and implementation of a new business is part art and part science. This text lays out a process for the "science" of forming and managing a new small business in a clear, sequential manner that is rich in its practical application as well as well grounded in research. The "art" is a matter of practice, example, and the skill of the founder or founders of the new business. The text encourages you as you go through the process of developing your ideas and work to develop your own business plan. While we will not be with you as you actually found your business, the goal of this text is to help you have everything as well developed as possible before you actually found a business. Generally, more than 50 percent of new businesses fail during their first four years, and in some industries that number tops 80 percent.[6] We believe that the principal way to be a part of the group that survives and thrives is to thoroughly plan and lay a solid basis for the business.

economies of scale
A condition that allows the long-run average cost to continue downward as production increases. It leads (in its most extreme case) to a condition where a single firm making 100 percent of the product is the most efficient. In reality this condition is moderated by the ability of management to control the size.

LO 1.2 A Brief History of Small Business in the United States

Before we start looking at small business today, it is important to note that small business has always been a critical part of the country's success. Alexis de Tocqueville was a Frenchman who toured the United States in the early 1830s and wrote a famous analysis of the country. One of his observations was that the United States was not so much a nation with ventures that were marvelous in their grandeur, but instead, a nation of innumerable small ventures. Thus, the history of the United States has always been intimately tied to small business. In fact, until the mid1880s, almost all businesses in the United States were small businesses.

The 1880s saw the initial development of the nation's large industrial base. It was from these beginnings that the robber barons developed. We associate their names today not only with great success but also with great abuses in business. They took advantage of the economies of scale that were suddenly possible with the industrial age and quickly came to dominate new sectors of the economy (as, for example, Andrew Carnegie's domination of the new steel industry). However, the robber barons were coming to dominate industrial sectors that had not existed historically, so they generally did not put small operations out of business. In fact, small business continued to thrive during these times as new businesses grew up to serve the needs of these new industrial sectors.[7]

The Great Depression of the 1930s was harder on small business than on large business, and it encouraged industrial concentration. The result was that following World War II, small business as a percentage of the economic output of the United States began to decline. It was during this time that Charles Wilson, Secretary of Defense for President Eisenhower, made the famous statement that "what is good for General Motors is good for the nation." The implication was that what was good for big business would be good for all of the people in the country.

In the late 1970s and early 1980s, the nation was in economic turmoil. Many of the large firms that had grown to dominate the U.S. economy were having difficulty. Entire industries, such as steel and automobile manufacturing, were in decline. It was during this time that President Jimmy Carter described the country as in a "malaise." The Japanese were in the dominant economic position in the world, and the widely discussed fear was that the United States was in decline much as the British had been 100 years earlier. However, the decline of the large multinational firms in the United States opened new opportunities which small businesses rose to fill. The economic growth and success that the nation experiences today is due to small firms that grew very rapidly, such as Microsoft, and a vast number of small businesses that are still small that push innovation and efficiency to new levels.

Therefore, as you begin your study of small business you should recognize that you are examining a domain that has historically been the backbone of the economic success of the nation. Small business today continues to play a dominant role in the ability of the nation to adapt quickly and to make economic progress. The time line of business in the United States (Figure 1.1) highlights the central role of small business. Note that some firms have been in operation since before the signing of the Declaration of Independence.

LO 1.3 Who are Small Business Owners Today?

Small business owners can be motivated by as many different factors as there are small business owners. However, there is some consistency within the variety of motivations. Particularly, small business owners have two common motivations: (1) the desire to be their own bosses,

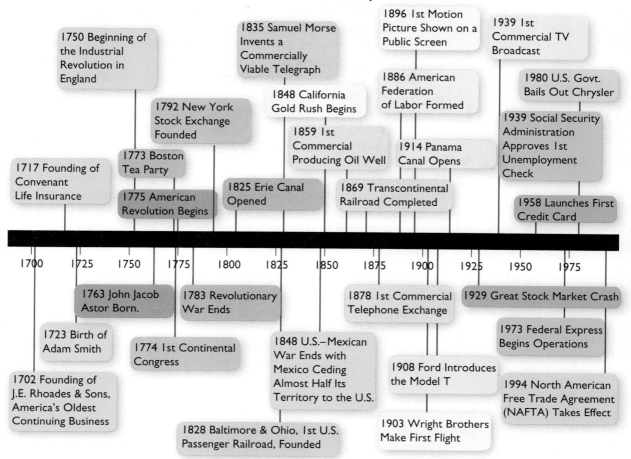

U.S. Business History

1750 Beginning of the Industrial Revolution in England

1835 Samuel Morse Invents a Commercially Viable Telegraph

1896 1st Motion Picture Shown on a Public Screen

1939 1st Commercial TV Broadcast

1886 American Federation of Labor Formed

1980 U.S. Govt. Bails Out Chrysler

1792 New York Stock Exchange Founded

1848 California Gold Rush Begins

1939 Social Security Administration Approves 1st Unemployment Check

1717 Founding of Convenant Life Insurance

1773 Boston Tea Party

1859 1st Commercial Producing Oil Well

1914 Panama Canal Opens

1775 American Revolution Begins

1825 Erie Canal Opened

1869 Transcontinental Railroad Completed

1958 Launches First Credit Card

1700   1725   1750   1775   1800   1825   1850   1875   1900   1925   1950   1975

1763 John Jacob Astor Born.

1783 Revolutionary War Ends

1878 1st Commercial Telephone Exchange

1929 Great Stock Market Crash

1723 Birth of Adam Smith

1774 1st Continental Congress

1973 Federal Express Begins Operations

1702 Founding of J.E. Rhoades & Sons, America's Oldest Continuing Business

1848 U.S.–Mexican War Ends with Mexico Ceding Almost Half Its Territory to the U.S.

1908 Ford Introduces the Model T

1994 North American Free Trade Agreement (NAFTA) Takes Effect

1828 Baltimore & Ohio, 1st U.S. Passenger Railroad, Founded

1903 Wright Brothers Make First Flight

Figure 1.1
Business Time Line
The time line of business provides both constants and natural evolution.

which allows them the opportunity to act in the manner that they think is best for themselves and their family, as well as for the business; and (2) the potential for significant personal and financial rewards.

Small businesses clearly provide the setting where business owners can be their own bosses. As we will discuss in Chapter 2, small business owners are the most important factor in the business's success. The new business owners have both the opportunity and the responsibility to be their own bosses. However, while the small business owners want this independence, they also needs to recognize they are not alone in the business; there are other important **stakeholders.** These are individuals or other organizations that may impact the success of the business. Relationships such as those with key suppliers and customers are critical to the success of the new business.

It is true that the rewards of owning a small business extend far beyond the financial; just one of these is the joy of building something. However, the financial rewards can be stunning. In their book entitled *The Millionaire Next Door,* Thomas Stanley and William Danko highlight statistics that demonstrate the potential for financial rewards from small business.[8] For example, they highlight that almost two-thirds of the millionaires in the United States are self-employed, despite the fact that self-employed people make up less than 20 percent of the

stakeholders

Individuals or other organizations that impact the success of a business.

THE
PHENOMENAL
#1
BESTSELLER

THE

MILLIONAIRE

THE SURPRISING

SECRETS OF

AMERICA'S WEALTHY

NEXT

DOOR

Thomas J. Stanley, Ph.D.
William D. Danko, Ph.D.

MORE THAN THREE YEARS ON THE
NEW YORK TIMES BESTSELLER LIST!

The Millionaire Next Door is a fascinating study of success stories associated with small business ventures. What would you consider to be a successful small business venture?

EXERCISE 1

1. Name some successful small business entrepreneurs that you personally know.
2. What types of businesses do they run?
3. Why do you think they are successful?
4. How would they define success?

workers in America. They go on to highlight that 75 percent of these self-employed millionaires are entrepreneurs, with the other 25 percent being self-employed professionals, such as doctors and accountants. Thus, the vast majority of millionaires in this country are entrepreneurs. These are the individuals who start a business, run it well, and over time build their financial success. Thus, the majority of millionaires are actually the individuals you know in your community that are successful small business owners. In many cases, the businesses they run are not high-technology, high-profile types of businesses, but they are nonetheless solid businesses that mow lawns, repair plumbing and electricity, or provide some other highly valued service or product. These individuals achieved this success by taking the significant step to actually start and run a business. The same step you are taking in this class.

Some of the financial rewards are overwhelming for successful entrepreneurs. For example, Bill Gates (Microsoft), Michael Dell (Dell Computer), and Richard Marsh (Tritech International) started out with small endeavors aimed at exploiting an opportunity. Michael Dell started his business in his dorm room, putting computers together for friends and other students. The business kept growing with some skilled management and a favorable business model, so that today it is a multi-billion-dollar business. While Dell Corporation is large today, it started out, like virtually every other business, as a small business.

LO I.4 How Does Society Benefit?

Small business development is an important driver of the economic success of a community, a region, and a state. As a result, civic leaders increasingly look to small business as a means to promote economic strength. There are some well-known areas where such efforts have been widely publicized, such as North Carolina's research triangle; Austin, Texas; the Denver–Fort Collins Innovation Corridor; and Boston's 128 corridor. These areas are well recognized for small businesses generating new employment, providing a growing tax revenue base, and providing a basis for significant improvements to the area's economic vitality.[9] The success of these areas has encouraged others to seek to promote entrepreneurship and small business to a much greater degree. For example, the Chicagoland Entrepreneurship Center estimates that small business growth over the past 10 to 15 years has outstripped the rest of Chicago's growth by 20 percent or more.[10] This success has led to an expansion of entrepreneurship and small business to a large number of areas beyond Chicago, which may not have emphasized it in the past.

Small business acts as a catalyst for societal change in other ways as well. Small business has the ability to garner profits in markets that have been ignored by large corporations. Small business is more flexible, and its owners and employees have an understanding of the local community not easily obtained by a large conglomerate. For example, after a large military base or factory closes, there is economic damage to that region, as the businesses that catered to the base or factory must either reset their target market or close their doors. Examinations of such areas suggest that a crisis like this can lead to the formation of a much higher level of new small businesses. Those individuals who have lost their jobs tend to form new businesses which, in many cases, can turn the economic fortunes of the area around.[11]

In 2001, the federal General Accounting Office did an analysis of the impact of the closure of military bases. They found that in areas such as Salt Lake City, Kansas City, and San Jose, the areas around the bases had unemployment rates lower than the national average and income growth higher than the national average. There had been large initial job losses in these communities; however, the individuals involved and the community leaders had responded to the closing of the bases with tax breaks and programs to support the development of new businesses. The result was that numerous new small businesses rose up to fill the economic gap that had resulted from the closing of the bases.[12]

Some interesting initial evidence indicates that small business has the same potential to turn around the economy of a historically depressed area. For example, beginning in the 1970s and continuing into the early 1980s, Pittsburgh, Pennsylvania, was severely hurt by the decline in the steel industry. However, today, the growth in small businesses (many of those businesses in high-technology domains) has largely offset those troubles.[13]

Small business provides more than just jobs; it also provides a means to meet the varied demands that individuals face in a society. Individuals can become frustrated with large corporations over the lack of promotion opportunities, or the inflexibility of the corporations in dealing with the needs of family and children. Starting a new business may allow individuals to meet these demands in their lives in a way that large corporations cannot.

The number of women starting new businesses has increased to the point where they are now the largest single group of new business founders. In part, this growth has come from the fact that women are often frustrated by what is referred to as the "glass ceiling." This refers to the fact that women, like minorities, may be hired by large firms but experience real limits placed on their advancement. As a result, these individuals may leave the large firms and start their own small firms. Women entrepreneurs also start small businesses to allow them to have greater control over their lives so that they can better manage such circumstances as their family and children's needs. A small business

What is the goal of business? Milton Friedman (among others) has argued that the only goal of business should be to make a profit. If the business owner pursues anything other than a singular focus on profit, then that person is diverting the money from the investors who rightfully own that money. On the other hand, a wide variety of people have argued that all businesses are part of a larger society and, as a result, should seek not only to make a profit, but also to try to better society by providing employment, making wise use of resources, giving back to the community, and supporting the efforts of the community to provide a better place to live for all people.

Does a business have an ethical obligation to do more than observe the laws of a society? While the absolute minimum requirement may be that a business-person must observe the laws, ethical decision making is the conscious examination of a wide variety of issues, including the purpose of the business. All business owners need to examine these issues, and different ones will likely reach different answers.

DISCUSSION QUESTIONS

1. How do you weigh the importance in business of making a profit versus providing broader benefits to society?
2. Do you believe that obeying the laws is sufficient for making an ethical choice?

---

may provide a valuable safety valve so that the citizens of a society can address the demands and needs in their lives.

To illustrate, consider Charlotte Fowkes. She was fired from a job with a large corporation when (in their opinion) she took too much time off to care for a sick child. As a result, she took her skills as a computer programmer and developed a new business called Baby-Cakes (www.Baby-Cakes.com). The firm sells goods for a baby that are packaged together to look like a cake. For example, her tallest cake is 22 inches tall and is made up of 55 diapers. Around those diapers are 25 to 30 other items for the baby that vary with the theme of the cake. In the well-known HBO television series *Sex and the City*, which is still popular in reruns, one of the actors in the show was having a baby, and a Baby-Cake was the focus of the episode. Ms. Fowkes has also been featured on the well-received TV show *The View*, whose primary audience is women. The business has continued to grow and prosper—but for Ms. Fowkes, it is the flexibility to be with her family that continues to be a major attraction of the business.[14]

Therefore, small business provides valuable benefits not only to the individuals that start the business but also to society. Individuals who may feel they have progressed as far as they can in a corporation or wish to have more flexibility for their family find that small business gives them new options to do things for themselves and overcome those obstacles.

LO 1.5 Small Business Around the World

Small business is critically important not just in the United States but also around the world. The World Bank estimates that one of the strongest factors in the growth in any nation's GNP is the presence of small- and medium-sized enterprises (SMEs). Today there are widespread efforts in almost all nations to encourage the development of small and medium enterprises. These governmental efforts range from very small contributions of capital or time to large, multidimensional programs that cross the boundaries of multiple nations.

EXERCISE 2

1. What motivates your interest in small business?
2. What opportunities do you see in your community?
3. Have these opportunities attracted other businesses, large or small? Why or why not?

Some of the efforts to encourage SMEs around the world are quite small, but still have a big impact. For example, microloan programs have been in existence for years to encourage self-development. These loans are often for only a few dollars each and are made directly to entrepreneurs, particularly women. The businesses founded through such loans are often as simple as delivering lunches, sewing baskets, or washing clothes. However, the success of such loans has been substantial, with great strides being made in many desperately poor nations. It is interesting that the repayment rate on such loans is typically 99 to 100 percent, a much higher repayment rate than on most types of loans. The success of these loans has resulted in an increasing dedication of the United States aid budget to microloan grants for developing nations.[15]

At the other extreme are nations that have prepared a full range of programs to encourage new venture start-ups. A program underway in Singapore is aimed at encouraging high-technology ventures among highly educated individuals. The government is providing a range of services and facilities to assist in the development of these ventures and encourage the founding of firms that might result. While these two examples are at different extremes, they both demonstrate a high level of interest and investment by governments in small business initiation. The result of these efforts is that the pace of small business start-ups is increasing around the world.

LO 1.6 What Is a Small Business?

It is clear from the discussion above that small business has benefits for individuals and society within the United States and around the world. But what do we mean when we say "small business"? For classification purposes, the United States government considers any business with fewer than 500 employees to be a small business. We would suggest that a business with almost 500 employees is actually a large firm requiring formal personnel policies, specialized groups, and an administrative structure that is in no way close to the reality of most small businesses. For the vast majority of students in this class, the businesses you will form will have far fewer than 500 employees.

We suggest that there is a further level of definition that will provide some insight into studying small business. You will hear these types of businesses referred to as entrepreneurial businesses, as small businesses, or sometimes as small-to-medium-sized businesses or enterprises (SMB or SME). These terms are roughly equivalent, and do not specify the differences between the two main types of new business. Without an understanding of these two main types, it is difficult to discuss new ventures clearly. While all these types of businesses are founded by an entrepreneur or an entrepreneurial team, each type then takes a unique track. The two common types of new businesses are described below.

The first type is formed as a high-growth, often high-tech venture that has several unique characteristics and is generally referred to as an entrepreneurial firm:

1. The businesses are well-funded by venture capital or "angel Investment" In fact, without such capital it is virtually impossible to begin this particular type of venture.* Venture capitalists are a specialized type of investor; they typically do not invest less than $1 million and expect extraordinary returns.

2. The businesses are formed with a **harvest plan** in place; this is a plan to exit the business that allows the founders to take advantage of growth. A harvest plan may include selling the business to another firm, selling it to a group of investors, or even participating in an IPO (a public offering of stock). Size is the deciding metric in a potential public offering or sale to a larger organization.

3. As a result of the harvest plan, these firms are organized to grow as quickly as possible and are generally heavily laden with debt.

4. They have a developed organizational structure.

5. They often hire an experienced president to grow the company.

6. They tend to start operations in multiple locations simultaneously.

7. They are inherently risky operations whose growth is dependent on the exploitation of unknowns in the market (a new invention, unique patents, etc.).

8. These businesses either start or grow quickly to employ a relatively large number of employees.

The second type of business is a more common type of business, most often referred to as a small business startup, and is defined by these characteristics:

1. The start-up is self-funded or closely funded.

2. The development plan is oriented around positive cash flow.

3. The management structure is designed to take advantage of the skills of the founder or founders.

4. The operation is designed in the image of the founder(s).

5. The business is oriented toward the personal goals of the founder(s).

6. The number of employees may be zero or as few as one, and typically would not be expected to grow to more than 50 to 100.

harvest plan

A plan to exit a small business. Typically, the owners have the intention to sell the business to another firm or take it to an IPO.

---

* The concepts of venture capital and angel investors will be dealt with in greater detail in later chapters. For reference here, both are investors who provide capital to the start-up firm in exchange for ownership in the new firm. This ownership level can be and often is at over 50 percent of the firm.

Although Microsoft or Dell were founded as small businesses, we would more accurately describe them as high-growth businesses, since each quickly required millions of dollars of investment from venture capitalists to grow. In contrast, the businesses of the majority of millionaires, who made their fortunes in areas like lawn mowing, plumbing, and electrical work, were almost all founded in a manner consistent with the second type of small business. This text examines the issues and systems applicable to the second type of business founding and development. While some of the concepts are applicable to high-growth firms, the focus in this text is upon the systematic designing of a successful small business. Many of the legal structures in United States law begin to apply when a firm reaches milestones of 35 and 50 employees. As a result, firms that exceed that number of employees must develop new systems to operate and are more within the purview of established management practices. Thus, our focus here is on those firms which are truly small, those with fewer than 50 employees. It is important to remember that firms with fewer than 50 employees represent the majority of all firms in the United States, and also represent approximately 33 percent of all full-time employees in the United States.[16]

Bill Gates is a great example of massive small business success. His story is more the exception than the rule. What lessons can we learn from Gates's success that might apply to businesses on a smaller scale?

Business Plans—Another Difference in Types of Firms

Another critical difference between small businesses and entrepreneurial firms is in the size and detail required in their business plans. A small business's resources are significantly more constrained than those of entrepreneurial firms. While the entrepreneurial firm generally develops a business plan as a promotional tool to be sent to venture capitalists and other potential investors, the small business develops a business plan as a guide for the running of the business. Many entrepreneurial ventures hire professional consultants to assist them in the development of their business plans; in contrast, we strongly advise all small business owners to develop their own plan as a part of their process. A high-growth venture's business plan runs from 25 to 45 pages long. The business plan for a small business should be relatively short (on the order of 20 to 25 pages) and should be developed in a manner that helps the small business person understand the industry, the firm he wants to develop, and how he needs to go about being successful in that business. Thus, the business plan for a new small business is developed with three goals in mind:

1. To be a guide to managing the business in its early development.
2. To provide a self-evaluation: putting the information down in writing allows for evaluation and honest analysis.
3. To provide potential closely held investors with the critical information necessary to evaluate the key criteria of the business: its cash flow, management team, and competitive advantage.

The business planning process that we develop in this text is a very practical and logical guide for the establishment and initial management of a new business. We do not develop the long, intricate business plans

EXERCISE 3

1. Do you have any initial ideas for a small business? Write these ideas down. As we go through the course you will be asked to evaluate your business idea in light of the concepts presented in that chapter. Most ideas will undergo significant evolution as you begin to study the topic more.

2. How many employees would your initial business require?

that are sometimes written to attract venture capital. Instead, you will develop a working document that is grounded in the needs of the new business. A well-thought-out business plan has heightened importance for the new small business as a tool to think through a wide range of issues, as most small businesses will not actually obtain financing from formal investors. This type of business will either be self-funded or obtain financing from friends and family. These individuals are not looking for a slick five-year formal plan; instead, they are looking for a document that explains the value of the business and how it will succeed.

Therefore, we will not use any of the cookie-cutter business plan programs that are available. If you google the term "business plan," you will find any number of programs on the Internet which encourage you to plug in information and allow the program to "generate" a plan. We believe such programs really inhibit the process of designing a business. Each business plan, much like each business, should have its own voice, feel, and presentation. We suggest to you that a good business plan is best developed by the individual(s) contemplating the business, not by paid consultants who will have none of the enthusiasm of the founder(s). The fact that potential investors to a small business will be those closest to the founder makes it critical that the entrepreneur(s) seek to ensure the chances of success by doing thorough planning and thinking. It is one thing to lose money and close a business if the investment comes from investors you know casually. However, if the investors are your parents, in-laws, grandparents, or siblings and the business closes, it can be truly painful and may, in fact, cause ruptures in the relationships you hold most dear. A well-designed business plan has already helped the founder(s) consider every aspect of the new business and allows everyone else involved to have a true "feel" for where this opportunity is heading.

We believe that if you do the planning and thinking developed in each chapter of this text, the business plan for the new small business will develop naturally from the material. The final chapter of the book has a fully developed small business plan and a full discussion about each section of that plan. The plan in the appendix is one developed by students as a class project. Our hope is that you will be able to produce an equally detailed plan in this class. The business plan you produce should ultimately be a good solid start on a plan you could use to begin your business. You will want to refine the plan more after you leave the class, but the class will provide you with the tools to begin the process of forming your own business.

summary

This chapter began by discussing the impact that new and small businesses have on the economy. A brief history of new ventures was discussed, with the observation that every business you can think of, regardless of size, was started by one person or a small group of people. Given that, there are still two very distinct types of businesses: (1) those that are funded by large amounts of outside capital with the intent to grow them as fast as possible, and (2) those that are primarily in business for the benefit of the founders and their families. The second group is far more prevalent around the globe and is the focus of this text. The remainder of the chapter was a review of the outline for the entire text and an explanation of why we approach the subject in this particular manner.

key terms

conomies of scale 5
Fortune 500 4
harvest plan 12

stakeholders 7
United States Small Business
Administration (SBA) 4

review questions

1. How do small businesses impact the economy?
2. Name several entrepreneurs who have grown their businesses into major organizations.
3. Explain what is meant by the science and the art of starting and managing a small business.
4. What types of small businesses interest you most and why?
5. What aspects of those businesses are particularly appealing to you?
6. Do you see yourself as a small business founder in the next five years?
7. How has small business impacted the growth of the United States?
8. Why does "profit as a goal" present an ethical challenge to new business owners?
9. What differentiates a traditional small business from one that is oriented towards high growth?
10. Why do you believe that Stoner, Inc. was so successful?

group exercises

INTERVIEW AN ENTREPRENEUR

Early in the semester, form into groups and interview two entrepreneurs. You have wide flexibility as to the types of entrepreneurs you select. However, each entrepreneur must be the original founder of the business or the current owner, and should not be your close relative. Prepare a report on each entrepreneur interviewed. The report should be 3 to 4 typed, double-spaced pages long and cover three primary areas. First, discuss the background and characteristics of the entrepreneur, as well as the history and nature of the business. Second, discuss lessons learned by the entrepreneur as related to you by the entrepreneur. Third, include your evaluation of the entrepreneur, and state what you can personally take away from the experience. Your group will choose one of the two individuals that you have interviewed and make a presentation on this individual.

everyday edisons class discussion

Go to www.everydayedisons.com/lisaMary.html and read about Lisa and Mary.
1. How did the two women come up with the idea for the dog leash?
2. Why do you think it took the two of them rather than one of them alone?
3. What would be your advice for these two women?

Louis Foreman Everyday Edisons

Louis Foreman has been an entrepreneur all of his life. When he was nine years old, he decided to hold a Muscular Dystrophy Association fundraising event in his hometown. Louis solicited items and services from businesses in the town and put on an event that raised thousands of dollars—an unheard-of amount for a nine-year-old. Since that time he has successfully started five different business ventures. His first was launched from his fraternity room while a sophomore at the University of Illinois.

As a successful entrepreneur, Louis became well known as a great source of advice for other entrepreneurs. He was struck by the raw number of ordinary people who had great ideas for products and businesses. This led Louis three years ago to develop the concept for a reality show that would help make inventors' dreams come true—and perhaps educate America about what it truly takes to bring a product to market in the process. Today this reality series is known as *Everyday Edisons,* and its mission aligns with Louis's initial desire: to fuel the innovative spirit that has historically characterized our society, strengthened it, and distinguished it from the rest (www.everydayedisons.com). Throughout this semester you will have the opportunity in each chapter to watch one episode of this series. These episodes illustrate the processes involved in developing an idea into something that is commercially viable.

Having the idea for a show that wouldn't make light of people's efforts was one thing; actually making it happen required a bit more luck. An interview for a receptionist position led to the introduction of Louis to a man who had an extensive background in broadcast journalism. Michael Cable was a seven-time recipient of television's most prestigious award, the Emmy®. In 2005, he and Louis began crafting a show that would allow viewers to see the entire process of taking a raw idea to commercial success.

They crafted the show to be part suspense, part reality television, and part education. Each season kicks off with casting calls in cities across the United States. In 2008, the casting calls were held in Atlanta, GA; San Jose, CA; Dallas, TX; Chicago, IL; and Providence, RI. Tens of thousands of people attend the calls, where they each have the opportunity to pitch their product or idea to a team of judges. The very best of these are invited to join the show. That is where the hard work begins.

Each episode dissects a part of the multistep process involved in taking an idea to commercial viability, offering insider tidbits and even expert advice from the United States Patent & Trademark Office. Viewers also meet the team of experts behind the show and learn how each product is branded, packaged, and marketed.

"Everyone either has had an idea for a new product or knows someone who has invented something," said Michael Cable. "We hope to show the world that you don't have to be a rocket scientist to have a great idea; from stay-at-home moms to a retired New York City firefighter, our featured inventors are just normal people leading normal lives."

Rather than rely on the drama and emotion of the casting call experience, the show's real-life aspect comes into play as viewers enter the lives of each "Everyday Edison" and learn the stories that led them to develop their extraordinary ideas. Because of its reality format, *Everyday Edisons* documents not only the stories of success and obstacles overcome, but also the setbacks and failures each product experiences on the road to completion.

Hundreds of thousands of dollars are invested in each product as they are taken to market free of charge to the inventors. "The best part about the series is that all of our inventors are 'winners'—no one gets voted off an island or knocked out in a process of elimination," said Louis Foreman. "In fact, the inventors each receive royalties on their products for 20 years, which is the lifespan of a patent. We're about inspiring people to be innovative and helping to make dreams come true."

Everyday Edisons began its third season in 2009, having won coveted awards like the Emmy and the Telly. As noted earlier, each chapter of the text will include a reference to a particular episode of *Everyday Edisons.* We encourage you to watch the episode and discuss how what you learned in the chapter and saw on the episode can be translated into a new business idea for you to pursue.

Everyday Edisons has led to the development of the Edison Nation at www.edisonnation.com. Here you will find interviews of famous entrepreneurs, information about placing your ideas with companies, and numerous group discussion boards. Edison Nation is rapidly becoming the premier clearinghouse to help individuals get their ideas to companies that will both pay for those ideas and make them a reality. We encourage you to become part of the nation of entrepreneurs.

QUESTIONS

1. What lessons can be taken from Louis Foreman's experiences?
2. How does *Everyday Edisons* help entrepreneurs?
3. What are some of the risks associated with pursuing a business venture like those highlighted on *Everyday Edisons?*

Individuals and Small Business Start-ups

learning outcomes

After studying this chapter, you will be able to:

2.1 Explain how small business founders impact the business world as a whole.

2.2 Discuss the importance of an entrepreneurial orientation.

2.3 List the triggers that encourage new business formations.

2.4 Compare and contrast various types of small business supports.

2.5 Explain how you can evaluate those things that you enjoy the most and discover how they may lead to business opportunities.

Tiny Showcase

Shea'la Finch and Jon Buonaccorsi

Providence, Rhode Island, is becoming a showcase for up-and-coming artists, but you won't necessarily find their work in a gallery. Every Tuesday, Shea'la Finch and Jon Buonaccorsi display a new print of an original drawing or painting on their Web site, tinyshowcase.com, and sell 100 to 200 prints for $20 apiece. In three years, Tiny Showcase has given more than 100 artists an audience—the site receives up to 10,000 visitors on a busy night—and has made art accessible to those with modest means.

Finch, 29, and Buonaccorsi, 30, were living together in 2005, trapped in office jobs they hated. To keep up morale, they left each other funny sketches on the fridge. Then Finch, who has an art degree from Bennington College, thought of putting their sketches and other underexposed art online in limited editions. Buonaccorsi, a Web designer, created the site, limiting their start-up costs to only a few hundred dollars. Revenue, which reached $250,000 last year, comes from a 20 percent commission on artists' sales, and the business became profitable quickly. But the two still depend on day jobs to pay the bills.

In large, well-established organizations, no one person is crucial to the survival of the business, even the president of the company. This is due partially to the strong structures, such as written procedures, in place at most large organizations. Large organizations also have wide dispersion of knowledge throughout the business; in other words, there are multiple people who know about any given aspect of the business. As a result, if any single person leaves the organization, it has the ability to continue with minimal interruption. Finally, large organizations have greater excess resources, including financial resources, which allow them to hire outside experts to fill any critical need that arises. These excess resources are referred to as **organizational slack;** they allow large organizations flexibility that is not available to start-up and small business ventures.

A small business is started as the brainchild of a single person or a small group of people, each of whom has an ownership stake in the business. The small business has few formal procedures, a concentration of knowledge in one or a few individuals, and limited slack resources.[1] The absence of slack financial resources means the small firm does not have flexibility in responding to issues such as the need to hire replacements if the company loses key individuals. As a result, the founders of a small business play a far more critical role in the business's success than does the senior leadership of the typical large organization. The importance of the individual entrepreneur in the founding and managing of a small business leads to the focus in this chapter on the individual entrepreneur who starts a small business.

This chapter will include a discussion of why individuals are so important to the success of a small business. It will also provide ways for you to understand your own entrepreneurial orientation. The examination of your orientation will include an examination of your risk tolerance and boundaries that may exist in your perception of events in the environment. It will also include an exercise to test your own entrepreneurial orientation.

Every individual brings a unique set of supports she can call on to help her in the founding process, and these supports are critical in the success of a new business. Therefore, we will examine those supports, the most critical of which is the family. In some businesses the family will play an even more important role; these businesses are referred to as "family businesses." Family businesses have unique issues that extend beyond those of the normal new small business. We will address family businesses more at the end of this chapter.

The authors of the text have had extensive experience working with small business people as they start and run their businesses. Throughout this text you will find that many of these firms are used as examples. In particular, we will follow one specific start-up business throughout the text. Philo Asian Grille (not the firm's real name) will be followed from start-up through the actual running of the business.

The result of the three friends' discussions was that Doug and Jennie realized that they created monthly budgets in a very similar manner. They also sought to avoid credit card debt unless they could pay it off before the interest was charged at the end of the month.

This was in sharp contrast to their friend William. He had no family budget, nor did he track his expenses in any manner. In his household

organizational slack
Excess resources in an organization, typical of large organizations but not of small business.

Understanding and collaborating in small groups can be an essential part of small business success. What are some of the key characteristics you would look for in a partner?

In 2009 three friends increasingly talked of starting a business. The three had known each other since high school 20 years earlier. Jennie had gone to the state university and had taken a number of courses in business, but had not completed her degree. William had received an associate degree at the local junior college, while Doug had gone to a career school while working full time at a local office supply store. Despite their different educational levels, they each had ended up in roughly similar jobs, either managing a local restaurant or managing a unit of a restaurant chain.

The three friends were located in approximately the same geographic area; they had grown up in the area, and as a result, they knew the area and its needs very well. Over the years since they graduated from high school, each had gotten married and started to raise a family. However, all three realized that the things they hoped to provide their families would require significantly more income than they currently earned, or would potentially earn in the near future. Finally, they also increasingly wanted the benefits from their hard work. They felt that in their current positions, they were working very hard, but receiving only limited direct rewards for that effort. They observed numerous other individuals in similar roles in other units of their business that worked much less and yet earned more. The three friends realized that increasingly, they wanted more control over their lives. These issues pushed the three to talk about starting a business. The discussions initially were little more than talk. However, in the past few months these discussions had become more serious. They were not sure what type of business to start or how to start it, but they knew they wanted to start a business.

Doug's uncle had founded several small businesses and appeared to understand what it took to be successful in small business. The three friends sought him out for advice on the type of business to start. In their first conversation with him, he advised them to spend a little more time investigating their motivations and personal risk orientation before they actually considered the type of new business to begin. He related the story of his first business, which he had started with his best friend. The two had been lifelong friends and thought they knew all there was to know about each other. Not only had they been friends since childhood, but they had also been best men in each other's weddings, and were the respective godfathers for each other's oldest children. While they thought they knew each other well, when it came to money and the level of risk they were capable of handling, they were substantially different people. The uncle was very frugal, while his partner believed that money needed to be enjoyed today. Ultimately their business partnership fell apart. While the financial loss was significant, even more devastating was the loss of the friendship between the two and their families. The uncle has always felt the experience was a significant failure and not one he wanted to repeat.

The uncle has had other businesses and partnerships since that initial failure. He now thinks that while he needs to like a person in order to work closely with them, it is much more important that they agree on key issues like money and risk.

Therefore, the uncle suggested the three do some simple things:

1. Compare how each of them prepared the monthly family budget.

2. Discuss how much debt they were each willing to have on credit cards.

3. Discuss whether they were willing to loan family members' money, and the reasons for their answer.

4. Each answer this question: If you inherited $50,000, what would you do with it?

The outcome of this exercise for our three potential small business owners will be discussed after Exercise 1 on the next page.

the family simply spent all the money that came in each month. It was frequently a stretch at the end of the month for him and his family to pay the bills that arrived. He and his wife made frequent use of credit cards, which allowed them to continue until they received their paychecks. Unfortunately, as a result of this continual behavior, William and his wife had built up considerable debt on those credit cards.

1. Evaluate your own views on the issues specified by Doug's uncle. Discuss your results with others in your class. What is the range of answers that were given?

2. What other measures of risk taking can you suggest?

3. Have you ever lent money to a relative? Have you heard stories of those that have? Would it be different if it were a close friend that you went into business with?

As you can easily imagine, Doug and Jennie soon figured out that they were more compatible as partners. They realized that if they went into business with William, they would soon have significant conflicts regarding both the approach to and the actual finances of the new business. The result would most likely be a loss of their friendship with William and also the failure of the business. The discussions among the three friends also brought these issues home more clearly to William, who ultimately decided that a small business was not for him. He realized that because of his current debt, if the business needed more money, he would not be able to put that money into it; also, if the business failed, he had so few resources to fall back upon that he might have to file for bankruptcy.

LO2.1 Founders Are the Reason Why Small Business Works So Well

New businesses have some significant advantages over large businesses. For example, the very size of small businesses results in those firms having greater flexibility. Small firms can respond quickly to changes around them, whereas a large firm tends to use many committees to approve the work of other committees. This feature alone allows the small firm led by the aware entrepreneur to respond quickly to opportunities or threats as they arise. Small firms can also fill niches that large firms simply cannot afford to fill. Large firms do have an advantage in those situations where there are truly economies of scale, the ability to do things cheaper when they are done in a large volume.[2] However, there are many small niches where large firms cannot afford to compete. The large firms' systems may be efficient, but not able to handle doing small volumes of a particular activity. These niches are ideal for small business.

While these advantages can be substantial, the greatest advantage for a small business is the fact that the small business is owned and run by the same person. Contrast this to most large corporations, where there is a division between owners and managers. Those individuals that manage the operations of the firm do not typically have substantial ownership in the firm. The managers (agents of the owners) may own some stock, but in a large firm like General Motors they own a very small percentage of the total stock.

Agency theory

A managerial theory that argues that individuals act to maximize their own benefit. Thus, in settings where there is a split between ownership and control (as in most publicly traded corporations), the agents (managers) must be monitored or they will act to maximize their own benefit, not necessarily that of those who own the firm (the shareholders).

Agency theory suggests that individuals act to maximize their own individual benefit.[3] The result in a large corporation is that the manager of a business will tend to act to maximize his own benefit, not necessarily that of those who own the firm (typically the shareholders). This does not mean that the manager seeks to steal from the firm; instead, in subtle but pervasive ways, the manager will act for his own benefit. In contrast, the individual who owns the business will always act to maximize the value of the business, since her interest and that of the business itself are aligned: If the business makes money, the owner makes money.

To illustrate, the manager of a large firm can easily justify why it is important that she fly first class across the country to a meeting in New York City. She might argue that she needs to arrive fresh and needs the space in first class so that she can think and work during the flight. This trip may easily cost $4,000 if the ticket is bought on short notice. Unfortunately, this comes out of the corporation's income, money that really belongs to the shareholders (the owners).

The cost of luxuries like first-class airfare is an extravagance few small businesses can afford. How would you, as a small business owner, decide what constitutes a luxury and what is a necessity?

Compare this with the typical behavior of the small business owner. An airline ticket is an expense for the small firm, as it is for the large one. However, in this case, there would be less money for the owner/manager if she spent $4,000 on an airline ticket. The small business owner is more likely to go on the Internet and find the cheapest ticket possible. The small business owner would also like to arrive fresh and be able to work during the flight. However, for the sake of the cost difference, she is likely to fly economy class, be a little more cramped, and save perhaps $3,000 or more. If the large, established business is doing poorly, the manager is still collecting a salary and benefits, while the shareholders (owners) are getting few rewards. The manager will move on to another firm if the business collapses, having no significant stake in the financial failure of the previous firm. In contrast, if a small business is doing poorly, the owner may ultimately have to close the firm and be responsible for any debts that have accumulated. As a result, the small business owner will treat the costs of the business very differently than will the manager of a firm. (When we deal with the legal structure of the small business in Chapter 7, we specify in greater detail if and when the small business person is responsible for the debts of the business.) If the manager of a large firm had to spend her own money, or were responsible for the debt of the organization, agency theory would argue that the manager would behave in a thriftier manner.

Thus, one of the greatest assets of the small business is the owner of the business, and his involvement in, and dedication to, the business. It is because of the owner's importance to the business that students need to consider their own abilities and resources early as they begin to look at building a small business.

EXERCISE 2

1. What will you do if the business fails?
2. How much time are you willing to dedicate to the success of the venture?
3. How much of your personal assets are you willing to put into the venture?

LO 2.2 Evaluating Your Entrepreneurial Orientation

There are a number of issues that potential entrepreneurs need to consider about themselves as they look at starting a new business. Examined with some depth, these issues will shape the small business person's analysis of the potential of any business idea. These include (1) risk tolerance, (2) prior experience, and (3) personality orientation of the individual.

Risk Tolerance

The potential small business owner must determine her own individual level of tolerance to risk. You are probably familiar with the concept from dealing with your own financial investing. The typical advice provided to most individuals is to build an investment portfolio in a manner consistent with your risk tolerance.[4] We use a similar concept here, but we use it more broadly, asking you to consider your tolerance to a wide range of potential risks that extend far beyond just financial considerations. Initially, an individual needs to evaluate whether she has the risk tolerance to actually start a small business. She then needs to evaluate what level of risk she will accept in a given small business situation.

To illustrate, a potential small business owner needs to first determine if she has the risk tolerance to open a small business. If you work for a large corporation, there is relatively low individual financial risk. In a normal economic environment, even if a large corporation has a poor year and loses money, it will still meet payroll, pay the workers' benefits, and not close its doors on short notice. On the other hand, the small business owner is faced with a substantially different situation. When starting a business, it takes time for the business to reach a level where revenue coming into the firm is sufficient to cover expenses. (We examine this in significant detail in Chapter 6; this point is referred to as a **break-even point**.) However, the small business may quickly reach a point where its funds have run out and it needs to close its doors quickly. If the business does close, then the small business owner(s) may find that he has to pay the debts of the firm that are left, since he had to sign personal guarantees for the loans of the business. Thus, the financial risk for the small business owner can be quite high. As a potential small business owner, you will need to consider how much debt you are willing to take on. In general, the greater the debt you are willing to take on to start your business, the higher your risk tolerance.

The potential new business owner needs to determine what risk level he is willing to accept in a new business and let that information help him decide which business to pursue.[5] There is not a correct answer as to what level of risk tolerance you should be willing to take on. Instead, the key is that the individual small business owner must be aware of his own tolerance of risk and establish a business in a manner that is consistent with that tolerance. The new business owner

Evel Knievel has become a cultural reference point for risk taking. An interesting counterpoint to this image was Knievel's very vocal stand against the risks associated with taking drugs. This dichotomy illustrates that risk levels can vary, even within the same person.

break-even point

The time when a new business has reached a level where revenue coming into the firm is sufficient to cover expenses.

EXERCISE 3

To help you figure out your own tolerance for risk, answer the following questions.

1. How much debt would you be willing to undertake to provide a footing for your business idea?
2. How much of your personal savings would you be willing to risk on your business idea?
3. At what point would you close the business?
4. If you were the recipient of a $100,000 inheritance, what portion would you be willing to invest in your business?

Given your answers to the above questions, how would you rate your financial risk tolerance?

---

needs to be sure that the level of risk is consistent with his background, values, and family situation. Evaluation of the risk profile for a particular type of business is more art than science.

Fran Jabara, a well-known entrepreneur from Wichita, Kansas, provides valuable advice on risk tolerance.* His argument suggests that one never do anything that does not allow one to sleep at night. This rule of thumb can help a small business owner to determine the risks with which he will be most comfortable. In future chapters we will return to the evaluation of risk as we look at specific risks, such as financial risks, strategic risks, and market retaliation risks.

Prior Experience

The second element of entrepreneurial orientation is prior experience. Every individual brings to a new business her own view of the world. This view of the world places boundaries on what a decision maker will consider as she makes decisions. These boundaries are set by experiences, history, culture, and family values, among other things. Boundaries help each of us make sense of the world. For example, in the United States, when you see a red octagonal sign at a corner, you typically assume it is a stop sign. You automatically assume that it is a stop sign because of your history and experience.

However, if you were in another country, such an octagonal sign may not be a stop sign; it might be a warning to slow down before a curve. Our experiences, history, culture, and values not only help us interpret the world, but they also place boundaries on how we see that world. Thus, our experiences, history, culture, and values also establish what we consider to be both possible and practical. This is referred to as the individual's **bounded rationality**. It is the presence of bounded rationality that often leads young people to be pioneers in an area, as they are not limited by the restrictions of the past.

Bounded rationality is the reason individuals from outside an industry are able to establish a new business in a manner not previously considered. To illustrate, cattle processing was historically done by large, established firms in meat processing centers such as Chicago, Fort Worth, and Kansas City. The cattle were shipped there and processed by well-trained butchers from the moment of slaughter until they were ready for packaging. An entrepreneur had an idea for viewing the entire process differently. Rather than shipping cattle to a central location, why not process the cattle where they are raised? In addition, instead of well-trained butchers, why not use individuals that make the same cut repeatedly, in an assembly-line manner? This small business idea grew quickly, others copied the model, and today virtually all beef is processed this way. Those individuals that had grown up in the beef industry believed that cattle processing had to be done in a given way. Others came from outside the industry and saw new ways to do things. Their analysis was not bounded by history in the industry.

bounded rationality
Rational decision making that is constrained by the background and history of the person making the decision.

---

* Fran is head of Jabara Ventures, a large and very successful merchant banking firm. He was also founder of the entrepreneurship program at Wichita State University. His students went on to found such ventures as Pizza Hut.

In a similar vein we could consider the airline industry and industry maverick Southwest Airlines. Today it is a major employer, but it started as a small business with a few rented planes. At the time everyone felt that air travel had to be done with what is referred to as a hub and spoke system. That is, the planes would fly into a major center such as Chicago or Atlanta from all the airports in that region. Then, people from all of these feeder airports would be placed on the same flight to a given location. Southwest wanted to go back to the way air travel used to be. Among many other things, this meant lots of short-haul flights of less than an hour between airports. Herb Kelleher (one of the founders of Southwest) was trained as a lawyer and brought fresh insight on how to compete in the industry.

It is important for individuals to understand how their decision making is bounded by their own version of rationality. It is important to know your potential partners' backgrounds and how their decision making is impacted by their history. These issues will impact how you and your partners act. It will also impact a wide range of issues, from how you set up the business to how you run the business.

Personality Orientation of the Individual

The third element of entrepreneurial orientation is an examination of your own personality. There is a wide variety of personality tests available to assist individuals in an analysis of their traits and tendencies. These tests should not be used to judge whether you are right to start a small business. There will be successful business people in all personality categories. Additionally, in general, you as an individual will probably score differently on the same test if you take it on different occasions.

Therefore, you can use these tests to help better understand yourself and your strengths, but you should not use them as a guide for your career. In general, if you are very outgoing and extroverted, you may wish to focus on a small business in which you have extensive interpersonal interactions. In contrast, if you are more introverted, you may wish to focus on a small business, such as an Internet business, in which interpersonal interactions are more limited. In this section, we review

There are varying aspects to everyone's personalities. How might knowing your strengths and weaknesses impact business decisions?

some of the major personality tests that are available. If you enter the names of these tests into a search engine, you will find that there are numerous versions of the tests available on the Internet, often for free.

Myers-Briggs. This is one of the most widely used tests for personality evaluations. It was developed in the 1940s by Katherine Briggs and her daughter Isabel Myers. The rationale for the test is drawn from Carl Jung, a Swiss psychoanalyst who broke from Freud and sought to incorporate broader issues into his analysis. The test focuses on four pairs of variables: extroversion-introversion (focus on outward world or internal); sensing-intuiting (how people gather information); thinking-feeling (how they make decisions), and judgment-perception (order vs. flexibility). The different potential arrangements of variables are believed to indicate the different ways that individuals deal with other people and their environments.

Enneagram. The underlying philosophy of this test is that a person is the result of all the experiences in his life. Thus, the factors in childhood are central in developing who we are today. As a result of this foundation it is also believed that as adults we will not change this personality over time.

The test believes there are nine different types of personalities. Through a series of questions, the test assigns you to one of these primary types. These nine types and a few of the characteristics of each type of individual are as follows: reformer (idealist/perfectionist); helper (caring/good interpersonal skills); achiever (competent/driven); individualist (sensitive/dramatic); investigator (cerebral/focused); loyalist (committed/pessimistic); enthusiast (fun-loving/impatient); challenger (action oriented/cynical), and peacemaker (easygoing/passive aggressive).

Big Five Test. The Big Five is a popular personality test in universities. It is composed of five factors: open-mindedness, conscientiousness, agreeableness, emotional stability, and extroversion (the factor names vary a little among authors). These are considered by many researchers to be the five key components of an individual's personality.

The Big Five test was developed by two independent research teams. These researchers asked thousands of people hundreds of questions and then analyzed the data statistically. The researchers did not set out to identify the five factors; instead, the factors emerged from their analyses of the data.

LO 2.3 Triggers for Starting a Business

Starting a new business is often the result of some particular event or condition within an individual's environment. These triggers tend to encourage the forming of new small businesses, as they encourage individuals to think creatively. Individuals get comfortable with their lives, and it takes a trigger to force them to think in new ways. You may not be faced with such triggers as motivations, and still decide to start a small business. However, many people do start their businesses when one of these triggers is present, and therefore it is useful for you to understand them. The triggers in the formation of a new small business can come

One of the important choices that every person has to deal with is what she may take with her when she leaves a business. This becomes more critical when the person leaving is starting her own new business. Whether it is voluntary or involuntary, leaving a job can be frustrating, and sometimes individuals are frustrated enough to wish to do harm to the firm they are leaving. Beyond that, there is a question as to where the line between personal and business information exists. If the person leaving does something that harms the prior business, then the prior employer can sue the former employee. The impact on a fledgling business can be substantial.

To illustrate, consider an employee who has worked for a large plumbing or electrical firm. In her former position, she had the opportunity to obtain the firm's customer list. However, if she takes that list and uses it to generate her own customer base, the former employer can sue her over the lost business.

QUESTIONS

1. What are some ways you can build a customer base when you leave a firm without running into problems with the former employer?

2. Beyond the customer list, what would be other things you could take from a firm that would present an ethical problem?

from either positive or negative stimulus that occurs in an individual's life. Some typical triggers include the following:

1. Being laid off from established employment.

2. Being approached by one or more people with a new business idea.

3. Reaching a point financially where the risk/return level is tolerable.

4. Having very little to lose financially by a failure.

5. Developing a concrete idea to improve a given situation.

6. Being spurred to action by attending a seminar, reading a book, or talking with successful entrepreneurs.

7. Experiencing a mid-life (or early-life, or even late-life) crisis.

8. Observing the establishment of an incubator or business development effort within the community.

9. Experiencing the inability to climb the corporate ladder due to circumstances beyond one's control. These might include not having graduated from the "correct" school, being female in a male-dominated business, having a marketing background in a manufacturing business, etc.

Often, more than one of these triggers may be present at the same time. For discussion purposes, we segment these triggers into two categories: personal motivations and circumstance motivations. While the exact dividing line between these two categories is somewhat fuzzy, this categorization will allow for the examination of the various issues involved in starting a business.

Personal motivations are driven internally by the individuals themselves, and as such are the strongest motivations available. Personal motivations drive people to make career and life-altering moves irrespective of "practical" advice. Small business founders driven by personal motivators will tend to be more proactive, and drive relentlessly toward their goals.

Circumstance motivators tend to result in more of a defensive positioning. The environment and environmental changes make opportunities available to potential business owners, but the motivation is substantially different. This is an opportunistic start-up whose staying power is more determined by other competing opportunities.

To illustrate personal triggers, consider that today one of the fastest growing groups of small business owners are women. In large part, women are starting new businesses when their career opportunities are blocked at larger corporations. The barrier is often referred to as the "glass ceiling." It involves not formal rules, but the practical reality that in some organizations there are limits to the level in the corporate hierarchy to which women are allowed to progress. If you question the presence of such ceilings, simply note how many women are in senior management positions at most major corporations. A particularly fast-growing segment of small business owners are minority women owners. Minority women–owned firms are expanding at an estimated rate of 31.5 percent per year.[6]

An illustration of a circumstance motivator exists when individuals are laid off by their prior employer. Human nature is such that most people get comfortable with their current status and financial position. When individuals are laid off, are demoted, are forced to take reduced pay, or even survive a layoff, they are forced to think about new opportunities that they never would have considered previously. For example, research has found that when a factory or military base closes, there is a blossoming of new small businesses in that area.[7]

Our opening story of Philo Asian Grille illustrates how personal and circumstance motivations merge. The three individuals who considered establishing their new small business felt that they had little chance for significant career advancement in their current jobs. They started looking for new areas that would allow them to build a business that would provide significant opportunities for themselves and their families. These individuals all had small children, and they wanted to provide a better standard of living for them. In this case, the three potential business founders not only had one of the strongest personal motivators available to individuals—that of providing for their children—they also had a strong desire to change their overall circumstances.

LO 2.4 Supports

This chapter focuses on the individual entrepreneur who starts the small business. It has been stressed in the chapter that this individual is central to its success. Generally, she is far more important than a single individual in a large firm.

This does not mean that an individual, or team of individuals, creates a successful small business without help. There are supports and resources available to the entrepreneur. No one of these supports or resources assures success, but the small business person should evaluate which resources and supports she has access to in an effort to increase her chances of success.

Like a classic architecture, a solid business is built upon a variety of support systems.

The supports and resources available are typically unique to the entrepreneur and where he lives. Not all individuals come to the process of founding the business with equal endowments or supports. The entrepreneur should avail himself of all the supports possible to make his entrepreneurial efforts successful. The support and resource areas the small business person should examine include (1) family, (2) social networks, (3) community, and (4) financial resources.

Family

Few people know you—including your abilities and shortcomings—like your family does. These individuals are a resource for support, guidance, suggestions, and potential funding for a small business. A spouse who is willing to handle the financial burden while you begin a new venture, a parent who will contribute time and money, an uncle who has been in the industry and is willing to review your plan and advise you so that you might avoid basic pitfalls—all are immensely valuable to the new small business owner. We advise potential new entrepreneurs to work with their family members not only for their advice and potential funding, but also as a reality check and support structure. Family members are in a unique position to provide you with key insights when you may be pursuing the wrong approach to an issue. Too many other individuals will not be willing to tell you when you may be wrong. Most individuals will tell you only positive things. In addition, you will need your family's support to push forward to success, since there will be times that you will have to deal with significant discouragements.

To fully utilize your family resources, we suggest you list those family members with whom you have regular contact, and also list the capabilities those individuals possess that might provide support to the new business. The benefit of such an activity is that it will allow a small business founder to think systematically through the items that need to be discussed with various family members. The small business owner needs to make sure she obtains the resources desired from family members without wasting the time and effort of these individuals simply because they are very familiar to her.

The role of family is so critical to the success of a new business that many small businesses in fact end up being what are referred to as family businesses. In such firms, the principal staff members of the business are family members. There may be other employees in the firm, but typically, family members hold the key managerial decision-making positions.

The long-term management of family businesses is unique when compared to that of non-family-owned small businesses. In the initial stages of formation, the support of the family can help the small business person overcome many difficulties that might cause the failure of non-family-supported small businesses. For example, when family members are the principal staff, a month in which payroll cannot fully be met by the company is more acceptable. These individuals' level of commitment to the founder may be high enough that they are willing to take only a partial or no salary that month. These individuals also are often willing to work at times and in conditions that other employees would not accept. For example, Christmas season is critical to all retailers, but paid staff may not be willing to work the extra hours needed at this time, while family will. It is this level of commitment that has produced such success for many immigrant families that open a restaurant or a service business, such as a grocery store or a dry cleaner. In these settings, the reliance on family is a key reason the firms are able to survive and prosper.

However, there are also potential negative long-term issues that accompany a family business. While family members have a greater commitment to you as an entrepreneur because of your close relationships, those close relationships make issues such as firing family members difficult. If a family member is not a good employee, how will you fire him, or even reprimand him, without rupturing the close relationships in the family? Similarly, since family members know each other so well, they are willing to say negative things to a small business owner that a regular employee would never say. These negative things may have no connection to work, but might be issues that are simmering in the family. These negative comments can be particularly caustic in the firm, since the owner may be hesitant to fire the family member, and can finally rupture all relationships with the individual and other extended family members. Finally, the presence of family in the firm can cause difficulties with other employees that are not family members. As will be discussed in Chapter 10, human resource management is one of the most important and contentious issues in a firm. Unfortunately, if it appears there are different expectations and rewards for workers depending on whether they are related to you, it can cause turmoil among employees.

Family is usually an important resource for a new business. The new entrepreneur needs to consider the balance of benefits and drawbacks to building a family-based business.

Networks

Beyond your family, another key support is the network of individuals in your life. These networks may have formed from former employers, individuals you know from a fraternal organization like the Rotary Club, friends at school, or individuals you know from another organization like a church or synagogue. Individuals in your network can be particularly helpful in providing some legitimacy to your business, in addition to providing feedback and advice to you.

To illustrate, a small start-up manufacturing business would be considered high risk until it developed a steady flow of customers and revenue. Established businesses are often hesitant to buy from a start-up small business, since it is not clear if it will be able to fulfill an order or service the product in the future. Thus, many firms will initially buy only small amounts from a new small business in an effort to observe the quality and reliability of the new firm. Similar effects are also experienced with suppliers, such that the new firm may not be able to obtain

the rodriguez family business

Alex Rodriquez was attending career school while working full time in an auto parts store. He knew that he wanted to eventually own his own auto repair shop, but Alex was not sure if he would ever be able to achieve that goal. On the way home one day, Alex noticed that the local auto repair shop where his family had taken their cars for years had closed. Over the next week, he found out that Mr. Jones, who had originally owned the shop, had died unexpectedly, and no one in Jones's family wanted the business. In fact, it appeared to Alex that the family wanted to be rid of the business quickly.

On Sunday, Alex's extended family traditionally gathered for lunch. This lunch included not only his father, mother, and sister, but also his uncle and aunt whose children were grown and lived away from the city, his other uncle and aunt and their two college-age children, and his grandmother. During the lunch, Alex brought up the death of Mr. Jones. While everyone was sad to see a good neighbor pass away, they also began to talk about Alex's goal to have an auto repair shop. His father and mother noted all the potential problems with such a shop; however, they then surprised Alex by saying he

should seek out the Jones family and see if they would make a deal on the shop and its equipment.

The discussion quickly evolved within the family to how everyone could do their part at the auto repair shop. Alex's older uncle suggested that while he did not know how to change a lightbulb, he could make a small loan to Alex to help start the business. His sister said she could apply her knowledge in accounting to help set up the books, while his two cousins both offered to work in the shop. His grandmother even offered to answer the phone.

The result was that Alex quickly moved from believing that he would never be able to own an auto repair shop to thinking about how he could start the business. It quickly became clear to Alex that while he alone most likely could not own the business, the family could own it and make it a success together. As a result, that night after everyone went home, Alex began to make a list of what each of the family members could perhaps bring to the business. He also carefully noted what they wanted to do. The two were not always the same. For example, his younger aunt had offered to manage the office. However, she was known to be very temperamental and difficult to work with. That said, she had great computer skills, and could be a real asset in setting up computer inventory systems and accounting systems. Alex knew in his heart that with the support of his family, he would be able to make his dream come true.

---

credit from a supplier for some time. Only after a history of prompt payment is built up might the supplier allow the new business to carry credit. A network can help overcome some of these debilitating issues early in the life of the business by providing a level of legitimacy. Support from companies in your network cannot only provide revenue, but can also help to indicate to others your seriousness and staying power.

Community

There are also more formal community supports that can lower the overall risk for a new small business in the community.[8] For example, many communities have small business **incubators.**[9] These facilities house new businesses, providing many critical services for them. An incubator will provide all of the typical office machines, basic furniture, phones, fax and copying equipment, and maintenance necessary for a business to begin operations. As noted above, one of the difficulties for a new small business is the establishment of some level of

incubator

A facility that houses new businesses and provides many critical services for them.

legitimacy. Those businesses that look like they are businesses may have more opportunities. Most new small businesses cannot afford a receptionist, while in a business incubator there is a common receptionist. This individual is typically trained to answer your phone calls from a central location, using your firm's own name. The impression made by such simple things can be significant. In contrast to an answering machine, the ability to have a message taken by the receptionist can help build credibility.

A business incubator also typically offers its space to tenant firms at subsidized rates. There are professionals such as accountants and lawyers available to help the new businesses. Local community leaders hope that all this aid will lead to businesses that are more likely to succeed than unsupported new small business start-ups. Thus, if a small business founder can locate the business in an incubator, then the firm's risk of failure drops. Business incubators work best with office-based service firms or small manufacturing firms. Clearly, a business incubator cannot effectively house a restaurant. A restaurant needs to be located somewhere near a flow of people. However, even for such a firm there are supports available. In most communities there are **Small Business Assistance Centers**. These centers are funded by the Small Business Administration and advise individuals wishing to start new businesses. The supports vary widely, but usually include research aids such as information on funding sources in the area for small business. There are other services available, such as counseling provided by the Service Corps of Retired Executives (SCORE). These retired executives work with small businesses as advisors on a wide range of issues. Still other supports are available at centers tailored to aid women or minority entrepreneurs. One specialized program is the Minority Enterprise Development Program. There are also programs targeted to veterans or those firms that are geared to export.

Each community has its own unique set of resources. The federal government provides some of the funds, but it encourages the local administrators and government entities to tailor the services to what is needed locally. Therefore, each potential small business person needs to survey what services she has available. A quick review of the Blue Pages (those focused on government) in the telephone book under titles like Economic Development will provide an entry into these services. The potential entrepreneur would be well served to take an hour or two to visit the offices identified and obtain information on their services. The potential entrepreneur should also ask these entities for leads on other agencies that have services for the start-up business. Almost all such agencies work with each other and want entrepreneurs to take advantage of all resources available, whether from them or from other agencies.

Small Business Assistance Centers
Centers funded by the Small Business Administration that advise individuals wishing to start new businesses.

Financial Support

Another key element for a new business is the financial support it develops. The detailed evaluation of financial resources will follow in the text. Specifically, in Chapter 9 we will examine the financing issues related to starting a firm. However, a few points need to be made briefly here. Potential small business owners need to have a full understanding of the cost/benefit of the small business.[10] In particular, the entrepreneur

Using the chart below, begin to fill in the supports and resources you might be able to call on. Describe briefly the support and resource that you list. Fill in the chart as much as you can now. In the accompanying workbook, you may expand on this table as you build your actual business plan.

Category	Source	Description
Family		
Network		
Community		
Financial		

needs to account for the financial resources that may be required by a small business. It is simply good business practice to ensure that sufficient financial resources are available prior to the start of that business. It may be a waste of effort to go forward if the goals of an individual are widely divergent from the financial resources that are available. The development of the small business is not "blue sky" thinking. The processes detailed in this book are a practical and applied effort to make the small business a reality.

From an individual evaluation of capability, nothing more is required at this point than a realistic vision of what resources are needed and available. If, for instance, a potential entrepreneur is considering starting a restaurant, then he needs to recognize that the equipment and setup for even a very small, modest carry-out restaurant may exceed $150,000. This cost goes up dramatically unless the potential small business owner buys used equipment. Regardless of the type of business contemplated, it is critical that the entrepreneur be able to fund that business or obtain the necessary funding. Therefore, the potential small business owner needs to have a broad understanding of what financial resources he possesses and a realistic idea of what he will need to expend. Chapter 6, titled "Cash Flow," devotes an entire section to this exact issue. Here, we stress that even at this early stage, the potential small business owner needs to have in mind how much money he and others starting the business may be able to generate.

Mary hates to cook, but her family really wants her to take over the family restaurant. What are some of the potential risks for Mary to head a business she lacks passion for?

LO 2.5 Form a Business Doing What You Like

This chapter has emphasized that small businesses are so often successful because the small business person both owns and runs the business. You bring to the small business a focus on the business that simply does not exist in large businesses. You also bring unique supports which can help make the venture successful. Ultimately, the greatest contributor to your success is that you are doing something you enjoy.

A small business person will need to spend considerable time at the business if she is to be successful.[11] In fact, the small business owner will likely spend more time starting and running the business than doing anything else in her life. Consider that in a typical day you have 24 hours, out of which you might typically sleep 7 hours. If you work 8 to 10 hours at a minimum in a business for five days, plus half a day each weekend, you will be spending the greatest amount of your time either sleeping or working. You need to enjoy what you do. If you do not enjoy weather extremes, do not seek to establish a heating and air conditioning business that requires you to work on broken air conditioners and heaters (which always seem to need repair in the extremes of weather). If you do not enjoy working with people, do not establish a retail shop where you must work with the wide variety of individuals who walk in the door. On the other hand, if you like people and find conversation easy, a retail business would make much more sense than an Internet business where you see very few people and primarily work alone. It is quite possible for someone to see great potential in a new business idea; however, if the new small business is not something that the entrepreneur has a passion for, history suggests that the business is not likely to be successful.

Our consideration of your time commitment also brings forward the issue that you need to clearly recognize the time commitment and the return you expect from your venture. While clearly part of the equation, the time/reward relationship in a small business involves more than simply financial reward. We will deal more with profitability as we consider the finances of the firm in Chapters 6, 9, and 12. However, your time is your most valuable asset and should be treated as such. This text is designed to help you think through the small business process in a formal manner and provide you with the tools necessary to be able to start a small business. By the end of the semester, you should be able to clearly understand what is needed to start your business and the rewards you can expect so that you can clearly evaluate your choices.

summary

The most critical resource that the potential small business person has in forming a small business is the entrepreneur himself. The founders are the reason small businesses are so successful. In forming a new business, the entrepreneur's choice of business needs to be consistent with his own individual risk tolerance. The small business person also needs to be aware that his own biases and bounded rationality will shape how he interprets opportunities.

The thought process associated with developing the small business needs to be consistent with the actual resources that are present. The process of developing the business is both time consuming and rewarding. There are many supports available to anyone wishing to pursue this course of action in business. The potential entrepreneur should look to her family, networks, and communities for assistance and honest feedback.

key terms

agency theory 22

bounded rationality 25

break-even point 24

incubator 32

organizational slack 20

Small Business Assistance Centers 33

review questions

1. How does the lack of "slack" resources impact new ventures?
2. What started the three friends thinking about an Asian grill?
3. What did you think about the method they used to determine compatibility?
4. Why is founder involvement in a new venture so critical to its success?
5. How would you evaluate risk tolerance?
6. What is your risk tolerance? Why?
7. Is there some minimum level of risk tolerance required to start a business? Explain.
8. How does bounded rationality affect the way an entrepreneur determines what type of business to start?
9. Which of the methods of personality assessment do you prefer? Why?
10. Do personality differences matter in the starting of a business?
11. List some triggers that push people into starting a new business.
12. Have you experienced any of these triggers? Did it cause you to consider starting your own business?
13. Which supports do you believe you might rely on the most if you started your own business?

individual exercises

1. Individually list up to five small businesses you could happily work at every day.
2. Do the same thing for five small businesses you would not enjoy working for every day.
3. How do your personal interests impact these choices?
4. As a group, discuss the commonalities and differences between the choices of the group's members. Why do these exist?

group exercise

FAMILY-OWNED CORPORATIONS

It is estimated that up to 25 percent of the Fortune 500 are family businesses. These are corporations in which a single family owns a high enough percentage to have control. Recognize that control does not require owning a majority of shares; control can be maintained with ownership of as few as 5 percent of the shares. Identify one of these corporations. How is this family-owned corporation different from more typical corporations?

everyday edisons class discussion

Look at Michael's story at www.everydayedisons.com/michael.html

1. What are the difficulties in Michael's life that encouraged him to form his business?
2. The United States has a strong history of immigrants leaving difficult settings, moving to the United States, and becoming successful entrepreneurs. Why do you think they are so successful in the United States?

Dee Silva–Dee's Place

As her children grew up and became more independent, Dee Silva decided it was time to go back to work. She wanted to do something she really enjoyed, and she knew two things about herself. First, she liked to be with people, and second, styling hair had always had a great attraction to her. She had done her own hair and styled hair for family members and friends for some years, but wanted to do more. Therefore, she and her husband used student loans so that she could attend a nine-month styling school program. (Interestingly, the cost today is about the same for styling school.) The decision to go to school and really hone her skills turned out to be a wise one for Dee. Her husband experienced an unfortunate accident and suffered a serious injury. As a result, her desire to earn a living while still having the flexibility to help her husband and the children still living at home was strong. The need for flexibility pushed Dee to set up her first business in a unique niche: the elderly who could not leave home. Dee correctly reasoned that it is difficult for the elderly to leave home and run errands,

like getting a haircut. However, the elderly still want their hair maintained in a neat, fashionable manner. Dee's new business plan was to go to individuals' homes and cut their hair. This approach allowed Dee to have full control of her schedule. If she needed to make a change in an appointment, this also was relatively easily to do, since the individuals were largely homebound. There was also very little competition in this niche. She had no advertising expenses, since she relied on word of mouth. Dee served this market niche for the next 12 years.

Eventually Dee decided that a bit more permanence would be nice, and she went to work in an established chain. This decision led her to be the manager of a store for a major chain for most of the next six years. During this time she worked for two different hair styling chains. In these positions she had responsibility for maintaining the store, maintaining the stock of the store, and maintaining the records, but not for hiring. The result was that she had tremendous responsibility but very little control over the key choice of the employees for whom she would have responsibility. The regional office had the responsibility for hiring. This produced great frustrations for Dee. Her salary as a manager was over $30,000 a year, but she ultimately recognized that she could earn the same amount working for herself.

Dee determined once again to run her own operation, but this time she set up her own styling salon. In the large Southwestern city where Dee lives, there is a facility that rents only to stylists and those in related professions. For approximately $300 a week, Dee was able to rent, in this facility, a private room that she shares with another stylist. They split the rent but have complete control over when they work and what equipment they have in the room. Dee and her friend maintain their own supplies and make their own appointments, although they support each other where they can. The utilities for the room are covered in the rent, and the facility provides items such as the large hair dryer, chairs, and wash bowl. Thus, the major items that Dee must provide are her own supplies, including shampoos, conditioners, curling irons, and hair colors.

Today Dee typically works five days a week; she takes Tuesdays and Wednesdays off. The reason she chose this schedule is that for most working people, Saturdays and Sundays are the days they have off and can come in to the salon. In addition, most beauty salons in the city where she is located are closed on Mondays, giving her a competitive advantage on that day. Thus, Dee again tries to serve domains where there is less competition, just as she did when she first started. There are several other things Dee does that help to ensure her business success. For example, many older women still like to have their hair curled with rollers. Therefore, she is still willing to do roller sets, whereas many younger stylists will not. She also makes sure she has a full set of colors that may be needed, since she knows she cannot stop what she is doing to go and get a supply. When you are the only person in the business, you need to be prepared for every possibility. It makes the old Boy Scout motto sound like a business truism: Be prepared. Dee's initial cost for her hair color inventory was over $700. Fortunately for her, Dee was able to bring many of her loyal customers with her when she left the large hair styling chain.

Dee's pricing strategy is also geared to maintain a strong customer base. Her price for a haircut is $12. Many comparable stylists charge $30. However, Dee has been able to use pricing to help her build a very loyal customer base that will come to her for more expensive treatments later. Her experience has been that she could give fewer haircuts at a high price or give more cuts at a low price. The income would be relatively constant with either strategy. However, her customer loyalty is higher with the lower price. In this time of economic contraction, this strategy has been particularly useful to her. Many higher-priced stylists are finding their customers are leaving, while Dee has maintained and even picked up customers.

Dee had several suggestions for students thinking about setting up their own salons.

1. *Love what you do.* If you do not love it, you will ultimately not be able to do it in a manner that is successful. Dee was in stylist school with over 200 people. Only a few years later, fewer than 5 were still styling hair. If you do not love what you are doing, the long hours to start a business will simply wear you down. Twenty-one years later, Dee still loves her work.

2. *Go to work for a large chain before you start your business.* Dee did not do this, but she wishes she had learned more while supported by other people's money. Rather than learning with your own time and money at risk, learn on the job from a chain. Then take that knowledge, and probably many of your customers with you, to start your own styling salon.

3. *Get good equipment.* Plan on spending about $8,000 in equipment and supplies when you start. Individuals can get cheaper equipment, but it costs them in the long run.

4. *Take walk-in customers when they come.* The key to business success is to build loyalty with your clients. Everyone who walks in is giving you the opportunity to build that loyalty. If you serve customers well that first time, they will be back. A stylist needs to be flexible and take advantage of those opportunities that appear. Dee does not advertise. Instead, she relies on the loyalty of customers and the ability to prove herself when an opportunity appears.

Dee has been able to do something she loves for 21 years. She has been able to earn a good living and have control of her own schedule during those times she worked for herself. Thus, she is the classic happy small business owner.

QUESTIONS

1. In Dee's first business venture, she found a market niche, in-home haircuts for the elderly, which had not been tapped into. How might that strategy work in other areas of business?

2. Dee stressed the importance of doing what you love. How has that impacted her career decisions? How has it impacted yours?

3. Flexibility is often cited as a major area of consideration in starting a small business. How does this impact your decision-making process?

learning outcomes

After studying this chapter, you will be able to:

3.1 Describe a systematic means for examining skills in order to generate new business ideas.

3.2 Discuss the elements of opportunity analysis.

3.3 Analyze how to choose a business.

Business Idea Generation and Initial Evaluation

DREAM DINNERS, INC.

Sometimes businesses are born when personal experience comes face to face with market demand. Such was the case for Stephanie Allen, a stay-at-home mom with some catering experience who for years had been efficiently preparing good meals for her family. Once a month she developed a menu of 12 different entrees which fed a family of 6. She would gather the ingredients, then prepare, pack, and freeze her meals in batches. She did not cook the meals prior to freezing them; instead, she prepared the meals ready to be cooked. This approach allowed the meals to sustain their taste and yet saved her hours of preparing the meals each evening. Over the years her friends begged her to teach them her methods. Allen finally organized a party at her house, prepared the menus, bought all the ingredients, and invited a dozen friends. They had only to bring their own baking pans and cover the cost of the food. It was a major hit, not only for the food but also for the socializing. Within a week Allen was being besieged with calls, checks, and requests to "join the club." She realized she had a business idea!

Allen enlisted Tina Kuna, a friend of hers who had more experience with the financial side of a business, and the two formed Dream Dinners. They initially rented out a commercial kitchen, but quickly opened up a second kitchen in the Seattle area so they could handle up to 1,800 customers a month. Each client chooses 12 entrees out of 14 possible, and then she selects the kitchen station she desires and proceeds to prepare the 12 meals, all for about $250.

The company moved quickly to franchise the business. The popularity of the model led to explosive growth for the company, but before long, the model frayed under changing market conditions (grocery price rise and a severe recession). With its two company stores and the franchise operations, Dream Dinners was initially profitable, but the business has turned sharply negative in the past two years. More stores are closing than are opening, and the future of the entire meal assembly industry is in question.

Sources: www.dreamdinners.com; A. Y. Pennington, "What's for Dinner?", Entrepreneur.com, August 2003; J. Gill, "Can Cooking Dinner Really Make you This Happy?", WorkingMother.com, February 2003; C. A. Tice, "A Full Plate: Meal-Preparation Firm Signs Up 36 Franchisees," *Puget Sound Business Journal,* January 19, 2004, http://seattle.bizjournals.com; M. Lindner, "Taking on Restaurants and Grocers," *Forbes,* May 8, 2008, www.Forbes.com.

Individuals come to the decision to begin a small business from many different perspectives and backgrounds. From this widely diverse group of individuals come many successful business ideas. Research shows that successful new business ideas are not determined by who your parents are, your race, your gender, or your religion. Instead, quality ideas are a function of the creativity and thoughtfulness of the person creating the business.

So how does someone come up with an idea for a new business? Many times the idea for a new business comes from the entrepreneur's professional background or hobbies. These are domains that the individual knows very well, so that he can easily see shortcomings in the current offerings in these areas. Great insight can also be gained from individuals that the entrepreneur respects or those who have been successful in founding a business themselves. Thus, there are a wide variety of sources that can be called upon for ideas about potential businesses. In this chapter we identify a systematic way in which to generate a list of potential businesses. The initial steps in evaluating the viability of these ideas will also be presented as a key element in this process.

Following is a description of the processes that the founders of our running case, Philo Asian Grille, went through in generating the idea for their business.

LO 3.1 Generating Business Ideas

While individuals may determine that they want to open a small business, the exact type of business to open is much more difficult to determine. We encourage everyone, even individuals that feel that they firmly know which type of business they wish to open, to examine all options through the processes detailed in this chapter. We have found that potential new business owners often feel strongly about the type of business they wish to open, and yet, upon a more systematic examination, move to an alternative idea. Frequently, they do find an opportunity in the market, but it may not be the exact business concept that they initially conceived. Alternatively, they may conclude after their analysis that the business they conceptualized would not be successful. Therefore, rather than reacting in a knee-jerk manner to what appears to be an opportunity, or even worse, quickly dismissing a promising idea, an individual needs to make a rational evaluation of a business opportunity and its potential.[1]

As discussed in Chapter 2, the desire to own/operate a business is a first step—but what business might that be? The generation of business ideas is not something that occurs automatically. Rather, it is a process of identifying the skills of the potential small business owners, identifying opportunities in the market, matching the initial financial funding available, and then marrying these together into a business idea that interests the potential founders. As noted in Chapter 1, the establishment of a successful small business is challenging. The high demands

The two potential entrepreneurs, Jennie and Doug, had determined that they wanted to start a small business and that they had a similar propensity for risk taking, as discussed in chapter 2. Realizing that they had significant skills in the restaurant industry, they knew that the new business needed to be related to restaurants. That said, they were not sure whether they wanted to develop a new restaurant, buy an existing restaurant, or develop a business that supports restaurants. The founders talked between themselves about ideas for businesses but had not been able to determine what business would best take advantage of their backgrounds and interests. They knew that there was a very high failure rate among restaurants, so they wanted to be sure to carefully examine their business ideas so that they would not be one of the failures. Therefore, they visited with the most successful restaurant entrepreneur they knew, an individual who had founded a number of successful businesses, including a restaurant in the area.

This successful entrepreneur gave the two potential business owners some general ideas about the key issues in starting a new business, but also suggested that the two of them needed to conduct an audit of themselves to better understand what type of business might be best to open. This audit would help them to determine their views on a number of topics. From this understanding the two potential entrepreneurs could help to focus their analysis of possible businesses to start. The successful entrepreneur suggested that the audit should include questions such as these:

1. What skills had they developed in their prior work experiences?

2. What special hobbies had they pursued?

3. What things about the restaurant industry (either owning a restaurant or supplying them) did the two really like?

4. What did they want to achieve with a new business?

5. Were there businesses in other countries and/or other parts of the country which seemed interesting but had not yet reached their area?

The two budding entrepreneurs initially answered these questions separately and then they summarized their answers as follows:

	Jennie Williamson	Doug Cheng
Skills/ experience prior work	1. Inventory control 2. Operating a retail business 3. Managing people	1. Connecting with people on an individual basis 2. Customer service management 3. Menu design
Hobbies	Cooking Interior design	Cooking Sailing
Industry Hope to Achieve	Retail/Wholesale Security	Retail/Wholesale Security
Trends	1. The slow economy had increased the price sensitivity of buyers. 2. Growth of specialty retailers such as coffeehouses	1. Greater price sensitivity of consumers. 2. Dominance of retailers such as Walmart in many domains. 3. A tendency toward individuals starting their own businesses

The hopeful entrepreneurs discovered through this process that there were some similarities in their answers and that their thoughts on which business opportunity to further investigate were clearer. Specifically, the two shared a common interest in retail and dealing directly with customers.

In a somewhat serendipitous fashion, both potential business owners were invited to an auction being held by a large restaurant in the area that had recently gone bankrupt. The two decided to go to the auction together and see what they thought of the opportunity to acquire used equipment for a restaurant. While at the auction, they were amazed that not only was every part of the business for sale, but also the lease on the space was part of the deal. The space of the restaurant being auctioned had

(continued)

originally been a BBQ restaurant, something that did not appeal to the founders as an effective concept.

The insight from the auction (that there was used equipment readily available) combined with their insight about themselves from the audit, leading the two to investigate restaurants that had failed in the past few months, as it seemed this might offer a real opportunity. A little investigating over the next several weeks found that eight restaurants had failed in the past two months. Only one had been through an auction, while real estate firms were trying to sell the others somewhat intact. Furthermore, the prices being asked for these places suggested that there were some amazing bargains available, especially if they could minimize the investment to get the restaurant started. The number of failures brought home to the two friends the risk they faced. Still, they felt that the key would be to match what was available with a restaurant concept that would give them an advantage. They really felt that they should be focusing on a concept that would attract a higher-end customer, but also had a clear theme that would separate them from other restaurants. With these ideas in mind, they landed on an idea to start an intimate, upscale Asian restaurant that focused on the variety and quality of its dumplings; these dumplings are small pieces of meat or vegetable filling wrapped in dough that is either steamed or fried.

placed upon everyone involved in the process necessitate that the founders truly enjoy what they are doing. The process presented below is intended to be an open one that considers passion and enjoyment as important elements to success.

While not a sequential formula, we would suggest the following approach to the development of a quality business idea. First, the founders should list and evaluate their personal skill set. These skills may arise from hobbies, current work, past work experience, and/or family history. The next step is to carefully analyze the market and look for a gap, or some need that is not being met effectively. Finally, the potential founders need to compare their ability to fill those gaps with the opportunity that seems to be available. We suggest the means to do this is the development of a chart that allows for an open, systematic examination. We will now look at each of these steps in turn in more detail.

Skills Analysis

Why do we start with the skill set of the entrepreneur rather than an "opportunity" in the market? There are literally millions of "opportunities" in a wide variety of fields, but without the requisite skill set, pursuing these opportunities would be a frustrating exercise of wasted money and time. There may be tremendous opportunities in the spa services business. However, if a potential business owner had no skills in this area, then those opportunities would not be easily available to him; nor could any initial advantage be held for long when faced with competitors that did have the necessary training in the area. The small business person must have not only the necessary skills, but also a depth of understanding, so that he can build a long-term advantage in his domain. Perhaps as important as the small business owner's skills in a particular area is the need for the potential owner to have interest in or passion for starting a business in that domain. Without a passion for the business the entrepreneur will not be willing to devote the time and energy necessary for the business to be successful.

As we mentioned previously, skills come from a variety of areas and are relatively idiosyncratic to the individual. In general, skills are derived from our history, experience, and interests. Several specific areas that potential business owners might examine include hobbies, education, work experience, and family history. Each of these will be examined in turn.

Hobbies

Your hobbies can impact how you approach business ventures. Do you have any hobbies that might lend themselves to a solid business idea?

Hobbies are those pursuits that an individual does as an avocation. Since the individual does these things because they are enjoyable, there is typically great passion associated with them which can help encourage the success of the small business. A rule of thumb in the founding of businesses has always been that the owner whose business is both her vocation and her avocation is difficult to beat. The questions the potential business owner should probably ask herself include these:

- What hobbies do you pursue on an active basis?
- What hobbies have you pursued in any manner over your lifetime (whether or not you were serious about them)?
- What is it about your hobbies that really excites you?
- What were the specific skills that these hobbies required?
- What have your experiences in the hobby taught you that could help others?
- What products and services did you use in these hobbies?

Education

The second set of skills is education, either formal or informal.

- What courses did you take that were particularly enjoyable?
- What courses did you take where the material came to you very easily?
- Have you attended any unusual education programs?
- Have you taken specialized training in any specific area?
- If you had to do it all over again, what areas would you pursue now?

Work Experience

Another set of skills comes from work experience. Such skills typically have direct applicability to the pursuit of a new business. In each job, individuals build up skills that they take with them when they start a new business.

- What businesses have you worked in?
- What skills were critical to the jobs you performed?
- What positions have you held in business?
- In what areas would you be considered a type of expert?
- What did you *really* enjoy about the positions you have held?
- What frustrated you about the positions that you have held?
- When were you the most excited about your work?

Your family can be a great help in developing a business. What are some of the risks and rewards that you associate with the idea of working with your family?

Family History

Your family history is an often overlooked source of skills. As we all know, every family is unique. There are often things that you do with your family in which you develop expertise. Many times potential entrepreneurs overlook this area of developed knowledge. If you regularly go hunting with family members, perhaps a business related to that hobby could be a great use of your skill set. To illustrate, one of the authors regularly hires a guide when in Sedona, Arizona. This particular guide grew up hiking and exploring the Sedona area. After working for the park service for many years, he decided to open his own tour operation. He takes individuals or very small groups on customized adventures that cater to the desires of the customer. He turned his passion into a business that has grown to include other guides and is a year-round operation. Your pursuits can similarly be the source of a unique skill set for a business.

- What is your family history with new business ventures?
- What types of travel/vacations does your family enjoy?
- What skill sets exist within your nuclear family?
- What are the financial resources of your extended family?
- Are there unique things your family does that others seem very interested in?

Additional Skills

Beyond these categories, we suggest that you also ask yourself the following questions:

1. What are your top three personal skills?
2. What things do you like doing best each day, each week?
3. When you look back over the past year, what one or two things did you enjoy more than any others?
4. What are the magazines and books you read?
5. What are your three greatest accomplishments in life? What skills were involved in these accomplishments?
6. Do you enjoy working with people? Or would you prefer to be left alone to concentrate your efforts in a particular area?
7. What industry (retail/wholesale/manufacturing/service) would you prefer to work in?

Clearly, the goal from all these questions is to explore the range of potential skills and abilities that each of us possesses. A few more

rodriquez family auto repair shop

Alex was now excited that he might be able to open an auto repair shop. However, as he talked to friends over a beer after work, a number of other good ideas kept being suggested. His friend Joe suggested he should instead look at opening an auto parts store just like the one where he currently worked. Another friend, Stella, thought he should instead open a home health service. Her cousin across town had started one and he was doing great in his business, which arranged for practical nurses and nurse aides to visit elderly shut-ins. Similarly, a friend of Stella's suggested setting up a computer business that enters medical records for doctors. Each of these ideas seemed viable to Alex. While he felt in his heart that he wanted to run an auto repair shop, he thought he owed it to himself to look at other businesses to ensure he was doing the right thing.

As Alex considered the last two businesses suggested to him, he quickly came to the conclusion that they were not for him. Both businesses required extensive computer and sales skills. Alex was competent at both, but he did not want to have to rely on those skills. Additionally, he called on several of the types of businesses his friends had suggested that were in another part of the city; the owners of these businesses often had MBA degrees. Alex was attending a career school, taking a few classes, and was considering working on his undergraduate degree, but he had no interest in waiting to obtain an MBA to start his business. In fact, he questioned whether there was a real need for an MBA to be able to run a business. Additionally, both types of business typically required extensive staffs. The person running the business rarely did the work. Instead, the owner was a manager who supervised and sold the service to others. Alex was much more hands on. Therefore, he quickly eliminated the home health and data entry businesses.

However, analyzing and contrasting the auto repair and the auto supply companies took more time. After greater study, Alex realized that the auto supply company would take extensive capital to start. The auto parts were expensive and the shops expected the parts store to keep a wide variety of products on hand at all times. The auto supply business also would need to supply shops throughout a very wide region to be successful. As the region to supply became larger, Alex would have to be able to compete in parts of the city he knew nothing about. In contrast, each auto repair shop covered only a small area. In addition, the auto parts supply industry seemed to be going through large-scale consolidation, with large chains quickly replacing the previously independently owned firms. Finally, if Alex did enter the auto parts supply business, he would be in direct competition with his current boss, Mr. Jackson. Alex's boss had always been very fair to him and Alex did not want to violate that trust. Beyond that, Alex felt that if he did open up an auto repair shop, Mr. Jackson would actually give him a high level of credit, which no other new shop could expect.

Therefore, after his analysis of ideas, Alex was more convinced than before that he should focus his efforts on auto repair.

questions can help you tailor your business to your unique skills and personality:

1. Do you prefer to work extensively with people or not? If not, you need to focus on a business that has minimal interpersonal demands (an Internet-based business, or a business that performs tasks for other businesses by handling back-office operations like bookkeeping, billing, etc.). If you thrive on people and have the corresponding skills, then a retail or service business may be ideal.

2. Do you have an intense detail orientation? If you are very detail oriented, then a business that is procedurally complex and involves managing a wide variety of details may be appropriate. Remember that there are many people and companies out there that will pay handsomely for someone to manage the details of life. For example, a supply company to large manufacturers that customizes a

product on a wide variety of details might be appropriate. Alternatively, an individual who finds this level of detail frustrating should pursue a business with a simpler business model.

3. Are you trained in the area you want to work in? Your experience and educational skills will have a critical impact on the direction of the business. Someone may believe that there is a need for a computer repair shop in your part of the city. However, if the individual does not have the skills from either educational training or experience to do such repairs, it does little good to consider such a business.

What is clear from the above is that in this text we believe that the founder(s) of a small business need to be intimately involved in the design, funding, and running of the new business. Often you will hear individuals quickly claim that they are "idea" people and plan to simply hire everyone needed to run the business, design the procedures, etc. These folks are not founders; they are bankers with vision. They are simply providing funding and the concept. Such a model might work for businesses that enjoy high profit margins, but for small businesses with fewer than 50 employees, this model is difficult to pursue successfully. Therefore, in this text in general, and this chapter in particular, we utilize the basic assumption that the founder will be intimately involved in the new business.

LO 3.2 Opportunity Identification

Once you have developed a list of your skills, abilities, and interests, the next step is to examine the marketplace for opportunities to utilize these in a business. The method that we use and recommend is a form of **gap analysis.** In such an analysis, individuals identify a gap or opportunity that exists between the demand by customers and the supply provided by firms in the market. The new business owner must then determine if she has the skills and abilities to fill that gap.

gap analysis

A relatively simple process of systematically examining the difference, or gap, between what is expected and what occurs. One type of gap analysis, called opportunity analysis, examines opportunities in the marketplace side-by-side with the individual's ability to address those gaps.

Potential Businesses

There is a variety of ways to identify gaps, or business opportunities, in the marketplace. These include the following:

1. Examine trends around the region/nation/world that may not have reached your particular geographic location. Trends do not start uniformly. Notice that a number of regional coffee chains have developed significant businesses in smaller cities throughout the midwestern United States. These chains developed by examining how firms such as Starbucks were achieving success in major cities. These businesses achieved a strong local position before the national firms could reach their markets.

2. Interview and talk about opportunities with key successful entrepreneurs in the area. Most successful entrepreneurs are great sources of ideas that have the potential to be successful given the right set of circumstances and people. From their own experiences, these individuals have a keen eye for what businesses are needed in an area. However, these individuals often have too much to do with their own ventures to pursue new ventures themselves, so they are willing to share their insights. The result is that they are more

than willing to advise new entrepreneurs, as well as to identify and perhaps fund such opportunities. In effect, they become mentors to those new entrepreneurs.

3. Discuss potential businesses with family members. Your family members know your abilities and disposition. Furthermore, they are uniquely positioned to provide a much-needed honest perspective on your efforts. Particularly if any of these individuals have a small business of their own, they might be useful in the process of helping you decide which businesses work best with your particular set of skills.

4. **Brainstorming** with key entrepreneurs and family members can also be useful to the potential small business owner. Brainstorming is a creative process where a group of individuals are brought together and asked to generate ideas related to a specific topic or problem, with little effort given to evaluating the true potential for those ideas. In this case, the scenario might be one where a group is provided information on the skill set of the founder and asked to generate a list of businesses that might be appropriate. The interaction within the group leads to a dynamic that can lead to new, innovative ideas. Such brainstorming sessions work well in informal groups. Think of friends or family gathering over a meal and talking in depth about the options that are available; this is brainstorming. The conversation in Chapter 2 in which Alex's family initially talked about the options for Alex to take over the auto repair shop was a form of brainstorming.[2]

5. Take a look at the things that frustrate you and your family. Daily frustrations are an incredible source of ideas. How would you solve the frustration? What is it about the frustration that needs to be solved? You will find that you might have as many as a dozen aspects that could be solved, but only a few that truly fit with your capabilities and interests. Most (if not all) needs in society are currently being met. However, the degree, level, detail, efficiency, effectiveness, politeness, or access all provide means for improving the satisfaction of a particular need.

6. If the potential small business owner has an interest and skill set based in technology, one of our personal favorites for the generation of business ideas is the examination of patent files. There are hundreds of thousands of patents that exist and are maintained by the original inventors that have never been the subject of a commercial attempt. We recommend an examination of patent files (available at www.uspto.gov/) to find several that interest the potential entrepreneur. We suggest that you contact the inventor (all of the contact information is included with the patent) to see if she would be willing to work exclusively with you in the development of a commercial business.

We have worked with entrepreneurs who started with their interest area, found a set of patents that had not been developed into businesses, successfully contacted the inventors, and then based their business in part on those patents.

EXERCISE 2

1. Create a list of ideas in each one of the six idea categories listed above.

2. Do any of these ideas strike you as particularly intriguing? Why?

LO 3.3 Choosing a Business

The process of generating ideas is not something that is done in a single sitting. Instead, it is a process that takes time, interaction, consideration, evaluation, and iteration. These steps do not occur in a linear fashion, but should occur in an interactive manner. For example, if a successful entrepreneur suggests a new business that seems to fit well with your skills, then an investigation into the opportunity may be warranted. In discussions with trusted friends and family, the idea will morph and be refined. New skill sets may need to be brought to bear by the inclusion of others on the founding team. As a result, the generation of ideas is truly a process that takes time and interaction. However, done well, this effort should lead to a list of three to five businesses where the founders have the appropriate skills and there appears (at least on the surface level) to be an opportunity.

To illustrate, we worked with a small business owner who had strong retail experience. This individual enjoyed working with people, and had great orientation to detail. Three opportunities were initially identified by the individual. First, several family members who operated a flower shop in another city were encouraging the individual to pursue a similar business in his city. These individuals thought the potential entrepreneur had the skills for that business and they could coach him in the business. Second, some experienced business people in the area that he knew identified a gap in the printing services that were available. There was a chain copy shop in the small "downtown" area in the town, but that shop did not provide any really high-quality business printing, despite the relatively large number of small businesses in the area. The focus of the chain store was on individuals, self-service, and low-volume printing jobs. Finally, this individual had noted a trend on the West Coast of the United States (not his area of the country): the growth of restaurants that were between fast food restaurants and full-service restaurants. These restaurants typically focused on a regional food such as Cajun or Asian. The restaurants had an upscale decor, but individuals ordered at the cash register and had their food delivered to them at the table. Thus, it was a different format for a restaurant than he had noticed in his area.

Each of these businesses had a relatively high level of detail involved in the operation of the business, and the processes to operate the businesses were relatively well known. Additionally, each of the businesses required high levels of interaction with customers, and customer service seemed to be a critical element of the business model. The background and skills of the potential business owner appeared to fit with all of these businesses. Now the small business owner would have to pick one business idea.

Initial Analysis

The potential business owner, just as in the example above, will likely have several ideas, but will need to identify one business on which to perform a due diligence analysis. Chapters 4, 5, and 6 identify the process for performing an in-depth analysis on that single business idea. It is possible that after doing that in-depth analysis, the potential business person will decide not to pursue the business and therefore begin the analysis of business ideas all over again. However, the nature of the effort required to truly perform an effective due diligence study necessitates a focus upon a single business concept. The analysis and thought processes require focus, time, and some financial investment. If the potential business person is to be successful, she will need to move from the three to five ideas initially generated to a single idea on which to focus. Thus, the would-be entrepreneur in the prior example had to determine whether to focus further analysis on the flower shop, the printing business, or the restaurant. One means to identify which business to pursue is through a gap analysis.

Gap Analysis

How do you decide that a sufficient business opportunity exists and that you have the resources necessary to take advantage of that opportunity? Starting with the list of three to five ideas that you have generated, you can now develop a chart that examines the issues that impact the potential success of the new business. The business ideas are listed down the first column, with a brief explanation of what each idea entails. (Later, each of these descriptions will be put into a short paragraph explaining the business and its opportunity for economic success. You should be able to tell anyone succinctly—in less than two minutes—what your idea is and how it will bring substantial success. Taking more time simply indicates that you have not clearly identified the opportunity or how it will work.) We refer to this as gap analysis, and it should look roughly like the one in Table 3.1. We have filled in the three business ideas generated by the small business founder discussed in the previous section (flower

Table 3.1

BUSINESS IDEA	CATEGORY	OUR RESOURCES	RESOURCES REQUIRED	DEFICIT
Printing Shop High-quality Printing—commercial				
Flower Shop Family history and support				
Restaurant Positioned between fast food and full service				

shop, printing shop, and restaurant). However, you would use this form for your own business ideas.

In the second column, next to a given idea (and this may take several spreadsheet pages), list one category you will use to analyze the idea. We urge you to consider, one at a time, at least these five categories, which are crucial to the founding and successful running of a business: finances, time, nonfinancial resources, risk, and competitors. Each of these categories will be discussed in greater detail once we illustrate why this is a gap analysis.

In the third column, the potential business person should provide a realistic estimation of his resources in that category. In the fourth column, he should list his estimates of what resources are required for success. For the last column, the potential business person then qualitatively compares his skills/resources with the perceived requirements of that particular business, and records the perceived deficit, or gap. Then he can answer an important question: Is that deficit surmountable, or is it one that kills the idea?

This qualitative chart can be completed with minimal or no research. What we are looking for at this stage of investigation is a gut-level, reasonably quick analysis to see if the business passes an initial test. The gap analysis is intended to be completed by the entrepreneur or entrepreneurial team in a very short time period.

The second column lists "categories." These are categories that will be used for analysis. There are a number of categories which the small business person needs to consider as he conducts a gap analysis. Following are the five important categories we have listed briefly. The list below is not meant to be exhaustive, as every type of new business will have its own unique categories.

1. *Finances.* You must examine the finances required to start and operate the business. A principal cause of small business failure is insufficient financial resources at founding. A new business person may have a good idea, but run out of funds long before a sufficient client base can be built. This will be discussed further as we examine cash flow in Chapter 6. However, we feel that at this stage of analysis, the small business person needs to have a basic understanding of the financial demands of the business.

   a. Your resources—What financial resources do you have that you can realistically commit to the new venture? This should include estimates of savings, retirement accounts that may be closed, your spouse's salary, etc. Do you have family resources that could be committed to the effort? How much money could you realistically raise on short notice?

   b. Business need—Estimating at a very high level, how much money do you expect to need in order to start and to stay in business for one year? Without a lot of investigation, consider the following: rent, furniture, utilities, advertising, renovation, equipment, supplies, an employee or two, taxes, and fees. Take whatever number you develop and add 50 percent to it. New start-ups take twice the money that was initially forecasted to achieve a sustainable level of operation. Is this number within the range that you would be willing to commit?

2. *Time.* It takes time to start a business. You will hear many successful small business people say that they estimate the time it will take to do something from scratch and then triple it. Again, you need to assure that you have the time necessary to start the business. Each type of business started will require different time frames. This is an area that many small business people grossly underestimate.

   a. Your resources—If you are currently employed, how much time can you dedicate to starting this new venture? Will you quit your current job to work in the new business? How much time on a weekly basis are you willing to commit to the business once it is up and running? What other time commitments have you made? Does your family support your efforts?

   b. Business need—What will the hours of operation require? How many additional hours will be required to manage the operation? Do you need staff early in the life of the business? When do you eat, sleep, etc.?

3. *Nonfinancial Resources.* There are other resources the new small business will need beyond financing. This list can be long and include such things as special contacts with suppliers or customer groups and the physical location of the business. This is a category where the small business person should exercise some creativity as she analyzes her situation and the needs of the business.

   a. Your resources—What do you bring to the business beyond the financial? What unique capabilities/experiences/knowledge provide you with a competitive advantage? Are these visible to the rest of the world? Are there others, such as family members, that can provide other critical needs of the new firm?

   b. Business needs—What unique skills will be required to run the business? Can you contract with individuals for the areas that you are missing? Can you obtain the resource in short order? (For example, to open a printing business, it would be very helpful to have wide experience on various types of printing presses. This could be gained by going to work for someone else for a period of time or by taking training classes offered by contractors or the printing press company.) What unique resources are necessary to develop a competitive advantage in this business?

4. *Risk.* All small businesses have an inherent amount of risk associated with the starting and operation of the business. While it is determined by the entrepreneur, the level of risk needs to be commensurate with the rewards and within the tolerance level of the individual involved in the business founding. To determine your own risk tolerance, you should look at your own life over the past few years. When the economy is not in a recession, do you invest primarily in high-risk stocks or in safer places like savings accounts? If you invest in savings accounts, then you are probably somewhat risk adverse. There are two types of specific risk you should consider: personal and business.

a. Personal risk—Risk at a personal level has many definitions and potential means of examination. It is certainly well beyond just the financial. What level of personal reputation risk are you willing to live with? If the business fails, what will you do? There is a strategic risk to starting a business when you are not ready, not committed, not sufficiently funded, etc. A failed business idea may lead to others imitating your idea and doing it better, or may affect your ability to pursue that or a similar type of business in the future.

b. Business risk—How aggressively does the business need to grow? Is there a competitive advantage that is fleeting? What level of product or geographic breadth is necessary to not only be a player, but be a success in the industry? What are the limiting factors in the growth of this business?

You can also characterize and examine business risk by considering three threats to business success: (1) threats to the profit margin, (2) threats to sales generation schemes, and (3) threats to operational financing.[3] Each of these areas represents a systematic examination of business risk.

1. **Threats to Profit Margin.** A significant threat to the success of a new venture is its ability to establish and maintain a high-margin product or service. That is, the firm is able to make a high level of profit on each unit of product or service sold. What might inhibit your pricing or cost structure? Who are your significant competitors? Why do people shop with your competitor? How will you attract people to bypass your competitors?

2. **Threats to Sales Generation Schemes**. A new venture must have the opportunity to sell to many customers and to obtain repeat business. The ability to develop a sales scheme that is broad enough to appeal to a wide variety of customers is critical to the development of a successful business.[4] Can your competitors meet or exceed your quality? Undercut your price? Position themselves better physically? Lock you out of suppliers?

3. **Threats to Operational Financing**. There are a number of specific threats to the new venture in obtaining the necessary financing for its growth. Some such threats are high development costs, rapid expansion plans, high inventory needs, and/or an entrepreneurial team with a low asset base. As will be discussed in Chapter 6, one of the greatest risks to a new business is fast growth. Typically, you will be selling things on credit but having to pay cash for your inputs as a new firm. Thus, rapid expansion can quickly overextend your financial resources. Research has shown that firms with higher initial capitalization have the opportunity to grow faster.[5]

4. **Competitors**. The small business also must be realistic about its competitors. If the new business is going to have to compete directly with Walmart, then the level of difficulty will rise substantially. A firm like Walmart obtains the products it sells cheaper than any other firm, since it buys in such volume. It also has some of the cheapest retail space available, since it develops all of its own properties itself. Combine this with the fact that

The risk of a business increases dramatically as the investment in the business is provided by family members. It is one thing to tell an outside investor that you lost their money; it is an altogether more difficult conversation when the investment came from your sister. Before you accept money from your family or close friends, consider how you will handle that money in your business. All new ventures are inherently risky. As part of your risk analysis, you have to consider how much financial risk you are willing to commit to personally and with funds provided from those close to you. How would having your grandmother's retirement funds invested in the firm affect your judgment of the risk of a venture? What if the business investment included your own children's college funds? What if those funds had been left to your children by a relative? How does the risk equation change if your children are still very young?

Walmart is so wealthy that it could lose money for years without going out of business. As a result, if your new business tried to compete directly against Walmart as a low-price operation, then you would likely lose that war. We would generally suggest that the small business look for a fragmented market with relatively weaker or more dispersed competitors.

How would you plan for competition like Walmart?

To illustrate how critical the accurate evaluation of these issues is to success of the new firm, consider a business we worked with at the onset of the Internet boom. This firm proposed to use the Internet to automate (and make remarkably more efficient) a process that previously had been done only through extensive use of the telephone—one call at a time. The former process involved making 30 or more phone calls to various individuals and then trying to coordinate their activities in a stepwise fashion while waiting for each to return the call (which usually came in while the initial caller was on the phone with another individual—these were the days before call waiting). The product developed by the small business was a Web page–based product that would perform this function. The initial response was immediate and positive. The software behind the product was modestly complex; nonetheless, once it was available and visible, it could be imitated by a well-heeled competitor in just a couple of months. The real key to the business was to obtain commitments from the key customers (of which there were less than 300). Once these customers (who were widely dispersed across the United States) were exclusively tied to the system, there would be an effective barrier to entry.

The founders really believed that the Web page approach, not the early commitment of customers, was the key to their success, and that the rollout could be incremental. They wanted to limit their risk and use cash flow to fund their expansion with a systematic plan to expand the business slowly. We pointed out that the critical limiting factor was obtaining exclusive commitments from as many of the 300 core customers as soon as possible, before the competition realized what our owners were doing. This examination of the importance of the customers changed the whole approach for the new business. The owners decided that rather than rolling the business out incrementally, they would seek to sign up the core customers as quickly as possible. The solution chosen by the entrepreneurs was to hire a sales company that put 35 contract salespeople on the project for 90 days. The cost and risk of this approach was significantly higher for the founders. However, the result was that before competitors even realized that there was a new company in the field, the founders had locked up over 210 of the 300 customers. The first competitor showed up 70 days after they started their operation and was able to sign up only 14 customers after a year in business.

For this new business, there was a significant strategic risk of misreading the critical factor(s) in the business, and a great idea could have simply limped along because of a poor implementation decision. If the business founders had not recognized the risk of their business idea being copied, they might have implemented the wrong approach and would likely have been replaced in the market by a larger, richer firm. You can see that a business founder needs to develop an in-depth understanding of his deficit analysis on each business idea before moving forward.

Now let's go back and take a look at our entrepreneur who is debating between a printing shop, a flower shop, and a restaurant. The entrepreneur contemplated the situation and developed the following insights. The printing shop would not have to be in prime retail space, since it was not going to focus on retail customers like the large chain near campus, but instead was to focus on business customers. The flower shop needed to be in prime retail space to obtain the impulse purchases that are a high percentage of the flower business. The size of the space needed and the need for excellent access to customers would make the restaurant's location the most expensive of all three.

The flower shop's competition would be the strongest, and the profit margins in that industry were lower than in the other two industries. The printing shop had good profit margins, but the investment in the equipment necessary was relatively high. The restaurant seemed to have the highest risk. The nature of eating out is both eclectic and faddish. Individuals might desire one type of food for a while, then switch to another type of food. Thus, this year it may be gourmet burgers, but next year it may be Thai food. Additionally, returns in the overall restaurant industry are historically low, although individual restaurants can be quite profitable.

The time needed to start up the flower shop and the printing shop would be shortest. The time it takes to set up and start a restaurant can be quite high, due to the nature of the finish to the interior that is required in the restaurant itself. The restaurant will have a developed character and must be decorated, while the print shop might just have white walls. Additionally, there is a far bigger staff in the restaurant, so the need for extensive hiring and training is an inherent and integral part of the business.

The entrepreneur had financial support from his family as well as some personal savings; had been laid off from his job, so he had lots of time to dedicate to the business; was single; and was dedicated to starting a business. The deficit analysis for these three factors is provided in Table 3.2.

As a result of this analysis, the potential small business owner decided to focus his due diligence on the printing business. The due

BUSINESS IDEA	CATEGORY	OUR RESOURCES	RESOURCES REQUIRED	DEFICIT
Printing Shop High-quality printing—commercial	Finances	Savings and some ability to get loans	Printing equipment, cheap rent	Medium
Flower Shop Family history and support		Savings, loans, family money	Coolers, basic equipment	Low
Restaurant Positioned between fast food and full service		Savings, loans	Significant equipment, expensive Location	High
Printing Shop High-quality printing—commercial	Time	Full time	8-5 and high-volume work	Low
Flower Shop Family history and support		Full time, plus family time and experience	8-5, need support for customer traffic, delivery	Medium
Restaurant Positioned between fast food and full service		Full time	11-9, need lots of support, service, cooking, cleaning	High
Printing Shop High-quality printing—commercial	Resources	Little knowledge	Printing expertise and experience	High
Flower Shop Family History and Support		Significant knowledge in family	Arrangements, design, stocking	Low
Restaurant Positioned between Fast Food and Full Service		Little knowledge	Food preparation, legal requirements, system for efficient delivery and payment	High

Table 3.2

diligence proved that there was a need for the business (this concept will be discussed more in Chapter 4); that a successful and sustainable strategy had the potential to be developed (this concept will be discussed more in Chapter 5); and that the potential business had the opportunity for positive cash flows (this concept will be discussed more in Chapter 6). As result of that due diligence process, the small business person established the business, and has made it a success.

summary

In this chapter we presented a method for the potential new business person to develop and perform an initial evaluation of her business ideas. This process starts with an evaluation of the skills that the individual brings to the new business. What education, experience, hobbies, etc. do you already have in your pocket when the new business gets founded? The next step is to look at the world around you and systematically evaluate the potential opportunities. There are literally millions of ideas out there. The real question is, Do you have the ability to successfully take advantage of those ideas to create a successful business? Finally, we presented a deficit analysis methodology that has been used successfully for some time.

key terms

brainstorming 49
gap analysis 48
threats to operational financing 54

threats to profit margin 54
threats to sales generation schemes 54

review questions

1. Based on your *education*, what are the skills you have that could be the basis for a business?
2. Based on your *work experience*, what are the skills you have that could be the basis for a business?
3. Based on your *hobbies*, what are the skills you have that could be the basis for a business?
4. What are your top three personal skills?
5. What things do you like doing best?
6. What magazines and books do you read?
7. What are your three greatest accomplishments in life? What skills were involved in these accomplishments?
8. Do you enjoy working with people?
9. What general industry (retail/wholesale/manufacturing/service) would you prefer to work in?

Conduct the following for yourself to determine which businesses would be an appropriate match for the skills and traits you determined above.

1. Think about what trends around the region/nation/world you know about that have not reached your area.
2. Interview and talk about opportunities with key successful entrepreneurs in the area. Where do they find a match between opportunity and your skills?
3. Discuss with family members what potential businesses they believe might be best for you.

Take the business ideas that have met your criteria thus far, and perform a deficit analysis of those ideas. Which idea has the most potential for success, given your resources, time, risk position, etc.?

group exercises

1. Break into teams of three to four. Present each of your personal deficit analyses. Help each other think through their accuracy and the means by which you could overcome any shortcomings in skills or resources.

2. The team has a combination of experiences and resources. If the team, instead of just one person, were putting together a business, how would the analysis change?

everyday edisons class discussion

Go to www.everydayedisons.com/matthew.html and read about Matthew and how his hobby led to a business.

1. How did his hobby lead to a business?
2. What creativity is needed to take such a hobby and create a business?

John Hughes: Camel City Café & Wine Bar

It is said that success is where opportunity and preparation meet. This is certainly the case for John Hughes and his Camel City Café & Wine Bar. John Hughes started in the restaurant business when he was 14 years old in Memphis, Tennessee. The manager was hiring new employees and several of John's fellow basketball players had already been hired to work at the restaurant in various capacities. John began to work at the restaurant and by the time he was a senior in high school, he was the manager. This experience taught him that the restaurant industry could be a great place for a young person who had a dedicated work ethic and who was willing to learn the ropes from the ground up. In his sophomore year in college, he was offered the position of food and beverage manager at the Sheraton Inn–Medical Center, which was one of the largest hotels in the city. John was a superior performer at the hotel and was offered the opportunity to join a new team being formed to run a resort off Lake Martin in Alabama. John became the Port Aquarius Resort's food and beverage manager. While at the resort, he developed a plan to one day own his own restaurant, and thus began a process of learning, planning, and looking for the right opportunity.

To start his own restaurant, John knew he needed to learn more. He had solid skills in operations but wanted to learn the best methods in the nation for managing operations. He also knew that he needed to learn more about the business side of the operation. He approached a fee-paid recruiter and specifically asked to be placed with the best-managed restaurant business in the United States so he could learn those skills. He landed a position with Magic Pan, a national restaurant chain that specialized in crepes which was widely hailed as one of the best-run restaurant operations. He stayed with them for four years, learning the business side of the trade. Approaching the same recruiter again, he expressed his desire to move to managing multiple locations, and landed a position with T.G.I. Friday's in Charlotte, North Carolina. These experiences working for restaurants with a national reputation helped him build a wide range of skills. John later moved to Winston-Salem, North Carolina, when an opportunity to be partial owner of a restaurant was made available to him.

Four years later John opened his own consulting business (Hughes Restaurant Consultants). The business was founded upon the notion that good restaurant management is a skill that can be taught. John specialized in taking troubled restaurants and turning them around. Unable to stay away from the retail business for very long, he saw an opportunity in the area to satisfy his other passion: wine. He initially opened the Triad Wine Company in Reynolda Village (a high-end shopping area near Wake Forest University). He also started two "smoothie" shops called Groovy Smoothie!, one of which operates to this day out of the Central Winston-Salem YMCA.

In late 2001, just after 9/11, a friend who owned a restaurant equipment supply company had a client go out of business. Faced with repossessing the equipment, he called John to suggest that he look at the location as a possibility for a new restaurant. John had been intrigued by the idea of combining his knowledge of food with his knowledge of wine. He saw the location in December 2001 and opened for business on March 8, 2002. His concept was to offer a high-end food and wine bar. He knew that five wine bars had gone out of business over the previous two years in the same area, as a result of either poor food management or poor beverage management. John felt he had the skills in both areas that would allow him to succeed. Therefore, he felt that the opportunity was ripe to try his hand at creating his dream restaurant.

Located just a few blocks from downtown, his new restaurant was actually a well-known location in the Winston-Salem community. The location had been in continuous use as a restaurant for the past 70 years. Generations of locals had eaten at that location, originally called the Toddle House. However, the restaurant itself was exceedingly small. John put a new door into the patio area and then had the entire area enclosed with a high-quality, year-round tent! This more than doubled his seating area and created an ambiance that works for the high-end clientele that he sought. Interestingly enough, due to its configuration in this city founded by tobacco (R. J. Reynolds), Camel City Café (a name that has its historical roots in tobacco) was not permitted a smoking area. The limited backroom space also prevented him from running both a lunch and a dinner operation. Therefore, he was only open for dinner. In just over two years of operations, John had virtually paid off his bank note, had established his business in the community, and was planning to move his operation to a much larger space in the central downtown area. His 36-seat restaurant was constantly full.

Camel City Café opened its doors at the new restaurant location in August 2005, shutting down the former location completely. Located at the corner of Fourth Street (aka "Restaurant Row") and Marshall, the restaurant is now located within walking distance of most of the area's largest businesses, including the M. C. Benton Convention Center. The restaurant's new home is a large facility on the ground floor of the North Carolina School of the Arts building with two separate dining rooms, an outside patio, and a full-service bar, "The Oasis." In addition, John also has a banquet facility on the tenth floor of the same building. However, the change in location actually changed the business model. Although the distance of the new location from the old location is just six blocks, John found himself having to develop a whole new clientele. Winston-Salem is still not an urban market like Los Angeles or Chicago, where people are used to parking and walking some distance. In Winston-Salem, the average customer wants to park outside the business and walk in. This is difficult at the new location. Thus, the new location means that John's customer base has shifted from locals to the tourist/conventioneer who stays in one of the downtown hotels and attends events at the convention center, and thus can walk to the restaurant.

John firmly believes that the number one challenge in any start-up is marketing the business. "You must look for ways to get the customer into your operation. The product must be high quality, but not necessarily high priced, to keep the customer. You have to find a way to get them to come and see you. Without marketing you will not succeed. Develop that plan carefully. We are proof. My old, established restaurant lost its base, even though we moved only six blocks. They did not want to park and walk half a block? Go figure."

Camel City Café is thriving in a developing downtown area that has seen an explosion in new condos and business activity. More information can be found about Camel City Café at its Web site: www.camelcitycafe.com

learning outcomes

After studying this chapter, you will be able to

4.1 Describe how to examine the industry that the new business plans to enter.

4.2 Discuss how to create a profile of the target customers for a new business.

4.3 Explain how to categorize competitors of the new business using external analysis.

4.4 Explain how to construct competitive maps.

4.5 Ensure that the entrepreneur has considered a full set of concerns in his or her external analysis.

4.6 Differentiate between those elements of the business which provide a competitive advantage and those that do not.

External Analysis

GUAYAKÍ SUSTAINABLE RAINFOREST PRODUCTS, INC.

Products and services that are popular in one part of the country or world may be very effective models for business start-ups. However, to be successful in starting this type of new business, the small business person must ensure that he understands the interests of his potential customers and has the ability to educate his own market about the product. Based on a student project to develop a new business, Alex Pryor built a small business selling a drink in the U.S. that was wildly popular in his native Paraguay (Yerba Mate). This product is a coffee substitute that seems to have many other benefits, including being an energy enhancer, a body system balancer, and an appetite suppressant.

Alex's friend Steve Karr joined the business in 1996 to form Guayakí Sustainable Rainforest Products. Their goal from the beginning has been to capitalize on the desire of many people to live an ecologically sustainable lifestyle. Funding in their early days included several SBA loans, Karr's entire life savings, and lots of credit cards. The founders traveled and served Yerba Mate from a rainforest mural–painted RV while operating the business out of a one-bedroom apartment. The market developed slowly as each customer was educated in the uses of the drink and the goal of the organization. While they provide a sustainable drink product, their organizational goal is to create economic models that drive reforestation while providing employees a living wage. They have established a carbon-neutral business model and have recently become a significant buyer from women-based businesses that are driving the charge to eliminate poverty, malnutrition, and destructive land practices from the area.

Guayakí is now one of the leading providers of organic, fairly traded, rainforest-grown yerba mate in North America, with products sold at thousands of natural foods stores, cafes, and supermarkets.

Source: Stephanie Huszar, "South America's Secret Weight Loss Tea," *Woman's World,* October 21, 2003; Joan Caplin, Ellen McGirt, and Amy Wilson, "Fortune Hunters," *Money,* August, 2003; www.guayaki.com; Jad Josey, "Yerba Mate: Real Amazon Gold," *Vision Magazine* ??, 2003; http://www.csrwire.com/News/13524.html

Starting a small business should be based on the observance of an opportunity.[1] The recognition of an opportunity may come from a frustration with the way that existing businesses operate (poor service, lack of selection); a new technology that makes an idea that was previously impractical become available (i.e., an Internet-based service, computer animation); a hobby that provides you unique skills and insight; or a new vacancy at the perfect location for a business. However, while there are many ways to identify an opportunity, the new business person must ensure that what she is observing is truly an opportunity. What may appear to be a great opportunity to you may in fact not be viable as a business. The key to opportunity recognition is a detailed understanding of the external environment.

There are a number of critical steps in examining the nature of the external environment. These include the following:

1. Define the industry in which you are competing.

2. Define your customers.

3. Research theindustry yourself.

4. Identify competitors within that industry.

5. Research those competitors.

6. Draw a competitive map.

7. Examine and develop insights about additional economic aspects of the industry, including substitutes, elasticity of demand, ease of entry/exit, benchmarking, and industry trends.

8. Determine your competitive advantage.

We shall look at each of these steps in turn in analyzing the external environment.

LO 4.1 Defining Your Industry

The first part of an external analysis is to determine the industry within which the new business will compete, as well as the general makeup of the industry.[2] In doing so the small business person should seek to be as specific as possible. For example, one might ask, In what industry does a new ice cream store compete? Clearly, the industry will include other ice cream stores. However, if the ice cream store will make a significant part of its revenues from selling ice cream cakes, then the industry might be best viewed as including a broader group of dessert providers, such as bakeries and other businesses that sell competing products. If the ice cream store has both dipping operations where the ice cream is sold in cones and prepackaged gallons of ice cream, perhaps the industry includes grocery stores that also sell gallons of ice cream. Defining the firm's industry is not something that should be taken lightly.

Basic information on the industry chosen can be obtained from the Internet, at the library, or via a magazine or journal that covers a broad category of firms to which you believe your new business will belong. While there are many ways to obtain this categorization, there are two relatively simple means available. The first is to locate your industry's NAICS (North American Industry Classification System) code for the industry. An NAICS code is a code that can vary from 2 to 7 digits in length (the more digits, the more specific the classification); the codes were generated by the U.S. government in an effort to gather, track, and publish data on specific industries. You can locate this code either at your local library or on the Internet (www.census.gov/epcd/www/naics.html). The second way to find nationwide information is to locate a public company that might be a direct competitor to the new business and simply use its NAICS code to look up overall industry data (via Dun & Bradstreet, LexisNexis, etc.).[3]

At an aggregated national level, the data gathered on a firm's industry has some value; however, it is the rare new business that intends to draw customers from across the United States at its founding. Most of the data available will be on a national basis, which provides the new business person some information on national trends, but provides little understanding of the local competitive environment. The national industry may be doing very poorly, while your immediate area might contain virtually no competitors and have the potential to do very well. For example, in the recent recession, housing construction businesses in California, Florida, and Nevada were severely hurt, while at the same time the housing construction industry in Texas and Missouri experienced limited economic slowdown.

The new business person should define the industry in which he will compete broadly enough to be inclusive of all potential competitors, but not so broadly as to be overwhelming. If you are starting a new jewelry store, it is most likely that not even all the jewelry stores in your area are likely competitors. If your store will be in a shopping mall, clearly, other stores in similar malls will be competitors. However, if there is a Tiffany's in the same city, it might or might not be a direct competitor, depending upon the specific customer market that you are seeking to serve. Someone who buys jewelry at Tiffany's is not likely to purchase items in a small, shopping-mall store, and vice versa.

Even more important, the small business must be clear about the practical level of actual competition. For example, what is a reasonable geographic customer draw for a new small business? Opening up a sandwich shop in the downtown area of a city means that the shop most likely competes with other sandwich or fast-food shops within a one- to two-mile radius—and perhaps less, if walking is the primary means of transportation for downtown lunching workers. There are limits to how far someone will travel for a sandwich. Drawing a practical radius around your potential new business location will also help target the customers that are most likely to patronize your business. This raises an interesting question for our case firm, the Philo restaurant: How far do you believe a potential customer would travel to get to such a restaurant?

Specifically for a small business, the **industry** is defined as those companies within a specified geographic radius that will be in direct competition for the same customers and sales as that of the new business. Thinking about Philo demonstrates some of the difficulties that many new businesses have in their planning. If the founders defined their industry as "dumpling restaurants," this would likely be too narrow to be of practical value. While there are some individuals that are driven to eat only dumplings, the reality is that for most individuals, the choice of restaurants is a smorgasbord. There is a range of choices for restaurants. For Philo to define the industry even as broadly as "Asian restaurants" is probably too narrow. A person normally chooses from a

industry

Those direct competitors selling similar products/services within a specified geographic radius that is consistent with a customer's willingness to travel to purchase those products/services.

wide variety of restaurants within categories such as price, class, ambiance, and location.

LO 4.2 Defining Your Customers

Once the industry is broadly defined, then the exact nature of the customer should be developed. It is important to define a narrower group of individuals who you believe will constitute your most likely customers. Where are they located? Where do they currently obtain the product/service? A new burger place opening up near a university is not competing against all burger places in the country, so overall industry figures for the nation, state, or even city are of little assistance. Instead, the customers are going to be the students, faculty, and staff of the university, and the immediate residents of the university area.

In defining the customer, the new business owner should be diligent in the effort to be as accurate as possible. We will discuss promotional activities such as advertising in Chapter 11 ("Marketing"), but here we note that defining the customer to which your company caters is important for the effective use of your marketing dollars, as well as the satisfaction of core, repeat customers.

One potential restaurant owner told us that he viewed his target customer market as those individuals from ages 2 to 90, from all income ranges, anywhere within a 50-mile radius. Indeed, he became quite upset when we suggested that this was unreasonable. His view was, why not seek every potential customer he could?

What would this type of definition mean to the operation of the business? He would have to have food items that appealed to children, teenagers, adults, and senior citizens in all price ranges. His original concept for the restaurant was that it was to be an upscale restaurant with some "flash" oriented around the extensive wine selection. However, if he defined his customers as everyone aged 2 to 90, his wine selection would have to run the gamut from alcohol-free wine to jugs of cheap wine and to rare vintages, because the range of customers he was targeting would demand to be satisfied, and all of these customers would be equally valued. This egalitarian approach is probably appropriate for a political movement, but is a poor approach to business success.[4]

Once the owner realized the expansive—and expensive—scope of the plan, he decided to narrow his true target to adults aged 30 to 50 with a median income of $60,000 and who lived within about 20 minutes' drive from the restaurant. This is not to suggest that he will, or would want to, turn away anyone who wishes to dine at his establishment. It does, however, suggest that the only patrons that he specifically caters to are those in his demographic. An outcome of this approach is that if a college-aged couple comes in and complains about the wine selection being too expensive, the owner no longer has to feel the need to appeal to them and provide inexpensive wines. They are not his target customers.

This approach helps the small business clearly focus on its core customer. It also helps the new business maintain a strategic distance between itself and its competitors, since the firm is not trying to do what everyone else may do. Finally, a clear understanding of the business's customers assists the owners in controlling expenses, as the business does not try to be everything to everybody.

As we have discussed previously, Doug Cheng and Jennie Williams are developing a restaurant that will sell Asian dumplings as its core product. This restaurant is unique in that it will specialize in selling a wide variety of dumplings. Understanding the potential competitors, the nature of the industry, and potential sales levels is critical in determining the opportunity for Philo Asian Grille. Below are the initial parts of Philo's external analysis, conducted by the founders as part of their business plan.

Industry

Philo is a specialty restaurant that will sell a wide range of dumplings. The industry in which it will compete is broader than "Chinese food restaurants"; instead, it is "all restaurants in the Uptown market." Consumers normally will not consider only Chinese food for a meal, but instead, will look at and choose from all businesses that offer an alternative to cooking at home. However, the distance that the consumers are willing to travel is relatively small: one mile or less.

Customers

Philo will be located in the heart of Uptown Charlotte. Our customer base will be people within a three-mile radius of Uptown, with an initial focus on those living in, working in, and visiting Uptown Charlotte.

The Uptown area is the center for many upwardly mobile, affluent, professional consumers in the 25- to 44-year age range. These consumers typically stay on top of the latest trends in dining, music, fashion, and technology. Psychographics for this group include a propensity for dining out an average of three or more times per week, frequenting lounges or nightclubs, and attending various Uptown events. These will be the target customers for Philo.

Competition

Within the Uptown market, there are 47 fast-food restaurants, 31 casual restaurants open for lunch and dinner, and 12 moderately upscale restaurants. Philo will directly compete with two distinct categories of restaurants, since its customers are relatively higher-income individuals. The primary category is "moderately upscale restaurants attracting both business professionals and Uptown entertainment seekers." These competitors are full-service restaurants open for lunch, dinner, and late-night dining and featuring prominent bar areas that offer expanded appetizer menus.

The secondary category of restaurants with which *Philo* will compete is "Asian-cuisine restaurants in Uptown." There are currently eight Asian restaurants in the Uptown area. These restaurants are bland and do not provide excitement or energy as part of the dining experience. Most include dumplings on their menu only as an appetizer. Any that have a bar or lounge have it only as an afterthought.

Following is an overview of Philo's primary dinner competitors within a one-mile radius.

Town

Town is a moderately upscale restaurant featuring a prominent bar and lounge area situated in the middle of the restaurant. Town's core clientele is stylish professionals that live and work in Uptown Charlotte. The food is progressive American cuisine with heavy Asian influences.

Blue

Blue is an upscale restaurant that features Mediterranean-style dishes. Blue is known for hosting the "Who's Who" crowd of chic and powerful people. The restaurant features live jazz weekly, which furthers solidifies its cool, trendy, and elegant reputation.

Cosmos Cafe

Cosmos is known for drawing the younger and beautiful crowd to its very active bar. In addition to serving dim sum and sushi, Cosmos has a variety of pizzas served from its wood-fired brick oven.

Aquavina

Aquavina is an upscale seafood restaurant located on the second floor of The Green on S. Tryon Street. The cuisine is innovative, contemporary seafood. Aquavina has recently opened a wine bar and attracts the affluent residential crowd and business executives from neighboring buildings.

Zink American Kitchen

Zink attracts a business crowd for lunch and dinner, but transitions to a younger, single crowd later in the evening. Zink's location is clearly its main driver for success; however, it does enough things right to pose formidable competition for business and late-night patrons.

LO 4.3 Developing the Information for the External Analysis of Competitors

The Philo founders were able to develop some very good information for their external analysis. They accomplished this with a lot of legwork and using publically available information. Next we discuss a number of ways to conduct such research.

Research Your Industry Yourself

At this point in your efforts to start a new business, you should have defined the industry that interests you, determined who your potential customers might be and why they might want to buy from your business, and gathered some information on these domains. The next issue is to identify the exact competitors within that industry. These competitors are those firms that directly compete for the same set of ideal customers as your proposed business. If the new business owners are very clear regarding their customers' needs, then the ability to identify direct competitors becomes significantly easier. As obvious and mundane as it sounds, the places to look for these competitors can be as simple as the local telephone book and the front seat of your car.

While it is certainly possible to hire a consulting company to perform the type of customer research service discussed above, the entrepreneur will gain invaluable insight by handling this process personally. Let us provide an illustration. A small group of golf professionals had the idea of developing an affordable, non-member 18-hole golf course in the Dallas–Fort Worth (DFW) metroplex. Their idea was to offer a country-club-level course without the membership commitment and expense involved with playing on some of the area's quality courses. The group had a tract of land that had been in the family of one of the potential founders and had been given to him upon the death of his father. While this was substantially larger than the ordinary small business idea, we believe the concepts point out the critical issues that any potential entrepreneur must address.

Knowing your market is important. What activities would you want to control personally when developing your business?

At the first meeting, the golf professionals were clear that they knew the market and what the market needed. However, basic market questions kept coming up that they were unable to answer. Some of the questions raised for which they had no answers included these:

1. How many 18-hole courses are there in the DFW metroplex?
2. How many of these courses are not tied to a country club?
3. How many rounds of golf are played on a typical weekend at these courses?
4. How far does the average golfer drive to play a round?
5. Are there capacity problems at some of the more popular courses?
6. How much does the average golfer spend in food/drink while playing 18 holes?

7. What is charged to play at various times of the day/week at each of the open courses?

8. Where is the population growth area for golfers?

9. What is the profile of a typical golfer?

It was clear that these individuals who wanted to start the business loved golf and thought they had a great understanding of the local industry, but had not done a true in-depth study of the market. These individuals were frustrated when they realized that they did not have a detailed understanding of the potential customer. In response, they were ready to hire a company to collect this information, despite the high cost of pursuing that option. Instead, we encouraged them to collect this information themselves. Doing so would make them the experts in the area and enable them to develop a plan for a business that would give them a competitive advantage. The benefits of planning and analysis are the insights it provides the individuals performing the activities. Hiring a company to gather information not only is expensive, but also limits the insights that can be obtained.

Therefore, the founders prepared a list of questions about a golf course that would help differentiate their business. After doing some quick research to find every 18-hole course in the metroplex, they divided up the courses and individually visited each one. The questionnaires that they developed were completed after each visit and an overall analysis was completed describing the entire market.

> ### EXERCISE 2
>
> Using the golf course initiative as an example, pair up with one other person and explain your business idea to her. Have the person role-play a friend who would be investing in your business. Have the person ask you questions about what the customer desires to get out of the product/service. Use the list as a starting point for your own competitor analysis.

Defining Competitors

An effective industry analysis starts by identifying every potential competitor within that previously defined reasonable distance from your planned establishment location. What a reasonable distance consists of is a matter of interpretation, and the interpreter is the new business person. While someone could argue with any individual's assessment of that distance, it must be established, and this is much more a matter of art than a matter of science. In any case, the first step is to define a radius from which you believe you will draw a majority of your customers. Make this distance reasonable, not just a wish.[5]

A woman in Knoxville, Tennessee, was planning a quick-serve, breakfast-oriented restaurant. She needed to define a reasonable radius from which she would draw her ideal customers. She originally said that she would draw customers from the entire metropolitan Knoxville area, and (much like our previous restaurant owner) was adamant that she didn't want to forego any business. Once again, we certainly don't suggest that you forego business unnecessarily, but an assessment that a business draws from an entire region is unreasonable for many reasons. Just one is that if you try to cater to everyone in a metro area, you will distort your advertising efforts, and you will dramatically increase your costs. Instead, this business founder needed to focus on customers within a reasonable commuting distance from the restaurant. She eventually narrowed that distance to 20 minutes of driving in traffic. While you may indeed draw customers from outside this area, they are not your primary group at the outset. If you need to rethink this distance as your operations mature, then you can. The core information is already in hand and will still be relevant if you expand or contract the market radius later.

Once she had identified the area she wanted to serve, she began driving the area, to see what competitors might be in the area. She also identified businesses through the phone book. The end result was that with relatively little expense, she was able to identify those restaurants that would be her direct and indirect competitors.

Once you have established a reasonable radius from which you will draw your primary customer, the next step is to examine each of your potential competitors. It is easy to discuss practices in the industry in general terms. For example, you might hear that at all the area photocopying places, service is poor, wait times are long, and the equipment is of poor quality. These general feelings about the industry may help an entrepreneur see an opportunity, but actually running a business requires specific knowledge about your competitors.

fragmented markets

Markets in which no one competitor has a substantial share of the market and the means of competition varies widely within the same market space.

As we observed about Philo, small businesses typically compete in what is referred to as **fragmented markets**.[6] These are markets that have no clear dominant competitor and are instead made up of a large number of similar-sized small firms. If the small business is competing directly with large firms, this virtually guarantees that at a minimum, the small business will be operating at a cost disadvantage, and will have to compete on some other basis. In any case, the number and size of all competitors needs to be detailed. Additionally, the differences in how the various businesses compete and their competitive advantages also need to be understood.

In the Knoxville restaurant example above, the ability to drive by and visit the various restaurants allowed the small business person to understand the situations with each of those establishments, and which might be the strongest competitors. Straightforward observations made by a small business owner who understands the competitive issues of the industry can provide valuable insight. However, there is another tool available to the small business person that can provide additional information. Specifically, an analytical tool that has the ability to digest information and display this information to others is a **competitive map**.

competitive map

An analytical tool used to organize information about direct competitors on all points of competition.

LO 4.4 Developing a Competitive Map

At this point in the process, the amount of detail that needs to be organized raises the need for a systematic means to categorize that information. Thus, the next step in your external analysis is to develop a competitive map in order to better understand competitors and their capabilities.[7] While there are many companies available who are in business to examine competitors, as we have stated previously, we recommend that the entrepreneur develop this map personally, for the following reasons:

1. It is less expensive.
2. Knowledge of what is right and wrong with each of the competitors allows the entrepreneur to better position the new business.
3. Insights will be developed regarding positioning, pricing, and facility layout.

rodriquez family auto repair shop

Alex was continuing to make progress on his business plan for the auto repair shop. He was now conducting his external analysis and seeking to define his industry, customers, and competitors. He had thought he knew exactly what he wanted to do when he first talked with his family about the shop that first Sunday. He now realized that there were numerous choices that had to be made. He found several auto shops in the area that had a very specific focus. For example, there were a few that focused only on rebuilding engines, while there was one that focused only on vintage cars from the 1960s and 1970s. There were also quick oil change shops—but he was not sure if these were really his competitors. Alternatively, if oil change shops were competitors, then were the national chain stores in the area that only serviced tires his competitors as well?

Alex decided that his industry was "general auto repair." Specialty repair shops, such as those that serviced only vintage cars, or focused on only one type of car function were not his direct competitors. The national chains focused on a single activity and performed that activity at a very low cost, but they did not try to build relationships with the customers. Alex knew he could never achieve a lower cost structure when compared with the national chains, and he also wanted to build a relationship with his customers. In addition, he knew he could not develop the extensive expertise necessary to be successful in a very specialized area like vintage cars.

Considering what his customer base might look like in his area of the city, Alex determined that his target customer would have an average household income of $50,000. He would focus on the households in the area, not on the public housing complex that was approximately a mile away. Alex's decision had nothing to do with the people in public housing as people. It had much more to do with the fact that he wanted to ensure that people could pay for the services delivered and that his customers would not be trying to find the lowest price possible. The population in this area of the city was relatively dense; therefore, he determined he would target customers within 7 miles of his business. This produced a population of approximately 50,000 people to serve. In his immediate area, there were only two other general auto repair shops that offered a similar set of services.

4. A competitive map, once developed, can be updated easily, providing a constant track on the industry.

5. The obtaining of any financing needed by the firm will be greatly enhanced with a detailed knowledge of the industry.

Developing a competitive map requires that the entrepreneur visit ALL of the potential competitors. Furthermore, we recommend that you be a customer at these competitors' places of business. There is nothing quite like the customer perspective from a series of such visits; the comparisons to your potential competitors become easier with this type of insight. With this in mind, the entrepreneur must develop a list of criteria that she wishes to take away from each visit and record that information after each visit. While this list might change depending upon the type of establishment, we suggest a list of potential items to consider:

1. Parking availability (how many spots and what quality?).

2. Access from road.

3. Nearby attractions for customers.

4. Size of facility.

5. Décor.

6. Pricing.

7. Product breadth.

Chapter Four External Analysis **71**

8. Product depth.
9. Staffing (number and quality).
10. Capacity.
11. Brochures/advertising material.
12. Customer traffic at several different times of day.
13. Average sale.
14. Friendliness/helpfulness.
15. Unique features.
16. Suppliers (what company is delivering to their business?).

An example of a competitive map is shown in Table 4.1. This competitive map (for the Dallas–Fort Worth golf course discussed earlier) encompasses a number of criteria that could be used in the evaluations of the business. The 8-mile radius employed in this map is based on the distance the partners determined from their research that someone would drive to play golf.

Table 4.1
Competitive Map: Golf Course (8-Mile Radius)

	COMPETITOR #1	COMPETITOR #2	COMPETITOR #3	COMPETITOR #4	COMPETITOR #5
Population in area					
# of households in area					
Household income					
Average age in area					
# of driving ranges					
# of golf shops in area					
# of customers – weekday					
# of customers – weekend					
Average # of customers/hour					
Peak flow of customers					
Average charge/ transaction					
Tee charge – peak/ off-peak					
Clubhouse feel					
Course feel					
Variety of menu offerings – clubhouse					
Variety of menu offerings – course					

Some of these items (and there will be other ones for your venture) can be easily categorized and analyzed. Others are more descriptive and give you a rich sense of what is available to customers right now. We have included a description of some of the findings from the group seeking to establish the golf course.

At this time the DFW area has 74 golf courses. However, it was determined from surveys with potential customers that on average, individuals will drive no more than 30 minutes one way to the golf course. Therefore, rather than examine all 74 courses, we chose to examine only those courses in Fort Worth and those no farther than 30 minutes from downtown. This resulted in our visiting 24 golf courses, 25 percent of which were private. The private courses in this particular area are very difficult to join. The membership/initiation fees at these clubs are quite expensive, several are at capacity, the current members appear to be very particular about who is a member, and the benefits of belonging to the club are more oriented to social/business connections than to golf. Therefore, the focus shifted to the remaining 18 non-club courses.

Five of the 18 public courses appeared to be poorly maintained. However, the other 13 were in good shape, with at least 6 of those in excellent shape. In visiting with golfers at the courses and playing the courses themselves, the potential founders discovered that there was no difficulty in getting on the courses. Both the access and the nature of the courses were generally excellent. The fact that they were public courses was a result of city government subsidies.

After completing their map, the potential founders concluded that the competitive landscape was not at all what they had initially thought. They concluded that the DFW area was overbuilt and that the presence of public subsidies for many courses distorted competition. They decided that the market was not as attractive as they originally had thought.

EXERCISE 3

Develop the basis of a competitive map for your proposed venture. Outline in columns each of the items that you would like to observe while visiting your competitors. Present this to the class and ask for help in developing a complete map.

LO 4.5 Additional Issues for External Analysis

There are a number of other economic issues that founders of a new business will want to consider as they develop their external analysis. These include substitutes, elasticity of demand, ease of entry/exit, benchmarking, and industry trends. Each will be discussed briefly.

Substitutes

The potential new business person should keep in mind potential substitutes for the activities of their business. A **substitute** exists if the service or product performs a similar function or achieves the same result as the planned business, but is not a precise imitation.[8] In the case of golf, a substitute might be tennis or boating. Any other sport that the customer can pursue in place of golf could be a substitute.

In developing a competitive map, the small business person needs to be aware of such substitutes and the potential impact they can have. However, it is also important that the new business person not overwhelm himself with so many potential substitutes that it appears that

substitute

A product that performs a similar function or achieves the same result, but is not a precise imitation.

there is no way to compete in the industry. Each new business person must judge the potential impact of a substitute, but the important issue is the recognition that at some price tradeoff point, customers will switch to substitutes. While the substitute is not the desired activity or product, it will be chosen under some circumstances. For example, if you charge $500 for a single round of golf, individuals will eventually seek out other means of entertainment. Thus, substitutes can help form a ceiling on the price that can be charged for the product/service.

Elasticity of Demand

Elasticity of demand refers to how easy it is for a customer to switch to substitutes or not use a product as the price of the product rises.[9] A product/service for which customers are willing to pay virtually any price is said to have a very inelastic demand. In other words, for your cancer medicine, the price is irrelevant; you will still seek out the medicine and buy it. In this case, substitutes have very little impact. However, for a product that has elastic demand, such as rounds of golf, a price increase of $25 for a round may create a significant substitute impact. Chapter 11 will deal more in detail with the marketing and pricing of goods; it is sufficient here to say that the presence and power of substitutes need to be considered by the new business person. When developing your competitive map, you will need to include those companies that are close substitutes for your product/service and determine how to evaluate a trade-off value.

Ease of Entry or Exit

Another issue that needs to be considered is the ease of entry to and exit from the industry. Once a business is in operation, then expenses are being incurred. If those expenses are such that a small business person cannot easily recoup the investment, then the level of competition will be more intense. This is considered an **exit barrier**[10]—that is, a barrier that keeps an entrepreneur from leaving a business she has invested in. For example, the principal investments for a clothing store are the clothes in the store. Clothes tend to be very seasonal. If a piece of clothing is not sold in season, then it likely has limited value in the near future. Think about the value of white polyester suits if you need to be convinced. To close a clothing store is easy, but to recover the initial investment is not. The owner will need to sharply discount the price of the goods, often to the detriment of the store and its direct competitors, just to bring in some money before she has to close the store.

In our golf example, the initial investment for the golf course is very high, but the ease of exiting the business is also very high, since the real estate could be converted to another use, such as a housing tract. If a business owner cannot easily exit an industry, then that owner is more likely to use predatory pricing in an effort to generate cash flow and survive. The ability to exit the industry must be taken into consideration when evaluating the competitive threat posed by existing businesses. A clothing store would have very high competition, while a golf course would have somewhat less. In contrast to the clothing store, a liquor store's principal investment is alcohol. If a liquor store is not doing well and needs to close, there is always a secondary market for its goods. There is little need to have deep price discounts to seek to recover the investment. Thus, exit is relatively easy, and competition would be expected to be a bit lower. The

How far can or should you go to collect information about your competitors? Most competitors will be private companies, and their financial information will not be part of the public record. Is it appropriate to be a customer of your competitor in order to collect competitive information? Can you hire a private investigator to find out information that is not in the public domain? What if the existing firm is owned by a friend? At what stage can you copy ideas from your friends and maintain your ethical standards?

ability to exit a business relatively easily tends to limit the intensity of competition in the industry and reduces the threat posed by a new entry.

Benchmarking

There may be specific areas in your business that you have identified as potentially providing you a competitive advantage. To strengthen those areas, you may consider **benchmarking** a business that is very successful in that particular arena, but that does not compete in your industry.[11] The ability to provide a top-flight call center for your business could be dramatically improved by your looking to companies in other industries that have excellent call-center operations. Most companies are more than willing to share their knowledge as long as you are not a potential competitor.

benchmarking
Working with and learning from a company outside of your industry that has a particular skill that is potentially critical to your operation.

Industry Trends

An overarching part of any analysis of competitors is an understanding of the trends in the industry. These trends shape the long-term perspective of the industry. For example, U.S. society is moving toward a more self-service economy, and companies that can move that process forward or take advantage of this movement appear to have an opportunity for success. Another example might be restaurant patronage. While the number of people eating at restaurants has not changed dramatically over the past few years, what they eat has been changing in a consistently predictable manner. Healthy, mid-price-range restaurant sales have been increasing dramatically. Thus, the percentage of individuals that are willing to pay a little more than fast-food prices for different fare is steadily increasing, while there has been little change in those willing to pay for very high-end restaurants. As a result, a restaurant that enters an emerging market (utilizing the Atkins Diet or another diet craze as a menu theme, for example) may be able to be among the first to enter that niche, and gain an advantage over other firms.

LO 4.6 Competitive Advantage

Once the industry, customer, and competitor issues have been clearly identified, the new business must develop a deep understanding of its competitive advantages. A **competitive advantage** is made up of those things that your business does uniquely well, or better than anyone else in your industry (remember, the industry is defined by you, and consists

competitive advantage
The edge a business has over competing businesses, made up of those things that the business does better than anyone else in the industry.

of those businesses in direct competition with you in your area). This is the last step in your external analysis. We will discuss competitive advantage in greater detail in chapter 5; it is important at this point to understand that these advantages (we hope there will be several) will ultimately be the reason that individuals come to your business and not to that of one of your competitors. Those areas that provide you with competitive advantages are the ones that are valuable, allowing the business to charge a price that exceeds that of its direct competitors while maintaining costs at an equivalent level.

A competitive advantage must provide the new business with the opportunity to make money in excess of the competition. Few new businesses perform better than their competitors in all areas, nor should they be concerned about doing so. Instead, there are many functions that a business must perform (and perform well) simply to be a player in the industry. In most industries the new business is similar to its competitors, but there is one (or hopefully, several) fundamental characteristic(s) by which the firm exceeds the performance of the industry. These characteristics constitute the business's competitive advantage. In order to be able to define the potential areas for this advantage, it is imperative that you have completed the competitive map and are able to discuss the strengths by which each of your competitors stands out.

The source of the competitive advantage can be an activity of the firm, such as service or product selection. It can also be something structural, such as a high-quality location. The new business must be clear about what its own competitive advantages will be, as well as about those of its competitors. One of the causes of failure for new businesses is a lack of focus on their competitive advantages. Individuals might believe they have a great idea and work hard to implement it, but they may not clearly understand why someone chooses their business over that of their competitors. Your customers will have reasons to consciously choose your business, and you must know what those reasons are to maintain your advantage. In thinking about competitive advantage, it is helpful to examine the business as consisting of performance within two areas. The **orthodox** (normal) parts of the business must be done and done well, but there is little reason to do any of these things any better than the average in the industry. The **unorthodox** (unusual) parts of the business should be the focus of the energy, money, and time of the business, since they are the means by which a business can differentiate itself from its competitors. What is orthodox and unorthodox varies by industry, and it varies with time in an industry. The standard practices in an industry move, and they inexorably move to greater and greater heights. For example, when the frequent flyer program was initiated, it was unorthodox and allowed the pioneering airline to stand out, gaining customers and profit at the expense of its competitors. However, today virtually every airline has a frequent flyer program, and indeed, many have shared programs. What starts out as unorthodox will (if it is effective) lead to imitation, and thus become orthodox in the industry. That said, we suggest that the new business person examine his competitive map carefully. What is orthodox in the industry—that is, what does virtually everyone do just to be a player in the industry? These are the standard things you will have to provide just to be a business in this arena. What is unorthodox in your industry? What are competitors doing that varies from one to another? What can you do that is unorthodox and might form a competitive advantage?

orthodox

Describing those areas of a business that are simply standard practice in the industry and are necessary for the business to be a player.

unorthodox

Describing those areas of a business that are unique or unusual when compared to the standard practices of the industry, and that provide the opportunity for the business to gain value over and above the ordinary returns in the industry.

NORMAL BUSINESS RESOURCES & CAPABILITIES (ORTHODOX)	UNUSUAL BUSINESS RESOURCES & CAPABILITIES (UNORTHODOX)
A storefront	A small, intimate facility
Tables	Fixed tile tables
Chairs	Roller, cushioned chairs
Floor covering	Tile floors
Lights	Mood lighting throughout
Cash register	Card swipe machines at each table
Signs	Custom neon signs
Menu	Touch screen at each table
Kitchen equipment:	
Freezers	
Refrigerators	
Sinks	
Stoves/ovens	
Cookware	
Safety equipment	
Fryers	
Plates, cups, silverware, napkins, salt & pepper shakers, sauce dispensers	
Shelving	
Tables & chairs	
Desk/work area	
Time sheets	
Staff:	
Cook staff	Trained chefs
Wait staff	Unique outfits; Experienced, highly training staff requirements, formal
Bartenders	
Cleaning crew (tables, etc)	
Host crew	
Management	
Trash cans (internal and external)	
Utilities	

Table 4.2
Company Evaluation of Resources & Capabilities

The need to be complete in this area is critical. Table 4.2 explores the competitive advantage of a new restaurant. Although not complete, it provides a bit of insight into this process.

While this chart may appear to be a bit excessive, it is not nearly complete. It would be difficult for us to overemphasize the importance of developing this chart prior to beginning operations, so that entrepreneurs are clear as to what might form a competitive advantage for them. We have found few tools more helpful in defining the uniqueness of the potential start-up, as well as defining the potential start-up expenses.

EXERCISE 4

Develop a two-column list for your new business. Label the first column "Normal" and the second "Unusual." In the "normal" column, list everything that you will need to have (physically) and do (actively) just to be a player in the industry. In the second column, explain what your business will have or do that is rare or unusual compared to your competitors.

Resource-Based View

resource-based analysis

A theoretical approach and methodology that examines the functioning of a business in terms of whether a product/ service simultaneously meets the criteria of being rare, durable, non-substitutable, and valuable.

To understand the unorthodox (unusual) resources and capabilities of a business and develop a competitive advantage, the new business owner should utilize a technique known as **resource-based analysis.** This tool helps the entrepreneur delve deeper into what creates that unorthodox ability. In the prior list of unorthodox actions for a restaurant, it was noted that tiles on the table could be an orthodox item. However, upon further consideration, the tiles are really just part of a larger resource that relates to the ambiance of the restaurant. The tiles themselves are good, but they need to be part of something more significant to have an impact. Resource-based analysis has been developed over the past 50 years by a variety of researchers;[12] it has become one of the most effective tools in defining a business's competitive advantages and in differentiating these from their competitors'. While we will cover this topic in depth in the next chapter, we feel that some introduction to this topic is warranted in the discussion of positioning relative to your competitors. The focus of this application is solely upon the unorthodox (unusual) products/services that you will offer in your business.

To develop into a competitive advantage, the unorthodox products/ services need to meet all of the following criteria: They must be rare, durable, valuable, and relatively non-substitutable to develop into a competitive advantage. "Rare" describes a quality that competitors will find difficult to obtain. For example, a particular chef might be unique, or a location may be particularly valued. "Durability" has to do with the length of time that you might be able to gain and hold a competitive advantage. How long would it take for a competitor to imitate you or to wash away your advantage? "Valuable" refers to your ability to gain extraordinary returns from your product/service. A product/service might be rare and durable, but if you cannot obtain returns in excess of your competition from its sale, then it will not provide you with a resource-based advantage. Finally, the new business person must determine whether the product/service may be easily substituted by something else that a competitor could provide.

As you examine your list of unusual products/services for the new business, consider each one on these four dimensions. Those items that meet all four criteria are your primary points of competitive advantage. These are the points on which you should concentrate your resources, time, and effort. These are the areas that will provide you with a competitive advantage relative to your competitors, and will be the reasons that customers choose you over the competition. We will discuss this in much more depth in the next chapter.

summary

This chapter examined the reasons and methods for the potential small business person to develop a complete, well-reasoned, and personal knowledge of the competitive conditions within her market. This analysis is fundamentally founded upon the idea that the entrepreneur decides what constitutes her "industry." For a new business person, her industry does not include (except in unusual circumstances) the whole country or the world. It is important that she limit the defined "industry" as it relates to her specific business, in order to effectively analyze the competition and the potential competitive threat. We have provided these highly practical tools for the founder(s) to personally develop their own analysis of the environment and their ability to compete within that environment.

key terms

benchmarking 75

competitive advantage 75

competitive map 70

elasticity of demand 74

exit barrier 74

fragmented markets 70

industry 65

orthodox 76

resource-based analysis 78

substitute 73

unorthodox 76

review questions

1. How would you advise a potential entrepreneur to define the industry for his new business?
2. How should a new business develop a profile for its potential customers?
3. Why should a potential entrepreneur research the industry personally?
4. What techniques would you recommend for identifying competitors within an industry?
5. How would you recommend developing a complete analysis of the competitors to a new business?
6. What elements are in a competitive map?
7. Finish your competitive map. Starting with the phone book, identify every potential competitor in your specific area and add each one to the spreadsheet you developed earlier in this chapter. Then, using your map, visit the first two competitors on your list, and adjust the map according to reality.

   a. What additional items might you add to the map?
   b. What areas of competition that you thought were unorthodox were actually orthodox?
   c. What qualitative areas of competition did you add to your map?

Using the material that you have developed in the previous exercises, write a two- to three-page description of the competitive environment in which your proposed new business will compete.

group exercises

1. Look at the list of orthodox and unorthodox items for the restaurant in Table 4.2 in this chapter. What would be the resources that would drive the unorthodox items?

2. Take the material that you developed outside of class. Break into small groups. Present your material to the group. Create a list of resources you will need to develop your unorthodox items for the firm.

everyday edisons class discussion

Go to www.everydayedisons.com/mingwei.html

1. With whom do you believe Ming Wei will be competing?

2. Who would be the perfect customer for the device?

Rod Long and Rick Restivo—Team Trident

One of the best pieces of advice that Rod Long and Rick Restivo have for people considering starting a new business is to "stick with what you know." They argue that this one piece of advice helps focus your attention on areas where you have the potential to be better than your competition.

Rod and Rick were both looking for something more in life. They had been through similar experiences since each graduated from Texas A&M University in the 1980s.

Rod was commissioned in the U.S. Marine Corps and served in Desert Shield/Desert Storm. He served for 10 years on active duty and continues to this day to serve in the reserves as a lieutenant colonel. Most of his civilian career up to founding Team Trident was spent in the oil and gas industry. Rick spent 10 years in the Navy and transitioned out as a lieutenant. Much like Rod, he spent his entire civilian life in the oil and gas industry. Rick earned an MS in physics from the Naval Postgraduate School and an MBA at Tulane University.

As luck would have it, Rod and Rick ran into each other at a tailgate party at an A&M football game and started talking about a new business idea. They wanted to do something that combined their backgrounds in the military and their desire to be in business for themselves. After several conversations they focused their ideas on how to combine their oil and gas industry knowledge with their military backgrounds. This knowledge let them see the following in the oil and gas industry:

- The oil & gas industry had suffered decades of infrastructure stagnation and was faced with an aging set of workers who knew the industry.
- Technological advancements across the industry were requiring more highly qualified and technically oriented employees.
- Production was moving to isolated locations like deep offshore sites, the Rockies, and parts of Canada, and to dangerous parts of the world, such as West Africa.
- Many companies recognize that the work environment in such isolated environments is challenging, even for workers accustomed to it.

At the same time, Rod and Rick noted an opportunity. They noted that there were relatively large numbers of skilled technicians transitioning out of the military, and observed these things about them:

- The average military technician receives between six months and two years of training and acquires four to eight years of on-the-job experience before the end of service.
- Service members are accustomed to the living conditions required offshore and in isolated locales.
- The military has high standards for ethical behavior and has zero tolerance for drug use.
- Approximately 240,000 people leave the service each year after honorably completing their obligation—providing an abundant and renewing source for quality, experienced individuals.

Luck has a significant role in starting any new business. However, luck should be defined. The same opportunity can be presented to a hundred people without a single one seeing the business potential. Luck is where perspiration and preparation meet. Rod and Rick had examined the market, understood a competitive gap, realized that they possessed the talent to take advantage of that gap, and had the confidence that this was a great opportunity. They developed a basic plan for a new business that would place trained ex-military personnel with oil and gas industry employers. Still, they both had good jobs and families to take care of. Making the leap into a new venture was going to take a stroke of luck.

Luck arrived at a restaurant bar one night when Rod had been stuck in classic Houston traffic and decided to wait it out. He became engaged in a conversation with an individual who turned out to be the president of an oil and gas services company. As the conversation progressed, this individual offered Rod the opportunity to put the idea he had developed with Rick into action. The company president loved the concept and needed to fill 20 "tough to fill" technical slots in the next six months. He hired Rod and Rick to do the job and fronted them half the fee so that they could get the firm started.

Rod and Rick named their new firm Team Trident. The company seeks the very best of the best of those leaving the military, and then seeks to place those individuals with employers whose needs exactly match the retiring service person's capabilities. They use their contacts within the military and their own very detailed interviewing processes to determine if the candidate is really of the caliber they are looking for. A Team Trident candidate is one who loves what he does, is extremely good at doing it, can handle living conditions that many civilians would find unpleasant, and enjoys getting paid well for this combination of skills. A classic civilian employee arrives on an oil platform and is taken aback by the rustic living conditions, lack of personal space, and round-the-clock mindset. A Team Trident candidate views the same conditions as a vast improvement in living conditions compared to those on a war ship, is used to a round-the-clock mentality, and appreciates the pay for doing what he loves to do. It is Rick and Rod's deep examination of potential candidates and their understanding of the oil and gas industry due to their civilian experience that has separated Team Trident from its competitors.

Most of Team Trident's competitors are too broad in their scope to really compete directly. Rod and Rick refer to their competitors' standard approach as "speed dating." They use job fairs and huge numbers to make connections. Whether the candidates work out or not is irrelevant. The competitors see it as a numbers game: Place any candidate in the job, and if she leaves . . . earn another fee finding a new employee.

Team Trident takes a different approach. The company guarantees its clients that the candidate will work for the firm for a given period of time. While the industry norm is to guarantee that a new employee will last 90 days, Team Trident guarantees six months; in reality, the company will execute a new search for free if one of its placements leaves within a year of hire. For the firm hiring the employees, this is a far better arrangement.

Team Trident has a small central office in downtown Houston. Each of the five employees for the firm telecommutes. They meet each morning on a conference call they call "The Huddle." It is a fast, get-to-the-point-about-each-search meeting using a free conference call service (www.freeconferencecall.com). The company has been growing at a rate of 20 to 30 percent per year. The company just added a recruiter from Tulsa, Oklahoma, and is bringing technical talent to clients all around the world as a result of the oil and gas industry's global reach.

When asked for the four lessons that they have learned in the first years of being in business, Rod and Rick responded quickly.

1. Don't try to be everything for everybody. Keep a focus so that everyone knows exactly who you are and why they should trust you.

2. When you make a mistake, own up to it immediately and correct it. Rod and Rick will do whatever it takes to make the client happy and develop a true, trust-based relationship.

3. Be careful to hire excellent internal employees. Rod and Rick say that hiring internal employees is the toughest job in the business. They found that they were exceptional at evaluating talented technicians for clients, but had no idea what made a great recruiter for their firm. They have gone through a number of what they love to call "bone-headed hiring decisions" to get to the point where they now understand the talent that it takes to work in their company. Employees in this type of organization work from their homes; they have to be organized and on point; and they need to leave their egos at the door.

4. Start your business as inexpensively as possible. As was mentioned earlier, Rod and Rick highly recommend this. They say that the trappings of a business are exactly that. Keep control of your costs.

Team Trident was founded in late 2005. More information is available at www.teamtrident.com/index.htm

learning outcomes

After studying this chapter, you will be able to

5.1 Recognize how mission statements guide a new business.

5.2 Explain what constitutes a sustainable competitive advantage.

5.3 Identify a new business's assets and capabilities.

5.4 Distinguish which of those assets and capabilities are standard and which are extraordinary.

5.5 Apply a resource-based analysis approach to arrive at a list of true competitive advantages.

5.6 Determine a strategy to match the new business mission.

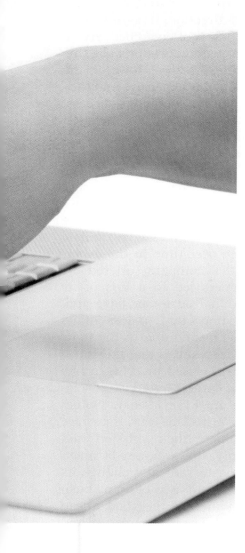

Business Mission and Strategy

VOSGES HAUT-CHOCOLAT

Vosges Haut-Chocolat was founded in 1998 by Katrina Markoff and a partner. Ms. Markoff was 27 at the time and, while working for her uncle's mail-order delivery business, she was asked to find truly exceptional chocolate products. She quickly recognized that while there are numerous large manufacturers of chocolates, their products are intended to have a long shelf life and be available to a large number of customers. The quality is consistently low and there is little in the way of uniqueness in their offerings. She thought this was particularly true of truffles, or chocolates that are filled with various fillings. As a result, she experimented, and developed a series of different types of truffles that offer a unique chocolate experience. For example, she has one called Budapest, which contains dark chocolate and Hungarian paprika, while another is Funk & Disco, which is a milk chocolate truffle with buttermilk banana pudding.

Ms. Markoff developed her business out of her apartment, and her first sales occurred when she convinced Neiman Marcus in Chicago to offer some of her chocolates for sale. This early experience has led her chocolates to be offered in most Neiman Marcus stores, as well as other high-end retail operations, such as Bergdorf Goodman in New York City. The company has now expanded operations to include a retail outlet in New York City and is developing a LEED-certified green manufacturing plant in Chicago.

The chocolate experience offered by Ms. Markoff is a true differentiation strategy, as she charges a higher price for a premium product that is not widely available. The focus of the business is on maintaining a high-quality product, sold only in high-end stores. She was named the 2007 Woman of the Year by *Entrepreneur* magazine and American Express. Her business has become a favorite for gift-givers and "foodies" around the world.

Source: Heather Kenny, "Mane Attraction," *Inc. Magazine* (August 1, 2003), p. 66; Margaret Littman, "Katrina Markoff: Sweet Taste of Success," *Crain's Chicago Business* 25 (November 4, 2002) p. E1;C. Greenwood, "Success Stories – Katrina Markoff," *Success* (January 6, 2009), www.successmagazine.com

mission statement

A brief statement that summarizes how and where a firm will compete.

strategy

The broad approaches a small business will use to accomplish its mission.

Defining the new business's mission and then formulating a consistent strategy for the firm are two of the most difficult and critical elements in the success of any businesss. A firm's **mission statement** is a brief statement that summarizes how and where the firm will compete.* From the firm's mission, the business then develops its **strategy,** which specifies the broad approaches the new business will use to accomplish that mission.

LO 5.1 Mission Statements

It is crucial to establish both the mission and the strategy of the new business prior to its inception. The mission and strategy guide the business development at its most crucial stage. As the business grows, it gets progressively more difficult to change its direction. Imagine establishing a new business oriented toward high levels of customer service with experts in each area of the business. The customers appreciate this extensive expertise, and as a result the business grows. However, the founders find that the model they have developed is expensive and they wish to increase their profits. Therefore, despite the company's success, they decide to use cheaper labor without the expertise. The reaction from their established customer base will likely take place over time. It will not be a dramatic drop in one month, but over time customers will begin to cease doing business with the firm.

This is precisely what happened to Circuit City. Started in 1949 (originally as Wards in Richmond, Virginia) as an entrepreneurial venture based on a well-defined strategy, the company grew to be one of the largest electronic goods providers in the United States.[1] A dramatic change over time in the expertise the company offered its customers led to a loss of its traditional customer base and, more important, a loss in its unique positioning in the market. The result is that the entire business closed in 2009, in one of the largest retail store closures in U.S. history. Sometimes firms find that they have to change their mission and strategy. However, any business seeking to radically change its fundamental way of doing business will find the road ahead difficult. The firm's mission and strategy are central to the new

What lessons can be learned from Circuit City's change to its mission and strategy?

---

* Larger firms typically have a vision statement that is a very broad statement of the firm's direction while the mission statement is a more specific statement. For a small business we believe that mission alone is appropriate. The goal is to help direct the firm in its actions and not create unnecessary work. For a small business to try to differentiate between vision and mission would be splitting hairs. Thus, the student should recognize their differences in theory, but also recognize that here they are treated as the same item.

business's maintaining a clear vision about what it wants to be and how it will accomplish that plan.

We use the term "mission statement" here, but there are many terms used in creating the overarching goals of an organization. It is quite easy for a business person to become consumed in the proper labeling of the action rather than focusing upon the goals of the organization. As a result, you will likely see terms as varied as "company mission," "vision," "overall strategy," "goals," "simple rules," and "statement of purpose" to describe what we call "mission." The important point for the new business person is to be concise and well understood by everyone she works with as to what the company does and does not do.[2] We choose to use the term "mission," but we do recognize that others may use another term.

The firm's mission helps the venture by targeting its efforts in specific arenas and on specific opportunities. No firm generally, nor any new firm specifically, can serve up all things to all people. Instead, the new business needs to focus on performing those activities where it has competitive advantage, or doing some set of activities better than everyone else. The firm's mission helps the new business specify what the business does best in its industry (keeping in mind that the industry consists of those businesses you believe are your direct competitors). However, the mission statement also helps the small business stay away from things that opportunistically sound promising, but which take the business away from its principal focus. Realize that if you start wandering off to another area of competition, you will lose focus in your core area of business. If that occurs, there are always single-focused companies in any market that are ready to capitalize on your judgment errors.[3]

To illustrate the benefit of a mission statement in targeting a firm's activities, let's take a look at another restaurant business. The mission statement of this restaurant read as follows (with some minor changes to protect its identity):

The Gourmet Mediterranean (Italian) Meal Experience in the Heart of the City.

While this mission statement is very simple, it ultimately helped the business owner tremendously. The city was opening a new central high-school basketball arena and needed someone to run the food facilities. The head of the school board asked the owner of the restaurant to consider running the concessions for the arena. The idea appeared to have the potential to be very profitable. However, the food that would be sold at the arena would be very different from what the restaurant traditionally sold. Thus, the expertise that the small business owner held would largely not be applicable. Additionally, new suppliers would need to be located, since the concession stands and the restaurants would use different quality inputs. The operation of the concessions would also take the small business owner's attention away from what she knew best: running a high-quality Mediterranean restaurant. Thus, while both the restaurant and the concession stands involved the preparation and selling of food, in reality they were really two distinct businesses. A clear mission statement helps the new business person focus her efforts on her expertise. The ability to be successful with one type of business does not mean that she will be successful with another type of business, even one within the same broad domain. The earlier business person's mission statement helped that owner keep the business targeted where it needed to compete. The owner passed on the offering of food in the basketball

Jennie and Doug are aware of how important a mission statement can be for a new business. As a result, they developed the mission statement below:

Mission Statement: *Philo is a small, intimate Asian dumpling restaurant in Uptown Charlotte that is known for its dedication to authentic food, creative drinks, and exceptional service.*

Key Issues This Mission Statement Reflects

Positioning Philo will be positioned as an intimate Asian restaurant. The focus on authentic cuisine and outstanding service indicates the firm will charge a premium for its product and seek to attract above-medium-income customers.

Product Mix Philo will serve hot, fresh, delicious Asian dumplings, innovative Asian dishes inspired by dumplings, other wrapped foods, and creative cocktails.

Staffing The staff will focus on excellent service. Thus, this will be one strong focus of the business.

Location The restaurant and lounge will be located in Uptown Charlotte at a site that is easily accessible, is visible, and will have high vehicle and pedestrian traffic and available parking.

arena and instead continued to build her restaurant to be one of the most successful in the area.

There are books galore regarding the development of mission statements, and the opinions seem to be as diverse as the individuals who hold them. There is, in fact, little empirical evidence regarding the most effective type of mission statement. We suggest that an effective mission statement and sustainable competitive advantage are inseparable. It should be recalled from Chapter 4 that the resources of the firm are generally constrained.[4] As a result, it is particularly critical that the new business conserve its resources and focus them upon those areas that have the potential to maximize the firm's success.

A key aspect to that success is the firm's **capabilities,** or those resources which combine to allow the firm to perform better than its competitors.[5]

EXERCISE 1

1. From the information provided, what is your assessment of Philo's mission and positioning?

2. What ways would you offer to Philo to better focus the firm?

capabilities
Resources which combine to allow a firm to do things better than its competitors.

Designing a Mission Statement

In developing the mission statement, there are several key characteristics that should drive the new business founder(s).

1. Keep it short—Does it fit on a coffee mug?

2. Keep it simple—It has to be something that everyone in the company can learn and understand.

3. Make it universal—It should be able to guide every individual in the company each and every day.

4. Be specific—Tell everyone exactly what you do, and by definition, you will tell them what you do not do.

5. Establish measurable goals—Develop a metric for every part of the statement.

Keep It Short We cannot overemphasize this fundamental aspect of a mission statement. The statement must be understandable and memorable for all those who come in contact with it. While it principally is written to guide the employees of the company, it must also speak to customers, suppliers, etc. It is not a tome that describes everything that you have done and might do, and how you will do it, so that the organization can impress external parties! It is a short, direct statement that is designed to guide the organization each and every day.

The mission of a firm is not "to make money"; that is a by-product of a good direction, and it is significantly more likely that the organization will indeed make money if the mission statement is clear, succinct, memorable, and known. We offer some past mission statements from established businesses as wonderful examples of effective and ineffective mission statements. The poor statements typically are too long and too vague to be of use for employees of the company. See Table 5.1.

Table 5.1
Mission Statements

EFFECTIVE MISSION STATEMENTS	INEFFECTIVE MISSION STATEMENTS
Positive News Network The vision of the Positive News Network is to create, produce and promote an alternative news service that will focus on positive people, stories and solutions.	**General Intelligence Corporation** We view the Internet as just another medium similar as such to television. And, just as how television programming comes to you via the networks at no cost to you, so too does our Webhosting service. But make no mistake, it's not FREE. It's just that YOU are not the one to pay us. Our service to you is advertising sponsored. In exchange for a cost-free basic website design and hosting we reserve the right to place one or more advertising banners on your web-pages, just as ad pages are placed in a magazine. We then help you to succeed because, the more "hits" your site gets, the more attractive will be our server to our advertising sponsors. We see this as a win-win situation. Can you live with that?
American Red Cross The American Red Cross is a humanitarian service organization, led by volunteers, that provides relief to victims of disasters and helps people prevent, prepare for and respond to emergencies.	**University Career Services** University Career Services, an integral part of the educational process, assists students and alumni in assessing their career possibilities, setting their personal goals and achieving their objectives toward becoming productive citizens in the global community. While assisting its clients in identifying professional employment opportunities, University Career Services also provides the university community with insights into the ever-changing world of work to help develop realistic ways to better educate tomorrow's leaders.
Division of Geriatrics at UNTHSC The Division of Geriatrics will promote health and quality of life for older adults and caregivers in the communities we serve through education, research and clinical care.	**AmeriCredit** To create value for our stakeholders by constantly improving our services, investing in innovative solutions and information-based strategies, and promoting a culture of teamwork, excellence and integrity.

Keep It Simple A mission statement that is not shared has little, if any, value to the organization. We have watched people spend countless hours crafting a statement only to have it poorly communicated and/ or not reinforced by the senior management of the company. The new business owner must ensure that every employee can understand the statement and how it can be applied to his day-to-day decision making. The key to the ability to communicate a mission easily is that the statement be simple, direct, and appropriate.

As the firm is developed, the founder needs to ensure that the mission statement is at the center of the various activities that are developed. Whether the firm is a new high-technology firm with Ph.D.s on the staff or a quick-order restaurant where many employees have no high school education, the workers will come closer to having an understanding of the mission of the organization if the statement is simple. The firm needs to ensure that the words and concepts employed in the statement are straightforward and have a clear meaning to all that hear or read them. A great line in the 2003 Disney movie *Pirates of the Caribbean* illustrates this concept wonderfully. The captain of the ship, somewhat taken aback by the demands and high-brow, patronizing language of his recent captive, tells her, "I'm disinclined to acquiesce to your request," pauses for a moment, and turns back to her and says, "Means NO." Avoid the use of lots of adjectives or descriptive language about how the company will accomplish its mission.

Make It Universal It takes extraordinary care to develop a mission that guides the entire organization, and yet, for the mission to be effectively utilized by every member of the company, it must have direct applicability to even the most entry-level employee. Imagine the employee assigned to handle the customer service lines who is faced daily with customers calling in with concerns and complaints. If the mission of the organization is a long tome that fundamentally says "do good," or if it is like so many and simply exhorts the employees to "act like owners and maximize shareholder value," then what is the customer service employee to do? She will try to follow procedures and not get in trouble. Hiring people to follow procedures, rather than to use their skills and creative abilities, limits the employees and eliminates one of the differentiators of a new venture.

The mission of the business needs to be actionable. That is, it needs to help the employees to make active decisions in the moment, without having to refer everything up the chain of command. An advantage to a well-developed mission statement is that it is able to guide everyone in the organization toward the goals that the owners have set. A well-developed mission statement helps ensure that everyone in the organization is heading in the same relative direction, so that, although there will be some variance, there will not be decisions made that are counter to what the founder of the new business would choose.

Be Specific In order to accomplish the three keys thus far listed, it is necessary that the mission be so specific that it clearly tells everyone what you do *not* do. Take a look again at the mission statement for one of the restaurants discussed earlier in this chapter: *The Gourmet Mediterranean (Italian) Meal Experience in the Heart of the City.* We know from this statement that it does not serve Chinese, or barbeque, etc.

We also know that it is located in the city and (at least with this statement) should not look to expand into the suburbs. It provides an "experience" that includes ambiance, certain types of wine, food, service, etc. It should not consider adding American cuisine, French wines, or rap music. The value of this limitation should be clear to everyone every day. Employees are constantly faced with decisions that appear to be of little importance, whereas they do have both individual and cumulative impact. A strong focus on a single mission statement keeps everyone in the organization constantly striving to achieve the goals of the owners.

Establish Measurable Goals A **metric** is a measure used to evaluate whether a person or firm is meeting its goals. From the mission statement, a new business owner should be able to develop a set of metrics that are meaningful to judge if the mission is being accomplished.

metric

A measure to evaluate whether a person or firm is meeting stated goals.

Greater specifics on metrics and developing them will be presented in Chapters 9 and 12; however, a few brief comments are appropriate here. We typically recommend that each organization develop between five and eight measures of success for its venture. These are broken up into two categories: (1) quantitative measures—those that are tied to the financial or strategic goals of the organization and are easily measured; and (2) qualitative measures—those that are tied to the strategic goals of the organization but have more to do with the "feel" of the organization.

To illustrate, below are some of the metrics used by our high-end restaurant:

Mission: *The Gourmet Mediterranean (Italian) Meal Experience in the Heart of the City*

Metrics   The Gourmet

 1. Number of chefs who have graduated from gourmet schools
 2. Ranking in annual Zagat guide
 3. Quality of reviews in local papers

Mediterranean Meal Experience

 1. Closeness in appearance to actual Mediterranean restaurants
 2. Number of employees from Mediterranean region
 3. Service measure as compared to actual restaurants in Mediterranean

Heart of the City

 1. Proximity to city festivals/events
 2. Do people refer to other stores, events, etc. by referring to our restaurant as the starting point (i.e., "Just down the block from XX restaurant")?

Metrics are best established at the founding of the business and are evaluated on a recurring basis. The baseline position is not nearly as important as the vector (direction and level of change) that the metrics are taking. We want to see positive movement on each of the metrics. They are the direct measure of the business's mission, and the more the

A mission statement has been called the guiding principle of a business, and yet many companies take the approach that the mission statement simply sounds good and that it should be carefully worded so as not to upset any potential constituency of the business. From this perspective, the real mission of the business is to make money. In fact, the real mission might be to make as much money as possible.

Customers, employees, suppliers, and the community at large all recognize that companies are in business to make money; however, no one buys from a business because it needs to make money. You don't use a dry cleaner because it really needs your money. You don't go to a convenience store simply because the store really needs you to shop there. Are businesses justified in not being clear in their mission statement?

business improves on each metric, the closer it is getting to its fundamental mission.

Mission Statement Impact

To illustrate the range of decisions that are impacted by the mission of the organization, consider three domains (advertising, location of the business, and staffing) for the Philo example in this chapter and how they are impacted by market choice:

1. If Philo chose to pursue multiple client bases at the same time, where would the firm advertise? Each market has substantively different outlets to reach its respective customers. Which magazines do different groups of people read? What endorsements would each group of potential customers consider important? What organizations (NASCAR, the North Carolina Dance Theatre, the Charlotte Bobcats, and/or the United Way) might you support, given your desired customer?

2. The location chosen for each type of business would differ significantly based upon the mission. The dance company might find an uptown location more appealing, while the local rotary club might prefer a mall location; still another might prefer a neighborhood feel.

3. Personnel and staffing size would vary from firm to firm as well. The style, sophistication, and approach from the staff would vary dramatically with different target audiences.

Thus, before founders can begin to build the new business, they must be clear about where and how they will compete. Almost all new ventures have a wide variety of activities that can be pursued. The mission statement should help by clearly specifying in which market the firm will compete, how broad a geographic range the firm will serve, and the major ways in which it will compete. If these activities are not precisely defined, the new owners will find themselves building an entity that in some ways is targeted to one business, and in other ways targeted to another related, but inconsistent business. Having everyone in the business moving in the same direction, toward the same group of customers will provide immense benefits to the new firm.[6]

LO 5.2 Sustainable Competitive Advantage

It was noted in Chapter 4 that a firm needs to ensure that it has a set of *competitive advantages,* or areas of separation where the firm performs better than anyone else in the market that it serves. Here we will go into more depth on this critical topic and discuss how it impacts the implementation of the mission statement. In particular, we will examine competitive advantages in terms of a **sustainable competitive advantage**—that is, a set of advantages that provides you with the opportunity to make money where other businesses cannot easily copy your advantages.[7]

sustainable competitive advantage

An advantage that others cannot immediately copy.

All competitive advantages eventually disappear as the industry generally trends toward those areas that are providing some companies extraordinary returns. However, all businesses should seek to maintain an advantage for as long as possible by continually refining their business model. A key part of building a competitive advantage is having a deep understanding of your customers' needs.[8] For example, a new business may decide that it will develop its business around the best customer service in the replacement/repair of any item it sells. However, if customers do not really value the ability to quickly repair the product, then this service (which is quite expensive) will not provide a sustainable competitive advantage. Consider another example: a small business that sells and repairs vacuum sweepers. Typically, customers want their vacuum sweeper repaired and back in their hands in a timely manner but do not care if it is the same day or within a few days. Thus, focusing your competitive advantage on the ability to repair sweepers within a few hours may not provide a financially rewarding sustainable competitive advantage.

Traditionally, new businesses find that their greatest source of sustainable advantage is the personal relationships with their customers.[9] The development of a compelling personal relationship is something that large organizations find quite difficult. Building the relationship with the customer for the small firm may be as simple as acknowledging the customer when you see him, or as complex as knowing what he buys and contacting him when a new shipment arrives. The long-term difficulty for the small business owner comes from setting expectations now that you will be able to maintain in the future.

Prior to developing an effective mission statement, the small business must first develop a detailed list of what might constitute or what will constitute its competitive advantages. There are three steps to the process of identifying a new business's sustainable competitive advantage. While it is quite tempting to skip ahead, we suggest that the process itself leads to unique insights and will help the founder craft a business that has a long-term opportunity for success.

Identifying a Sustainable Competitive Advantage

Step 1: Develop a list of your business's assets and capabilities

Step 2: Break that list into two groups: standard and extraordinary

Step 3: Evaluate the extraordinary resources/capabilities

Table 5.2
Tangible & Intangible Assets

TANGIBLE ASSETS	INTANGIBLE ASSETS
Building location	Industry experience
Equipment (list)	Contacts
Initial financing (equity or debt)	Previous start-up experience
Inventory	Education
Patents or patents pending	Unique knowledge of the industry (usually from previous research)
Software and systems for business	Skill set of founders (presentation, innovation, etc.)
Build out of facility (list detail)	Name branding
– Walls, fixtures, built-ins, etc.	

LO 5.3 Step 1: Develop a List of Your Business's Assets and Capabilities

The owner, or founding team, needs to develop a complete list of all the physical and intangible assets that the company will have at its founding. **Tangible assets** are those hard assets such as equipment or a location. The intangible assets are those things that are not physical but are just as critical to success, such as relationships with key suppliers. A key part of the **intangible assets** are the capabilities and skills of the founders or employees.[10]

While this inventory process may seem a bit mundane, it is absolutely critical to the later steps and the development of an effective and focused mission for the organization. In evaluating the intangible assets and capabilities, the small business founders need to develop a clear and precise list that encompasses the breadth of knowledge within the founding team. This list will tend to be a bit long and should include absolutely *everything* that the company has now or will have at the point that it opens for business. See Table 5.2 for an example.

tangible assets

Hard assets such as equipment or a location.

intangible assets

Things that are not physical but are just as critical to success, such as a relationship with a key supplier.

LO 5.4 Step 2: Split the List into Standard and Extraordinary Assets

The tangible and intangible assets can be further separated into standard and extraordinary, much in the same way we categorized actions of the entrepreneur and firm earlier as either orthodox or unorthodox. Most of the assets listed by a firm are standard to be a player in the industry. For Philo, those assets might include a wide range of items, such as its building, computer systems, and business license. These assets allow the firm to operate. They are not things that provide a competitive advantage to the firm.

Similarly, most capabilities, or skills of the founders and employers, are also somewhat standard for the industry. For example, serving customers in a timely manner may be done very well by a new business; however, the standard expectation of most customers is that you will have a strong capability in this domain. Therefore, this capability cannot be a source of sustainable competitive advantage.

Some of the assets/capabilities that the entrepreneur or entrepreneurial team has and perhaps some of the tangible assets, like location, are potentially extraordinary. These are resources and/or capabilities that are unique, allow the business some period of time without a matching competitor, and cannot easily be matched by anyone else. There is a reason that individuals, or other firms, do business with a particular firm. The nature of individuals is that they are driven by inertia. Thus, individuals or businesses are not willing to make a change unless forced to for some reason. Your extraordinary capability will be the source of that motivation to change to do business with your new business. The previously discussed personal relationship is just such an extraordinary capability.

To illustrate, if you were to consider opening a new video store in a strip mall, what would you consider to be your competitive advantages? Why would customers come to it rather than a major national competitor such as Blockbuster or the new RedBox outside most grocery stores where you can rent directly from the box? Would your new firm have different movies when compared to the major firm? Would the firm's movies be rented more cheaply than those at the national firm? Would access to the business be easier? If you are going to do the same thing that other firms do, why will anyone switch to you?

The new business must have something that will motivate potential customers to select that business; these are your extraordinary resources and capabilities. It will be these extraordinary assets (or resources, if we consider the term more broadly) and capabilities that form a competitive advantage for new business.

There is a wide range of potential resources and capabilities that can be the source of the competitive advantage. For example, customer loyalty can be obtained if customers are driven principally by something other than cost and the firm is the first to market. This is referred to as a **first mover advantage,** and those firms that come later are referred to as **followers.**[11] Such firms can benefit by learning from the mistakes of the first movers, but may not be able to obtain the loyalty of customers if there is any to be had. For the new business, this does not mean that you have to be the first to the market with the broad concept as long as you bring some unique resource/capability to the idea. A new business could never be the first to market with a general concept such as that of a mid-priced restaurant. However, you may recall from Chapter 4 that new businesses do not compete against the entire industry. Instead, there are limits to how far someone will drive for a restaurant. Therefore, a new business only needs to be the first in the industry that is relevant to that firm. In many fast-growing suburban areas, a restaurant may be the first of its type in the area; it would then be the first mover in that area.

There are other ways that a small business can build a competitive advantage. For example, a firm can have special relationships with suppliers. There are a number of Amish carpenters that make furniture. A small retailer may wish to carry that furniture, but would need to have a relationship with those specialized suppliers before such opportunities could be arranged. Location can be another source of advantage;

first mover advantage
The benefit of gaining customer loyalty by being the first firm to the market.

followers
Firms that enter a market after the first mover.

EXERCISE 2

Develop a complete list of resources/capabilities for your proposed new venture. Then break the list into two sections based upon whether each one is standard or extraordinary for your industry.

those firms with prime locations that have easy automobile access might have an advantage over those businesses that are hard to access. The range of potential sources of a new business's competitive advantage is as wide as there are activities in the firm. But a small business's competitive advantage also needs to be defensible. That is, the advantage must be something that is not easily substituted away or matched by established competitors.

LO 5.5 Step 3: Evaluate Competitiveness of Extraordinary Resources/Capabilities

Once you know what resources/capabilities your new business might have that appear to be extraordinary, you will need to examine each before you can claim any of these as a source of competitive advantage. Successful businesses generally have several sources of the competitive advantage. The new business may have a capability or resource that is extraordinary, but as noted before, that may or may not be the best resource on which to center a new business. To illustrate further, in a manufacturing business we may be able to offer 24-hour customer service in an industry that does not value 24-hour operations. The new business needs to focus its efforts on those areas that have the potential in the market to provide the greatest competitive advantage to the business. We refer to the financial gains garnered from an asset or capability that are in excess of the ordinary returns in that particular industry as **economic rents.** Ordinary returns in an industry suggest that you are doing no more nor less than the average of the industry. This should be accomplishable by simply matching the industry average for behavior, location, etc. Economic rents imply that the new business not only matches the norms for the industry, but in several areas, far exceeds the industry in a manner that allows it to charge well in excess of its additional costs. [12]

There are several means with which to analyze these resources and develop a small list of resources/capabilities that truly provide the new small business with the potential to obtain a sustainable competitive advantage. We have found the resource-based perspective to be the most effective method. For new businesses, there are four elements that seem to be most effective within this evaluation system. Each and every resource/capability that is listed as unorthodox in the previous step must be subjected to the following four questions. As mentioned at the end of Chapter 4, only those unorthodox resources/capabilities that meet all four criteria are truly the keys to the new business's strategy.

Is It Rare?

You must evaluate the uniqueness of each resource/capability relative to the competitors in your market. Is the resource/capability relatively unique for your industry? Can a competitor easily copy it? If it can be copied, how perfectly can it be imitated and how long would it take? These are qualitative judgments based upon the research and experience of the founder.

economic rents

Financial gains garnered from an asset or capability that are in excess of the ordinary returns in that particular industry.

Is It Easily Substituted?

For every resource/capability that you determine to be indeed rare, you will evaluate the market for a close substitute. A substitute is not provided by a direct competitor, but is something that satisfies the same basic need that is satisfied by your product/service. If we started up a small electronics repair operation, then our direct competitors would be other businesses that repair electronics in our area. Substitutes would consist of self repairs, manufacturer's warranties, or throwing the item away. As you can see, these are not particularly great substitutes, and that is the question every entrepreneur needs to ask himself. How close are the substitutes for your extraordinary resource/capability, and are they good substitutes?

Is It Durable?

If you have determined that an unorthodox resource/capability is both rare and not substitutable, then the next step is to determine how long you might be able to hold onto those advantages. As noted before, no advantage lasts forever, but the new business person wants her advantage to last as long as possible. The time lag between the development of the competitive advantage and the point where competitors can match your advantage is the window where the small business can earn extraordinary returns. In some industries a competitive advantage will last only a few months, while in other industries years would be more appropriate. This evaluation is done by estimating both the amount of time you believe it would take for a competitor to match you in a particular area and whether you believe they would actually try to match you. Many companies have the resources to match the offering of any new business, and yet they don't. The entrepreneur's estimation of the time frame in which she will be able to enjoy the benefits of an unorthodox advantage is a critical element in this evaluation.

Is It Valuable?

The customer must be willing to pay extra for these extraordinary resources and/or capabilities. A key decision, then, is which resource/capability the customer will pay the most for. It is not uncommon to have a resource/capability meet all three criteria above, and yet be unable to attain value in one or more of the three means for doing so: (1) charging more; (2) obtaining more customers; or (3) reducing costs relative to the competition.

Table 5.3 summarizes these concepts.

LO 5.6 Strategy

While we have presented the content thus far in a sequential manner, the reality is that much of this is and should be done concurrently. The firm needs to build on its mission and develop an effective strategy for the new business. This building process in which the mission is the firm's foundation explains why such extensive attention is given to the development of a mission statement. The firm's strategy is how the firm plans to accomplish its mission. Thus, the mission is the foundation that the firm's strategy is built on. Strategy is a complex field of study,

CRITERION	MEANING	ILLUSTRATION
Rare	Few firms have it.	There are only four corners at an intersection. Once they are used, no other firms can locate there.
Non-Substitutable	It cannot be replaced by something else easily.	Your firm may be able to supply original auto parts for automobiles from the 1950s. However, newly produced auto parts for such cars would substitute for those parts easily.
Durable	The length of time that the advantages will last before competitors match the offering.	Can firms match what you do in days, months, or years?
Valuable	Customers want it.	What you do is something that customers value and so they will pay more than what is charged by your competitors.

Table 5.3
Components of Resource-Based Analysis

and we do not presume to cover the entire subject in this text. Our goal is to present the concepts we believe will be most valuable to a new small business start-up.

Michael Porter argues that there are fundamentally two broad means to view a business's strategy: low cost or differentiation. A low-cost strategy is one where the firm seeks to be the lowest-cost competitor in the industry. A differentiation approach is one where the firm finds a unique position in the market through product, service, location, etc. He then goes on to argue that firms can narrow these two approaches to focus on smaller niches within those broad markets. He refers to this concentration on smaller niches as low-cost focus or differentiation focus.[13]

As a practical matter, most new firms pursue a combination of these two broad categories. A small business is only rarely the absolute lowest-cost competitor in an industry (especially in an industry that is well established). There are actually several reasons for this, but one clear reason is that large businesses can typically obtain what are referred to as economies of scale.[14] There are simply many logistic/process areas that operate much more efficiently and cheaply on a large scale. The ability to gain those efficiencies from operating a large operation is called economies of scale. For example, a large firm (Kellogg's) owns

What would you need to do to alter your strategy from Keebler's, if you went into the cookie-making business?

Keebler Cookies. You may make wonderful cookies that you want to get into stores, but Keebler will obtain its inputs much cheaper than a small firm because of its systems and size. Similarly, its shipping will be cheaper and it will be able to rent store space much cheaper, putting the new small business in a position where it would be virtually impossible to be a lower-cost competitor than Keebler. As a result, if you wish to open a new cookie company, you will need to utilize a differentiation strategy of some type.

The new business will also find it difficult to be differentiated along all dimensions of a product or service (and actually may not really wish to be). Thus, the new business commonly will have what would be called a differentiation focus strategy. In choosing the elements where they may effectively differentiate, new business owners should reexamine the prior discussion in this chapter on competitive advantage. The resources/capabilities upon which the new business differentiates itself will constitute the key elements on which the firm builds its competitive advantage. To illustrate, the firm may believe that customer service will be one of its competitive advantages, so that should also be where it builds its differentiation and value strategy.

There are four logical steps in developing the firm's strategy.

Step 1: The firm's mission statement is employed to specify where the firm is to compete and how.

Step 2: A detailed strategic plan is laid out specifying a series of items that will be used to meet each part of the mission/strategy. This plan should include the area of the mission that is being addressed, the strategy employed, the specific action, the result desired, the person responsible, and the status of the action. This can be developed in a spreadsheet format for ease of analysis. A brief example is shown in Table 5.4 for our Mediterranean restaurant example.

Step 3: Following the approach outlined earlier, the strategy needs to meet the criterion of being defendable for some length of time (depending upon the industry, the length of time that would be considered sufficient may vary). The strategy should also provide the founder(s) economic returns above the industry average. If these two criteria cannot be satisfied, then the firm's strategy needs to be reexamined. However, if these two criteria can be met, then the firm should move forward with a focus on those activi-

Table 5.4

MISSION	STRATEGY	ACTION	RESULT DESIRED	RESPONSIBLE PARTY	STATUS
Gourmet	High-end, well-known chefs	Hire a chef from one of the top schools	Recognized in community	Founder	
			Has a short spot on TV news show each week	Founder	

ties that are defendable and have the potential to provide economic rents. The firm does not have to be excellent in all areas. Instead, it needs to have only those two to three competitive advantages that are its means of value differentiation.

Step 4: The firm's strategy needs to be constantly reevaluated. As noted, no competitive advantage or means of differentiation lasts forever. The small business must constantly evaluate its performance and its means of competitive advantage relative to its direct competitors to ensure that they are still relevant. This control function will be discussed in greater detail as we discuss analysis techniques in Chapter 12.

Applying the Strategy

Implementing a strategy is about fit and alignment within the business. The key is that the firm seeks out a consistent set of activities around what typically will be a focus differentiation strategy. Greater detail will be discussed in Chapters 10 and 11 on how to build a consistent set of activities around the strategy of the firm. However, to illustrate the key role that strategy can play for the new business, consider another illustration from the restaurant industry. A restaurant was founded by a Greek immigrant located close to downtown in a large Midwestern city*. The principal customers were expected to be the individuals that lived in the apartments and condos that were close to the downtown area. The restaurant started as a café with cheaper Greek entrees, but over time it developed a dinner clientele that wanted more sophisticated menu items, so the owners upgraded a number of items on the menu to the point where a standard dinner entree cost $15. Due to inertia and a desire to hold onto their roots, several of the original items were still on the menu. Then, the founder of the restaurant wanted to expand his customer base. He noted that Cajun food was gaining popularity in the region, so without regard to his position as a Greek restaurant, he added Cajun food to the menu. The market already had several restaurants that were part of large chains that offered Cajun food in the downtown area.

Piece by piece the owner of the Greek restaurant was working his business away from what he wanted it to be and muddling the perception that potential customers had of his establishment. Customers making a decision to go to dinner might have found the Greek atmosphere and food appealing. As the atmosphere and offerings moved away from this Greek atmosphere, customers were confused by the menu choices and the eclectic nature of the offerings. The restaurant was losing its appeal and becoming undifferentiated in a market that has thousands of choices.

---

* We have referred to restaurants on several occasions as classic examples of strategic management not because we believe they are the only examples, but because they are well-known types of establishments and their positioning is obvious to even the most casual observer. They also are classic small businesses with an owner-manager who typically has high involvement in the business. These businesses can be founded by anyone with a passion for the business and do not generally require the special training that a high-technology small business may require.

The owner of the restaurant decided that his business was on its way to being a generic restaurant (and would probably need to close if changes were not made). He decided to refocus the organization around a succinct mission statement for the firm and then build a strategy or set of actions consistent with that mission. It had become obvious that while he thought he had seen an opportunity, he had failed to define his true competence and focus. As a result the owner centered his business strictly on Greek food, eliminating the Cajun offerings. The owner also determined that his fundamental skill set was oriented toward more sophisticated meals, so he chose to offer a differentiated product at a premium price.

The owner then set out to align his business in a manner consistent with the differentiation strategy that would focus on sophisticated Greek food. The simpler, cheaper offerings were eliminated from the menu. This rationalization of the menu also allowed the owner to more efficiently use the food that went into making the products. In this industry, a key success factor, especially for a small restaurant, is control of the cost of inputs. The cost to the firm of ordering a large variety of food items entails significant storage and spoilage expenses in addition to an increase in complexity in virtually every aspect of the business. Thus, focusing strictly on Greek food and eliminating lower-priced items helped the efficiency of the whole organization, as well as situating it in a unique position within the market.

Consistent with this approach on food, the restaurant began offering only Greek wines. Previously the restaurant had served beer, but consistent with its differentiation focus, the owner wanted to focus on wine as the drink of choice, and specifically Greek wines. The hiring of staff also became much more clearly focused. There were a number of Greek immigrants in the city with detailed knowledge of this cuisine who were willing to work in a restaurant. The owner decided to hire these individuals, actually paying them a premium, in order to have highly skilled workers who understood what they were serving.

Finally, rather than advertising in the newspaper that went to all parts of the city and to numerous individuals who would never come downtown or, even if they did, would not patronize a high-end Greek restaurant, the owner began to focus his advertising. These are the specifics:

1. Since the restaurant is a part of the downtown area, the owner began to work with the concierge operations at the major hotels in the area in order to become one of their suggested specialty restaurants.

2. The Greek community in the city was strongly associated with the local Greek Orthodox church. The owner opened a Greek restaurant because that was the food he knew. Only later did he realize that the Greek community was willing to travel from around the city to have good Greek food. Therefore, the owner began to advertise in publications and activities associated with the church to better reach that audience.

The result was that the restaurant built a consistent set of activities around its mission and strategy that helped to focus the firm clearly on what played to its strengths and gave it the best opportunity to make economic rents.

Alex had been advised by the Small Business Assistance Center to develop a mission statement. He understood that he wanted to be in the auto repair industry (recall the discussion of opportunity identification in Chapter 3). In addition, he knew he wanted to have a neighborhood auto repair store whose product was targeted to middle-income individuals within a seven-mile radius (recall Chapter 4, as he analyzed his external environment). However, Alex was not clear how he wanted to compete in this domain. He had been told, and it seemed reasonable to him, that he should focus on cost or on providing premium service. However, he did not know what this meant in terms of strategy.

Alex had developed relationships with other Hispanic owners of auto repair shops. He received particularly good insights from one of these owners, who had loose connections to his family but operated his business in another city. This owner's grandparents and Alex's parents had emigrated from the same region in Mexico. The auto shop owner described his strategy to Alex as charging a premium for his service. His charges were less than those of the nearby large auto dealers, but they were still higher than those of many small shops in the area, or those of individuals that worked on cars in their home garages in their spare time. His rationale was that he wanted to do business with people he had a relationship with. He believed that individuals who bought on price alone would change their auto repair shop every time they found something cheaper. He wanted to build his business on relationships in the community, charge a slight premium, but also be more responsive to these individuals' needs. Thus, rather than just trying to sell a person as many services as he could at one time, building a relationship meant the owner would need to do the work necessary, but only the work that was necessary.

This was the approach that Alex also wanted. This led Alex to develop the following mission statement:

To establish a neighborhood auto repair shop that is part of the community and which provides exceptional service.

summary

Small businesses need to ensure that they develop a business mission, whether they are forming a new business or running an existing business. In both cases the firm must clearly define how the business will compete. It is easy for a small business to lose focus and try to pursue too many activities in a chase after sales. A good mission statement that is effectively implemented with a consistent strategy will help everyone involved in the organization overcome those tendencies.

Developing the Mission Statement

1. Keep it short—Does it fit on a coffee mug?
2. Keep it simple—It has to be something that everyone in the company can learn and understand.
3. Make it universal—It should be able to guide every individual in the company each and every day.
4. Be specific—Tell everyone exactly what you do, and by definition you will tell them what you do not do.
5. Establish measurable goals—Develop a metric for every part of the statement.

The strategy puts that mission into action. The steps to put all this into action are as follows:

Identifying a Sustainable Competitive Advantage

Step 1: Develop a list of your business's assets and capabilities

Step 2: Break the list into two groups: standard and extraordinary

Step 3: Evaluate the extraordinary resources/capabilities

1. Is the resource/capability rare?
2. Is the resource/capability durable?
3. Is the resource/capability relatively non-substitutable?
4. Is the resource/capability valuable?

key terms

review questions

1. What is the value of a mission statement for a new organization?
2. How should a mission statement guide the actions of employees?
3. What makes a good mission statement?
4. What is the difference between a tangible and an intangible asset?
5. Why do assets/capabilities have to meet all four requirements of the resource-based analysis to provide the company with a competitive advantage?
6. Why is it important to identify the orthodox (ordinary) elements of a new business?
7. What are the core assets/capabilities of the business that you are contemplating?
8. What mission statement would you write for your new business and why would it be a good one?

group exercises

1. Using the Internet, identify three large corporations and their mission statements. For these corporations, how would you evaluate the mission statements in terms of clarity and fulfilling the goals of a mission statement identified in the chapter?
2. Discuss in your group how these mission statements might be different if they were for small firms.
3. Take one of these organizations and list your suggestions for what might be orthodox and unorthodox.

everyday edisons class discussion

Go to www.everydayedisons.com/james.html and read about James.

1. What do you think James's mission statement would look like?
2. Are there specific things that James should seek to avoid in his business that his mission statement could help him with?

Dan Davis—Davis Appliance Repair

Dan Davis started his appliance repair business eight years ago. However, it was a lifetime of preparation that allowed him to start the business and grow it to a success. Today, the joy of owning his own firm and the independence it gives him is something that he would not give up even if offered twice the money by a large corporation.

Approximately 30 years ago, Dan left the military after being trained as an electrician. With that skill set and a strong recommendation from a family member, Dan obtained a job as a repairman with the dominant appliance manufacturer of the time: Sears. The corporation provided valuable training to Dan, and the steady schedule of the work also allowed Dan to obtain his bachelor's degree in management and marketing at night during the next seven years.

With his degree in hand, Dan ultimately hoped to move into management. He left Sears and through hard work he was able to become manager of service for a private retailer and later for a large store that was part of a

national chain. In both cases, he managed a large number of technicians and was responsible for a key part of the store's profit. Regardless of whom he worked for, Dan felt very frustrated by the lack of control he had within the company. He dealt with situations where top management did not back him up on key decisions involving personnel. At the same time that management was not backing him up on personnel decisions, he was being held responsible for the performance of those employees. The result was a classic "Catch 22," where he could not effectively discipline employees but was responsible for their behavior. The resulting pressure produced so much tension in Dan's life that he ultimately asked to go back to being a repair technician for the large national chain.

As a repair technician Dan had far less pressure, and made a good living earning roughly $25 per hour. (You can take hourly wages and multiply them by 2,000 hours to get an estimate of yearly salary.) He won numerous awards for being the best technician in regional and national competitions for the retailer. He likely would have continued in this role, but the retailer decided to exit appliance sales, a move that quickly pushed the chain into bankruptcy. The bankruptcy resulted in Dan's taking a severe hit to his savings plan, which had been invested in the company's stock. However, it also created an opportunity for Dan when the firm offered additional severance to those technicians that stayed with the firm until it actually closed its doors. This severance pay would become the basis for Dan's ability to start his business.

Dan had thought about starting a repair business before, but realized that he would need to have a solid customer base. Appliance repair is a different type of service business from hair styling or auto repair. In those service businesses you typically see the person providing the service frequently, whereas your appliance repair person might be seen only once or maybe twice a year. Thus, you need to have a very large customer base in order to have a consistent flow of appliance repair business. Dan had talked to several independent repair business people prior to starting the business. This need to have a large customer base had led these other repair businesses to make a strategic choice that Dan thought was wrong.

Specifically, the other repair businesses were not concerned about repeat business. They priced themselves for a service call at a level that seemed cheap. However, the repair businesses had predetermined levels of services and parts that each job required. The result was that their price was often quite a bit higher in the end. The tactic led to higher single billings, but made the customers so angry that they rarely called again.

Dan determined that his pricing would be focused not on being the cheapest initial price, but instead on creating value for the customer and building a relationship. As a result, he billed $65 for the initial call. This was not the cheapest in the area. However, for most repair people, that initial call fee is just the cost to get them to come to your house. For Dan, this fee included the first 30 minutes of the repair. For over half of the repair calls he makes, this is all the time that is needed. In addition, while Dan is outgoing, he makes a point of working the full time he is in someone's home. Many repair people end up charging customers for the time they spend talking to them. Dan may talk, but he ensures that he is working during that time as well.

Since the chain was going out of business, Dan was allowed to use his own records of the service calls he had made for the company to build a customer base. (Typically, building your customer base from your work with your prior employer is something to do very carefully, since you cannot take records from a prior employer. However, in this case it was Dan's own information and the firm was going out of business.) Dan selected the geographic area that he wanted to serve and took the addresses of the jobs he had done in that area. This did not include all of the repair jobs he had done, since the large chain would often send him far distances in the metropolitan area. However, for his own business he knew he wanted to serve only a given part of the metropolitan area so he would not be driving all the time.

He then wrote to each of those individuals whom he had worked for in the past for the large corporation. He simply told them that the large corporation was going out of business, as a result he was setting up his own business, and he would appreciate their work. In this business he also sent a magnet for their refrigerator with his business name and phone number on it. He sent similar letters to the members of his church. Finally, he also wrote the individuals on a voter list for the small suburban town in which he lived. The result was that he sent out 3,000 letters with magnets with his phone number on them. Since that time he has only done very limited advertising, and a few other types of business generation. Largely through word of mouth, he is constantly busy.

Today he typically works five to six calls a day, five days a week. He tries to not work Saturdays or Sundays since those are the days he enjoys for himself, although sometimes there is just too much work and he has to work on Saturday. His son has now joined him on many of his jobs. Dan pays him an hourly wage and expects that someday his son will take over the business. Dan's business grosses $80,000 a year. Starting the business took less than $500 in small hand tools. Over time, more specialized tools that allow the work to be done faster were added for $1,000. In addition to these start-up costs, Dan carries parts in his truck that allow him to do 70 percent of the jobs he is called on. These parts are worth around $1,500. The start-up costs are not the key issue in this business; it is the customer base and how you develop it. Dan has one other key piece of advice for those that want to start such a business: Treat your customers like you want to be treated yourself. If you do that, then they will be back and you will have a long-term business.

learning outcomes

After studying this chapter, you will be able to

6.1 Recognize the fundamental importance of cash flow analysis.

6.2 Prepare a cash flow statement and a budget.

6.3 Identify other financial tools.

Analyzing Cash Flow and Other Financial Information

OPTIMO FINE HATS

Graham Thompson, owner of Optimo Fine Hats in Beverly (an area on the south side of Chicago), has for years gone to Ecuador to buy toquilla straw for Panama hats and to Italy and Portugal for fancy felts for fedoras. Now the hatmaker wants to reverse at least some of that trade flow—by opening stores in London and Milan. A shop in downtown Chicago is also on the to-do list.

Thompson, 36, who grew up in Oak Brook, had hat dreams as far back as the eighth grade, idolizing men in hats from 1930s and '40s movies. As a teen, he hung out with South Side master hatter Johnny Tyus and ended up buying Tyus's business, paying him $75,000 from cash flow over three years.

Today, Optimo draws locals willing to spend $500 to $20,000 for custom-made hats, though it boasts celebrity clients, too, including bluesman Buddy Guy, comedian Bernie Mac, and actor Andy Garcia. Thompson also has made hats for movies, including *Road to Perdition.* He worked on Michael Mann's Chicago gangster film, *Public Enemies,* starring Johnny Depp and Christian Bale. To supply his new stores, Thompson plans to jack up production to as many as 100 hats a week, from 36 today. Revenue should hit $1 million in 2008, he adds, up from $700,000 in 2007 and $100,000 when he opened in 1994.

Source: Excerpt from "Fresh Entrepreneurs: Brimming With Business." Reprinted from April 2, 2008 issue of *BusinessWeek* by special permission. Copyright © 2008 by The McGraw-Hill Companies, Inc.

At this point you have generated the basic concept for a business, analyzed the potential of that business for success in the external environment, and determined what strategy the new business will use to compete in the marketplace. The next step in the due diligence process is to develop an actionable financial plan for the business. In fact, the next analytical step is perhaps the most critical in the due diligence effort, as the financial analysis of the business will most likely determine whether there is actual financial opportunity for your small business. Specifically, a new firm must decide whether there will be sufficient cash flow for the proposed business to survive its early days and then thrive as an established entity. A good idea that is unable to generate minimally sufficient cash flow in some reasonable time is not a practical business idea.

cash flow

Actual cash that flows into the firm, minus the cash that goes out of the firm.

When we discuss **cash flow,** it is important to understand that cash flow in a business is not the same as profit.[1] A firm obtains profits when its sales revenue is higher than its expenses, including depreciation of assets. However, generating profits does not put cash in the bank for a business. It is quite common to have products "sold" with no cash coming to the firm. Credit accounts may have terms that range from 30 to 90 days, which means you will not receive payment for your services or goods for 30 to 90 days. In fact, some percentage of these credit accounts will go past due and some will ultimately be uncollectible. Even simple items such as checks you receive from out-of-state banks may not be paid immediately, since a bank has the ability to hold them for up to 10 days after the check is deposited. Thus, you will not likely receive the money for your business immediately once you sell the product or service. On the other hand, a new business must generally pay in cash for its goods and supplies since it has no credit history. Carrying inventory of any type results in payments for those supplies taking place long before any cash is received by the business. Thus, while many small firms appear to be making a profit, they are suffering with a negative cash flow. Ultimately, the danger is that the small business will need to make payments in cash for its inputs but will have insufficient cash available from sales. This cash crunch is actually exacerbated when sales are growing. A doubling in orders in a single month sounds great, but it means that twice the inputs must be ordered and paid for while there is no cash coming into the firm to pay for the dramatic increase of inputs needed until those goods are paid for by the customer. The result is that cash flow is one of the most critical areas in the survival of a new business, and it is typically the absence of sufficient cash flow that is the greatest reason that a new business fails.[2]

To prevent such a cash crunch, it is important for a new small business to carefully, thoughtfully, and accurately forecast its real cash flow. In its simplest form, a cash flow statement is a comparison of cash inflows to cash outflows. In this chapter we will present a thorough method that will help ensure that the small business has a clear picture of its cash flow situation.

EXERCISE 1

1. What additional items would you like to see included in Philo's cash flow statement?

2. Do you believe that the numbers above are realistic? Explain.

3. For which items would you like to have additional information? How might this be best presented?

4. Solely based upon the cash flow statement, would you believe that this venture was worth investing in if you were an investor?

To illustrate the fundamentals of cash flow analysis, let's examine the cash flow developed by Philo Asian Grille as the two friends evaluated the potential financial viability of the new venture. The Philo founders' initial analysis of their projected cash flow is listed below.

The cash flow statement reflects the firm's plan for $100,000 of equity investment by the two founders and the acquisition of a bank loan in September. The founders tried to include every actual expense that would be incurred in the first six months of operation. The receipts were estimated by observing their competitors and considering the nature of their location.

	July	August	September	October	November	December	Total
Receipts (Sales)	$ 0	$ 0	$ 31,000	$55,000	$78,000	$91,000	$255,000
Debt Financing	$ 0	$ 0	$50,000	$ 0	$ 0	$ 0	$ 50,000
Equity Financing	$100,000	$ 0	$ 0	$ 0	$ 0	$ 0	$100,000
Input (Food) Purchases	$ 0	$10,000	$30,000	$25,000	$35,000	$38,000	$138,000
Liquor & Beer	$ 0	$ 8,000	$14,000	$ 7,500	$13,000	$18,000	$ 60,500
Equipment Purchases	$ 22,250	$ 3,850	$ 2,500	$ 500	$ 1,500	$ 0	$ 30,600
Salaries	$ 4,167	$ 4,167	$ 4,167	$ 7,500	$ 7,500	$ 7,500	$ 35,001
Payroll Taxes	$ 375	$ 375	$ 375	$ 675	$ 675	$ 675	$ 3,150
Health Insurance	$ 900	$ 900	$ 900	$ 1,350	$ 1,350	$ 1,350	$ 6,750
Professional Fees	$ 7,500	$ 2,500	$ 0	$ 0	$ 0	$ 0	$ 10,000
Restaurant Lease	$ 5,208	$ 5,208	$ 5,208	$ 5,208	$ 5,208	$ 5,208	$ 31,248
Utilities	$ 750	$ 500	$ 500	$ 550	$ 600	$ 750	$ 3,650
Phone Expense	$ 0	$ 850	$ 900	$ 1,000	$ 1,000	$ 1,000	$ 4,750
Music & Entertainment	$ 0	$ 0	$ 500	$ 500	$ 1,000	$ 1,000	$ 3,000
Insurance	$ 1,350	$ 0	$ 0	$ 1,350	$ 0	$ 0	$ 2,700
Advertising	$ 0	$ 7,500	$ 3,500	$ 1,500	$ 2,500	$ 5,000	$ 20,000
Office Supplies	$ 500	$ 1,000	$ 250	$ 250	$ 500	$ 500	$ 3,000
Repairs & Maintenance	$ 0	$ 0	$ 250	$ 500	$ 750	$ 1,000	$ 2,500
Interest	$ 0	$ 0	$ 0	$ 417	$ 417	$ 417	$ 1,251
Taxes	$ 0	$ 0	$ 0	$ 0	$ 0	$ 1,695	$ 1,695
Beginning Balance	$ 0	$57,000	$ 12,150	$30,100	$31,300	$38,300	
Cash In	$100,000	$ 0	$81,000	$55,000	$78,000	$91,000	
Cash Out	$ 43,000	$44,850	$63,050	$53,800	$71,000	$82,095	
Net Cash Flow	$ 57,000	$44,850	$ 17,950	$ 1,200	$ 7,000	$ 8,905	
Ending Balance	$ 57,000	$ 12,150	$30,100	$31,300	$38,300	$47,205	

LO 6.1 Understanding Cash Flow

The role of the cash flow statement developed in the due diligence stage of a fledgling venture is substantially different from the financial analysis developed for an ongoing firm. An established business will develop a series of financial reports for both investors and founders over some time period such as a month or a quarter. The data generated will include an actual cash flow statement, but will also include a balance sheet, an income statement, and a small series of industry-specific reports. Each of these financial statements provides a unique look at the operation of the business and each is valuable in its own right. We will briefly examine these statements in this chapter, and then in Chapter 9, we will provide a detailed examination of the means to use such financial reports once the business is up and running. For a proposed business, the financial analysis focuses almost exclusively upon its ability to generate positive cash flows in the shortest time possible.

This focus on cash flow is due in part to the fact that in the new business, the management of the firm will also be the owners of the firm. Profitability is applauded in the public investing community, where the members of management are generally not the majority owners and therefore there is a split in ownership and control. When there is a separation between management and ownership, profits are a useful measure as a means to evaluate performance, since such firms are typically larger and have numerous slack resources. However, for owners of the small firm, the focus is on value and the viability of the business. Particularly for a new business, the viability of the firm will be decided by cash flow, not profitability. The ability of the new business to generate strong profits on each item sold is indeed important; however, profit should not be the principal focus in the analysis of a potential new business. Profits have little to do with whether the business will be viable over the long term. The key to the success of a new venture (as simple and obvious as it seems) is its ability to bring in more cash each month than it spends and, more important, to bring that cash in on a cycle that is faster than the payout cycle.

One of the authors of the text assisted a start-up company whose founders had developed a device that sold for $199 and was used in the construction industry. The founders and their investors had invested almost $80,000 in the business (the firm's **equity**). The small business had been in operation for approximately four months when the founders asked him to come to the office for a celebration. Upon his arrival there were drinks and balloons to celebrate the first sale of the product produced by the firm. One of the founders proudly announced he had just made $100, a profit margin of about 50 percent on this first sale of their product. The owners were totally focused on that profit margin and had visions of a business that would now grow and provide them a solid living for the rest of their lives. However, the owners had burned through almost $38,000 to make that $100. Total cash that had flowed into the company was $199; total cash outflow had exceeded $38,000, for a net cash flow of a negative $37,801.

Regardless of the profit margin of a company's product, there is a need to bring in sufficient cash to pay all of the bills. That small business was going to have to generate many more sales to have any potential for staying in business. Unfortunately, while the firm generated lots of interest and started to gain contracts for its product, it went through all of its cash reserves before it could bring in sufficient cash from sales for the firm to survive. This was another great idea that had lots of potential and a good profit margin, but failed to produce a long-term business due to the absence of cash flow.

equity
Investment into the small business by the owners of the firm.

Of course the new business person wants to make a profit, but cash pays the bills and the payroll. As we stated earlier, a new small business will have to pay its vendors cash. Even after a small business is well established, it may have only 30 days to pay vendors, while its customers, particularly if they are large firms, may take upwards of 90 days to pay their bills. The small business has to cover that period of 60 days between when it had to deliver the product and when it receives payment. It may even be a longer period if your customer was a government entity of some type.

This situation represents an important concept or term in cash flow analysis: **float.** This term reflects the setting where there is a difference between when the money goes out and when it comes in.[3] Banks commonly use float to their benefit. You as a business owner may deposit a check from an out-of-state buyer. For some period of time your bank account reflects no inflow to you. However, the bank generally receives the money for that check within 24 hours. This is because the bank is legally allowed to hold an out-of-state check for clearance for pre-assigned time periods. Thus, the bank has free use of the money during that period when it has received the cash but is not yet required to reflect it in your account. While the float from one out-of-state check may be very small, when those amounts are aggregated by large banks, they can involve millions or billions of dollars they have the ability to use at no cost to themselves during a year.

float

The difference between when the money goes out and when it comes in. For example, if you deposit a check today in payment for some good, you typically do not receive cash when you deposit it. Instead there is a period of float before it is credited to your account.

The small business owner can also benefit from float. Credit card charges (not including cash advances) are typically a free form of cash float, since the new business owner does not have to pay interest unless the bill is not paid in full each month. For anywhere up to 25 days a month, the owner has use of the funds without having any outflow to pay the bill. This is a positive cash flow situation for the small business owner.

An interesting fact, and one somewhat counterintuitive to most new business owners, is that one of the most dangerous situations for a new venture is rapid growth. Growth requires funds to build products or provide services immediately, in a situation where the revenue from those activities will not be in hand until sometime in the future. The revenue from the sales can actually be far in the future, depending upon the nature of the business. As a result, the time lag during a rapid buildup of the business causes a cash crunch and is one of the leading sources of new business failure.[4] Active, accurate, realistic cash flow projections are critical to ensure that the new venture can survive by showing the founder of the new business what the cash flow should be over a given period of time.

Cash Flow Versus Budgets

A cash flow statement is not a budget and should not be confused with a budget. A **budget** projects all the costs that will be incurred by the organization over some period of time (a year, for instance) and allocates that expense evenly over the relevant time period. This is similar to what you might do for your household expenses as you set aside money each month to pay the annual life insurance payment or school tuition. At any one time the account for that expense usually has excess funds (except for the month in which the bill comes due). An example might be an insurance payment. The annual cost might be $1,800; thus, the budget would reflect $150 per month.

budget

Statement that projects all the costs that will be incurred by the organization over a period of time and allocates those expenses evenly over the relevant time period.

BUDGET

Receipts:		January	February	March	April	May	June	Total
	Sales	$ 1,000	$2,500	$3,000	$ 5,000	$ 7,000	$10,000	$28,500
	Consulting	$ 5,000	$5,000	$5,000	$10,000	$10,000	$10,000	$45,000
Total Receipts		$ 6,000	$7,500	$8,000	$15,000	$ 17,000	$20,000	$73,500
Disbursements:								
	Salaries	$ 4,000	$4,000	$4,000	$ 5,500	$ 5,500	$ 5,500	$28,500
	Travel	$ 1,000	$1,000	$1,000	$ 1,000	$ 1,000	$ 1,000	$ 6,000
	Car Leases	$ 1,000	$1,000	$1,000	$ 1,000	$ 1,000	$ 1,000	$ 6,000
	Rent	$ 900	$ 450	$ 450	$ 450	$ 450	$ 450	$ 3,150
	Payroll Taxes	$ 300	$ 300	$ 300	$ 300	$ 300	$ 300	$ 1,800
	Insurance	$ 121	$ 121	$ 121	$ 121	$ 121	$ 121	$ 725
	Fuel/Maint.	$ 150	$ 150	$ 150	$ 150	$ 150	$ 150	$ 900
	Benefits	$ 350	$ 350	$ 350	$ 350	$ 350	$ 350	$ 2,100
	Advertising	$ 300	$ 300	$ 300	$ 300	$ 300	$ 300	$ 1,800
	Inventory Inputs	$ 50	$ 50	$ 50	$ 50	$ 50	$ 50	$ 300
	Utilities	$ 200	$ 200	$ 200	$ 200	$ 200	$ 200	$ 1,200
	Misc.	$ 250	$ 250	$ 250	$ 250	$ 250	$ 250	$ 1,500
Total Disbursements		$ 8,621	$ 8,171	$ 8,171	$ 9,671	$ 9,671	$ 9,671	$53,975
Beginning Balance		$ 0	$7,379	$6,708	$ 6,538	$ 11,867	$ 19,196	
Equity Investment		$10,000						$10,000
Net Profit		($ 2,621)	($ 671)	($ 171)	$ 5,329	$ 7,329	$ 9,196	$ 18,392
Ending Balance		$ 7,379	$6,708	$6,538	$ 11,867	$ 19,196	$28,392	

Table 6.1

Example Budget for Start-Up Software Firm

An example budget for a start-up firm that sells software is shown in Table 6.1.

This is the actual budget prepared by a new small business that sold software to other small- to medium-sized businesses (the founders had developed a small software package and sales consisted of a CD-ROM and a small manual). This budget was what the firm relied on as it started its business and it showed that the small business should have consistent positive cash balances. Note that virtually all of the amounts in each category were the same from month to month.

A cash flow statement does the exact opposite of a budget. In the example above of an insurance payment, in each month in which no actual cash outflow occurs, the category receives a zero, and then in the month that the payment is due, the account will record a cash outflow of $1,800. While budgets are helpful for planning purposes, nothing brings home reality like the recognition that the company must have X amount of actual cash in order to pay this month's bills.

Compare the example firm's budget with its actual cash flow statement in Table 6.2.

CASH FLOW STATEMENT

Receipts:		January	February	March	April	May	June	Total
	Sales	$ 350	$ 550	$1,200	$ 9,400	$12,200	$13,000	**$36,700**
	Consulting	$ 3,000	$ 3,500	$5,000	$ 0	$ 3,000	$ 3,500	**$18,000**
Total Receipts		$ 3,350	$ 4,050	$6,200	$ 9,400	$15,200	$16,500	**$54,700**
Disbursements:								
	Salaries	$ 4,000	$ 4,000	$5,000	$ 5,000	$ 5,000	$ 5,000	**$28,000**
	Travel	$ 2,304	$ 365	$ 558	$ 846	$ 1,368	$ 1,104	**$ 6,545**
	Car Leases	$ 1,000	$ 1,000	$1,000	$ 1,000	$ 1,000	$ 1,000	**$ 6,000**
	Rent	$ 900	$ 450	$ 450	$ 450	$ 450	$ 450	**$ 3,150**
	Payroll Taxes	$ 240	$ 240	$ 300	$ 300	$ 300	$ 340	**$ 1,720**
	Insurance	$ 0	$ 0	$ 0	$ 1,450	$ 0	$ 0	**$ 1,450**
	Fuel/Maint.	$ 13	$ 21	$ 46	$ 361	$ 468	$ 502	**$ 1,412**
	Benefits	$ 350	$ 350	$ 350	$ 350	$ 350	$ 350	**$ 2,100**
	Advertising	$ 28	$ 44	$ 96	$ 752	$ 976	$ 0	**$ 1,896**
	Credit Card					$ 500	$ 2,000	**$ 2,500**
	Supplies	$ 17	$ 20	$ 31	$ 47	$ 76	$ 112	**$ 303**
	Utilities	$ 174	$ 213	$ 208	$ 189	$ 132	$ 188	**$ 1,104**
	Misc.	$ 67	$ 81	$ 124	$ 188	$ 304	$ 764	**$ 1,528**
Total Disbursements		$ 9,093	$ 6,784	$ 8,163	$11,433	$12,424	$ 9,810	**$57,708**
								$ 0
Beginning Balance		$ 0	$ 4,257	$ 1,523	$ 60	$ 27	$ 2,802	
Equity Investment		$10,000						**$10,000**
Credit Card Advance				$ 500	$2,000			
Net Cash Flow		($ 5,743)	($2,734)	($1,963)	($2,033)	$ 2,776	$ 6,690	**($ 3,008)**
Ending Balance		$4,257	$ 1,523	$ 60	$ 27	$ 2,802	$ 9,492	

Table 6.2
Example Cash Flow Statement for Start-Up Software Firm

The firm developed this cash flow analysis after several months of operation, when it became clear that the budget document was not proving helpful in the management of the firm's cash. The cash flow statement that was developed for the company showed some shortfalls that should scare a firm founder. The company (which started with $10,000 from the founders) was completely out of cash by March and had a negative cash position of almost $2,000 in April. The firm actually covered this shortcoming with credit card cash advances and was able to survive. Note that the company founders did not account for the interest on those advances which accrued from the date of the transaction—a cost they should have accounted for to better understand their financial standing. One of the fundamental realities of starting a new business is that it takes a period of time for the new venture to ramp up sales and then to obtain cash from those sales. Much of the difficulty with this small business could have been avoided with a cash flow projection prior to

CASH FLOW STATEMENT

Receipts:		January	February	March	April	May	June	Total
	Sales	$ 350	$ 550	$ 1,200	$ 9,400	$ 12,200	$13,000	**$36,700**
	Consulting	$3,000	$ 3,500	$ 5,000	$ 0	$ 3,000	$ 3,500	**$18,000**
Total Receipts		$ 3,350	$ 4,050	$ 6,200	$ 9,400	$ 15,200	$16,500	**$54,700**
Disbursements:								
	Salaries	$4,000	$ 4,000	$ 5,000	$ 5,000	$ 5,000	$ 5,000	**$28,000**
	Travel	$2,304	$ 365	$ 558	$ 846	$ 1,368	$ 1,104	**$ 6,545**
	Car Leases	$ 1,000	$ 1,000	$ 1,000	$ 1,000	$ 1,000	$ 1,000	**$ 6,000**
	Rent	$ 900	$ 450	$ 450	$ 450	$ 450	$ 450	**$ 3,150**
	Payroll Taxes	$ 240	$ 240	$ 300	$ 300	$ 300	$ 340	**$ 1,720**
	Insurance	$ 0	$ 0	$ 0	$ 1,450	$ 0	$ 0	**$ 1,450**
	Fuel/Maint.	$ 13	$ 21	$ 46	$ 361	$ 468	$ 502	**$ 1,412**
	Benefits	$ 350	$ 350	$ 350	$ 350	$ 350	$ 350	**$ 2,100**
	Advertising	$ 28	$ 44	$ 96	$ 752	$ 976	$ 0	**$ 1,896**
	Credit Card				$ 500	$ 2,000		**$ 2,500**
	Supplies	$ 17	$ 20	$ 31	$ 47	$ 76	$ 112	**$ 303**
	Utilities	$ 174	$ 213	$ 208	$ 189	$ 132	$ 188	**$ 1,104**
	Misc.	$ 67	$ 81	$ 124	$ 188	$ 304	$ 764	**$ 1,528**
Total Disbursements		$ 9,093	$ 6,784	$ 8,163	$ 11,433	$ 12,424	$ 9,810	**$57,708**
								$ 0
Beginning Balance		$ 0	($5,743)	($ 8,477)	($ 10,440)	($12,473)	($ 9,698)	
Equity Investment								**$ 0**
Credit Card Advance								
Net Cash Flow		($5,743)	($2,734)	($ 1,963)	($ 2,033)	$ 2,776	$ 6,690	**($3,008)**
Ending Balance		($5,743)	($8,477)	($10,440)	**($12,473)**	($ 9,698)	($3,008)	

Table 6.3
Modified Example Cash Flow Statement for Start-Up Software Firm

deciding whether to pursue the business or not, and then with use of that cash flow projection to ensure an increase in the initial equity position of the new firm.[5]

We utilize a rule of thumb (and it is only a rule of thumb) when examining the initial equity needs of a new venture that has proved to be very helpful in ensuring that the new venture has sufficient cash to achieve a market position. Calculate your entire cash flow projection without adding in any equity investment, and look for the point where the ending balance is at its lowest. Take that number and multiply it by 150 percent. We argue for multiplying by 150 percent because it always takes more cash than you expect. (It also takes more time than you expect.) That number is what we would recommend for the initial equity or equity-plus-debt investment.

For example, we take the exact cash flow statement from Table 6.2 and remove the equity-plus-debt investment from the projection to produce Table 6.3.

CASH FLOW STATEMENT

Receipts:		January	February	March	April	May	June	Total
	Sales	$ 350	$ 550	$ 1,200	$ 9,400	$12,200	$ 13,000	$36,700
	Consulting	$ 3,000	$ 3,500	$ 5,000	$ 0	$ 3,000	$ 3,500	$18,000
Total Receipts		$ 3,350	$ 4,050	$ 6,200	$ 9,400	$15,200	$ 16,500	$54,700
Disbursements:								
	Salaries	$ 4,000	$ 4,000	$ 5,000	$ 5,000	$ 5,000	$ 5,000	$28,000
	Travel	$ 2,304	$ 365	$ 558	$ 846	$ 1,368	$ 1,104	$ 6,545
	Car Leases	$ 1,000	$ 1,000	$ 1,000	$ 1,000	$ 1,000	$ 1,000	$ 6,000
	Rent	$ 900	$ 450	$ 450	$ 450	$ 450	$ 450	$ 3,150
	Payroll Taxes	$ 240	$ 240	$ 300	$ 300	$ 300	$ 340	$ 1,720
	Insurance	$ 0	$ 0	$ 0	$ 1,450	$ 0	$ 0	$ 1,450
	Fuel/Maint.	$ 13	$ 21	$ 46	$ 361	$ 468	$ 502	$ 1,412
	Benefits	$ 350	$ 350	$ 350	$ 350	$ 350	$ 350	$ 2,100
	Advertising	$ 28	$ 44	$ 96	$ 752	$ 976	$ 0	$ 1,896
	Credit Card				$ 500	$ 2,000		$ 2,500
	Supplies	$ 17	$ 20	$ 31	$ 47	$ 76	$ 112	$ 303
	Utilities	$ 174	$ 213	$ 208	$ 189	$ 132	$ 188	$ 1,104
	Misc.	$ 67	$ 81	$ 124	$ 188	$ 304	$ 764	$ 1,528
Total Disbursements		$ 9,093	$ 6,784	$ 8,163	$ 11,433	$12,424	$ 9,810	$ 57,708
								$ 0
Beginning Balance		$ 0	$ 13,257	$10,523	$ 8,560	$ 6,527	$ 9,302	
Equity Investment		$ 19,000						$ 19,000
Credit Card Advance								
Net Cash Flow		($ 5,743)	($ 2,734)	($ 1,963)	($2,033)	$ 2,776	$ 6,690	($ 3,008)
Ending Balance		**$13,257**	**$10,523**	**$8,560**	**$6,527**	**$9,302**	**$15,992**	

Notice that in April the low point for the ending balance is ($12,473). Multiplying that number by 150 percent yields a recommended initial investment of $18,709, or roughly $19,000. With that number inserted into the initial equity investment for the firm, we see that the cash balance remains well above zero. This provides a cushion to the new firm which enables it to pursue options it did not consider at founding, more easily handle rapid growth, and/or handle unexpected external shocks to the organization. See Table 6.4.

In developing a cash flow projection, the new business owner should contact vendors/suppliers to ask about payment terms and also check with credit card companies to get exact information about when accounts will be processed and what percentage will be charged to the company for each transaction. These interactions also allow the new business owner to seek out the best terms possible from vendors and suppliers. In the next section of this chapter, we will suggest a specific series of items to be accounted for as you develop your cash flow statement. Once the venture begins operations, actual cash flow should be compared monthly to the projected cash flow statement in order to produce a **deviation analysis,**

Table 6.4
Finalized Example Cash Flow Statement for Start-Up Software Firm

deviation analysis
Analysis of the differences between the predicted and the actual performance.

an analysis of how the predicted and actual cash flows differ. This will not only assist the new business owner in developing realistic forecasts for the business in the future, but also point out differences between actual performance and predicted performance at a point in time. Taking the time each month to examine this allows the new business person maximum flexibility in making changes to the business as it grows (a habit that will help keep the venture responsive as the venture develops). Chapter 9 will go into greater detail on such comparisons and how to analyze and respond to the deviations that are identified. To illustrate, you can see in Table 6.5 the cash flow deviation analysis from the software firm we have been discussing.

In this example, the software company's revenues fell $2,650 short of the owners' predictions and their expenses were $693 more than they had expected. While the firm will still have positive cash balance, this type of cash analysis provides valuable information to the owners of this new company. Why were sales so far below expectations? Why was travel more than double the projection? We note that the firm did virtually no advertising; perhaps this is why sales were less than expected. Some expenses need to be made in order to increase the opportunity for success on the revenue side, so we are not suggesting that the new venture attempt to cut its way to success; instead we suggest a careful monthly analysis of all actual revenues and expenses.

Table 6.5
Example Deviation Analysis for Start-Up Software Firm

DEVIATION ANALYSIS

Receipts:		January – Predicted	January – Actual	Difference
	Sales	$ 1,000	$ 350	($ 650)
	Consulting	$ 5,000	$ 3,000	($2,000)
Total Receipts		$ 6,000	$ 3,350	($2,650)
Disbursements:				
	Salaries	$ 4,000	$ 4,000	$ 0
	Travel	$ 1,000	$ 2,304	$ 1,304
	Car Leases	$ 900	$ 1,000	$ 100
	Rent	$ 900	$ 900	$ 0
	Payroll Taxes	$ 300	$ 240	($ 60)
	Insurance	$ 0	$ 0	$ 0
	Fuel/Maint.	$ 150	$ 13	($ 137)
	Benefits	$ 350	$ 350	$ 0
	Advertising	$ 300	$ 28	($ 272)
	Supplies	$ 50	$ 17	($ 33)
	Utilities	$ 200	$ 174	($ 26)
	Misc.	$ 250	$ 67	($ 183)
Total Disbursements		$ 8,400	$ 9,093	$ 693
Equity Investment		$10,000	$10,000	$ 0
Net Cash Flow		($ 2,400)	($ 5,743)	($3,343)
Ending Balance		$ 7,600	$ 4,257	($3,343)

LO 6.2 Developing Cash Flow Statements

There are several key issues that should be noted in developing a cash flow statement. The first is that a cash flow statement for a new business is substantially different from the typical publicly traded corporate annual report that you may have seen. New businesses, unlike established companies, are unlikely to have either investing activities or financing activities (interest on notes/loans is included in the operations section of new business cash flow statements). New business ventures typically have only one type of activity: operations. Everything that involves cash in/cash out is related to the operation of the business.

The cash flow statement is used to describe all of the activities that provide and use cash during the period being examined (we would recommend that the statement be done monthly until the business is well established). Used effectively, this statement helps the owners accurately keep track of the overall cash position of the business and provides a well-respected and accepted means of displaying the ability of the company to meet its obligations. As the business grows, a well-developed, accurate long-term track record of cash flow statements and their comparison to plan will go a long way toward assisting the company with loans, credit lines, infusions of equity capital, and even valuation, should the businessperson want to sell the company.

Generating the cash flow statement should actually begin with the expenses of the organization, for the very simple reason that they are easier to accurately forecast than are revenues. Expenses fall into a number of categories that are inclusive of, but not limited to, the following list:

- Salaries
- Basic Benefits
- Taxes/Fees
  - Payroll
  - Income
  - Local
  - State
  - Business
  - Licenses
- Cost of Goods Sold
  - Manufacturing
  - Packaging
  - Direct Labor
  - Shipping
- Utilities (Electricity, Gas, Phone Service, etc.)
- Security Systems
- Tools/Machinery
- Office Supplies (a big and often underestimated expense)
- Travel Expenses
- Insurance
- Advertising
- Furniture/Computers

- Telephones
- Maintenance of Equipment
- Cleaning (either a service or supplies for your use)
- Rent/Mortgage Payments

In short, all actual expenses must be accounted for in the cash flow statement. If your specific business has unique expenses that do not fit into these categories, note that you also need to add those expenses to this list.

Revenues (cash inflows) should be separated into as many categories as possible in order to provide maximum insight to the owner. The firm's revenues can come from a wide variety of sources that may not automatically be recognized. A new firm may sell computers, but it may actually make more money from servicing those computers. Separating out revenue lines aids both in predicting where the firm's revenues will come from and in analyzing the actual revenue sources for the new firm. Once there is a fine-grained understanding, then those categories can be collapsed together if a more general-level categorization is desired.

To illustrate further, a lawn care company found from its cash flow analysis that its cash inflow was more positively impacted by what appeared to be an ancillary portion of the business (planting the flowers for a commercial building). The firm had to have the contract to mow the lawn to get the business, but it was planting the flowers that actually had a greater positive impact on the cash flow. Thus, the firm reexamined its pricing and priced the mowing so that the firm was certain to get the lawn mowing contract, with flower planting and other landscaping activities providing the substantial portion of the positive inflow of revenues.

Several examples of the breakout in revenues that we have seen are listed in Table 6.6. These include revenue statements from a restaurant, a clothing store, and a retail office supply operation. Note that these examples focus only on revenues in order to provide you an idea of how to develop this aspect of cash flow statements. We will discuss expenses later in the chapter.

As the examples above suggest, generating a cash flow statement should be tailored to the information needs of the new venture. The lists above are not meant to be exhaustive. In general, we recommend that each unique area of the business that generates income should be given a separate revenue line item.

A final comment regarding cash flow statements concerns the development of a **sensitivity analysis.**[6] The cash flow statement developed above could best be labeled a "most likely case" scenario. It is also quite prudent to look at a worst-case and a best-case scenario to examine the sensitivity of the potential cash flow to dramatic changes in the revenue or cost stream when conducting due diligence on a business idea. The sensitivity analysis is a judgment call by the new business person about whether the business could survive the worst-case or successfully carry out the best-case scenario.

To better understand your financial situation, our advice is that you take the revenue figures developed in your most-likely scenario and create two new cash flow statements. One increases monthly revenue by 25 percent and the other decreases monthly revenue by 25 percent. What is the effect upon your net cash flow? Could your new venture survive

sensitivity analysis

An examination of the best- and worst-case cash flow scenarios.

RESTAURANT CASH FLOW STATEMENT

Receipts:	January	February	March	April	Total
Food	$1,300	$1,800	$2,300	$2,400	$ 7,800
Drink	$ 350	$ 490	$ 600	$ 605	$ 2,045
Alcohol	$ 450	$ 770	$ 780	$ 810	$ 2,810
Misc.	$ 110	$ 200	$ 205	$ 399	$ 914
Total Receipts	$2,210	$3,260	$3,885	$ 4,214	$ 13,569

CLOTHING STORE CASH FLOW STATEMENT

Receipts:	January	February	March	April	Total
Men's	$1,100	$ 900	$ 880	$ 850	$ 3,730
Women's	$ 800	$ 1,300	$3,900	$ 4,010	$10,010
Children's	$ 210	$ 800	$1,460	$ 1,503	$ 3,973
Shoes	$ 0	$ 130	$ 468	$ 890	$ 1,488
Accessories	$ 35	$ 473	$ 608	$ 950	$ 2,066
Total Receipts	$2,145	$3,603	$7,316	$ 8,203	$21,267

OFFICE SUPPLY STORE CASH FLOW STATEMENT

Receipts:	January	February	March	April	Total
Paper	$ 110	$ 400	$ 900	$ 1,450	$ 2,860
Calculators	$ 0	$ 340	$ 0	$ 110	$ 450
Computers	$ 0	$4,060	$1,300	$ 9,400	$14,760
Peripherals	$ 460	$2,389	$1,600	$ 2,450	$ 6,899
Furniture	$ 0	$ 0	$ 0	$ 199	$ 199
Writing Instruments	$ 280	$ 300	$ 460	$ 730	$ 1,770
Presentation Materials	$ 505	$ 695	$ 803	$ 477	$ 2,480
Impulse Display Items	$ 34	$ 79	$ 672	$ 309	$ 1,094
Cards	$ 250	$ 150	$ 172	$ 220	$ 310
Services	$ 120	$ 420	$1,200	$ 1,833	$ 3,573
Other	$ 96	$ 388	$ 700	$ 271	$ 1,455
Total Receipts	$1,855	$9,221	$7,707	$17,449	$35,850

Table 6.6
Revenue-side examples for
Three Different Businesses

The Rodriquez family had identified the issues for the auto repair shop, including the supports they would use, strategy, and key operational issues. However, Alex initially developed only a budget for the business. When he and his uncle Fred (who was helping to fund the business) went to the Small Business Assistance Center for advice on their plan, they were told that a budget was simply not enough. It was then that Alex learned about the differences between a cash flow statement and a budget.

It was like a light came on for Alex. He had always heard the owner of the auto parts store where he worked talk about how "cash was king." He knew that some of the auto repair customers took upwards of 90 days to pay their bills. However, he also knew that the large national auto supply chains where the store obtained parts demanded payments within 30 days, after which they invoked significant penalties. A small auto parts store represents only a speck in the total parts sold nationally, so the auto parts store where Alex worked had very little leeway as to when payments were due to the national suppliers.

The result of this insight and the advice of the Small Business Assistance Center was that Alex developed two cash flow statements: a best- and a worst-case example. The basis for these two cash flow estimates was his discussions with others on what a shop of his size should produce. Using the Internet and the local Yellow Pages, Alex contacted dozens of auto repair shops, most of which would not be in direct competition with his proposed business. While not all shop owners would talk to him, an amazing number would, particularly other Hispanic shop owners who could relate well to his efforts. One part of the insight that Alex obtained from these discussions was that much of his cash would actually come from doing things other than repairing the engines of the cars. Prior to the discussion with the other owners, Alex's vision was that he would be rebuilding engines most of the time. However, the individuals he talked with made it clear that he would be getting much of his cash flow from such mundane tasks as changing oil and belts. They also gave him insight as to the percentage breakdown in the various activities. The income side of the cash flow statement he developed is below.

CASH FLOW STATEMENT
BEST CASE

Receipts:		January	February	March	April	Total
	Oil Change	$ 4,960	$ 5,010	$ 5,440	$ 6,000	$ 21,410
	Air Conditioning	$ 4,400	$ 3,200	$ 8,600	$10,900	$ 27,100
	Brakes	$ 3,200	$ 3,800	$ 5,900	$ 5,900	$ 18,800
	Belts	$ 1,300	$ 1,860	$ 2,550	$ 2,650	$ 8,360
	Engines	$ 6,890	$ 7,400	$ 8,100	$10,900	$ 33,290
Total Receipts		$20,750	$21,270	$30,590	$36,350	$108,960

CASH FLOW STATEMENT
WORST CASE

Receipts:		January	February	March	April	Total
	Oil Change	$ 3,120	$ 3,800	$ 3,940	$ 4,300	$ 15,160
	Air Conditioning	$ 2,850	$ 1,890	$ 4,800	$ 5,800	$ 13,340
	Brakes	$ 1,800	$ 2,100	$ 4,300	$ 3,800	$ 12,000
	Belts	$ 800	$ 1,300	$ 1,650	$ 2,100	$ 5,850
	Engines	$ 3,850	$ 4,600	$ 5,100	$ 6,800	$ 20,350
Total Receipts		$12,420	$13,690	$19,790	$22,800	$ 68,700

either of these situations? What changes might you make to accommodate the new outcomes?

The owners of a print shop developed best- and worst-case scenarios in their cash flow projections. The worst-case scenario painted a picture of events which the founders of the small business could not survive. This did not lead the entrepreneurs to give up. Instead, they worked to control their immediate costs through methods such as negotiating with their landlord to pay lower rent until they reached the break-even point. Additionally, this situation encouraged the founders to secure several definitive contracts from the city for printing. The result was that the founders were able to revise their cash flows such that even a worst-case scenario would be survivable.

LO 6.3 Other Financial Tools

The focus thus far in this chapter has been exclusively on cash flow. This focus is consistent with the view that cash is king in small business. However, there are other financial tools that are very helpful in analyzing a new business idea. Specifically, a new business will likely want to create **pro forma** balance sheets and income statements. The term "pro forma" (Latin, meaning "as a matter of form") simply means that the small business owner estimates what the balance sheets and income statements will look like in the future, in order to plan well.

Balance Sheet

A **balance sheet** is a summary of the assets and liabilities of the small business. It is useful for the new business to analyze and understand the types of assets and liabilities the small business can expect. Once the firm is up and running, the pro forma balance sheet is also useful as a comparison in order to understand how assets are being used. The analysis of balance sheets in an ongoing business will be discussed more in Chapter 9. There are two basic types of assets that should be included as separate items in the balance sheet:

Current assets: Assets such as cash or those assets that can easily be converted to cash, such as accounts receivable and notes receivable.

Fixed assets: Assets that have a physical presence, including land, buildings, office equipment, machinery, and vehicles.

The balance sheet should include separate lines for each relevant type of current and fixed asset. The level of detail in this type of document is exclusively up to the small business owner; however, we would suggest that one err on the side of more detail early on in the life of the new venture.

On the other side of the equation there are two types of liabilities: current liabilities and long-term liabilities. The definitions of these two types of categories and explanations of what constitutes each are as follows:

Current liabilities: Liabilities or debts that the small business has to pay within one year. These include accounts payable, notes payable such as bank notes, and accrued payroll.

Long-term liabilities: Liabilities that are owed by the business and are ultimately due more than a year from the current date. These include mortgages payable, owners' equity, and stockholders' equity (the latter two are the investment by these individuals in the business).

pro forma

A term describing estimates (in our case, by the small business owner) of what the balance sheets and income statements will look like in the future.

balance sheet

A summary of the assets and liabilities of the small business.

current assets

Assets such as cash or those assets that can easily be converted to cash, such as accounts receivable and notes receivable.

fixed assets

Assets that have a physical presence, including land, buildings, office equipment, machinery, and vehicles.

current liabilities

Liabilities or debts that the small business has to pay within one year. These include accounts payable, notes payable such as bank notes, and accrued payroll.

long-term liabilities

Liabilities that are owed by the business and are ultimately due more than a year from the current date. These include mortgages payable, owners' equity, and stockholders' equity (the latter two are the investment by these individuals in the business).

We have noted that banks are able to accept a check from out of state, and yet they do not have to place those funds in your bank account for a period of up to ten days, even though the bank may actually obtain those funds earlier. The banks benefit from the float. Although this is a historic element of the business and certainly an element of the business model for banks, what is your opinion of the practice? Many small businesses use the same type of float to their advantage when they utilize credit cards during the month, knowing that they will pay off the balance before any finance charge is due. How could banking and businesses adjust this practice and gain a competitive advantage? Should other tools be employed along these same lines?

The assets minus the liabilities of the firm reflected in the balance sheet should total to zero. Thus, the assets and liabilities balance each other. A balance sheet is a snapshot of a firm at some point in time. For a new start-up small firm, the balance sheet is a pro forma projection of what is expected in the future. The estimate of the firm's current assets will be quite limited, as the firm will not yet have any operations. The fixed assets and liabilities can be more exact and should be estimated with some care, since the cost of items can be reasonably estimated, and issues like debt should be well known. Since the firm is a start-up, there will generally not be depreciation of items such as machinery. The text will discuss issues such as depreciation in Chapter 9, but for now you should know that it is basically a percentage of the value of equipment that is seen as the loss of value of an asset due to wear, tear, age, or obsolescence. The current assets minus the current liabilities are referred to as the working capital of the firm. This means, in effect, the liquid assets the firm could call upon quickly to meet needs that arose. Table 6.7 shows the balance sheet for a small manufacturing firm.

Income Statement

income statement
Revenue of the firm minus expenses.

A pro forma **income statement** projects the future income of the organization. The focus of the income statement is profit rather than cash flow. While we emphasize cash flow as a foundation for analyzing the potential viability of the new business, we believe an understanding of profit allows the projected business to understand its overall cost picture. It is not unusual for a new business to take a significant amount of time to reach overall profitability.

One of the keys to developing an income statement is predicting sales for the organization. While there is much more art than science to this process, there are some techniques available to assist the new business person. The new owner should initially look to similar enterprises and attempt to estimate or research their sales levels. If a restaurant with a similar format to yours is available, for example, you can estimate its sales by taking the average ticket price and multiplying that by the traffic flow through the restaurant. You can estimate traffic flow to the restaurant by sitting in the parking lot for one or two nights and keeping a count of how many customers go in the door. The ability to talk with entrepreneurs in the same domain against whom you will not compete was cited in Chapter 3 (identifying the idea) and in Chapter 4 (external analysis) as excellent sources of information. (This is what Alex Rodriquez was able

Table 6.7
Pro-Forma Income Statement

Assets

Current Assets

Cash		$ 50,000
Acct Receivable		$ 0
Total Current Assets		$ 50,000

Fixed Assets	Land	$100,000	
	Buildings	$150,000	
	Office equipment	$ 15,000	
	Machinery	$ 75,000	
Total Fixed Assets			$ 340,000
Total Assets			**$390,000**

Liabilities

Current Liabilities

Accounts Payable	$ 35,000	
Notes Payable (less than a year)	$ 4,500	
Accrued Payroll	$ 15,000	
Total Current Liability		$ 54,500
Long-Term Liabilities		
Mortgage	$200,000	
Total Long-Term Liability		$ 200,000
Owner's Equity		$ 135,500
Total Liabilities/Owner's Equity		$ 390,000

to successfully do in his auto repair shop.) These same individuals are excellent sources of information on what sales levels could be expected at various stages in the new business's growth. The key is to be conservative, since the reality is that things never happen as fast or as smoothly as you would hope in founding your business.

The entrepreneur may come to the conclusion that there are 25,000 people who live in the area around his appliance rental store that are potential customers. The store owner cannot (and should not) assume he will get all or even a majority of those customers. It is better to be very conservative and underestimate demand for a product or service than to overestimate demand. What percentage of the general population rents appliances on a weekly basis? What are the demographics of the typical appliance rental customer? How far will the typical appliance rental customer drive to rent an appliance? What are the primary drivers for the rental of appliances versus the purchase of them? How is the industry tracking? These and many other questions will assist the new business person in estimating the potential sales of his new venture. Additionally, the entrepreneur needs to realize that sales growth is a function of time, and should not assume that the new venture will

INCOME STATEMENT

Receipts:		January	February	March	April	May	June	Total
	Sales	$ 350	$ 550	$ 1,200	$ 9,400	$12,200	$13,000	$36,700
	Consulting	$3,000	$ 3,500	$5,000	$ 0	$ 3,000	$ 3,500	$18,000
Total Income		$3,350	$ 4,050	$6,200	$ 9,400	$15,200	$16,500	$54,700
Cost of Goods Sold								
	Inventory Inputs	$ 17	$ 20	$ 31	$ 47	$ 76	$ 112	$ 303
Gross Profit		$3,333	$ 4,030	$ 6,169	$ 9,353	$ 15,124	$16,388	$54,397
Other Expenses								
	Salaries	$4,000	$ 4,000	$5,000	$ 5,000	$ 5,000	$ 5,000	$28,000
	Travel	$2,304	$ 365	$ 558	$ 846	$ 1,368	$ 1,104	$ 6,545
	Car Leases	$1,000	$ 1,000	$ 1,000	$ 1,000	$ 1,000	$ 1,000	$ 6,000
	Rent	$ 900	$ 450	$ 450	$ 450	$ 450	$ 450	$ 3,150
	Payroll Taxes	$ 240	$ 240	$ 300	$ 300	$ 300	$ 340	$ 1,720
	Insurance	$ 0	$ 0	$ 0	$ 1,450	$ 0	$ 0	$ 1,450
	Fuel/Maint.	$ 13	$ 21	$ 46	$ 361	$ 468	$ 502	$ 1,412
	Benefits	$ 350	$ 350	$ 350	$ 350	$ 350	$ 350	$ 2,100
	Advertising	$ 28	$ 44	$ 96	$ 752	$ 976	$ 0	$ 1,896
	Utilities	$ 174	$ 213	$ 208	$ 189	$ 132	$ 188	$ 1,104
	Misc.	$ 67	$ 81	$ 124	$ 188	$ 304	$ 764	$ 1,528
Total Expenses		$ 9,093	$ 6,784	$ 8,163	$10,933	$10,424	$ 9,810	$55,208
Profit Before Taxes		($5,760)	($2,754)	($1,994)	($1,580)	$ 4,700	$ 6,578	($ 811)
Taxes		$ 0.00	$ 0.00	$ 0.00	$ 0.00	$ 0.00	$ 0.00	$ 0.00
Profit After Taxes		($5,760)	($2,754)	($1,994)	($1,580)	$ 4,700	$ 6,578	($ 811)

Table 6.8

Example Income Statement for Computer Sales & Services Firm

reach an established company's sales volume in the short run. The new business venture needs to make conservative predictions regarding demand. Again, discussion with successful entrepreneurs is the new business person's best resource.

The income statement provides both the gross and the net profit figures for the firm. In its simplified form, gross profit generally equals the sales of the organization minus the cost of goods sold. The firm then calculates all other expenses, such as salaries and benefits, to reach a total expense for the firm. Gross profit minus all other expenses yields net profit before taxes. Lastly, estimated taxes are calculated and subtracted from net profit, to determine the company's net profit after taxes. A sample income statement for the computer sales and service firm discussed previously is shown in Table 6.8. Note that the cost of goods sold is very small, since producing a computer disk and a manual are very cheap activities from the production standpoint. If this were a restaurant, the cost of goods sold would be much higher.

Break-Even Analysis

Now that you have developed a pro forma cash flow statement, income statement, and balance sheet for your proposed new venture, it is time to look at one additional analytical tool. The initial effort to project the cash flow is critical. However, the firm needs to extend this analysis. Specifically, what are the opportunities for the new venture to really generate significant returns for the owners? Individuals have numerous alternatives to starting a new venture, and we want to suggest that a **break-even analysis** of the projected position of the company will go a long way toward determining not only the viability of the new venture, but also the realistic assessment of whether this is the best path for the entrepreneur to embark upon. A break-even analysis provides some judgment about when the firm will reach a point of being self-sustaining after the business is begun.[7]

The break-even analysis recognizes that the growth in sales does not occur all at once. Instead, the sales of the business will grow incrementally once the firm starts. However, many of the expenses of the firm will start months before the first sale. Specifically, there are **fixed costs** (for example: rent, utilities, equipment leases, etc.) which must be paid regardless of the sales level. There are also **variable costs** that will fluctuate according to how many goods are produced. For example, if you manufacture something packaged in plastic bottles, you will have increasing costs as you produce more products, since you will need more bottles.

The traditional Fortune 500 approach to break-even analysis would suggest that once revenues exceed the total of the fixed costs plus the variable costs, then the firm has reached breakeven. In this approach the profit margin from each sale adds to the net profit for the firm. For firms operating in a project-by project-environment, this type of analysis is relatively effective. These firms are simply trying to compare investment in one project to investment in another, as shown in Figure 6.1.

However, entrepreneurial ventures need to operate in a fundamentally different manner, and we calculate breakeven using cash flow rather than profit. The initial investment in the new venture is an item of concern that is not normally included in most corporate cash flow

EXERCISE 2

You have all the basic tools now to create a projected cash flow statement for your proposed business. Categorize all of your income-generating areas and carefully develop a complete list of your expenses (review the list provided earlier in this chapter). Using the examples in this chapter, develop a six-month projection and then present it to a group of your peers.

break-even analysis
Tool for the estimation of when a business's income exceeds its expenses.

fixed costs
Costs that must be paid no matter how many goods are sold, such as rent for the building.

variable costs
Costs that vary according to how many goods are produced.

Figure 6.1
Classic Break-Even Diagram

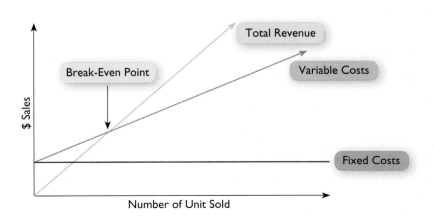

Figure 6-2
Entrepreneurial Break-Even Diagram

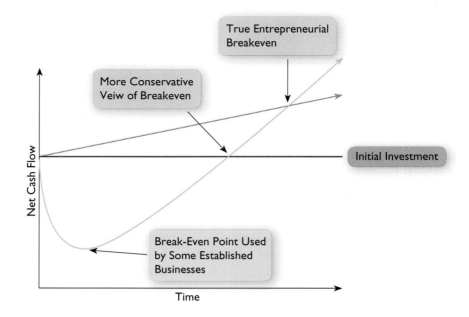

analyses. Accounting for the initial investment allows the new firm to discuss the true economic returns, or economic benefits, from the business. (Recall that we discussed earlier that the small business person wants to be sure that her business is providing the economic return she envisioned and that she is not working essentially for free.) Figure 6.2 demonstrates this relationship. We begin this diagram with an initial investment level. As the new firm begins operations, it is burning cash (from both a fixed and a variable cost standpoint) and reporting a negative net cash flow. Depending upon the venture and the industry in which it is operating, this negative cash flow can go on for some time. However, at some point a successful business turns the corner and begins producing positive cash flows. This has been called the break-even point for the company, that is, when the firm's costs equal its sales. However, we believe that until the new venture's positive cash flows exceed the initial investment, true breakeven has not been achieved. This analysis can be further enhanced by taking into consideration the issue of time value of money.[8] There are other uses of your investment dollars and your raw time. With inflation, $1000 received today is far more valuable than $1000 will be if received 10 years from now. Thus, if you invest in a business today, you will want it to produce a return that is greater than the return you could have made if you simply had put the money in a savings account. Calculating the **time value of money** gives the initial investment line in Figure 6.2 an upward slope and creates an entrepreneurial break-even point that is farther out, but infinitely more realistic from an investor point of view.

time value of money
The value of money over time at a given rate of inflation or other type of return. Calculated as the value of your investment in time and money if you did not do the proposed venture.

summary

The decision process for starting a new small business is fraught with the unknown. This chapter has focused exclusively upon the analysis tools that are the most critical in determining the financial viability of the proposed new venture.

A detailed examination of cash flow, its inputs, and its uses was provided. A brief examination of the balance sheet and income statement were provided, and finally we discussed the unique nature of an entrepreneurial break-even analysis.

key terms

balance sheet 119
break-even analysis 123
budget 109
cash flow 106
current assets 119
current liabilities 119
deviation analysis 113
equity 108
fixed assets 119

fixed costs 123
float 109
income statement 120
long-term liabilities 119
pro forma 119
sensitivity analysis 116
time value of money 124
variable costs 123

review questions

1. Why is cash flow so important for a new business?
2. How are cash flow and profit related?
3. What are the basic elements of a cash flow statement for an entrepreneurial business?
4. Why is a budget statement not a cash flow statement? How do they differ?
5. How does float affect a cash flow statement?
6. How does a balance sheet relate to a cash flow statement?
7. Why is break-even analysis so important to a new business?
8. What elements make up a break-even analysis?
9. How is an income statement used by new business?

group exercises

1. Each person on the team should prepare a preliminary cash flow statement for his or her proposed venture.
   a. When will the venture achieve entrepreneurial breakeven?
   b. What other revenue categories could be developed to better focus sales tracking?

2. Use an Internet search engine to look for SBA cash flow loans.
   a. What are the basic requirements of these loans?
   b. Why do you think the government supports such loans for small business?
   c. What insights does this provide each person on the team about his or her own proposed ventures?

everyday edisons class discussion

Go to www.everydayedisons.com/markCody.html and read about Mark and Cody.

What do you think the items on their cash flow statement might include?

Jeremy Jones—Body Alive

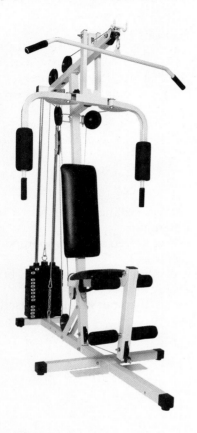

In January 2003 Jeremy Jones had an opportunity that he did not feel he could ignore. Jeremy had a lifetime passion for health and personal fitness. In the fall of 2001 he was selling fitness equipment for a chain of stores in the Dallas/Fort Worth area. The store owners felt that if there were a personal training facility near one of their stores, they would be able to sell more equipment. Jeremy had done a little personal training with individuals he had met at the gym or who had been referred to him, but the idea of opening a facility focused on personal training seemed like an ideal opportunity to him.

The owners suggested that Jeremy set up a personal training facility next to their store in one of the Dallas suburbs. They would sublease the space so that Jeremy did not have to sign a long-term lease and they would sell the equipment to him at cost. These two factors, which dramatically improved his initial cash flow position, were major motivations for Jeremy to start the business. The strategic position for this business would be that it would cater exclusively to personal training. Individuals would not be allowed to simply work out but instead would be trained by Jeremy or others he hired. A premium would be charged for this service, but he planned to charge only $45 per hour, less than personal trainers charged at local athletic clubs.

Jeremy studied the idea for the business for over a year. As part of his due diligence, he visited with a very successful small business person before he decided to pursue the new venture. The advice he received made him stop and think; the individual suggested that he needed to focus more on cash flow. The individual thought it was a good idea, but he was not sure how the venture could generate cash fast enough to cover the costs. Jeremy thought it was sound advice, but the willingness of the fitness equipment retailer to help sublease the space for the venture was a great incentive, since typically such space requires a commitment of several years and a significant initial payment. Therefore, he went forward with the venture.

Jeremy spent $15,000 on equipment and was required to pay rent of $1,000 a month, even for the two months when he was preparing the facility to open. He had some significant costs associated with preparing the facility and he chose to open in January, as that is one of the busiest times for athletic gym attendance (due to New Year's resolutions).

The customer base began to build for Jeremy after he opened but it was slower than he had initially predicted. It soon became clear to him that the facility's location was very dependent on the athletic equipment store to generate customers. The location was near a high-intensity retail location, but the actual location of the facility was relatively hidden from this retail traffic.

The result was that at the end of three months he was over $25,000 in debt. His customer base was growing, but not as fast as his debt. He estimated that if he stuck with the business, after approximately a year and half he might reach initial breakeven in this location. He then began to research other locations or taking on a partner. Despite several promising opportunities, he decided he would be better served by closing the business.

As a result, at the end of three months he had a debt of $25,000. He closed the business in good fashion so that the retailer of athletic equipment remained a supporter and actually would eventually hire Jeremy to manage one of its stores. He decided to keep the equipment and perhaps look for other opportunities in personal training.

Jeremy realized that one of his critical problems in the business was his cash flow. While his experienced entrepreneur friend had suggested that this was the critical issue, it took his own experience to understand the role of cash flow. Soon another opportunity presented itself, as Jeremy found that he continued to have some customers that wanted to be trained. The old customers were referring new potential customers to him, and his Yellow Pages advertisement was continuing to generate calls.

What he soon realized was that there was indeed demand for his services, as he had predicted when he opened his business. However, in an important insight he realized that it was not necessary to have the overhead of a facility to run his business. Instead, he could actually take much of his equipment with him in his van and actually go to the customers' homes to provide the training. In fact, he could charge more money for offering what could be described as a more tailored service since he went to their home. As a result, he increased his charge to between $65 and $80 an hour.

Overall, without the overhead costs Jeremy has been able to do what he has always wanted to do while producing a steady positive cash flow. One outcome is that Jeremy has not only been able to save money; he has also been steadily retiring his debt from his first venture. His customer base is building, although he supplements his income by managing a store for the athletic equipment retailer. However, he hopes that shortly he will be able to focus solely on athletic training.

In hindsight, Jeremy believes that experience is a critical teacher in starting a business. However, he also believes that it is critical that prospective small business owners focus clearly on costs and seek to maximize the net cash flow. Failure to do so can easily force a new business to close, despite its potential for profitability.

learning outcomes

After studying this chapter, you will be able to

7.1 Discuss the various legal forms of business in order to determine the best design for a proposed new business.

7.2 Explain the basics of contracts.

7.3 Define the role of leases in the legal formation of the new business.

7.4 List how laws, rules, and regulations benefit new businesses.

7.5 LO 7.5 Explain the importance of copyrights/trademarks/patents to small business.

7.6 Define the role that insurance plays in the risk portfolio of the new business.

7.7 Discuss how to develop an effective board of advisors and board of directors.

Establishing the Legal Foundation

AMERICAN HOME COLLECTION

 Most individuals think of a knockoff as being that designer handbag sold by an individual on the street corner of some large city for a fraction of the cost of an original. However, many small businesses have their designs stolen by large companies eager to take an advantage in the market. There are stories of small business people designing such things as innovative furniture or very compact ladders for escape from the home and then having these designs copied by large firms. The ability to protect your ideas through copyrights is a protection available for small business in these settings.

Judi Boisson is a quilt designer in Southhampton, New York, who chose to copyright her quilt designs. She ultimately noted that many large firms were producing quilts that were very similar to her designs. She produced her quilts in China and then also discovered that the larger retailers were using the same manufacturer she used to produce their quilts at a steep discount (primarily due to the volume the large retailers could order). As a result of her discovery she sued many of these large retailers. Since she had copyrighted the quilt designs, she was able to win lawsuits against major retailers including QVC, Target, and Burlington Coat Factory. She was also able to settle with Pottery Barn Kids out of court. Thus, her creativity was protected through her copyrighting of the design.

The cost of such litigation can be significant, costing $400,000 or more. A broad rule of thumb suggests that a follower firm must alter at least 30 percent of a product for it not to be considered an infringement of copyright. The ability of small firms to pursue such litigation can be prohibitive; however, small businesses without copyright or patent protection have virtually no opportunity to pursue efforts to protect their designs.

C. Adler, "Can you spot the knockoff?", *Fortune Small Business* 12, no.3 (2002), pp. 42–48; www.judiboisson.com.

Legal issues are critical for a small business to consider. The information in this chapter is not meant to be definitive or exhaustive of all the legal concerns for starting a new business. The material is factually correct; however, we strongly believe that you should hire a qualified attorney to assist you in building the foundation of the new business. The laws in each state vary and the consequences are often serious enough that you will want to ensure you have a full and complete understanding of the legal issues related to the business.

In the previous six chapters we have set out a means for you to develop the type of business that you want to create, determine its strategy/mission, and perform a detailed analysis of the potential cash flow position for the new firm. However, prior to the beginning of any actual operations, the founder must ensure that the proper legal foundation is established, and that all legal procedures, licenses, and authorities are granted or obtained.

Mature economies are based upon laws.* To fully appreciate the reliance in America on the legal institutions, one need only compare the United States to China.[1] There is a legal system in China, but in most cases this system can best be described as chaotic. Similar laws may exist in many nations, but the key questions are how are those laws enforced, and what are the penalties for violations of those laws? These two answers will vary widely between different provinces and even between different cities in the same province in China. Whether laws and their enforcement are the concern of the central government, province, or city is often unclear; instead, there are competing authorities who may interpret what is to be done very differently. To work in this environment, a business survives by developing good relationships with administrators, regulators, and/or the police. It will be the relationship between these individuals and the small business person that determines if the laws are enforced and, if so, how they are enforced. The relationship between business and government officials may originate from a variety of sources, such as being related by blood or marriage, going to school together, or making a payoff, but without such relationships the small business person will most certainly find that she has significant legal problems.[2]

In contrast, the laws of the United States and some other economies are relatively clear and reasonably well enforced, and the amount of corruption is among the lowest in the world. As a result, your legal conflicts are decided based on the facts, not on who you know. While this may indeed be the fairest way to decide business issues, the legal system is often a source of irritation with businesspeople. For example, obtaining a license to sell alcohol at your premises involves approval from numerous authorities—local, state, and federal (Bureau of Alcohol, Tobacco, Firearms, and Explosives). While it is potentially frustrating for you to file documents with all of these parties, it is important to realize that

---

* The law present in a country is referred to as an institution. Other issues such as culture and ways that a given profession may conduct business are also institutions. These institutions shape the way business is conducted in subtle and pervasive manners. To fully understand how business is conducted in a given area, such institutions must be understood.

legal structures in society are critical to you and your business. The abilities to collect money owed to you, to trust that contracts will be honored, to operate without fear of being arbitrarily shut down, and to insure your business against ruinous interventions by the government are all the result of laws. Indeed, in a developing country or one recently ravaged by war, one of the first major steps in building the nation's economy is to establish the police and the courts so that basic business can be transacted.

Our view is that small business people need to acknowledge the central role and importance of the legal system, recognize how it will impact their business lives, and be prepared to compete in that arena. The businessperson cannot ignore legal issues. As a result, small business people need to recognize that they will at some time probably need to go to court to solve disputes. If a supplier or customer did not live up to an agreement in China, you might go see a powerful person who would mediate the dispute between the two parties using his judgment and experience as a guide. However, if your relationship with that person were poor or the other party's were very strong, you would likely lose. In the United States, the entrepreneur has the ability to use the court system for a legal remedy that is bound by precedence and the Uniform Commercial Code. The nature of business is that there will be disagreements, and as a result, you as a small business person are likely at some point to be in court. While this may not be the ideal, it is better than the alternative of no legal system, or a weak one.

An important part of operating a business is having a fundamental understanding of the basics of commercial law and the potential remedies when there is a dispute. The establishment of a basic legal foundation will help the small business person navigate the legal environment much more easily. The Philo restaurant owners had to face the importance of their legal structure early in their operations, as we will see on the next page.

EXERCISE 1

1. What do you believe the liability issues are that concerned the potential investor?
2. Why does the legal form of a business matter to the founder(s) of a business if they are not seeking investors?

As has been noted, the legal environment can have a significant impact upon the operation of a business. The case of the Philo restaurant points out just one important concern of a potential investor: the type of business that is being formed. Significant time and effort can be saved in the long run with some careful thought at the founding of a new venture. This chapter will examine a number of legal issues that impact the founding of the new business, including these:

The forms of business

Contracts

Leases

Regulations, including licensing requirements

Copyrights/trademarks/patents

Insurance

Board of advisors/directors.

Philo's founders had determined the type, mission, and fundamental positioning of their new business idea. However, before they began operations they felt that this business idea might need another investor or two. The resources from these individuals would allow them to position the business to grow faster. The partners had started their discussion with several local bank managers and loan officers regarding their initial financing, but were stumped in the process when they were asked "what type of business" they had. They initially thought this question referred to their positioning or plan for success, but quickly found out that the financiers were asking about what legal type of business entity the firm would form.

Having given this topic very little thought, the founders were not sure they understood the different types of business formations, but they did not have time to worry very much about such issues (or so they thought). They wanted everything to be fair and even between the founders, and with very little thought, announced that they were going to form a "partnership." They mistakenly believed that this form of business would indicate their commitment to the business and their desire to have investors involved in the business. After all, in law firms and CPA firms, being made a partner is considered the highest honor and confers upon the partner rights to the profits of the firm.

The founders had made great progress in developing their business plan, and their next step was to approach the person they expected to be their key financial investor. This individual was a very successful entrepreneur that one of the founders had loosely known since childhood. He had a variety of retail businesses. While the investor had not had a restaurant, he was interested in the idea and was familiar with the business domain. His prior success in business led the founders to also believe he could provide great insight to them in running the business. The founders met with this investor and made a presentation of their business idea. It had taken two weeks to get on his calendar and the meeting was going to be quite brief. He was intrigued by the business idea and by their "numbers." However, he then asked them what type of business entity they had formed. The founders responded that they had formed a "partnership."

The potential investor was silent. After what seemed like an eternity, he responded that he would not invest in partnerships due to the personal liability and problems associated with the lack of liquidity. He said a few polite things, wished them the best of luck—and the meeting was over. The founders realized that the type of entity they wanted to form was of more than a passing interest to potential investors, bankers, and perhaps themselves. The legal foundation needed to be reconsidered and appeared to be more central to how they needed to proceed than they originally believed. The opportunity to obtain the investment from this ideal investor was lost forever due to the lack of an adequate legal foundation.

LO 7.1 | Forms of Business

There are three basic types of business: sole proprietorship, partnership (including both general and limited liability), and corporation (C, S, and limited liability company). Each of these will be examined below.

Sole Proprietorship

sole proprietorship

The simplest form of business organization, characterized by the fact that the person who owns the business and the business itself are treated as the same entity.

A **sole proprietorship** is the simplest form of business to establish, as the person who owns it and the business itself are treated as the same entity. On the principle that small business is good for the economy and should be encouraged, most communities have made the process for obtaining a sole proprietorship license quite simple. A quick trip to the local courthouse or public administration building, filling out a simple form, and paying a small fee is usually all that is required to establish a sole proprietorship. More and more communities are making this process even simpler with an online application. All of your business income and losses are treated as part of the individual's overall income and are reportable on schedule C of your 1040 tax form. Absent other licenses that may be required to operate your business (a topic that we will cover in more detail later in this chapter), the establishment of a sole proprietorship allows an individual to legally transact business.

The major benefit of this form of business is that it is very easy to form and easy to dissolve. There is virtually no separation between the founder and the business. There are strict rules regarding record keeping, and it

Many single-person businesses are set up as sole proprietorships.

is important that the founder maintain a firewall between personal and business expenses; however, you may deduct business expenses from your income.

The drawbacks to this type of business are numerous, and for businesspeople that develop a substantial business, these drawbacks will outweigh the ease of establishment. The first disadvantage is that a business that involves more than a single founder cannot be a sole proprietorship. Philo, by its very nature of having been founded by two individuals, could not be a sole proprietorship unless the founders placed 100 percent of the authority with a single individual. The law does not recognize other equity investors in this type of business. This limitation is a significant drawback for the growth potential of a new business not only from an initial investment perspective, but also because as the business develops it may need additional outside investment which often is in exchange for part ownership of the business. Such investment would be virtually impossible in this legal form. This inability to have additional owners also means that equity incentives to attract top employees/executives are not possible. This leaves the founder with two options: either obtain all new monies as debt instruments or go through the process of changing the legal form to a more robust one.

This brings up a second significant disadvantage of a sole proprietorship, that of liability. In the sole proprietorship form of business, all the liabilities of the sole proprietorship are the direct responsibility of the owner of the business. Thus, a debt for the firm is a personal debt for the business owner. The result is that if the business does something relatively risky, such as trading commodities, or even something mundane, like taking delivery of substantial inventory that ultimately cannot be sold, then those debts of the business are treated as debts of the owner. A third issue is one of legitimacy with suppliers and customers. Due to the fact that this legal form is so easy to dissolve, suppliers typically require personal guarantees for debts, and the value of the business is only as good as the reputation of the founder.

Thus, a sole proprietorship is very popular among individuals who:

1. Are unsure of their business idea and just want to see what might happen (if the business proves successful these individuals often re-form the business later, using another business form).

2. Have a small business where the time limitations of the founder will keep the business from growing significantly.

3. Have a small business where the costs of equipment are low and therefore so are the risks. For example, a small business that embroiders names on shirts and hats can have relatively low costs and low risks.

Partnerships

A more complex business form is a **partnership.** There are two types of partnerships: general and limited. The two differ significantly from each other and will be reviewed separately.

General Partnership If two or more people are involved in the founding of an organization, they can form a partnership. Similar to the founding of a sole proprietorship, the means of forming a basic partnership is relatively simple; however, it does involve an extra step beyond that of a sole proprietorship. When filing for a partnership, most local communities require a partnership agreement. While there is no set form that this agreement must take, these agreements generally specify who is involved; what each party is expected to contribute to the founding of the firm (whether it be cash, services, or property); how profits, losses, and **draws** by the partners are to be treated; how one partner can buy out the other(s) if she decides to leave; how new partners are brought into the partnership; and how disputes are to be settled.

We periodically hear from potential partners that they simply do not need such items to be specified. These individuals may have known each other for years and feel very comfortable with each other, so that they trust each other and are ready to tie up their combined financial wealth. However, recall what we stressed at the beginning. This is a legalistic society, and a business is fundamentally a financial transaction which should be treated as such. The time to prevent problems is early in the relationship, prior to any conflict (which, by the way, is inevitable in any interaction between two or more people). We recommend the early establishment of clear and legally binding dimensions of the partnership. Thus, our advice is to get aid from your accountant or lawyer in drawing up such an agreement.

To illustrate the importance of this process, we will describe a partnership we worked with that had been formed to develop a landscaping business. The business developed quite well for several years and grew to where the firm had more than 50 employees and annual revenues in excess of several million dollars. When the partners began, both were married, had known each other for years both personally and professionally, and attended the same church. One partner worked in the field operations while the other attracted new business for the company and managed the office operations. The wife of the partner who worked in the field was the in-house accountant for the business. Unfortunately, after several years it became clear that the partner working in the office and the wife of the field partner were having an affair. During the next few months, both partners filed for divorce and the pair having the affair moved in together. The rift in the business became obvious to customers, suppliers, and the employees of the business to the point that the business was on the verge of collapse.

The two partners had developed a short partnership agreement when they formed the business, but it was based on one they found in a how-to book from the local bookstore, and they had simply deleted passages that they did not want to address. The document they had generated was not clear on how they were to split the business if either partner wished to terminate the agreement. The result was that the case ended up in court connected to two messy divorces. As you can imagine, the business continued to suffer. Employees left, customers chose other landscaping companies, and suppliers changed their credit terms for the business, as they were concerned about the dissolution of the business. The result was a costly battle for each party, with the field partner retaining the business and the office partner receiving a cash payment. Unfortunately for the partner who got the business, there was no noncompete clause in the partnership agreement, nor in the settlement. Once the legal case was over, the partner that left with the cash payment began to set up a new business. In this business he immediately began to seek the best customers of the partner who had received the business in the termination of the partnership. In general, divorce has a negative impact on small business.[3] However, a better-constructed partnership agreement could have allowed for a fair and less costly dissolution of the partnership, plus it could have protected the existing company as it continued in operation.

If a partnership agreement is not developed and signed, the partnership will be governed by either the Uniform Partnership Act or the Revised Uniform Partnership Act. These partnership laws were developed as suggested formats and adopted by each state. Thus, while there is some variation among the states, they are nonetheless a relatively effective means to handle the basics of partnership. Although the laws vary somewhat from state to state, there are certain standards that are in place in the absence of a pre-formation agreement. The rules in the acts are reasonable, but they rarely match exactly what most individuals would like to do. For example, in these acts all assets are treated as equal for the partners. However, we find that rarely is there a 50–50 partnership. Inevitably one or more partners contribute more capital or take more of a role in running the business than the other(s). Given this situation, small business owners would likely want to write a partnership agreement that recognized the larger contribution and perhaps provided a larger ownership stake. Similarly, issues like noncompete agreements are not covered in these acts. Having one partner leave the business and set up a competing firm is such a negative event that it is highly preferable to have a signed partnership agreement in place with a rich set of contingencies specified.

A partnership has many of the same characteristics as a sole proprietorship. The owners report their shares of losses or profits on their own personal income tax returns in proportion to their interest in the firm. Business expenses have some flow-through to personal tax forms, but the restrictions are significant. Partnerships require little more in the way of formal paperwork than sole proprietorships and dissolution can be quite easy, although it does require a formal record with the local authorities.

Some of the drawbacks are the same as with a sole proprietorship. The issue of liability is usually a bit more of an issue than with a sole proprietorship. Partners are generally held to be jointly liable for all debts incurred by the partnership. This means that a debt agreed to by your partner for the business becomes your total responsibility if the partner fails to meet his obligations. Each partner is assumed to be involved with all decisions, which translates into a fiduciary relationship between partners. In other words, partners have the responsibility to watch out for the best interests of the other partners.

While a sole proprietorship virtually eliminates the firm's ability to bring in new equity investment, a partnership opens this door just a bit. In order to accept new equity investment in a partnership, each established partner must surrender a portion of her ownership position. This is usually a process in which the new "partner" buys out a portion of each of the existing partners in a transaction that also adds some financial muscle to the organization. A new partnership agreement is required each time this process occurs, and there are limits in some communities as to the number of partners in a business.

Limited Partnership Some of the drawbacks to a basic partnership encourage the development of another type of partnership: a limited liability partnership (**LLP**). In an LLP there are still at least two individuals who are partners in a venture (although technically, one person can form an LLP and declare a full pass-through (of all income) on his federal taxes); however, there are two classes of partners in such a venture. The first is a **general partner.** This individual is considered the manager of the firm and as such has unlimited liability for any debts or judgments against the firm. In contrast, the other partners are considered to be passive investors, and as such their liability is limited to their investment in the business. The other partners are called limited partners and can work for the firm, but must not be active in the management of the organization. Active management makes that partner a general partner. The only requirement of an LLP is that at least one partner is considered to be a general partner. Otherwise, the positives and negatives discussed in the previous section for general partnerships also apply to LLPs.

Corporations

The result of forming a sole proprietorship or a partnership is that the business debts flow directly to the owner(s), meaning that all owners are responsible for any debts of the firm that arise. Thus, owners can have their life savings disappear if the business goes poorly. The critical issues of personal liability and the desire to limit exposure to the original equity investment led to the development of other forms of organization. A corporation addresses both drawbacks by viewing the business not as synonymous with the individual but as a separate entity.[4] If a corporation suffers substantial losses, the founder(s) will lose only their investment in the business.

LLP
A limited liability partnership.

general partner
In an LLP, the individual considered the manager of the firm, who, as such, has unlimited liability for any debts or judgments against the firm.

What are the advantages of working for a corporation?

There are a variety of different types of corporations that have been developed, and we will address the three most common forms. Historically, a small business formed a simple protected corporate form known as a Subchapter S corporation, while a business that was large or one that was developing into a large business formed a Subchapter C corporation. These corporation types take their names from subchapters in the Internal Revenue Code. However, since its development, the Limited Liability Corporation (LLC) has become one of the predominant forms of business formation in the United States. We discuss S, C, and LLC corporations in greater depth next.

Subchapter S Corporation As with all corporate forms, the Subchapter S has the benefit of protecting the owner(s) by treating the firm as a separate entity. Thus, the liability is generally limited to any investment the owner(s) might have in the organization. However, a Subchapter S allows the owner(s) to treat the income as they would if the firm were a sole proprietorship or a partnership. Thus, the owner(s) report their income or losses on their own 1040 income tax forms. The business must file informational tax returns that report each shareholder's portion of the business.

> **Subchapter S corporation**
> An organizational form that treats the firm as an entity separate from the individuals. This allows the owner(s) to treat the income as they would if the firm were a sole proprietorship or a partnership. It has limitations in the number and type of shareholders.

Therefore, the benefits of a Subchapter S can be summarized as follows:

1. Limited liability.
2. The potential to consolidate financial statements for the tax benefit of the owner(s).
3. Relatively easy formation compared with a Subchapter C corporation.
4. Legitimacy in the market as a more established form of business (the ability to put "Inc." after your business name).

However, there are negatives to this form of business as well. While the effort to form this type of organization is substantially easier than that involved in forming a Subchapter C corporation, it is nonetheless quite cumbersome and expensive when compared to a sole proprietorship/partnership form. We strongly recommend that founder(s) wishing to form an Subchapter S corporation get an experienced professional (lawyer or accountant) to process the paperwork. A second consideration is the limitation to the number of shareholders in this type of organization. Historically, a Subchapter S corporation has had a numerical limit to the number of shareholders. Currently that limit is set at a maximum of 100 shareholders. This limitation is fine for a closely held or family corporation, but is a significant limitation to a rapidly growing organization or one that has any thought to going public in the future.

New York Stock Exchange

Subchapter C Corporation Subchapter C solves some of the issues raised regarding Subchapter S corporations, while creating others. Subchapter C corporations also have limited liability for the owner(s), but the corporation pays an income tax.[5] This leads to the situation where the corporation pays a tax on its profits. Then those profits after taxes can be paid as dividends to the owner(s). However, the owner(s) will have to pay taxes on their personal tax returns for that income. This is the double taxation situation that is often discussed in the United States.

> **Subchapter C corporation**
> An organizational form that treats the firm as a unique entity responsible for its own taxes. There are no limitations to shareholder participation and the "owners" are protected beyond their equity investment.

However, it is possible for the developing new business owners to mitigate this cost. The owner(s) are also employees of the corporation and as such are paid salaries and bonuses. The costs of these salaries and bonuses are expensed as costs. Thus, the owner(s) can pay themselves virtually all of the profits each year, so that little actual profit is reported, and therefore, little corporate tax is owed. Profits that are not paid out for such items as salaries, bonuses, and/or dividends are then retained by the corporation for future expansion. A Subchapter C corporation also has the advantage that fringe benefits that are paid out are not treated as income for employees. Thus, owner(s) can have their health insurance and other benefits paid by the corporation, which then expenses each of these as a cost of business.

A nice feature of a Subchapter C corporation is that there are no limits to the number of shareholders that the organization may obtain. The only real limit is the number of authorized and distributed shares in the organization. Shares in the firm must have an initial value at which they are offered, a "par" value. Thus, the corporation has a floor value which is equal to the par value times the number of shares distributed and this will be equal to the shareholder equity of the firm. We recommend that the par value be set very low so that the new company can authorize a very large number of shares (millions or even tens of millions). In both Subchapter C and S corporations, authorizing more shares; annual board meetings; and reporting standards to local, state, and federal authorities are among the issues that must be formally addressed. A Subchapter C corporation requires a rather detailed corporate charter and while packages are available to guide the new businessperson through the process, we strongly recommend that she again seek professional advice. At a minimum the entrepreneur will have to have the following:

1. A corporate name—the new organization cannot choose a name that is considered a replication of another company's name. Patent/trademark attorneys offer services that include detailed searches of company names (and that allow business owners some level of comfort with their choice) all the way to obtaining a nationwide trademark on the name.

2. Location of the corporate headquarters—for a new business this is generally the same as the business address.

3. General nature of the business, specified for the filing.

4. Names, addresses, and titles of all corporate founders and initial investors.

5. A so-called time horizon for the firm's existence—for all intents, this is usually "in perpetuity."

6. Authorized stock and capital—the par value times the number of shares issued is considered the initial capital of the organization. Some states require the company to have that amount on deposit in a business account with a bank.

7. By-laws of the organization. These are the basic rules that will govern activity in the new company.

Limited Liability Corporation In recent years the limited liability corporation (**LLC**) has become one of the most popular forms of incorporation for small business.[6] This business form is still relatively new; for

LLC
A limited liability corporation.

example, it was only in 1994 that California passed the law to allow such entities. The limited liability company has many similarities with the Subchapter S corporation. There is the limited liability feature, which exposes each shareholder to the amount of his investment. However, the LLC allows the new venture to have more than 100 investors, and it allows other corporations to hold stock in the company (a feature not available to Subchapter S Corporations). An LLC may have as few as one individual listed as an officer of the company, referred to as a "member" of the corporation. The LLC is similar to a C organization in that all of the information required is the same, but is unlike a Subchapter C corporation in that profits from the organization can be handled flexibly. The owner(s) are allowed to flow the profits through to their personal returns to avoid double taxation, which occurs with a C corporation. Furthermore, there is substantial flexibility (unlike with a partnership) regarding the amount of income that is designated for each individual. It does not have to be in proportion to that owner's holdings.

While the cost of formation is very low, this type of organization is formed by submitting the paperwork to the state government and having a charter issued prior to beginning operations. Therefore, dissolving these organizations is somewhat expensive and a relatively drawn-out process.

State governments establish how this business entity is formed and a few states, such as New York, also require that the founder of the new business publish notice of forming the limited liability company in the local newspaper. Some states limit their use and will not allow professionals such as accountants and lawyers to form such business entities. As we have stated before, professional advice in regard to what is appropriate within your state is money well spent.

> **EXERCISE 2**
>
> 1. What form of business do you believe will be the best for your new venture? Why?
> 2. Looking five years down the road, what form of business will be best if you meet all of your forecasts? If there is a difference in your conclusion, why would that be so?

LO 7.2 Contracts

Beyond the legal form of the new organization, there are a number of other legal issues that should be considered prior to beginning operations. A **contract** is an agreement between two parties to perform certain activities for some consideration. A contract does not have to be written, but consistent with the theme presented in this chapter; we strongly recommend that the small business founder employ formal written contracts whenever she has an agreement with another party.

A contract should include several items that are reasonably straightforward, including the following:

contract
An agreement between two parties to perform certain activities for some consideration.

1. Who the parties are in the contract. This preamble describes briefly who the parties are so that it is clear who is involved and in what manner.
2. What each party agrees to do and for what consideration (i.e., their cost, pay, product received, etc.).
3. When the transaction is to take place.
4. The timing of payment, if other than immediately.

Peter Roberts was a clerk for a Sears, Roebuck and Company store in Gardner, Massachusetts, in the 1960s. In 1964, when he was only 18 years old, Roberts invented the quick release socket wrench. He presented the idea to Sears's managers and waited to hear back from them while they did market studies and considered the manufacturing implications. He was offered $10,000 for his invention, which was a sizable sum of money for a teenager in the mid–1960s. Sears told him that they saw only limited sales for the product, but wanted to reward his ingenuity and also keep the rights to sell the tool. Unbeknownst to Roberts, Sears's market studies had suggested that the market would love the tool and the company had made plans to sell 50,000 per week. Roberts sued Sears for "willful infringement" and after more than two decades was awarded over $8 million. He later settled with Sears for an undisclosed sum of money.

Would you fight a legal case for more than 20 years? Do you think it was ethically wrong for Sears to tell Roberts that his invention was not very valuable when in fact it appeared to be a significant new product? Since both parties would like to benefit from a new invention, how should each approach a situation like this one?

5. When the activity is to take place and how long the contract is in place.

6. Warranties.

7. How the contract can be terminated. There may be damages specified.

8. Whether the contract can be transferred.

9. If the firms are in different states, which state's law applies.

LO 7.3 Leases

One of the most significant contracts that a new business is initially involved in is the lease where the business will operate. Lease contracts may be of any term length that is agreeable between the parties. Whatever the length of the lease, there are several issues that the new business owner should consider as he examines such contracts:

1. What exactly is the new business owner leasing? Beyond the basic address and exclusive access to the premises, leases should address utilities; access to parking (either exclusive or shared); responsibility for the external premises (including lawn care, painting, etc.); structural repairs/improvements; approval of lease-hold improvements; and responsibility for permanently installed equipment (heating/air conditioning, plumbing, electrical, etc.).

2. Is there an ability to renew the lease? The lease should specify how long the lease is in effect and if there is the opportunity to renew the lease. The actual space that is leased may not be critical for some types of businesses, such as an air conditioner and heating repair small business. Individuals call the business, and the technician comes to their home. (Keeping the same phone number is far more critical to such a business.) However, if you have a bakery that makes specialty cakes, your customers grow accustomed to where you are located. If you have to move such a retail-based business, there are significant limitations to maintaining a customer base

(see the end-of-chapter story about Camel City Café in Chapter 3). Regardless of the type of business, it is simply expensive to keep moving operations.

Leases help protect long-term businesses.

3. Who is responsible for improvements? Who has responsibility/authority for physical plant improvements? A lease that includes the responsibility for making improvements to the facility should be accompanied by a lower lease payment. One entrepreneur bought an existing barber shop and negotiated what he believed was a reasonable lease with the landlord. During the first summer that he occupied the building, the air conditioner stopped working, and the lessee found out that he was responsible for replacing the air conditioning unit; however, the landlord had to approve the unit. The landlord wanted a top-of-the-line unit to replace the old unit, while the lessee just wanted to install a functional mid-priced unit. The decision had to be made quickly, as it was midsummer in the southwest United States, with temperatures over 100 degrees. The owner of the business had no choice but to put in the unit the landlord wanted. The unit and the related improvements cost over $15,000.

4. Who has responsibility for maintenance and other facilities issues? Who has responsibility for issues like the utilities, landscaping, janitorial costs, trash removal, parking lot maintenance and security, window washing, and real estate taxes? Can you place the signage you want, or are there restrictions?

5. Who has to carry the liability insurance and at what level? Many leases require the tenants to carry insurance not only for themselves but also to cover any liability of the landlord. Insurance can be expensive and it merits particular attention to be clear who has what responsibility for insurance.

6. Can your landlord enter your place of business? Most leases give the landlord some rights to enter your business to inspect it. The landlord wants to make sure you are taking care of the rental location and that nothing illegal is occurring. However, it can feel like an invasion if the landlord comes into your business whenever she wants.

7. If there are problems, what are the procedures for addressing and resolving them? If you cannot use all of your space and have a financial need, can you sublet some of your leased space to others? Many leases prohibit such subleasing. Most leases also do not allow you to cancel the lease unless you meet the specified conditions in the lease. To illustrate, recently a small business

was looking for a location for a new retail store. There appeared to be a number of good opportunities in buildings with empty space. Unfortunately, the business owners found that one space they really liked was already leased by a business that no longer existed. The lease had been written with the personal guarantee of the small business founder. Most states do not allow a landlord to charge two individuals for rent on the same space. Interestingly, the landlords chose to leave the space empty and collect full rent for the remainder of the old lease rather than rent the space to the new start-up at a lower rate. The individual who had personally guaranteed the lease before going out of business could only get out of the lease by filing personal bankruptcy, which he was not willing to do. If there are other problems and disagreements between the landlord and the business owner, how will these be solved—mediation, arbitration, or other means? If there are problems, can you withhold your rent?

Hopefully you can see that a lease is multidimensional and should be carefully crafted before signing. Consistent with our belief stressed in this chapter, small business owners can prevent many problems by ensuring that legal issues are thoroughly investigated and that they employ experts where needed.

EXERCISE 3

1. Put together a list of all the items you feel are critical to discuss with your potential landlord.
2. What are the three or four most important items? Write down your minimal acceptable negotiation position for each.

LO 7.4 Regulations

Small businesses generally deal with fewer regulations than do large businesses. There are many regulations enacted by the federal government that do not apply to business with fewer than 50 employees (this number varies with the regulation). Some industries are highly regulated regardless of size, where others are only loosely regulated even for the large, well-established organizations. If a small business deals with toxic waste such as asbestos, it can expect to have to file extensive registration documentation and be subject to significant regulation once in business, regardless of the size of the firm. Thus, regulation-related issues need to be extensively considered when the business is developed. This same issue will also apply in industries involving alcohol, medical-related industries, and military-related businesses. However, at the other extreme, an Internet business that sells retail goods faces only minimal regulation.

There are some basic regulations that cut across the spectrum of businesses. If a small business has employees, then the business must have an Employer Identification Number. Additionally, the business will be required to calculate and deduct various taxes for federal, state, and in some cases, local authorities. The payroll requirements are specific and well developed. Thus, an entrepreneur can simply purchase a canned package for doing payroll and should be able to meet all of these various requirements.

Many states, such as California, have much more expansive laws governing small business practices. While environmental regulations at the federal level are typically designated for large businesses, in some areas the states will also apply those laws to small businesses.

Similarly, specific cities may have unique sets of special regulations. A city like New York has extensive additional regulations for small business. A restaurant in the city has to post information on the calories and fat content in all of its products and also deep fry its food only in particular types of oil.

Obviously, the special rules and regulations for your industry and location should be explored before you start your business to ensure that you are meeting all requirements. Excellent sources of information regarding regulatory requirements are the Small Business Assistance Center (run by the Small Business Administration) in your area, the state or local department of economic development, and the local chamber of commerce. Most states and cities are critically aware of the role small business plays in their economic viability. The result has been the establishing of offices to help new small businesses to navigate these laws and regulations.

Do you think the fast-food regulations are fair to small business owners?

One set of regulations that bears particular mention is the Americans with Disabilities Act (**ADA**). This law applies fully to any firm with more than 15 employees. Thus, many more small businesses will be affected by this law than by other federal laws. The law requires that there be no discrimination in the hiring, management, or dismissal of employees with disabilities. If the firm has someone with a covered disability, the business must make reasonable accommodation for that individual. Additionally, virtually all retail and most office businesses will also need to make their places of business accessible to people with physical disabilities.

ADA

Americans with Disabilities Act

Licensing

Related to the topic of regulation are the licenses that the business must obtain to operate. A license can be as simple as a business license that is used by communities to track business performance (and thereby tax income), or it may be specifically related to the fundamental operations of the business. Examples of licenses/permits include the following:

1. Local ABC (Alcoholic Beverage Control) liquor license.
2. Occupancy permits.
3. Federal liquor license (Bureau of Alcohol, Tobacco, Firearms, and Explosives).
4. Business license (from the local authorities).
5. Sign permits.
6. OSHA permit for food handling.
7. Fire safety permit.

At a minimum, most businesses must acquire a license to do business in the county/city in which they will be operating. This type of license is quite simple to obtain, as it normally requires only that one of the principals of the business fill out a form, pay a set fee (usually less than $100 and often quite a bit less), and agree to report basic information about the business's performance on a set schedule (again, usually quarterly at the most). While completing this procedure, which is normally transacted at a courthouse or government agency building, we suggest that the new businessperson inquire as to other licenses that might be required for his operation. Since lack of knowledge is no excuse for failing to have the proper licenses, we always recommend talking with current business owners concerning the procedures and licenses required in each locale. For those firms who are facing more challenging licensing, such as liquor businesses, it is best to visit with a lawyer.

LO 7.5 Copyrights/Trademarks/Patents

A topic that merits brief mention is intellectual property protection through copyrights, trademarks, and patents. A **copyright** can be claimed on creative materials generated, such as books, magazines, advertising copy, music, artwork, or virtually any other creative product, whether published or unpublished. In the United States, a copyright is assumed to apply to anything that is your own original work, although for a small fee you can file for an official copyright with the government. The copyright is valid for the life of the author plus 70 years.

A **trademark** is legal protection of the intellectual property that is associated with a specific business. This may be the name of the firm, a symbol representing the firm, or the names of its products. For example, you may not use the name Microsoft since it has a trademark. Similarly, you may not use a product's name such as Sprite, since it is the trademark of a specific product (here, of the Coca-Cola Company). Although not as universally recognized as a copyright, a trademark is assumed in place once a firm begins to use the symbol or name. However, a firm can and probably should register its use to ensure the protection of the trademark. A small business is well served to perform a search to ensure that it is not violating a trademark. A firm that is doing so can be sued and forced to not only pay damages but also change its name. A trademark is valid for 10 years and can be renewed as long as the firm or product is active.

The last intellectual property protection is a patent. A **patent** covers a specific innovation. A patent is good for 20 years and must be filed and accepted by the United States Patent and Trademark Office for it to be valid. That said, a patent has some legal protection from the moment that it is filed with the patent office. Patents are expensive to obtain and expensive to maintain, so they should be used only in the case where a patent is part of the sustainable competitive advantage of the organization. Patents generally apply to a physical invention; however, recently the U.S. Patent Office has considered granting process patents. A patent is a potent entry barrier for a business, as it prevents direct imitation for that period of time. Unfortunately, close copies may skirt the patent laws, so a patent should be but one avenue of competitive protection.

LO 7.6 Insurance

A topic related to the legal concerns of all types of business is insurance. One of the key concerns that should have been clear in the discussion of the form of organization is that the small business chooses the level of liability it is willing to risk. One means to limit liability concerns is through the effective application of insurance.

There are several basic types of insurance, including property, liability, employee bonding, and workers' compensation. Property insurance covers the building, fixtures, and inventory in all of the buildings in which the business has a function. One key concern is whether the insurance covers

---

copyright

The legal means to protect intellectual property. It grants ownership on creative materials generated, such as books, magazines, advertising copy, music, artwork, or virtually any other creative product, whether published or unpublished.

trademark

Claim of intellectual property that is associated with a specific business. This may be the name of the firm, a symbol representing the firm, or the names of its products.

patent

Claim of intellectual property that covers a specific innovation.

Alex was making progress on the planning for his repair shop. He initially felt that getting all the supplies in place would be the biggest time holdup to starting the new business. Several weeks into the process his uncle asked him about his business license. He hadn't gone down to the city building to get that, but decided to do it the next day. He was stunned to find out that there were a substantial number of licenses that he was going to have to acquire, and some were going to take some time. These included a wide variety of licenses:

1. A business license like that for any new business.

2. A license for an auto repair shop. Alex had known for a long time that the auto repair industry was known for charging for unnecessary repairs. In addition, there were firms that paid their employees on a commission basis and encouraged them to sell the customers a lot more than they actually needed. In his state, the legislature had passed a law requiring a specialized license for auto repair shops. A new department had been created to supervise auto repair shops (Bureau of Automotive Repair). To obtain the license, Alex would have to complete a number of education classes where information on the law for auto repair shops would be detailed. The state regularly sent around inspectors (both announced and unannounced) whose job it was to see if auto shops were abiding by the law.

3. A license from the environmental safety department. The cleaning of auto parts involves specialized solvents that can cause extensive damage to the environment. As a result there was specialized training and Haz-Mat (hazardous material) licensing that was required before undertaking any part cleaning operation.

4. A license for a sign. A recently passed city ordinance required each store owner to apply for a license to put a sign on the building and/or the street. The restrictions were substantial.

5. An independent auto dealer license. A part of any auto repair operation is the ability to acquire and sell automobiles. Customers who fail to pay their bills and/or find the repair bills unmanageable will allow the auto repair place to sell their cars. In addition, the employees might find a good value and repair the car in their spare time, then sell the car. For the auto shop to be able to do this, Alex had to get a separate license as an independent auto dealer.

6. Bonding. While bonding is not a license, it is similar in that each employee must be bonded at a level required by the state. Since Alex planned to give his employees wide latitude in making repairs, then he needed to cover any damages that might result. The liability laws in his home state are such that without bonding Alex could suffer serious financial harm from any lawsuits or complaints filed. (Bonding will be covered in more detail when we examine insurance mechanisms.)

On the whole, these licenses and insurance bonding were not particularly expensive to obtain, other than the bonding for his employees. However, the time and effort it would take to address these licenses was not a small matter. The regulation associated with each license had typically arisen in response to an abuse by business. Alex wondered as he began to allocate time to attend the classes for each license if the licensing was still relevant.

1. What are your thoughts on the nature of licensing for Alex's small business?

2. What do you think the licenses are that would be required for your business idea?

3. Check with the local Small Business Assistance Center to see if you are right.

replacement cost or current value. For example, you may have equipment that has only limited value in a resale market, but that would be very expensive to replace if you had to buy new equipment. The firm must decide what types of risks it will accept and cover itself versus those that it will purchase insurance to cover. It is fairly standard to obtain coverage for fire, windstorms, hail, and smoke. However, the firm may also wish to obtain a special form of insurance that covers issues such as floods and earthquakes. The greater the insurance coverage obtained by the small business, the greater the cost. Thus, each firm needs to balance risk and cost.

The firm can also obtain liability insurance, which covers lawsuit judgments. Such insurance does not cover intentional acts of malice; however, it does cover the business for accidents. Product liability insurance is expensive, but it can also be obtained in order to provide a legal defense fund in the case of a negligence lawsuit.

A small business should also explore whether it needs to have its workers bonded. Bonding is a type of insurance in which the business is covered in case the workers cause any damage in the performance of their work. To illustrate, a plumber may hire an assistant that makes some of the calls on customers. The assistant may make a mistake that leads to a pipe's breaking and flooding the house or apartment. The damage done can be very costly and perhaps even cause bankruptcy. However, through bonding, the insurance company agrees to pay for such damages. In an office setting you can also get bonding to cover losses from employee embezzlement.

Workers' compensation insurance covers liability for workers that are injured on the job. In many states, workers' compensation insurance is required and can represent a major expense for a small business.

We suggest that insurance is such a critical issue that it merits spending time with an insurance agent, or multiple agents, to discuss the needs of the new business. Discussion with multiple agents will allow the new businessperson to obtain different viewpoints on the issue. The new business owner should seek out agents with expertise in the industry in which the small business operates.

LO 7.7 Board of Advisors and/or Board of Directors

Two related entities that can help the small business owner foresee legal problems are boards of advisors and boards of directors. These boards are composed of people that have both insight and experience with which to advise the small business founders. An effective group of advisors will not only help the small business owner predict where legal problems might arise but also help the new business wind its way through a full range of other issues and opportunities where experience is the best teacher. As a result, the small business should have at least one of these entities to advise the founder. A business that chooses to form a corporation must have a board of directors. These are individuals who have a fiduciary responsibility to the shareholders of the organization. In new corporations, the shareholders and board of directors are often the same individuals. In contrast, a **board of advisors** may be formed at the discretion of the founders (regardless of the legal form chosen); it is composed of individuals outside the new business that advise the firm.[7]

While the size of the board is a matter of choice, as a practical matter it is better to have a few, well-placed individuals that are motivated to help the firm through the start-up process rather than a large number as a means of false showmanship. There are a set of basic needs for most new businesses; thus, we suggest individuals that have experience navigating the following:

1. Licensing requirements for your type of industry in your locality (if such licensing is relatively complex/difficult).

2. Regulations for your specific industry.

3. New start-up experience and success.

4. Financial/accounting background with new start-ups.

5. Human resources experience—especially establishing basic personnel criteria.

This board can formally meet on whatever schedule seems appropriate (we have used three times a year as a good standard); however, the beauty of this group is the ability to contact them as issues arise without the formality of a meeting in order to resolve problems. In keeping with the efficient operation of a new business, we have traditionally suggested that the board size be maintained at less than five individuals. Compensation is not much of an issue for these indiviudals. Some will be in a professional capacity working with the firm, while most get involved with start-ups because of their love of seeing a business flourish. As the firm develops, formality and compensation can be considered.

summary

This chapter covered a wide variety of legal issues related directly to the starting of a new small business. The legal form that the founders choose has implications from an operational, tax, and legal perspective. The new venture must be aware of and deal with regulations imposed by local, state, and federal authorities; obtain all relevant licenses; and be sufficiently savvy regarding the evaluation of contracts, leases, and insurance. All of these areas can be quite complex, and throughout the chapter we suggest that awareness of the issues is the first step, but that getting some professional advice is the most prudent move.

key terms

ADA 143

board of advisors 146

contract 139

copyright 144

draw 134

general partner 136

LLC 138

LLP 136

partnership 134

patent 144

sole proprietorship 132

Subchapter C corporation 137

Subchapter S Corporation 137

trademark 144

review questions

1. Why is a legal system so critical to a small business?
2. Do you think such legal protections are more or less important to a small business than to a large business?
3. What are the impacts on a business that chooses to form as a sole proprietorship?
4. What are the impacts on a business that chooses to form as a partnership?
5. What are the impacts on a business that chooses to form as a Subchapter S Corporation?
6. What are the impacts on a business that chooses to form as a Subchapter C Corporation?
7. What are the impacts on a business that chooses to form as an LLC?
8. What are the major differences between a board of directors and a board of advisors?

group exercises

Break into teams of three or four people. Develop the following information and then present it to the individuals in your group, discussing why you made those choices. The detailed information on question 2 you will need to collect outside of class.

1. Create a small chart outlining the broad types of people you would want to sit on your board of advisors and explain why you would choose them.

2. Make a contact list of seven to nine people to invite onto your board of advisors; include their names, addresses, telephone numbers, e-mail addresses, positions, and what they would bring to your new business. Review this list with your group. Rank the list and begin contacting each person in that order.

everyday edisons class discussion

Go to www.everydayedisons.com/sheldon.html and read about Sheldon and his bubble machine.

1. How do you think Sheldon legally protects his idea for the bubble machine, since bubbles have been around for so long?

2. If someone does copy his idea, what do you think Sheldon should do about it?

Thinking Critically

Shannon Shipp—SHS Associates, LLC

Shannon Shipp comes from a line of entrepreneurs including a father who was a serial entrepreneur, and he has always had the entrepreneurial bug. Shannon grew up sitting around the family kitchen table at meals talking about business and new opportunities. When he was 16 he convinced his mother to sew him a Santa Claus suit. Armed with the suit, he contracted out his services for parties, churches, and schools that had events for kids.

Since that time, Shannon has continued to pursue a wide range of business opportunities including commercial real estate development, the building and selling of portable buildings, and a record store. The last venture, the record store, was ultimately his largest venture. He initially bought a small record store that was having difficulty in a small midwestern city. The record store had suffered through some very poor management and poor oversight of the business for several years. The business was going to have to either close or be blessed with a completely new management team. The prior owners loved music but did not know how to run a business. Shannon was able to buy the store from them for the value of the inventory, a relatively low price. He restructured the store

layout and operations and then brought in a new manager for the store. In short order, the store was turned around and made quite profitable. These management changes included computerizing the inventory and establishing electronic ordering.

Shannon reinvested those profits in the store and expanded the operation into not one, but three profitable stores. At that stage, a large record store chain approached him to inquire about his desire to buy its 10-store operation in his region. The 10-store operation was owned by a larger corporation that was looking to focus on large stores in major cities. The large chain store management team knew Shannon and knew that he had a good reputation in the industry for being able to operate retail record stores even in hard times. As the chain was trying to entice Shannon to buy its operations, Shannon was doing his own due diligence. As he investigated the future of the industry, he became increasingly aware of trends in the industry that were troubling. It was the early 1990s and firms such as Walmart and Target were beginning to use music as a loss leader to get people into the stores. These large retailers would carry only the most popular music in the stores, but they would sell the CDs at a price cheaper than the wholesale price that Shannon could obtain. In addition, the wholesaler that Shannon used had recently been bought by Walmart. From his perspective, the future did not look bright for independent music retailers. Shannon did not buy the large chain and as a result of his own analysis, he also sold his stores.

At that stage Shannon began to look for new entrepreneurial ventures. He knew he wanted to be in an industry that would afford him some protection from the industry shock that he saw occurring in the music business. He also did not want to manage large numbers of people; avoiding the typical frustrations of trying to get employees to do their jobs was a significant objective in his search for a new business. His wife had a solid job at a publishing company, and he was employed as a professor of marketing at a university. Thus, he had the flexibility to look around. During this time period, a relationship with a friend who was a lawyer produced an opportunity to do an analysis of lost business wages and opportunity costs in a large commercial case the friend had coming to trial. The lawyer needed someone to do the analysis quickly and accurately and be willing to represent those findings in a court of law. Shannon took on the job in part because he didn't realize the amount of effort and time that would be involved. He read over 12,000 letters and legal documents in this process. However, he was able to write a report that was exceptional. The first act of the legal team in this case was to read Shannon's report into the court record on the first day of the trial. The offer of settlement from the opposing team went from around $500,000 offered on the day before the trial to over $6,000,000 immediately after the reading of Shannon's report into the record. The case was won and Shannon was paid well. More important, it led to the idea for his next business: consulting on lost wages and opportunity costs for lawyers and others in legal cases.

To set himself up in this type of consulting practice, Shannon wanted to buy into or buy outright an existing practice. While he had been successful in the first case, Shannon knew that he needed more skills to do really well in the profession. Consulting on lost wages is what is referred to as a boutique consulting practice. Most large firms are not active in this particular domain, and this creates more opportunity for smaller, specialized operations. It also means that getting to know those consultants who are active in this area is a little easier. Through a "friend of a friend" introduction, he met with a consultant who was looking to exit the business. He agreed to work with Shannon for one year and then sell Shannon the entire business. In addition to having the opportunity to work with an experienced consultant, Shannon was effectively buying a list of customers and a firm reputation. The selling price of a boutique consulting business tends to be quite reasonable, since customer retention is a real question mark.

Since that time, Shannon has been able to build the business. The company growth rate has been over 500 percent since his first year of consulting 12 years ago. One of the things Shannon has sought to do since buying the business is to create value in the business beyond the customer list. He developed proprietary software that helps him track all of his legal cases. This information is sent to him and to the attorney that has those cases so that they are not caught by surprise in court. He has also created software that tracks any other published data on the case, helping the attorneys who work with him and giving him a competitive advantage. Not only do these packages help him now, but they also provide some real value for the business for the day when he wants to sell the business. This software allows Shannon to manage far more cases than the prior owner could have imagined.

To help publicize his business, he has written two books that deal with how to evaluate issues like lost wages. While some may believe that writing books on his core subject would create new competitors, Shannon sees the real customers as the lawyers that need his particular skills. The books create an awareness of him and his business that traditional advertising simply cannot attain. This past year he served as president of the national association of individuals that prepare such economic analysis of lost wages: the American Rehabilitation Economics Association. This position allowed Shannon to increase his national reputation and the awareness of his business.

Today his business does very well, providing a wonderful income for Shannon, his wife (who works at the firm), another partner, and a secretary. The lessons Shannon would share with anyone seeking to set up a consulting business include these:

1. Don't be afraid to try your hand at lots of businesses. You will learn from each of them. The first one is not likely to be your most successful venture, but you will gain valuable skills from the effort. This knowledge will be your most valuable asset when you find the one business that is best suited for you.

2. Always use a lawyer in developing your contracts. For example, Shannon had a very good lawyer draw up the sales agreement when he originally bought the consulting business. In that agreement, there was a noncompete clause for the previous owner. It was not an issue for Shannon, but others who have not been as farsighted in their purchase of consulting practices have soon found themselves competing against the person they bought the business from.

3. Develop a business plan. It helps you communicate your ideas to others.

4. Always be on the outlook for new business opportunities.

5. To be an entrepreneur means you do not have to wear a tie—which is a good thing.

Establishing Operations

learning outcomes

After studying this chapter, you will be able to

8.1 Discuss the use of a critical path chart.

8.2 Describe how location can be used as a competitive advantage.

8.3 Discuss the important issues in the financing considerations of new firms.

8.4 Distinguish between the various methods with which a new firm establishes legitimacy in the market.

8.5 Explain the importance of production management in start-up ventures.

8.6 Explain how production charting is accomplished.

8.7 Describe the importance of quality as a competitive tool.

8.8 Discuss the type and condition of equipment needed at start-up.

8.9 Explain how timing is a competitive advantage.

8.10 Recognize the issues related to time management in the starting of a new business.

The Comfort Company

Renee Wood says she's used to weeping at work. She runs an online bereavement gift outfit, Comfort Company, from suburban Geneva, Illinois, and gets calls all day from people who want to buy something special for someone who has just lost a loved one. Compassion comes naturally to Wood—she was a social worker in a neonatal unit in Little Rock for years before she moved to Illinois—but it was only in 2000 that she figured out how to make money from it. Her sister-in-law's father died, and Wood couldn't find a suitable gift. She crafted a pendant out of her daughter's Play-Doh and took it to a silversmith to make into a necklace. Wood put a photo of the pendant on the Web and sold 150 of them. After getting a $6,000 home equity loan from Harris Bank, she went to gift shows and found more items to carry on her Web site, thecomfortcompany.net, including Christmas tree ornaments to remember lost ones at the holidays. Wood, 42, has added Spanish-language products and would like to expand her pet sympathy line. Revenue jumped to $625,000 last year, from $53,000 in 2003. "The more I grow, the more people I help feel better."

Source: "America's Most Promising Starups: Easing Death's Sting While Turning a Profit." Reprinted from March 18, 2008 issue of *BusinessWeek* by special permission. Copyright © 2008 by The McGraw-Hill Companies, Inc.

Planning is the first step in the small business development process. A great many individuals do little more than this initial investigation. During this process they find a fatal flaw, decide that the business is not nearly as lucrative as they had originally thought, or simply determine that they do not want to take the risk. The decision to not pursue the business is completely legitimate, and it is better to make it early if you believe that the business does not present the right opportunity for success. The process provided in this book, in fact, is designed to encourage the student to fully examine the business opportunity prior to actually starting a business.

However, at some stage the small business researcher must decide that she has investigated the idea sufficiently and that it is time to actually begin operations. While we would advocate good research and examination of your idea, the critical point of difference between an entrepreneur and someone with an idea is *action*. This chapter examines the practical, process-based actions that must occur to actually begin operations. To illustrate some of these actions and decisions that must be made, let's revisit Philo.

EXERCISE 1

1. What steps would you take now to start this business if you were in the Philo founders' position?
2. In what order would you suggest they proceed with these steps?

The position reached by Philo is actually quite typical of most new business start-ups. During the initial start-up period, the expenses of the firm are often higher than expected and the time to reach the break-even point takes longer than expected. A root cause of many of the problems for a new business can be traced to the lack of development/implementation of its operational plans.[1] It is this lack of operational plans that can lead to a cash crunch in the organization as the new firm stumbles while trying to actually put its ideas into action. As a result, the firm may have a great idea and be on a clear path to breakeven, but run out of cash before it has the opportunity to achieve that success. The firm should have a solid understanding of the specific operational issues related to that business prior to starting the new venture.

There are a number of distinct actions which must be taken in order for a new business to begin operations. Although there may be some crossover among these actions, we separate them into the following categories:

1. Critical path chart.
2. Location.
3. Financing considerations.
4. Legitimacy.
5. Production management.
6. Production charting.
7. Quality.
8. Equipment.
9. Timing.
10. Time management.

Each of these will be examined in turn.

The time had arrived for the founders of Philo to put their plan into action and start the business, redevote themselves to their current employment, or look for a new position or company. The founders realized this need to make a choice during a time when the economy in the area appeared to be taking a nasty turn for the worse, with many major employers in the city announcing plans for massive layoffs. In addition, both of the potential founders had been informed by their employers that there would be no raises during the next year.

These economic conditions might look like a poor time to start a new firm, but our founders viewed them as a good time to start their particular business. They knew from the analysis that their potential success depended on their customers. However, their customers were not the average workers in the city who were suffering. They were targeting young, upper-income individuals in the central business district. The central business district in their city was actually relatively prosperous. The city was centered in an area which was heavily dependent on energy and energy-related businesses. The recent expansion of energy prices had resulted in the city's young professionals doing particularly well. The national firms laying off workers were typically laying off hourly workers, who were not the target customers of the restaurant. In addition, the large state university in the city had just announced a major alliance with a Chinese university. This alliance had led to an increased interest in Asian-related activities in the city. The local art museum had announced a new Asia exhibit and a number of important acquisitions of Asian art. In addition, several of the small local manufacturers had found a significant new market in Asia. The result was a focused interest in Asian-related items in the city which seemed to fit well with the proposed restaurant. The issue that the founders next faced was to begin to actually set up the operations of the restaurant.

The founders took their business plan to their local bank and worked out an initial loan for the business, as well as a working capital line of credit for the business. In addition, each founder contributed $50,000 of his or her own money as initial equity in the business. Armed with this initial financing, they proceeded to complete the next critical steps in starting the business over a three-week period of time. The steps they took included the following:

- They employed a stationery store to design a simple logo for the operation. The cost was only $400 and would be zero if they purchased all their business cards, letterhead, and envelopes from the store. The founders realized that such visual items as letterhead and cards would help to legitimize their appearance (a concept discussed in more depth later in this chapter). This they agreed to immediately.

- They attempted to lease the restaurant location they had identified in their initial analysis. Unfortunately, unbeknownst to them in their initial planning, there was already a contract to purchase that facility, so it was unavailable to them. They called a commercial real estate broker and looked at more than 12 potential restaurant locations. They found one that met most of their criteria; however, it cost $1.50 a square foot more than their estimates. As the location was empty, they would be able to take possession (as a leaseholder) immediately. They signed a lease for two years.

- They contacted the phone company, electric company, and gas company (as the restaurant had a large central gas furnace) to establish service at the facility.

- They began to select equipment for the restaurant by contacting a used restaurant equipment contractor.

- They began contacting restaurant supply businesses to obtain other needed inputs.

- They agreed to take no salaries until cash flow was positive.

The partners had begun the operations of their small business. They had a plan for when they should reach breakeven, but unexpected expenses started almost immediately:

- An outdoor sign had to be obtained and mounted per the regulations of the city and requirements of the landlord. The total cost was $1,700.

- Once in the restaurant location, they found it was in far worse shape than their initial examination had revealed to them. They spent the next 11 days, with their families' help, cleaning up and putting the fundamentals in place for their operation. The cleaning supplies and meals for their families over this time cost almost $1,000. In their lease

(continued)

agreement, they had taken on the cost to upfit the location to their needs. However, beyond the basic cleaning, they began to realize that to bring the restaurant to the style they desired would be very expensive: approximately $80,000. They needed to buy tables and chairs, paint the walls, and decorate. All the inputs for the bathrooms were also needed. The bathrooms had appeared initially to be acceptable. However, as the partners studied revising the restaurant, they realized that the outdated toilet facilities also needed to be changed.

The cost for all of this was an additional $5,000, and only that low because the partners planned to do the work themselves.

The result of all this was that the start-up business owners almost immediately recognized that their plans for the operations of the business were not leading to the break-even point (the point where revenue equals expenses) that they had projected. Instead, the company was faced with a negative situation well beyond their expectations.

LO 8.1 Critical Path Chart

The first technique in this section is also one of the most popular for organizing a wide range of activities. An absolute imperative for any organization, but most especially for a new business, is the efficient use of time. Many tasks can be handled concurrently, but others must be performed sequentially. Identifying the actions which must occur, in what order they should occur, and what order will be most efficient is one of the first operational steps for a new business. While it is often not possible to identify every action item that will be required prior to the start of a new business, the effort to develop a complete list will allow the new business to have a faster, more thorough, less expensive start-up. Failing to plan may leave the new business waiting weeks for some small step that could have been completed earlier, concurrently with other actions taken by the firm. For example, items such as obtaining a state tax ID or a city license are not difficult but may take some time, depending upon the requirements. However, the firm may not be able to buy equipment for the business or rent facilities until these licenses are obtained.

While there are a number of methods and formats for completing a critical path analysis, we present a relatively common, easily understood format that we have used with a number of new start-ups.[2] Initially, the small business owner must identify the most likely amount of time it will take for each of the key tasks to be completed, the actual time one of the owners will be involved, any prerequisite tasks, and who is responsible for the task. The chart of critical activities might look something like the one in Table 8.1 for a small manufacturer.

Note that the assigning of responsibilities and estimated times is more than an intellectual activity. When you specify who will do a task, and how long it will take to be completed, you set for yourself a control mechanism to ensure that you are going to be ready when you intend to open. If you do not set timetables and responsibilities, it is possible for the founding of the business to drag on, using up precious financial and emotional resources. Thus, by setting the schedule the founders can get a solid handle on how soon they can begin

STEP	TASK	TIME TO COMPLETE	ACTUAL TIME INVOLVED	PREVIOUS TASK REQUIRED	RESPONSIBILITY
1	Establish Business Bank Accounts	1 Week	3 Hours		James and Margaret
2	Obtain Bank Loan	2 Weeks	4 Hours		James and Margaret
3	Establish Accounting System	3 Weeks	1 Week		Margaret
4	Lease Facility	2 Weeks	20 Hours	2	James and Margaret
5	Obtain Equipment (Office & Manufacturing)	4 Weeks	8 Hours	2 & 4	James (manufacturing) and Margaret (office)
6	Acquire Raw Materials	4 Weeks	30 Hours	2 & 4	James
7	Make Initial Sales Calls	8 Weeks	90 Hours	2 & 4	James and Margaret
8	Produce Initial Inventory	4 Weeks	150 Hours	4, 5, 6, & 7	James and Margaret

Table 8.1
Critical Path Table

operations. The owners understand that while they must wait on some tasks, they can complete other tasks so that their time is used efficiently. The owners also can set some priorities on where their time should be focused. For example, it would be difficult to acquire raw materials and have them delivered prior to the leasing of the facility. Thus, if the leasing of the facility took more time than estimated, then the entire process would be delayed.

Underestimating the amount of time it will take to begin operations is a mistake that harms many new businesses. You should estimate the times very generously, since many critical steps may take significantly longer than originally planned. New business people often do not recognize a given step they will need to accomplish in order to successfully develop their business. The listing of critical tasks and the resulting critical path chart can help to overcome this problem.

From the lists of critical tasks identified in Table 8.1, the new business can then develop a chart that demonstrates how the activities fit together. This is your **critical path chart,** that shows the set of activities which are dependent upon each other (i.e. the longest path) and which take the longest time. The chart listing the critical tasks provided in Table 8.1 will produce the critical path chart shown in Figure 8.1.

critical path chart

Chart that demonstrates how the activities necessary to start the firm fit together and build on each other. This chart allows you to understand which activities can occur concurrently and which must already be in place before the next activity can occur.

Figure 8.1
The Critical Path Chart

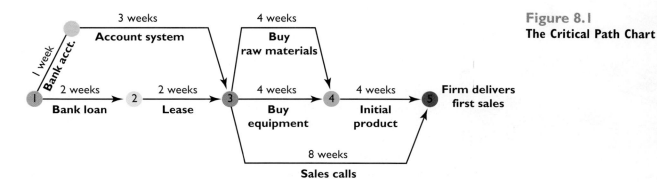

As you can see from the critical path in Figure 8.1, it will take a minimum of 12 weeks to open the business. There are some things the firm can do at the same time, such as setting up the firm's bank accounts and starting to work on bank loans. However, the new business will likely not be able to start to lease a facility until it has its financing in place. Potential landlords will initially screen out those individuals they do not feel are serious as they seek to lease a property.

The businessperson can make the critical path as detailed as he feels necessary. The chart for the small manufacturing firm in Figure 8.1 is actually quite simple. The new businessperson should be guided by developing a chart that provides the most assistance/information. The purpose of the chart is not to be a formal document to place solely in a business plan. Instead, it is designed to help focus the founders' efforts so they are not slowed down by some simple activity that was not visualized. Therefore, it may be useful for the founders to create a more complex form of critical path chart that can be developed by estimating three different time needs for each task: minimum, most likely, and maximum. For complex start-up operations, there are several project management software packages that will assist you in developing a task chart and producing a critical path chart. They are available at most office supply stores. The new businessperson must judge the level of detail that he desires in a critical path chart and whether purchasing such a program will aid him or not.

To further illustrate the importance of such planning, consider one of the small businesses that students in one of our classes wished to start. The students wanted to start a "Study Café" open from 4 p.m. to 8 a.m., seven days a week. The business design was simple but elegant and potentially quite lucrative. The café would provide a well-lit, open-forum, safe space to study individually or meet with groups. It would make a majority of its money by selling basic food and drinks, and leasing out the conference rooms in the facility. There was cheap space available close to the campus where a restaurant had gone out of business. (The prior restaurant had appealed to students, but closed every night at 9 p.m. and strongly discouraged students from "hanging out.") The stu-

Is the Study Café a lucrative business idea? Why or why not?

dents' original intent was to open just prior to the start of classes in the fall semester. However, after completing the critical path chart, they realized that they would complete everything necessary to open their doors in April. This would mean the business would open for operation at the end of the spring semester. The city in which the Study Café wanted to open was a college town where only the resident college students would be interested in staying up till the early hours of the morning. As a result, the business would have to suffer through the summer months of limited business while the expenses just piled up.

As a result of their critical path analysis, they approached their opening from a completely different perspective. Rather than starting the process immediately and seeing when they could open, they went to the end of the chart and set the opening date as August 1st. They then calculated the critical path chart in reverse, with the date they were to open being the starting (and therefore missing) element. Estimating the longest path for opening the Study Café, they were able to establish a date to begin the process of putting together the operations of the business so as to minimize wasted effort and money while still opening for operations by August 1st.

You should constantly update your critical path analysis as you develop the plan for your business. Share it with potential suppliers, friends, and industry experts—with anyone who will look it over for you and add, modify, or delete activities. The critical path analysis is a living document that should be modified during the process of actually accomplishing the tasks. We have worked with a number of new businesspeople who take large flip-chart sheets of paper and post a critical path chart on the wall of their home, office, etc. As tasks are accomplished, delayed, added, etc., the chart is continually updated.

EXERCISE 2

1. Develop a list of all activities necessary to start your business.
2. Develop a Critical Path Table of activities. Think very carefully about what activities can be completed concurrently.

LO 8.2 Location

One of the most important steps in the critical path chart will be the identification and purchase/lease of a location for the new business. The old axiom from marketing is that the three keys to business success are location, location, and location. While this might be a bit overblown, we certainly agree that location is a critical item in the successful operation of a new business.[3] How do you decide upon the best location for the money? The method that we utilize involves breaking the business down into the critical design features of the business. You may recall from Chapter 5 that you should develop a list consisting of all the resources/capabilities of the organization. These should then be divided into two categories representing the ordinary and extraordinary points of competition for the new business. Your location decision should address all of the orthodox points required for your industry and should enhance the unorthodox points. For example, an orthodox location for a restaurant is one that is visible and easily accessible to your target customers, while an unorthodox location may have a stunning view of the downtown skyline.

It is very easy to simply fall into the trap of trying to locate a business based upon the capital available or some convenience factor that has little to do with the actual strategy of the business. This is a mistake that can, by itself, send all of the other planning down the drain. For example, one of the authors met a young couple for dinner several years back, both of whom had been students in his classes. They were very excited because they had decided to open a restaurant and wanted us to come by once it was open. It was a reasonable restaurant idea, but its location constituted a fatal flaw. They were opening the business near their home because they knew the area "so very well." This decision also allowed them to return to the area where they had both grown up.

However, this area was more than 60 miles from any major city and, worse than that, they had selected as their location a **strip shopping center** with very cheap rent. A strip center is a small, one-story retail center typically located parallel to a well-traveled road. This type of center is referred to as a strip center since it was often developed on a strip of land irrespective of the development in the area; it generally has no major **anchor stores** to draw in customers. The fact that they were

strip shopping center

A small retail center located typically along a major road. The center has only small businesses and the center itself occupies only a small strip of land along the major street.

anchor stores

Major retail stores, such as department stores in a mall. They serve as the anchor for the retail establishment.

What businesses are best suited for a strip shopping center? What businesses might not work in such a space?

locating in the strip center itself was not the problem. Instead, it was the specific strip center that they had selected. The reason the rent was so cheap was that the shopping center was virtually empty. It was empty not because the center was too new to have tenants; instead, the customer base in the area was too small and poor to support any of the businesses that had previously operated there. Their proposed location was more than two miles from the interstate. Therefore, they would not be getting the interstate travel traffic that would be passing through this isolated location. Despite our warnings and suggestions, they went ahead with the business withtheir father's seed money (almost $50,000) only to see the small restaurant collapse within six months. Even the best idea can be killed by a bad location.

While there are many very sophisticated methods for performing a location analysis, in more simple terms locations can be graded by the type and amount of traffic that the particular location draws. If you are setting up a warehouse, then you neither need nor want an "A" location in a mall, on a busy street, or in a tourist-heavy downtown area. Match the type of business, its needs from both an orthodox and an unorthodox perspective, and the amount of money that you wish to invest in the first years of operation. Take the time to analyze the long-term as well. If you will need to move within a short period of time because you achieve all of your targets and outgrow your space, then you may want to consider a location that includes an option to allow for expansion.

To illustrate the rich options that a firm can pursue, we recently helped raise capital for a small business that started out as three people renting space from a travel agency (literally, three desks in the back of the building). As luck would have it (for the new business at least), the travel agency was struggling, which allowed the new business owners to rent more and more of the building as their business expanded. Within 18 months they were renting 80 percent of the building and approached the travel agency owner about taking over the entire building and setting up a lease/purchase agreement. The travel agency finally sold what was left of its operation to a larger travel firm and the small business owners were able to acquire the building location. Having established a client base, they really wanted to hold onto their location. As will be discussed later in this chapter, location is one of the things that provide a business with legitimacy. If you have a location and maintain it for some period of time, then you are more accepted and acceptable with potential clients and suppliers, since your business appears to be more stable.

Commercial real estate firms are a source of unparalleled information for the new business owners trying to locate their business. Building owners pay agents in a leasing agreement that is usually based

Location is a critical choice for a firm. Some entrepreneurs become completely enamored with what they perceive to be the perfect location. It is difficult for these people to see any way that the business can succeed unless they can operate in that one location. The same goes for the perfect piece of equipment, the rights to a critical license for the business, or any number of things or events.

1. What would you do to get something that you deemed to be critical for your new business?
2. What if you were prevented from obtaining it by someone you felt was just being vindictive?
3. Would paying double the true value of something be acceptable to you?
4. What if you had to sell part of your business in exchange for that perfect location?

upon a percentage of the first year's lease and the signing of a two-year lease. While commercial real estate agent income can be quite substantial, the commercial real estate market is relatively small and an individual's reputation is critical to future bookings. Therefore, agents focus extensively on ensuring that the new business signing the lease is successful. The fact is that the cost for all this expertise is paid by the building owner, and a successful business that pays its bills is very desirable. Thus, commercial agents can be a valuable asset to new business owners as they seek to locate properties that match their needs.

EXERCISE 3

1. What criteria are critical for the location decision of your new business?
2. What orthodox criteria must you satisfy to be a player in your industry?

LO 8.3 Financing Considerations

While not addressing the details of financing operations here (we will cover those issues in depth in Chapter 9), we nonetheless want to acknowledge the gamut of financial issues related to the operational start-up of a new business. Financing the initial operations begins with the variety of initial payments and the process of setting up the business, and ends with the first completed sale. The new organization has to be in a position to make initial payments for

1. Security deposits.
2. Utility set-up fees.
3. Purchase/lease of initial equipment and installation.
4. All licenses and inspections.
5. All initial supplies (this is a significant and oft-overlooked expense).
6. Hiring and training of initial staff.
7. Initial advertising expenses.
8. Bank set-up fees.

These costs can be substantial and the new business must ensure that it has the proper resources to conduct such activities. Recalling our critical path analysis, if one element, such as purchasing of some key inputs, must be delayed due to a lack of resources, the impact can be to place the entire development of the new business's operations behind schedule.

Point number 8 in the list of financial considerations on page 161 brings up the issue of establishing a bank relationship. The new business is well served to establish a variety of financial relationships with its bank. Some of these key issues include establishing a revolving line of credit (working capital), acquiring a business credit card account, and setting up a basic business checking account. These accounts should have a primary signatory and a confirmation signatory as an audit safety condition. No one individual should be able to write checks for the business in excess of a specified amount (usually $500) without a countersignature.

Picking which bank to work with is more than a choice of which branch is closest to you. Working with small businesses is a specialized skill that all banks will say they possess, but which in fact may be very limited at a given institution. Some banks develop expertise in large commercial accounts such as Fortune 500 customers. Other banks have an expertise in retail banking, primarily serving individuals. Still other banks have their principal focus on small and medium-sized business. A bank may have a range of customers, but you want to ensure that it has an expertise in your type of business and understands issues such as timing of payments from customers. If you have a small retail firm, you may need large draws on your lines of credit to get the Christmas merchandise onto your shelves. If you are a small oil and gas exploration firm you will have other specialized needs, such as determining the value of given leases that you include in your assets. Whether your bank can work with such issues is an important question for a new business owner. The expertise of other successful small business owners in your area provides valuable insight into these issues.

LO 8.4 Legitimacy

A topic rarely discussed in the establishment of a new business is the issue of legitimacy. **Legitimacy** is the term that we use to discuss acceptance by key stakeholders, such as customers and suppliers, that you are a genuine business that will still be in operation next year. Developing the perception of legitimacy for both customers and suppliers can be difficult, although it is critical to the long-term survival of the business.[4]

The new business will need to look like and act as an operation that will be in business for the long run in order to achieve some level of legitimacy. Customers and suppliers want to do business with someone that will still be in business next year. If a customer buys a product and the company is then no longer in business, who does she turn to when she has a problem? When a supplier sells goods on terms of 90 days, where will that firm get its payment if the firm that bought the goods goes out of business before the 90 days? Thus, both customers and suppliers want to ensure your business will be operating for the long term before they do business with you.

You will recall from our discussion of community supports in Chapter 2 that we discussed business incubators. These institutions are a potential setting for new businesses (especially non–food service businesses) to locate their initial operations. They offer new small businesses office space at reduced rates, as well as providing services such as a receptionist who answers the phone with the business name, conference room facilities, and basic office equipment (copying, fax, Internet, telephones). The effect of this is that it helps to build the legitimacy of the business with the look of a more professional presentation as well as the endorsement provided by the incubator operator. Incubators are usually swamped with new businesses that would like to be considered. The incubator operators try to pick those businesses that have the best chance for success.

EXERCISE 4

1. What do you look for in a business before you patronize it?
2. If you were going to sell equipment and supplies to a new business on credit, what would you want to see from the new business?
3. What small items might add to your legitimacy with little cost?

Regardless of the business location, the small business owner needs to consider the potential means with which to establish the legitimacy of the business in the eyes of the customers and suppliers. Below is a list of classic items that may help establish more legitimacy for your new business:

1. A business checking account with the firm's name printed on the checks; start the check numbering higher than 001 or even 101.

2. A business credit card.

3. A bank line of credit.

4. Professional business cards.

5. Professional letterhead, billing slips, envelopes, etc.

6. Professional advertising material.

7. The prestige of the business address

8. Job titles—titles cost you very little, use them liberally.

9. Telephone answering support.

10. A high-quality Web page.

11. A board of advisors/directors with excellent community visibility.

12. Endorsements from well-recognized and respected individuals.

You may have noticed that some items in the list above are quite inexpensive, while others are both time consuming and expensive. We suggest that all new businesses develop a plan to establish and continually enhance their legitimacy. Appearances are not everything, but they are important, especially at the outset of the business.

LO 8.5 Production Management

Another important element in the success of a new business is the establishment of a production management system.[5] A production management system is a fancy name for defining the steps that are involved in moving from your product/service offering to the point where you actually receive money. This importance is exaggerated in the early stages of a new business, as the firm has only limited resources, as well as strong time pressures to perform well at the outset. To illustrate, we worked with a small group of individuals whose rather simple but interesting plan to refurbish printer cartridges was targeted at college students. Their original plan had them handling the vast variety of cartridges on an individual basis. They would simply deal with each cartridge as it came in and depend upon their individual knowledge and experience to punch the hole in the cartridge, refill the ink, plug the hole, and finally seal up the cartridge for resale. They accepted the fact that they would develop procedures for each type of cartridge, but thought that this would develop over time. The process of discovery would allow them to handle a wide variety of cartridges early in the life of the company.

We pointed out that their projections depended upon their handling more than 10,000 cartridges a month by the sixth month of operation, and that an ad hoc system being handled directly by the owners would likely not lead to success. The time wasted as each cartridge was handled as a unique order would simply be unwieldy in a very short time period. As a result, they employed a mechanical engineer who developed a very simple set of procedures with fixed equipment to handle the most common types of cartridges. For these stations with fixed equipment, they employed individuals to process the most common cartridges. For all other cartridges they maintained a job shop section to develop procedures and process those cartridges. Over the next eight months, they developed a production management system and methodology that allowed them to dramatically cut costs. On more than one occasion they have commented to us that more time spent prior to start-up in developing a process would have resulted in enormous financial dividends to the owners. It is important to emphasize that all businesses have production systems, whether or not they are codified. All service businesses have preferred ways of dealing with items such as customers, paperwork, orders, and services. These constitute the foundation of a production system. Putting together a production management system to handle the most common and expected routines will ensure consistent handling and enable the employees to focus their energy on the unusual aspects of the job.

While this topic is quite complex and is its own field of study, we discuss the two most important elements to production management as they relate to small business. These are production charting and quality.

LO 8.6 Production Charting

There are many established software programs available for new business owners to help them establish the production processes they will use in their firms. To emphasize the importance of such methods, new business owners need only look to franchises. The text will discuss franchises in greater detail in Chapter 14. Here we simply point out that one of the reasons that franchises are so successful is that they have well-established methods of operation. The franchisors have prepared these methods for the franchisees in a plan detailing each step that occurs in the production process and when each step is to occur. This type of exercise is enormously helpful for all new businesses.

This level of detailed understanding about a firm's production typically comes from a **production chart.** You will recall that at the beginning of this chapter, we discussed a critical path chart. A production chart is similar; however, rather than focusing on the founding of the business, this chart details each step that must occur within the

production chart

A chart that provides a detailed understanding of a firm's production process.

production process. It takes the reader step by step through the processes necessary to provide the customer with the finished product. It starts with the order being received and finishes with the final delivery to the customer. The production chart is similar to the critical path chart in that some steps in the production process can occur simultaneously while others must occur concurrently. In presenting this chart, we have chosen a slightly different format from the traditional one used in most textbooks. Most textbooks focus on established company production processes and have many items occurring concurrently; however, we have found that new firms have limited personnel and the processes are more sequential. The process detailed in the production chart in Figure 8.2 is very simple: production of a plaque from a trophy shop. Even for early-stage ventures, the production chart can become complex quite quickly. Imagine the difficulty in producing meals from a menu that may have 25 different entrees with different vegetable selections. How does the restaurant assure that all of the items are produced so that those that take longer are started sooner, those that take less time are started later, and all items are finalized at approximately the same time and are delivered to the table when they are at their peak? Now add in complexities like appearance, appetizers, salads, and drinks. The production chart for a business that appears quite simple can, in fact, be quite complex.

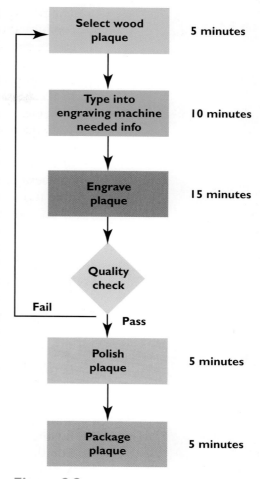

Figure 8.2
Production Chart

All businesses have a production process. It is easy to recognize such a process in a manufacturing setting. However, a small business owner should recognize that even a retail firm has a production process. Goods come into the store and then are counted, tagged, stocked, sold, detagged, and bagged, or if not sold moved to the discount area. If firms do not have a detailed understanding of the methods needed for these basic processes, it is quite easy to end up creating bottlenecks and procedures that negatively impact both customers and employees. One business that we got to know was in a tourist area and it catered to the tourist trade. To save money the owner decided to use a dial-up phone line for credit card transactions. As compared to a dedicated high-speed line, this choice meant an additional 45 seconds per transaction, and dialing delays/busy signals were a common problem. Complaints continued to rise and the owner noticed more and more people either walking out of the store or deciding, upon looking at the checkout line, to go elsewhere. He chose to move to a dedicated line. At the same time, he changed his required procedure that each item be recorded in a ledger by the cash register, as that process was slow and cumbersome. At some expense he moved to a bar code system in order to improve the throughput of customers. The dedicated high-speed Internet line and the bar code system were both more expensive, but once the owner realized the negative impact on his production process of not having them, the rationale for each became quite obvious.

In a similar vein, we once dealt with a clothing retailer who did not have a clear understanding of the store's current process, nor what processes should be in place. The owner would bring all goods in at cost and continue to carry all unsold items in inventory at their original cost.

The predictable result was an ever-growing percentage of the store being consumed by obsolete stock, and this eventually led to failure, as the firm ended up with a storeroom and retail space full of goods that appeared on paper to be quite valuable, but were in fact items that had little or no market value. The firm's bank eventually figured this out and due to clauses in the line of credit, cut the credit line of the firm to virtually nothing. This cash crunch resulted in an inability to place orders for goods the store needed in the upcoming year, and the store eventually closed. There is no universally "correct" way to deal with the issue of obsolete stock; however, it is necessary to establish a procedure for handling such stock.

There are many established production management systems available to new business owners. If you are starting a business that is part of an established industry, then you should talk to others in the industry regarding the popular packages for the management of your business processes. Starting one from scratch is a waste of time and money. A little effort investigating the industry should provide tremendous positives for the organization.

LO 8.7 Quality

Another important consideration in all aspects of a business venture is the investment in quality. In the recent past, designing quality into your product/service was a means to differentiate a small business from mass-market businesses. Increasingly, however, quality is an assumed standard whether the small business is in manufacturing or is a service business. Individuals have to look no farther than fast-food restaurants. For illustration purposes, look at a franchise like McDonald's. It sells a number of products for $1.00, has playgrounds for kids, maintains clean tables and restrooms, and even puts a toy in a meal for children. The playgrounds are expansive and expensive, while the food quality is guaranteed across the spectrum of all McDonald's restaurants. It is a tremendous value for a very small price, and each store opens with the full complement of offerings. If a new business is to compete against McDonald's, the firm will have to have a similar quality and quantity of offerings to be successful. Therefore, new businesses need to be clear about the expectations for quality in whatever business they pursue.

One of the keys to successfully delivering quality is the monitoring and measuring systems put into place by the founder(s). Dr. W. Edwards Deming is considered the father of the quality movement in the United States. One of his arguments is that quality needs to be constantly and consistently improved. Thus, there needs to be a continuous set of measures for each of the various processes of the organization. Without recorded data, it is impossible to judge the performance of the processes that have been put in place by the owner(s).

Deming went much further and argued that while the organization should set goals for quality in the organization, these goals are not to drive every action. If they did, the firm might make short-term decisions that were detrimental to the overall direction of the company. To illustrate, a firm may have a target for on-time delivery that it is striving to improve upon. While this is admirable and perhaps even a point of differentiation in the industry, if the firm gets so wrapped up in on-time delivery that this becomes the only focus of the organization, it can easily miss critical orthodox issues, such as delivering the correct item! Delivering the wrong item on time would result in great statistical success (concerning timing, at least) but would destroy value in the firm.[6]

Deming strongly suggests that the firm be guided by what he calls the "scientific method." In this method, rather than changing lots of things at the same time, the firm should change only one thing at a time, measuring the impact of that change. It is through this systematic method that a firm knows if it is moving in the right direction and also knows the true impact of each change.

Additionally, he suggests that rather than focusing strictly on obtaining the lowest prices for supplies, firms should focus on the quality of the inputs. He argues that without quality inputs, the output has no chance to be high quality. To illustrate, there was a large privately held bakery in Oklahoma that used 12 different types of flour. The owners shopped by price, so there were actually as many as 15 different suppliers they used at different points in time. The result was that the firm would use inputs that met the formal requirements for the flour, but each had slight differences in their characteristics, such as moisture content. These differences were very small, but they still led inexorably to differences in the baking processes. Thus, each time a new supplier's product was employed, the owner of the firm found that her workers had to test and adjust the production process. This sometimes took as long as three separate baking runs to effectively establish. After years of handling this situation, the owner followed the advice of a close friend who simply recommended that the bakery employ one supplier who would guarantee the quality standard. Saving the constant testing and product waste would more than make up for any additional expense. It is this type of realization that has moved firms to focus on forming **strategic alliances,** where firms join together to form long-term, mutually beneficial relationships. Firms, both large and small, now seek to establish a reasonable price for their inputs and then seek out a long-term relationship with a supplier that can meet that price and supply a consistent, high-quality product. A consistent input helps the firm produce a consistent output.

strategic alliances
The joining together of firms to form long-term, mutually beneficial relationships.

LO 8.8 Equipment

Acquiring the initial equipment for a business can be a daunting task. The basic equipment can easily be one of the most expensive elements for a new business. Clearly, a small manufacturer that needs to purchase specialized equipment will have a higher initial outlay when compared to a service business. Yet even a small business such as a restaurant or clothing retailer can incur significant expenses for equipment. It is important that the small business owner accurately evaluate the equipment needs while at the same time recognizing that there is a wide flexibility in the types, ages, methods of acquisition, and availability of all equipment obtained for the new organization. Purchasing new equipment may guarantee that it is the most current available and that it will be delivered directly to the new business; however, it is usually the most expensive method, and delays may be significant if the items are not in stock. Purchasing older equipment has its own risks with quality and availability, but should always be investigated. It is relatively common for new equipment to depreciate

Alex had started to generate a set of ways to show his potential customers and suppliers he was serious about the business and expected to be there for a long period of time—to establish what we have referred to in this book as legitimacy. He knew from his conversations with other repair shop owners that the first six months were critical to his success. However, he also knew that since that first six months would decide if he would survive, many suppliers would not provide goods at favorable terms, and some customers would not trust him, until they were sure he would be in business for a long period of time.

Alex had some benefits already going for him. His current employer at the auto parts store had appreciated Alex's hard work and had indicated he would be as generous as he could in supplying parts to Alex. In fact, he indicated that if Alex would commit to be his customer, his conditions at first would be very generous, and he would go to more of a market rate after six months. Alex also had the benefit of establishing his business in the same location where a well-respected auto repair business had been previously. He chose to not keep the Jones family name, as he wanted to reach out to the majority Hispanic clientele in the neighborhood. However, he felt that the presence of a well-regarded auto repair shop in the existing location should still attract some of Jones's regular customers.

Alex knew he would still need to buy over $100,000 worth of equipment, even if he bought used tools. In addition, he needed to build greater support in the community for his business. Therefore, he followed several major initiatives. First, he made contact with a local advertising group to design an initial professional advertising campaign in his very narrow neighborhood. One of the principals in the firm was an old high school friend, so he gave Alex a special deal. The size of the market to be served in such advertising was not to be large, but Alex wanted it to look good. His friend advised him to take advantage of his name and not call the business Rod's, as he had been planning to, but Rodriquez Auto Repair. Alex took his advice and changed the name.

In addition, he sought out individuals in the community to serve as a board of advisors. He looked for leading people in the community, including a priest at the local Catholic church and a Protestant minister who served another large church in the area. While he did not expect these individuals to endorse him, their presence lent credibility to the business. While it was not stated, Alex assumed that in gratitude for the aid of the minister and priest, he would be working on the vans of both churches. This was fine with him because he had already planned to give back to the community. He also asked an old friend who was a senior manager at a branch of a large bank in the area to join his board of advisors. Alex also completed a number of small steps, such as getting business cards and starting his checks at a relatively high number, to help establish his legitimacy in the community.

50 percent or more in the first year. Similarly, it is possible to lease equipment. The ability to lease the equipment is particularly attractive to new firms since it has the lowest initial costs. However, over the long run such leasing can prove expensive.

Therefore, the new business owner needs to clearly understand what equipment is needed, how long it will be before it will need to be replaced, and the long-term impacts of the decision. This understanding should also include both what equipment is needed to begin operations and how quickly the company might need more/bigger equipment. The new business owner should then prepare a chart comparing the price and the positives and negatives of buying new, buying used, or leasing that equipment. The positives and negatives should include not only the immediate cost and the ability to overcome the cash flow crunch that impacts all new businesses, but also the impact on the firm's quality, and the long-term impact if the small business grows.

LO 8.9 Timing

It is interesting to note that choosing when to start a business is an important operational element. The temptation for most new businesses is to start their operations as soon as possible. This is rarely an effective strategy. Instead the potential entrepreneur should select the time to enter the market based on when it provides the greatest competitive advantage.[7] The timing of your start is a function of several factors: (1) the general environment, (2) competitor moves, (3) cycles in purchasing/supply patterns, and (4) lifestyle issues.

The general economy moves in cycles of boom, slowdown, recession (or the million other terms that are used as euphemisms for this term), growth, and boom. While the general rule might be that you should open your business during or at the beginning of a boom, the reality is that different businesses depend upon different conditions. A fore-closure business depends upon poor economic times, and storage facilities do best when the economy is heading downward, etc.

Competitor moves may also dictate the opening of a new business. If your business plan is dependent upon having no direct competitors within a specified radius of your operation, a move by another business may accelerate or dramatically alter your plans. Alternatively, the failure of several similar businesses may suggest an alteration of your opening or strategic positioning prior to your actually opening the business.

Some (we might suggest most) businesses have cycles for their purchasing. Some suppliers have production runs that are scheduled a year or more in advance. Your ability to obtain critical supplies may dictate your lead time and opening time. It can be difficult to obtain significant Christmas inventory in September. The shipping time for these goods and other factors typically requires that a retailer make decisions much earlier.

A small business that we advised some years ago had a significant issue with the supply of wooden tubes that were needed for its production. The sole supplier of this particular size and quality of wooden tubes had a production run of eight weeks in March/April of each year for that particular product. All orders had to be in place by January. This new business reoriented its entire opening and operation around the acquisition of these wooden tubes. The owners placed an order in January, took delivery in three batches between April and June (storing all of the tubes in a warehouse that they leased), and began production of their product in November. Their first sale was in February of the following year, by which time they had placed yet another order for the following year. The ability of the new business to understand these timing issues required extensive planning and forecasting, without which it would have failed.

LO 8.10 Time Management

The last item is one that is meant to help the new business owners as they seek to manage this wide variety of operations. It is clear from the discussion provided here that the business owners will need to manage their own time efficiently if they are to be successful.[8] There are several steps that are helpful in this process.

1. Write down what has to be accomplished in all parts of the business formation.

2. Prioritize which tasks are critical and which would be helpful. Those that are critical must be done and should be the priority.

3. Segment items in terms of the time frame they need to be accomplished—short term and long term. The short-term items that are critical have to take priority. The fires that are burning have to be put out before the longer-term issues approach.

4. Allocate time that is strictly for dealing with operational issues. The more you become involved in establishing the business and its operations, the more individuals will wish to visit with you about the business. While some of these individuals will be helpful, many simply will wish to sell you something you do not need or to find out what you are doing. As your agenda becomes filled you must ensure that your attention is not diverted to nonproductive activities. This does not mean you should not be flexible when opportunities arise, but it does mean that you must have a clear vision of your work goals.

5. Write tasks down and mark them off when you accomplish them. As your agenda becomes more complex, you will gain satisfaction from seeing things being removed from it. However, this method also ensures that you will not forget key items (there should be a strong tie back to your critical path chart). In writing these things down, it is best if you can do this in a systematic, organized manner. Keep a notebook or use a PDA every day to see what you must accomplish and take notes about it. This approach can also be a valuable resource for keeping notes about meetings, issues that hit you as you think about the business, and issues that others raise with you. From these items and other information, you can keep track of issues to do today, this week, this month, etc.

summary

There is a wide variety of operational issues that must be considered as the new business begins operations. These include (1) developing a critical path chart; (2) establishing a location; (3) financing considerations; (4) legitimacy; (5) production management; (6) production charting; (7) quality; (8) equipment; (9) timing; and finally, (10) time management. Each is important to the start-up of a new business, and with proper planning and implementation, these various activities can substantially improve the opportunity for success.

key terms

anchor stores 159
critical path chart 157
legitimacy 162

production chart 164
strategic alliances 167
strip shopping center 159

review questions

1. What elements would you include in a critical path chart? How would you ensure that your estimates were accurate?
2. Why is a critical path chart useful to potential investors?
3. Aren't all locations equal?
4. What elements should be considered when leasing a new business location?
5. What would you recommend that a new business do to improve its acceptance and legitimacy in the market?
6. Why is a detailed chart of how business operations are conducted important to the new business?
7. How can quality be built into any product or service?
8. Should all new companies open as soon as they are physically ready? Why or why not?
9. Explain some key time management techniques that will benefit any new entrepreneur.

individual exercises

1. What are the "lease or buy" equipment issues you will face in your business?
2. Can you employ used, or will you need new equipment in your business?
3. What is the difference in price of new and used equipment in your proposed business?
4. What are the critical timing issues involved in your business?

group exercises

1. Establish a plan to address each of the critical issues related to the starting of operations for a new organization.
2. Imagine that your team has decided to franchise the business idea. Develop a set of processes/procedures that would allow a third party to become a franchise of your operation.
3. Present your operational plan to the class and ask for feedback.

everyday edisons class discussion

Go to www.everydayedisons.com/matthew.html and read about Matthew.

1. What would be the legitimacy issues he faces in making a table tennis game that is new?
2. Think of some of the critical path issues that Matthew has had to deal with and list those.

Keith Milburn—Milburn's Photography

Keith Milburn got his start in photography by shooting pictures of rock bands. A friend offered him a job photographing babies that paid four times as much as he was making with the rock bands. For the next six years he photographed babies and learned the ins and outs of the photography business. However, he wanted to start his own business and run it his own way. One day he called in sick to work and went to look at a commercial location for a business. Unfortunately his boss found out and fired him by noon that day. As a result, by 1:00 p.m. Keith had signed a lease and started a business.

Keith wanted to continue photographing babies and children as he had before. However, rather than photograph 20 sets of kids a day, he wanted to photograph fewer, with higher quality and for a higher price. He had built a large, loyal clientele at his prior employer. He saw and contacted those he knew well, and they quickly followed him to his new location. He funded the business with a 15-year small business loan of $15,000 that he was able to pay off in just two years. The collateral for the business was his car and his photography equipment.

Keith likes to say he learned at the school of hard knocks. When he started the business he had no concept about even the most basic of things, such as who pays for fixing up a new business location. He learned the hard way how to negotiate everything his business needed.

Today he runs his business out of a 4,600-square-foot facility. One of the beauties that results from photographing children is that they keep getting older, necessitating more pictures. Today he photographs the babies of those folks he used to photograph as children. He has two assistants that help him in the studio. One does the books and helps with the sessions. It can be an exhausting process trying to arrange babies to look good and happy. The other assistant helps with the production side of the business. After Keith takes the pictures, the family comes by to select the ones they want by looking at each on a digital screen. He sends the selected pictures to a production house to actually be produced. Up to this stage everything has been digital. The assistant works with the production house to ensure that the photographs are exactly as desired. She also works with packaging the pictures so that they are presented well and deals with the customers as they close the transactions. The firm also provides custom framing services for its customers. Keith's costs for framing are about one-third of what an art studio would charge. However, this part of the business is designed mostly as a convenience service to the customers, not as a high profit center.

The business markets itself via word of mouth. In addition, with Keith's focus on doing higher-priced, higher-quality photographs, he performs key volunteer work for social organizations as a means of getting his name out. One such function in this southwestern city is a ball that raises funds for a variety of charities. The ball organizers take photographs from the event and place them in a memory book for all key donors. Keith volunteers his time and photography skills. The reality is that when people come in to his business to pick a photograph for the memory book, they often buy pictures for themselves or their families. This has also introduced Keith to some of the wealthiest people in the city. The other major marketing effort he volunteers at also builds an e-mail list of potential clients. He encourages them to come in to the studio and take seasonal pictures. For example, he will offer pictures with Santa Claus at Christmas or bunnies and chickens at Easter. The result of these seasonal promotions is that he gets several very full weeks of photography sessions. He generally does not do school pictures, principally because that business tends to be highly competitive, mass production oriented, and cost focused.

As is often the case with small business people, Keith has learned a lot about how to run a business. He is now focusing on new streams of business. For example, he is setting up a blog on Google. Google charges each blogger a small fee to be listed on the sidebar as a firm or blog that deals with a given issue. In Keith's case this is dealing with Photoshop, including ways that others can do great things to a photograph such as take a photograph and turn it into a line drawing. The blogger pays a nickel for each person that clicks on his blog. Within the blog, there are firms that sell a given product or service. Each time one is clicked by someone who came to the site, the blogger earns money, and if someone buys something from him, then of course the blogger earns much more. Keith's goal is to earn several thousand dollars a month from this service.

Keith is also working on developing a franchise system that creates video resumes. He will bring the technical skills to this process, and will have a small ownership in each franchise sold while also being paid for the production of the videos. He can hire someone part time for $10 an hour to perform the basic work and then make the person full time when the business can fully support her. This is one of the opportunities that has the potential to produce a large income stream, but it depends on how the concept develops.

Keith also keeps his hand in photographing bands. He is now on the road taking pictures of a top rap star that has several leading singles. While not a major income stream for Keith, this does provide part of a lifestyle that Keith really enjoys. That is one thing Keith is very clear on: You do not have to be a conformist to be a successful small business person. Keith had his hair down to the middle of his back until very recently. He actually believes you need to be different to see some of the great opportunities that are out there.

Keith has a number of good suggestions for students looking to start a business.

1. Get a degree in business. He did not, and instead learned over time in the school of hard knocks. The money that those lessons cost him could have easily been saved.

2. Always pay the IRS. Never get in trouble with them. Interest and penalties just keep accruing. Obtain a good accounting software program and good accounting services to support you.

3. Find good people and delegate as much as you can. Keith could do photography 24 hours a day, 7 days a week. What tires him out is running the business aspects that go with it.

4. Keep technologically up to date. Everything changes constantly. You would think photography would be a mature industry. It is in a constant state of change and adaptation.

5. Always watch your competition and steal unmercifully. These ideas are not patented; look at what competitors are doing and match it if it fits with your business.

learning outcomes

After studying this chapter, you will be able to

9.1 Identify key financial issues involved with starting a business.

9.2 Discuss the basics of funding a business.

9.3 Explain the importance of proper accounting when starting a business.

Financing and Accounting

AIRBORNE, INC.

 Starting a new venture takes not only a creative idea, but often creative funding as well. Such was the case with Airborne, Inc. It was founded by Victoria Knight-McDowell, a second-grade teacher who was tired of getting every cold that her students brought to class; she embarked on a quest to help prevent colds in the first place. Having found standard cold medicines relatively ineffective, she experimented throughout the 1990s with various herbal, vitamin-based, and mineral-based (zinc, selenium) formulas. After going two years without a cold, she realized that she had hit upon an effective formula.

Using that formula, the company was formed and sold its first packages to a local drugstore. However, to sell more than locally, the business needed capital. That money came to it in an unusual form. Victoria's husband, screenwriter Rider McDowell, received a payment for writing and producing a movie. The couple decided to invest that money in the business and Airborne became a reality.

Sales were so slow at the beginning that Victoria and Rider would take turns going into the drugstores and buying Airborne just to get some turnover in the product so that the stores would keep stocking it. The couple cashed out all of their retirement savings and invested them in the company. They gambled on the business and its opportunity for success. Less than a year later, the company received its first big order—from Trader Joe's, for 300 cases (a $75,000 order). At that time Victoria was only working with the company part time and was still affixing labels individually. The product has since exploded in demand and is now available at Walmart, Rite Aid, Albertsons, Osco Drug, Trader Joe's, Walgreens, and other stores.

In 2008, the company agreed to stop claiming that its product could prevent colds and paid out a substantial sum in a class action lawsuit filed against the company. The company now simply claims that the product helps boost your immune system. Demand for the product continues to expand, and Victoria's and Rider's faith in their business has proven itself.

Source: www.airbornehealth.com; Rachel Konrad, "Out of the Cold: Teacher Serves Up Possible Remedy", *LA Daily News*, February 24, 2003; www.drugstore.com; www.naturallydirect.net; April Y. Pennington, "Cold Gold: Striking a Blow in the Age-Old Quest to Find a Cure for the Common Cold," *Entrepreneur Magazine*, March 2003 (www.entrepreneur.com); "Airborne Settles Lawsuit for $23.3 Million," CNNMoney.com, March 4, 2008.

Financing the start of a new business and establishing the accounting systems are central operational concerns in the start-up of a new business. In Chapter 6 we examined the basic financial analysis (on a pro forma basis) that should be used to evaluate the decision to start a business. Now we must consider the specific financing and accounting issues that impact the operational start-up of the business. Specifically, three questions are examined in this chapter:

1. How will the small business person fund the new business, and what funding level is really needed for the new venture?

2. What accounting records will you maintain, and how will you maintain them?

3. How will you manage the paper/data flow of the new company?

All of these issues are directly related to the establishment of the financial structure and record keeping of the new company. Too often new businesspeople put these issues at the bottom of their priority list (both during and after start-up) and do not devote much time to them. However, it is far easier to establish items such as a sound system to account for the transactions of the business at the beginning of the venture. Some forethought on the process will save lots of frustration after the business is up and running. This is illustrated by Philo's experience.

EXERCISE 1

1. Did Philo do the right thing by agreeing to host the event for the bank?

2. What would you advise the owners to do now regarding their accounting issues?

LO 9.1 Identification of Key Issues

As you read about Philo in this chapter, you will see that the firm's focus was on the shortcomings with its accounting systems. However, there are also a wide range of issues that new businesses need to be aware of that are related to financing of the start-up. The issues we address in this chapter are not ordered by their importance; instead these issues are intertwined with each other. The first is the funding and funding level of the firm. The next is the establishment of an accounting system. Finally, the flow of information in the new business needs specific attention. If the new business does not address these issues very early on in the process, then the owners will constantly be putting out fires related to these items rather than focusing on building the firm.

To demonstrate how these various issues interconnect, consider the case of Philo on the next page. You will ultimately see that the issue the owners were most concerned with related to their need for an effective means of accounting. This really stood out when they did not know the true cost of any individual item in their business (an important issue in this business). In developing a bid for the bank's work, the owners had not included the cost of hiring temporary workers to handle short-term event opportunities, and they had not figured on the need to purchase additional serving items that weren't in the plan for a standard restaurant. The opportunity to showcase their business as well as gain the event-based business was not something they had originally targeted in their business plan. In effect, Philo was diverting its focus from its business plan during its first days of operation and doing so without a clear idea of what it was actually getting involved with. Whether this catering was really an opportunity or not was truly unknown.

Philo had made the initial steps to make the new business a reality. The owners had established a bank relationship with the region's largest bank, found a place of business, obtained the required business licenses, and begun operations (they opened for business on a very limited dinner schedule to test out their systems). In this process they were spending money and receiving invoices. They were busy with the details of starting a business, but quickly realized that they needed a means to track their transactions. For the first few weeks they simply kept a classic accounting T-chart with all the expenses on one side and all the income (of which there was very little) on the other. During this time they also received their first bank statement and, more important, a call from someone in the bank who had gotten their name from their loan officer. The bank had decided to hold a series of evening events to kick off a new marketing program. The bank made a policy of supporting its customers and wanted to reserve the whole Philo facility for three straight nights for the marketing events.

The founders traveled to the bank and worked out a wonderful deal to host up to 210 people per night for three consecutive nights. There were to be 70 people at three times each night: 5:00–7:00 p.m., 7:00–9:00 p.m., and 9:00–11:00 p.m. The events would kick off in less than a week and Philo would require a substantial amount of additional help to make the events a success. The bank agreed to pay one-fourth of the total price up front, with the remainder payable within 30 days of the last event day. Doug and Jennie thought they would play it very safe and charge 100 percent more than all the costs they could think of. A contract was quickly signed and the two entrepreneurs began to prepare for the events.

Doug and Jennie were thrilled to get the business and went straight back to develop a plan for the logistics. They initially thought they could run ads and hire workers. However, as they thought more about this, they realized they did not have time. They contacted several temporary ("temp") agencies and began to realize that their cost estimates were not accurate when they found out the hourly rate that they were going to have to pay to get workers. They hired 24 people via one of the temp agencies. It was as they dealt with the temp agency that they realized the need to bring in all of these workers ahead of the event so that they could be trained. They calculated how much food had to be ordered for the event, quickly realizing that the food costs alone were more than 40 percent of the total amount that they had quoted the bank for the total event. They had thought they understood the costs well before they went to the bank. The food supplier had a policy with new restaurants that required full payment up front for the first 90 days that they did business together. After that time period, the supplier would start extending a 2/10, Net 30 policy to them. 2/10 meant that Philo could get a 2 percent discount on its purchases if the restaurant paid its bill within 10 days, and if the bill was not paid during that 10 days, then the full amount would be due in 30 days. However, for this event, all of the food had to be paid for up front.

The founders had reacted very quickly when the opportunity arose to host this event. However, when they returned to the restaurant and began discussing what they had done, they increasingly realized that they were not so sure that they had gotten a good deal. It would certainly be a great marketing effort if they pulled it off, but financially it was going to really test their cash flow.

1. They knew basics of food cost and preparation, but they had not effectively accounted for the dramatic increase in hiring that would be necessary. These hires were untrained and cost substantially more than they had counted on in their business plan projections.

2. Kitchen space was yet another concern. They had no real experience in estimating their space needs. They would need to store items in various states of readiness and needed lots of room for active preparation. The plan did not anticipate a restaurant that was packed each night, turning over completely three times in a night.

3. They would need to purchase a number of unique items to handle catering a party as opposed to dealing with sit-down guests. These items could be used again if the need arose, but how much and what to buy was all new to them.

4. The opportunity to use their facility for special events had never occurred to them. This now seemed like a potentially lucrative area, providing they could price the events correctly. They would have to acquire all the things necessary to run an event except for the expertise.

(continued)

The founders began to realize that they needed to track every item that was sold individually so that they could tell if their plan for a 100 percent markup would in fact cover their other costs. This deal had been put together on the fly, and they had no idea how much food would be consumed. The owners soon realized that their business was a lot more complex than they had initially realized and they needed to have a much better system to track all of their finances. The current system left them with no means of tracking the total costs of their food, preparation, and delivery. The realities of the business were facing them.

Doug and Jennie called an accountant they found in the phone directory. This individual told them that maintaining accurate records was going to be critical and the sooner they got a computer accounting package and used it, the better. The accountant recommended a straightforward package that was available at most office supply stores and was easily understood. They quickly acquired the package and went about learning it and setting up all of the business records. The result was that they were learning the system and seeking to adapt it to their needs while at the same time getting ready to run a restaurant and what appeared to be a large catering business. The founders were behind the curve spending valuable time taking care of financial and accounting issues, which was something they probably should have done prior to actual start-up.

Extra expenses, especially early on in a business's life when no (or virtually no) income is coming in, can quickly use up the cash intended to found and grow the business. By the time Philo pays for all the additional expenses related to this opportunity, the restaurant could well be out of cash. How much initial funding does a business need in order to survive the first year of operation? What type of financial cushion should be in place to help buffer the business when an unexpected cost like the one facing Philo arises? Central to a financial cushion is the nature of the firm's funding. When considering funding, the firm needs to evaluate not only the amount provided but also the sources of that funding. A key aspect of how the funding will be used is found in the information provided by the business, and that comes through the accounting system and the data flow management. Thus, all of these issues are interconnected and will be discussed in turn.

LO 9.2 Funding

Funding for almost any new business starts with the founder(s) and her own resources. However, at some stage (often prior to actual start-up), the firm will need to find other sources of funding. These sources may be small and receive no equity (ownership) interest in return for the funding. This funding may be a line of credit, where a person or a bank agrees to help finance certain functions for the business. This party is paid back with interest as the supplies are used and the money is received from the customer. The line of credit can go up and down, therefore, as the need for supplies rises and falls and the account is repaid. In contrast, others will make **equity investments,** where someone provides funding in return for some ownership in the firm. Each of these types of funding will be reviewed in turn. First, those funding sources that do not require equity in the firm will be reviewed. Then we will review equity investments, and then we will examine alternative

equity investment

Funds received by a business in exchange for a percentage ownership of the business.

sourcing tools. Separately the chapter will review how much funding the firm should ensure it has at the outset of the business.

Non-Equity Funding

There are several principal sources for non-equity capital to start a business. Debt is a major source of such non-equity financing and can come from banks, credit cards, asset leasing, and/or suppliers. Grants are another type of non-equity method that some businesses will have access to. A grant may come from the government or a nonprofit agency; it is simply money designed to help the new business begin operations.

Debt Debt comes in many forms, each with positives and negatives for a new business. Debt is any form of dollar infusion that must be paid back with interest. Debt allows the new business to manage its cash flow for various peaks and valleys in the operation of a business, or more important, to handle the disparity between when goods must be purchased and when money will be received from a customer to pay for those goods. The most common forms of debt for small businesses can be classified as follows:

debt
A generic term to describe any type of non-equity funding tied to the business.

1. Loans from
   a. Bank or finance company
   b. Individuals
   c. Founders
2. Credit cards
3. Supplier credit

Loans A **loan**, regardless of its origin, involves a contractual agreement whereby the business receives some amount of money that must be repaid over a specified period of time at a specified interest rate. Loans are repaid monthly from cash flow and, especially early in the life of a business, are secured by an asset or personal guarantee. In the case of dissolution, debt generally must be paid back prior to any equity investors receiving a distribution.

loans
Contractual agreements whereby the firm receives some amount of money that must be repaid over a specified period of time at a specified interest rate.

Banks have traditionally been a major source of funds for established firms but are quite restrictive in their lending to start-up firms, since the risk is perceived to be too high. However, there are some specific ways that banks lend to new businesses. For example, banks will make loans for the purchase of some types of equipment. In this type of lending, the bank will estimate the residual value of the equipment if the bank had to repossess the equipment and then lend the business a percentage of the difference between that number and the sale price. This discount is typically quite significant. This type of lending is referred to as **asset-based lending.** As discussed in Chapter 8, a relationship with a bank is critical to the small business's ability to obtain bank financing.[1]

asset-based lending
A loan provided for the purchase of a necessary asset for the business.

Banks will also lend money for the establishment and maintenance of inventory by arranging a revolving line of credit. A lender will periodically perform an on-site examination of the inventory to ensure that the inventory is being used properly. A particular problem with lines of credit for inventory is that a firm may have old inventory that has not been sold for a period of time. Such inventory needs to be discounted, as its value in the market has shrunk. Too often firms still reflect that old inventory on their books at full market value.

Individuals are also a wonderful source of funding for the firm. For example, loans can come from friends and family. While the conditions may be a bit more relaxed, the small business owner should view the loan as he would one from a bank. One issue to consider in such loans is that if the business fails, the inability to repay such loans can permanently rupture the family relationship or friendship.

The founder(s) of the business may also choose to lend money to the firm themselves. While it may strike some as odd to lend money to your own firm, debt is a secured investment. Therefore, if you lend your firm $1,000, then you, along with the other debt holders, have the right to the firm's assets if the firm fails to pay off that debt. An equity investor generally receives only those proceeds that are left after paying off all other debts.

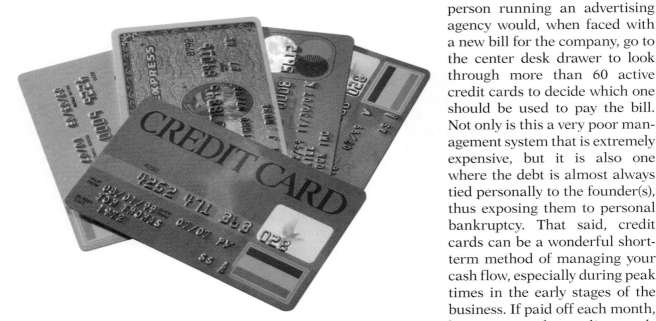

What are the risks and rewards of using credit cards when financing a business?

credit card

Card entitling one to revolving credit that is not tied to any particular asset, does not have a set repayment schedule, and is usually tied to a much higher interest rate than that of a bank loan.

Credit Cards Credit cards are another form of non-equity investment. A **credit card** is another type of credit. However, a credit card is not tied to any particular asset, nor does it have a set repayment schedule (other than a minimum payment), although it is usually tied to a much higher interest rate.

We have worked with a number of small businesses that decided early on to finance their operations with credit card debt. One small business person running an advertising agency would, when faced with a new bill for the company, go to the center desk drawer to look through more than 60 active credit cards to decide which one should be used to pay the bill. Not only is this a very poor management system that is extremely expensive, but it is also one where the debt is almost always tied personally to the founder(s), thus exposing them to personal bankruptcy. That said, credit cards can be a wonderful short-term method of managing your cash flow, especially during peak times in the early stages of the business. If paid off each month, business-issued credit cards provide the company with an excellent financial tracking system that can be divided up by individuals within the company, and payment can be delayed by up to 25 days, allowing for a unique positive cash flow situation. However, the small business must be able to carefully manage such debt if it is going to be employed.

Supplier Credit Supplier credit is another form of non-equity funding that is available.[2] Suppliers will generally provide credit on both physical assets (refrigerators, molding equipment, etc.) and the actual supplies purchased. A firm such as IBM Credit Llc is an example of a firm that you may be familiar with that exists primarily to fund the acquisition or lease of IBM products. The credit terms offered by such firms can be quite generous, but they are a liability for the company and need to be managed as such. Accepting **supplier credit** ties you to that supplier, limiting your ability to shop around for a cheaper source. The terms can be quite generous and the rates are usually more competitive than those available from traditional bank sources.

Grants The new small business should also explore **grants** from both governmental and private foundation sources. There are special funds that are neither equity nor debt funds that are designed to aid businesses in specific areas. These grants typically target disadvantaged groups, economic areas, or particular industries. There are also grants for target groups such as veterans. The presence of such grants varies widely based on the given funding year and where you live. Grants should be explored through groups such as your local Small Business Assistance Center.

Equity Funding

The new business should employ all non-equity funding mechanisms available to it. In the long run (assuming a successful business operation), the cost of such capital is generally less than that of equity investment. However, a growing small business might need to seek equity funding (investors' or founders' capital).

In the founding process, the business generally receives funds from the founder(s) as well as other investors. An evaluation is needed to determine the percentage of ownership each founder will have in the business and the percentage that will be reserved for investors. We will cover valuation of the business in Chapter 13, and we recommend that prior to allowing any nonfounder to invest in your new business, you have a fair and valid estimation of the value of your company. That said, we would like to address several key issues related to equity financing of the new business with outside sources.

Obtaining equity investment from investors has a number of potential operational impacts. Investors can be active or passive, majority or minority, companies that might ultimately wish to buy the whole new venture, and/or suppliers looking to add new volume for their products. Each of these potential sources has characteristics that can have a major impact on your business. Additionally, accepting an equity stake from an outside investor adds a dimension of accountability to the founding of a new business and opens the new venture up to new concerns. Therefore, seeking outside funding is a significant decision for the small business.

To illustrate the impact of outside investors, we worked with an entrepreneur who started a new high-end restaurant. The initial investment needed to make the venture work was substantial and well more than the founder could invest. She sought outside investors for the business from her country club, social friends, and business acquaintances. She ended up with 47 total investors with separate investments that varied from $8,000 to $110,000. The restaurant was built and opened to great fanfare. Thursday, Friday, and Saturday nights were packed, with an average wait for a table of two hours. The founder worked nonstop on those evenings, but had continuous problems with her fellow "investors." A number of these investors felt that they deserved preferential treatment

supplier credit
Another form of non-equity funding that is available. Suppliers often will provide credit on both physical assets (refrigerators, molding equipment, etc.) and the actual supplies provided.

grants
Special funds, neither equity or debt, that do not require repayment and are designed to aid businesses in specific areas.

at the restaurant since they were "owners." Many of them demanded special favors, such as being placed first in the wait list for a table; walking through the kitchen (not a helpful thing to do on busy nights); talking to the chefs; or even having their meals "comped" (received for free). Some investors similarly felt free to discuss employee performance with the individual employees. These individuals would also call at will to talk to the founder about the restaurant's direction, as well as expecting to be able to meet with the founder at their convenience. The small business owner finally had a meeting with all of the investors to lay out the problems involved with their behavior and the disruption to the success of the business. Several of the investors were indignant and demanded their investment be returned. This the business could not afford, and legally, it did not have to comply with their request. The result was fractious relations with some investors, and an enormous amount of time being taken away from the business to handle "bruised egos." A little care in the initial setup of these relations could have prevented a series of problems later in the operation.

Equity investment involves selling a percentage of the business to an outside party. This should be done in consultation with an attorney who is well versed in this area of the law. The founder(s) must be very clear that in the case of dissolution, each investor is entitled to the percentage of the break-up value equal to his investment percentage of ownership. However, even more critical to the success of the business is to carefully and clearly outline what rights and expectations each investor has as the business grows. Will the new venture divide up all profits at the end of each year? What will be retained in the business for future growth? How can each investor "sell" her shares? Does the company have first right of refusal? Working with an attorney to develop a clear document that details all of the concerns about an equity investor should be completed prior to approaching a potential investor.

As previously mentioned, the sources of equity investment include other firms, venture capitalists, and business angels.

Intel is an active equity investor in start-up firms. What are the pros and cons of equity investment from a firm like Intel in a new small business?

Businesses as Equity Investors Many established businesses are willing to make equity investments in other start-up firms. Large firms such as Microsoft, Intel, and Cisco have traditionally been among the most active equity investors in new start-up firms in the technology sector. Of two scenarios that we have dealt with regularly, one type involves a company that will invest in a new venture with the idea of ultimately purchasing the operation. The second type is a large supplier that is willing to invest in a new operation as an additional outlet for its products.

The company that invests with the idea of an ultimate purchase does so because it is one of the least expensive means for trying out new ideas/products/methods. For the established company to try to develop every idea in-house, it would have to redirect significant resources away from the core focus of its business. Instead, the large business invests in a series of businesses that are trying new things within its industry, and in effect, it has taken out a series of strategic options without having to detract from its core business.[3] Those options that turn out to be successes are then purchased and brought into the core organization. This can be a wonderful harvest strategy for a newly founded business; however, the founder(s) may not wish to sell the business at the exact point in time that the larger company wishes to close the sale. Depending on the nature of the investment, the founder(s) may not have the option to decide when the business is sold.

Having a supplier invest in your new business is somewhat simpler, in that the supplier is generally not trying to run your business, nor looking to take the business over if it does particularly well. Instead, the issue with this type of equity investment is one of restriction. The deal usually involves an exclusivity agreement to use only that supplier's products. This can be a significant (and in some cases a business-killing) proposition. The founder(s) must be careful not to trap themselves into an agreement that prevents flexibility that may be needed in the future.

Venture Capital (VC) A form of equity investment that seems to garner considerable press is venture capital. A **venture capital fund** is a fund that is usually organized as a limited partnership.[4] Limited partners in the fund, which may include very wealthy individuals, insurance companies, other businesses, and retirement funds, invest in such funds seeking high-returns. The general partner in the fund is the venture capitalist, who then investigates and invests in each new business. Venture capitalists might invest in less than one out of the thousand business plans they see in a year. They are seeking extremely high-growth businesses that have an opportunity to "cash out" with an IPO or sale to a larger company within a relatively short period of time. The result is that it is extremely rare for a VC to invest in a small business. Additionally, VCs are looking to make a significant investment, generally something greater than $1,000,000. As such, they are not a source of funding for very many small businesses, and we spend very little time in this text on venture capital.*

venture capital fund
A fund that is organized to make significant equity investments in high-growth new ventures.

Business Angels Business angels are a form of equity investors that are more widely available to small businesses. **Business angels** are high-net-worth individuals that invest widely in businesses.[5] These individuals may include small business people that have built one or more businesses and have cashed out (i.e., sold their businesses and have the excess cash in hand), executives with large organizations that have high incomes, professionals such as doctors and lawyers, and individuals with significant inheritances. These individuals can be very helpful sources of expertise and contacts in the area. However, the small business person should seek individuals that have relevant knowledge (not just money) to add to the firm. When seeking investment from such individuals, we suggest that you evaluate the nature of their advice, how intrusive they will be, the nature of their business experience, and what other contacts and relationships the angels may have that can help the new firm.

business angels
High-net-worth individuals that invest in businesses not as a business, but as an individual.

Other Financing Tools

There are several other financing tools that are available to the new business as it starts. These mechanisms include asset leasing and factoring.

---

* If the student wishes to locate more information on venture capital and venture capitalists in his or her area, the National Venture Capital Association is an excellent source of information.

Asset lease

A form of lease tied to a particular asset used by a business to conserve cash and maintain the latest versions of whatever equipment is available.

Asset Leasing A form of funding for a new organization is an **asset lease** arrangement. Similar to leasing a car, many of the assets needed by the new business can be leased from the manufacturer, or from a third-party reseller. Instead of owning the assets, the company simply leases what it needs. In fact there are companies (third-party resellers) that have a significant part of their inventory in equipment that they lease to other companies. The advantages are relatively straightforward. The new business is able to acquire the assets that it needs to begin operations with a minimal cash outlay. The company pays the lease from production that is a direct result of using the equipment that it has leased. Furthermore, it is not stuck with an aging asset. As newer, higher-quality machines become available, the small business is able to trade up.

The big disadvantage to leasing is that over time the small business may spend more money for equipment maintenance than if it had bought the unit outright. However, the net present value of the lease may actually work out to a net positive since the small business person does not have to put as much cash initially into the lease as in a purchase. Therefore, the decision should evaluate two areas: (1) How much cash does the new business have to invest in equipment up front? and (2) Given the pace of equipment obsolescence in that industry, would it be more advantageous to lease or own the equipment needed to operate the business?

Factoring With the exception of new businesses that operate strictly on cash, as the business begins to make sales it will generate accounts receivable—that is, sales that have been made, but not yet paid for. If the firm needs to generate cash in the short run, then these accounts can be sold at a discount via a technique known as **factoring.** There are numerous businesses that provide this service. They will discount the dollar amount of such accounts based on the quantity and quality of the receivables. The quality of the receivables is determined by such issues as: (1) who owes the small business the money; (2) the debt age; (3) the size of the transaction; and (4) the debtor's credit rating. For example, if a blue-chip firm like IBM or a government entity owes you the money, there is a virtual 100 percent chance of being paid. In contrast, if your accounts receivables are from a small building contractor (an industry segment with a considerable history of turnover), then the accounts will be more heavily discounted. The benefit for the small business person is that he gets the money from his accounts receivable immediately. Aside from obtaining the cash up front, the small business also does not have to spend time and effort trying to collect the accounts receivable. The negative is that the small business will not receive the full amount of the bill that is due to it.

factoring

Accounts receivable that are sold at a discount to another company in order to receive immediate cash.

Initial Funding

The new businessperson needs to calculate how much money she will need to acquire prior to start-up. Although it would appear that more initial funding would be somewhat better than less, it must be tempered by what the founder has to give up to obtain the money. In Chapter 6 we examined the financial issues associated with breakeven and basic cash flow analysis. The complexity of capital funding increases substantially as the new business requires external investment in order to begin operations.

To calculate the maximum amount that you may wish to obtain in outside financing, recall from Chapter 6 that we recommend that the small business founder calculate his entire cash flow projection without adding in any equity investment and look for the point where the ending cash balance is at its lowest point. A safe rule of thumb suggests taking that number and multiplying it by 150 percent. The resulting amount is what we recommend for the initial equity or equity-plus-debt investment. The new businessperson then connects this amount with the percentage of the firm that he previously determined would be made available to other investors. The two points frame the new businessperson's investment parameters. Consider the following example:

Value of the Firm Prior to Beginning Operations (See Chapter 14)	$100,000
Lowest Point in Projected Cash Flow	$ 20,000
Required Investment	$ 30,000
Amount Invested by Founder	$ 10,000
Amount Needed from Outside Investors	$ 20,000
Potential Percentage of the Business to be Expected by Investors (20,000/100,000)	20%

It is important to remember that negotiations between the founder(s) and your investor are just that, negotiations. It takes two willing parties to reach an agreement. You may see the investment in your firm as worth X, while an investor sees it as worth Y. It will take negotiation to determine the ultimate value. A review of Chapter 14's discussion of valuation and negotiation should be helpful in conceptualizing these issues.

EXERCISE 2

1. How much funding will you need for your new business?
2. How do you plan to fund the new business?
3. What assumptions have you made regarding your funding?

LO 9.3 Accounting

We do not presume in the next few pages to show you how to do all of the accounting that you will ever need to know to manage your business. There are many fine texts and courses available that focus tightly on this huge and complicated area of business. Furthermore, we covered the basics regarding the balance sheet and income statement in Chapter 6. That said, we would like to suggest that the needs of most small business people are very straightforward and can best be met with one of the numerous computer software programs available.

The new businessperson will need to quickly decide whether she will use a cash- or accrual-basis accounting system. In its simplest form, cash-based accounting recognizes expenses as they are paid and recognizes revenue as it is generated. Accrual-based accounting is the more typical form of accounting utilized, with expenses and revenues being recorded when they apply, regardless of when the cash is received. This type of accounting must be used if you have inventory; if you have gross sales over $5 million per year; and if your business is a Subchapter C corporation, partnership, or trust. The end result is that only the smallest businesses use cash-basis accounting.

The small business person will need to carefully evaluate which accounting program would be the best for his business. We believe that the key to evaluating these programs is knowing what you want to accomplish and what you really need and do not need. All of the major programs have vast capabilities to enter, track, and produce financial information. Following is information about some of the top accounting programs for small business. This information will ground you in the major programs that are available.

Simply Accounting Accounting Software
Simply Accounting is the full-featured, entry-level accounting solution for small businesses, providing quick setup, ease of use, and payroll functionality. /www.simplyaccounting.com/

MYOB Premier Accounting Software
Premier Accounting's complete feature set includes sales, purchases, banking, inventory, payroll, and more. www.myob.com

QuickBooks Accounting Software
Quickbooks is a popular, full-featured accounting and payroll program designed for small businesses. QuickBooks is available in a suite of packages, from a quick start version to editions for accountants. http://quickbooks.intuit.com/

Peachtree Complete Accounting Software
Similar to Quickbooks, the Peachtree offerings run the gamut from simple online systems all the way to professional systems used by accountants. www.peachtree.com/

These are just four of the numerous accounting programs that are available to small business. Choosing a package that will be useful for your business is a process of understanding your new business first and then finding a package that will accommodate your needs with the least impact on the business. Most of the packages will provide any report that could be demanded by the owner(s), potential investors, auditors, or loan officers. Some of the key reports that the new businessperson should be prepared to generate include these: (1) chart of accounts, (2) petty cash register, (3) check register, (4) expense accounts, (5) inventory accounts, (6) accounts payable, and (7) payroll.

Chart of Accounts

The chart of accounts is the master system for tracking the activity of the business. It requires a bit of care up front in its establishment and will

ACCOUNT NUMBER	CATEGORY	ACCOUNT NUMBER	CATEGORY
10	Basic Tube	142	Office Supplies – Other
20	Premium Tube	150	Internet Supplier
30	Basic Service	160	Auto Leases
40	Unlimited Service	170	Insurance
101	COGS – Wooden Tubes	180	Advertising
102	COGS – Diodes	200	Payroll
103	COGS – Circuit Boards	201	Benefits
104	COGS – Resistors/Capacitors	210	Telephone (Cell and Office)
105	COGS – End Caps	220	Licenses
106	COGS – Packaging	300	Production Machinery
107	COGS – Shipping	310	Tools
120	Utilities	400	Building Mortgage
130	Security System	500	Payroll Taxes
140	Paper	510	State Taxes
141	Letterhead/Business Cards	520	Federal Taxes

Table 9.1
Chart of Accounts—
Electronics Manufacturer

need updating as the business grows. This chart is not complex; however, the new businessperson needs to ensure that the system designed provides the information necessary to analyze the business and its performance. This topic will be discussed more in Chapter 12 as we examine business performance of the going concern and ensure that the firm is performing as desired.

A chart of accounts is simply a listing of each type of activity (income or expense) and each type of asset within the company. The account number used is completely at your discretion, but income categories are usually first, expense categories next, and asset categories last. You may use two-digit or three-digit numbers as you wish and in accordance with the level of detail you anticipate in the future. There are usually far more expense categories than there are income categories. Table 9.1 shows the chart of accounts of an electronics manufacturer which displays some of the expense categories for the firm.

The new businessperson will want to leave room for new account detail to be put into the chart of accounts. As the business develops, you will find that you want to obtain additional detail, as new income/expense categories will appear. Notice that the chart tracks not only income and expense accounts but also asset accounts as well.

EXERCISE 3

1. Develop a preliminary chart of accounts for your new business.
2. Have fellow classmates review the chart and add/delete as necessary.

Petty Cash Register

There are numerous expenses that are simply too small to write a check for, and there are times when a check is simply inappropriate (for example, if you had pizza delivered for everyone because the whole group was working late to meet a deadline). A petty cash fund operates much like a bank savings account. The founder purchases a small lockbox and writes a check to "Petty Cash" for whatever amount she would like to keep on hand (this is not the same as cash register money, which should be handled as a separate deposit/expense account). A register is maintained to track the amount of money in the box, much like a savings account register. For example, if you decide that $100 is the amount that you would like to have on hand, you would start the box off with $100. As withdrawals are made, each is recorded and all change is put back in the box. The founder should be able to glance at the register and know exactly how much money is in the petty cash fund at any point in time, as well as know how the money has been spent. As it depletes, a new check should be written to "Petty Cash" to fill the box back up to the $100 level.

Check Register

As simple as it sounds, it is important to create a listing of all checks that have been written and all that have cleared through the bank. Today, with online banking and the ability to transfer data directly, this process has become quite easy. Regardless of how the entrepreneur might maintain his personal checking account, it is very important to record and balance the company account on at least a monthly basis.

Expense Accounts

Depending upon the volume of business that your venture processes, you will have either a daily or a weekly listing of expenses. These will allow the new businessperson to perform a monthly tracking of expenses and ultimately form an annual record of all expenses. The process requires you to have both your check register and your petty cash register available to record all outflow of funds. Credit card payments should be handled by recording the interest as an interest expense, recording the payment made to the account, and then recording each line item with a notation of "Visa," "MC," "Am. Ex.," etc., next to the expense. The only other expenses that are truly handled in a different manner are those related to travel. The IRS has very specific requirements related to the record keeping necessary in order to deduct these expenses.

Inventory Account

Any business that has even a small inventory should maintain an inventory record that lists a description of the item, the quantity, an item number, a unit cost, and a total cost. Inventory should be taken at scheduled times during the year and an exact match should be completed between starting inventory, units sold, and ending inventory. A second record should be kept to track inventory ordered and inventory received. It is a fact of business that **shrinkage** will occur. This reduction in inventory can come from poor record keeping on any of the fronts mentioned previously, but can also result from either employee or customer theft.

shrinkage

The difference between what is sold and what was brought into the business.

Accounts Payable

A separate accounts payable record should be maintained for each creditor. All invoices received should be recorded and a record of payment toward each invoice should be included (Date Paid, Amount Paid, and Check Number/Transfer Tracking Number).

Payroll

A payroll record should be maintained for every employee, tracking time for hourly employees and attendance for exempt (salaried) employees. Additionally, an employee record should be maintained that tracks every payroll check issued to the employee. This record will list all of the items that make up the check:

- Date
- Check number
- Number of hours worked (or 40, for exempt employees)
- Base pay
- Overtime hours worked
- Overtime pay rate
- Gross pay
- Taxes (federal, state, local, Social Security, and Medicare)
- Benefit deductions (if appropriate)
- Net pay

The software packages mentioned earlier have the ability to produce all of these documents plus many more. These become both the control documents and the input documents to produce your financial statements (Cash Flow, Balance Sheet, and Income Statement).

One additional statement is a must-have for most small businesses and directly results from the effective collection of all this information: the **Profit and Loss Statement (P&L Statement).** This statement represents your business performance over time. It is a quick, easily understood document that should be prepared monthly. An example is shown in Table 9.2.

Developing and maintaining effective records is essential in the operation of a business, and some forethought to the process and needs of the business will pay off in the knowledge and understanding developed by the founder(s). We will examine a number of analysis tools in Chapter 12, but for analysis to have any value, good records must be kept.

profit and loss statement (P&L statement)

A financial statement that summarizes the revenues, costs, and expenses incurred during a specific period of time.

Managing Data Flow

The new businessperson needs to recognize that small businesses will differ in the time frame that they need to obtain data. The founder(s) should seek to visit with other similar firms and find out what reasonable time frames might be for the monitoring of data. The experience of other firms can be very helpful in the start-up phase of your business.

Table 9.2
Profit and Loss Statement

PROFIT & LOSS STATEMENT

Period:		Month		
Income	Gross Sales	$114,560.00		
	Less COGS	$ 34,900.00		
	Net Sales		$ 79,660.00	
	Other Income		$ 13,400.00	
	Total Income		**$93,060.00**	
Expenses	Acct #	120	$ 1,084.00	
	Acct #	130	$ 35.00	
	Acct #	140	$ 110.00	
	Acct #	141	$ 320.00	
	Acct #	142	$ 45.00	
	Acct #	150	$ 79.00	
	Acct #	160	$ 1,340.00	
	Acct #	170	$ 367.00	
	Acct #	180	$ 1,100.00	
	Acct #	200	$ 47,900.00	
	Acct #	201	$ 14,370.00	
	Total		$ 66,750.00	
	Misc. Expenses		$ 1,780.00	
	Total Expenses		**$68,530.00**	
	Profit (Pre-Tax)			**$24,530.00**

The path of well-established firms has been to aggressively use just-in-time (JIT) inventory. This method of management seeks to minimize excess capital investment in inventory. These firms seek to have inventory present only shortly before it is used. Small firms do not have the same complex data measurement methods of large firms, but they should be driven by the same basic philosophy. The key to this ability is obtaining data in a timely manner that is tied to the strategic needs of the organization. We worked with a restaurant that wanted to serve fresh vegetables and meats; however, the owner wanted to perform his inventory check only once a week. "Freshness" as a strategic position would dictate that the data collection cycle should be shortened. If deliveries are easy, then a high-turnover firm should monitor its inventory needs on a daily or every-other-day basis. The accounting system of a firm is a powerful tool that should be used as a fine-grained tool to provide data when and how it is needed.

EXERCISE 4

1. How could Alex have done a better job setting up the accounting system?
2. What kind of data flow system should Alex use to track his business?

rodriquez family auto repair shop

The Rodriquez family was luckier than most business founders, because not only did they have access to solid knowledge about starting new businesses, but they also were able to pool together the money for the business. Alex spent several weeks visiting an extensive line of relatives and friends of the family. Over that period of time, he was able to put together the entire $250,000 he estimated he needed to purchase the business and ensure its survival for the first year. He had more than 70 investors in the business. Some had invested as little as $250, while his uncle had invested $28,000.

Having cleared that hurdle, Alex faced a significant issue in the design of statements and tracking of funds in the business. He had no formal accounting training, and during several conversations with other entrepreneurs he had been told repeatedly to purchase an accounting software package—which he did. Not knowing what he might need for the business, Alex decided to just set up some rudimentary categories and then add new ones as

he needed. The business was developing nicely. He purchased the former Jones Auto Repair, which came with a lease that had seven more years before it would need to be renegotiated. While the business came with a lot of equipment, Alex was excited about the opportunity to buy the remaining things that he felt he needed on the used market. One of the parts suppliers told him about a big, national chain store that had closed less than 90 miles away. Alex contacted the agent handling the dissolution and was able to buy some of the store's more sophisticated equipment, which he really wanted for his business.

As the parts and equipment began arriving, Alex was simply too busy trying to set everything up to spend time entering all of the stuff into his accounting package. He wasn't worried because he had a good head for numbers and knew that he was right on track for what he had predicted for the business. He thought that he might ask his sister to enter the information from the invoices over the weekend. When he and his sister took a look at the invoices, the two of them quickly realized that Alex's temporary system was not very useful. There were bills that did not appear to be accurate, but no one had asked about them when the shipment of parts came in. Similarly, there were a few bills that had already gone past due.

summary

This chapter sought to examine two important operational issues directly tied to the start-up of a new venture. Obtaining sufficient initial funding is a key method to allow for the variances inherent in any business. We examined several means of obtaining that financing. We then examined the development of the firm's accounting system and method of data gathering/handling. Establishment of a quality method for data gathering at the outset will allow the founders to focus their efforts on the running of the business.

key terms

asset-based lending 179
asset lease 184
business angels 183
credit card 180
debt 179
equity investment 178
factoring 184

grants 181
loans 179
Profit & Loss (P&L) Statement 189
shrinkage 189
supplier credit 181
venture capital fund 183

review questions

1. How can using loans help the new business grow?
2. Explain the best use of credit cards in a new business operation.
3. What are the negative impacts of supplier credit on the new business start-up?
4. How can a new business take advantage of grants?
5. Why should a new businessperson be wary of equity investments by other companies?
6. How will venture capital impact a growing business?
7. What are the pros of having angel investors in a new business?
8. How can asset leases be used to improve the income generation of a new business?
9. Why might a business choose to factor its accounts?
10. How might a small business person find out how much her business is worth?
11. What factors impact how much equity a new business gives away for a set dollar investment?
12. How does a new businessperson utilize a P&L statement?
13. Why should a new business spend time setting up a chart of accounts?

individual exercises

1. Given the needs of your business, examine at least two widely available accounting packages and choose one for your business.
2. Why did you choose that one and not one of the others?
3. How robust is the package that you chose? Will it still be useful if your sales reach $1 million per year?

group exercise

In your group, take one of the companies that a group member is designing (or alternatively, use the Rodriquez Family Auto Repair Shop) and set up a spreadsheet in Excel (or other similar program) that will form the basic accounting system for the company. Here are suggestions for such a project.

1. Start with the Cash Flow Statement:
   a. Create a worksheet (tabs) for each of the 12 months and label each one.
   b. Enter all sources of income and all expenses that you can think of for January.
   c. Put in a formula to subtract expenses from income and determine the net cash flow.
   d. Copy January's data to the other 12 months and then modify any month that needs to be adjusted. Remember, this is just the start of the effort. You will have plenty of time to modify this spreadsheet as you develop the company.
   e. Create formulas on the Summary sheet to capture the data from the 12 months.
2. Repeat this process and create a Cash Budget.
3. Repeat this process again to create an Income Statement.

everyday edisons class discussion

Go to www.everydayedisons.com/ted.html and read about Ted.

1. What do you think is the type of debt and equity structure a business like this would need to have?

2. If you were a potential investor, what financial questions would you have for Ted?

Teresa Nelson—Teresa's Treasures

Teresa Nelson has overcome tremendous difficulties to start a successful small business. In 1992 she was in a terrible car accident while a senior in college. The accident resulted in the loss of her memory and all of her facial bones being broken. She was actually pronounced dead at the accident. She survived the car accident, but the university honors student with an IQ of 140 was reduced to having to learn to walk, feed herself, and talk all over again. This difficult journey included such things as having to color with crayons to bring back her coordination.

She was in the process of successfully overcoming the car accident when her doctors discovered a tumor on her brain stem. Given the difficulties that still remained from the car accident her doctors decided not to operate immediately, but to wait a year so that she would grow stronger. During that year the tumor grew to be the size of a softball. When they removed it, the resulting damage meant that once again she had to learn to walk, talk, and feed herself.

In an amazing success story, Teresa was able to complete college and obtained a job in investments. However, her continuing health problems resulted in her not being able to perform on her job, so in 1999 she took a leave. While at home, Teresa began to develop gift baskets for friends that contained items such as tea and candy. Over

a six-week period of time, what had begun as a few simple gifts for friends developed into a new business. The response to the baskets was so great that by Christmas of that year she had orders for over 1,200 baskets with essentially no advertising.

Today, Teresa Nelson and her firm, Teresa's Treasures, are in a pattern of consistent growth. In this gift basket industry there are numerous small competitors, but these firms typically go in and out of business. Nationally, there are only eight firms like Teresa's that have sales over $1 million, and Teresa's Treasures was named as one of the top 25 gift companies nationwide.

This growth has come from Teresa's focus and drive. The ability to overcome the difficulties she has faced has been significant and could only have happened with a strong level of commitment by her. However, there are many others that have supported her in this effort. One of her key mentors in the business was none other than Sam Walton of Walmart. While working in high school at the pharmacy at Walmart, she had the opportunity to meet and grow to know Sam. He was very generous with his time and support of her early in her career. One of the lessons she learned from him continues to be part of her core philosophy today: Treat your customers, suppliers, and employees like you would like to be treated and with respect. If you do that, almost everything else will take care of itself.

Teresa has also received strong support from her husband, Dennis, who works full time in transportation for a local bread company. He works second shift each day so he can spend the morning helping his wife with her business as vice president of distribution, overseeing deliveries and shipping. This support has helped to ensure the success of the business. Teresa's parents, Howard and Betty, are also supportive of the venture as the VP of operations and the VP of finance, respectively. Teresa still does very little advertising. Instead she relies on word of mouth and corporate awards for her success. Recently one award granted her billboards across the city for a year of free publicity. This low-cost approach in marketing has allowed her to sell her baskets at prices approximately 30 percent below those of her competitors. Teresa also maintains an active public speaking schedule. She speaks nationally on a wide variety of subjects, but is often called on to either talk about how to start and grow a small business or do motivational talks about overcoming adversity. These talks serve as great low-cost marketing tools for her business.

She wants potential small business owners to be aware of the numerous supports available in the community that provide advice and insight that can be helpful to a new entrepreneur. In the development of her own business, she was not aware of these supports and utilized very few of them. In hindsight she wishes she had known they were available. She is willing to help others, hoping that they do not face some of the difficulties she has had to overcome in starting a business, so she now volunteers as a counselor for the Fort Worth Business Assistance Center.

There are several key areas that Teresa advises new small business people to focus upon.

1. First is that the owner needs to have a vision of what she wants to accomplish. This vision is motivating for the small business person as well as for her employees. Those employees that understand what the owner is trying to accomplish will be the small business person's greatest asset and support in the process.

2. She also urges small business people to not become overwhelmed by the risk, because with risks come tremendous opportunities. A small business person might not want to plan, but the plan allows calculated risks, and should not be used to keep someone from trying. She highlights that the plans that a small business person ultimately develops should be both short term and long term. Thus, small business owners starting out need to plan for issues like the cyclical nature of their markets and the need for cash reserves to ensure they have time to build their businesses. (One of the classic mistakes that you will see this semester is that too many new businesses do not have sufficient cash reserves to ensure that the business has time to become established. A new business needs to double the estimated time that it will take to get the business to the point where revenue exceeds expenses.)

3. Lastly, she believes that small business people need to fully understand their market as they build their plans. She points out that for a small business person, great sources of information are other entrepreneurs in the industry who do not directly compete against the business. Competitors in your area may not want to share information with you, but if you are not a direct competitor, then most businesspeople are very willing to talk and share ideas and information with you. Other key sources of information as you plan your new business are your customers. Every businessperson needs to listen to his customers and find how to satisfy them. You are trying not only to sell to those customers but also to learn from them.

Teresa Nelson is a key part of her firm's success. That success builds not only from her but also from her key supports, such as her family. The success of the business also comes from her focus on planning, being proactive, and understanding the market.

Human Resource Management

learning outcomes

After studying this chapter, you will be able to

10.1 Explain the elements of human resources.

10.2 Discuss the process of hiring employees.

10.3 Analyze the means for retaining employees.

10.4 Determine the pertinent aspects of employee probation and firing.

10.5 Distinguish the unique aspects of human resources within a family business.

Military Service

 Jeff Forrestall is a Certified Public Accountant (CPA) and managing partner in a small (16-employee) accounting firm. Not only is Forrestall a small business person as a partner in the CPA firm, but in 2001 he and his wife opened a franchise operation of a child care center business. However, following the September 11th, 2001, destruction of the Twin Towers, as a reservist in the military he was called up to serve his country. He had no option but to go and leave his business interests.

As an owner of a business, he received no compensation for his absence other than his military pay. If Jeff had been an employee of the firm, the business would have had to let Jeff go and promise to have his job or a similar job available for him when he returned. Furthermore, many large employers make up the difference in pay between the deployed person's salary and that paid by the military. If a small business can prove that this absence caused a decline in its business, it can seek loans from the Small Business Administration to help. However, the business must show a measurable impact from the absence. Such impacts are more easily seen in manufacturing settings, where there are measurable units sold, than in a service firm like a CPA firm.

Forrestall's CPA firm includes other family members who have worked to cover his share of the load. However, as a small business owner, he recognizes that such obligations and requirements can have an important impact on the business. It is critical that every small business also recognize that it cannot discriminate against an individual who wishes to participate in reservist activities, even though there is this potentially negative impact on its business.

Source: Sloan, J. 2003. "Small Business Goes to War." *Fortune Small Business,* 13(2): 12–14.

philo asian grille

The restaurant was within a few weeks of opening and the founders of Philo hired 22 people to work in the restaurant. They were able to hire three experienced chefs, one of whom was a graduate of the California School of Culinary Arts and had trained at an Asian dumpling restaurant in Shanghai. The other two had specialized in Asian cuisine while receiving their cooking degrees—one at Johnson & Wales and the other at the Culinary Institute of America (CIA). All three were a bit temperamental, but seemed to get along well with one another during the interviews. The plan was that typically one chef would be in the kitchen at a time, but they needed to work well enough together that schedules and handovers in the kitchen would be smooth.

Two people were hired to assist in the kitchen, clean dishes, and give general assistance to the cooks. Two additional people were hired to serve the dining floor, bus tables, and be a general help in the restaurant itself. Eleven wait staff were hired to handle the dining room for the various shifts. Doug and Jennie planned to handle the host station, greeting people and ensuring that everything was running well in the restaurant. The last four employees hired were experienced bartenders, who would each work shifts based upon the needs of the business. The bartenders and wait staff would each keep their own tips and contribute 10 percent to a pool for the kitchen assistants and bus help.

While the chefs designed the procedures for the kitchen, Jennie trained the entire dining staff. She required that they start seven days before the official opening of the restaurant, and the training was set not only to discuss individual roles and learn the menu by heart, but also to refine the "means" by which she and Doug wanted the restaurant to run. Their approach was to stimulate the senses and calm the nerves. The place was to have energy about it where guests would feel extraordinarily taken care of and yet also feel comfortable enough to sit and relax. Philo wait staff was to be courteous, friendly, professional, and highly knowledgeable about both the food choices and also how to pair those with the appropriate drinks if requested. Jennie's goal was for all guests to be greeted within one minute of sitting down at their table, and for each guest to feel that the wait staff were taking care of only them in the restaurant.

The bar would specialize in wines selected to complement Asian food and also in Asian beers and cocktails. The lounge décor and contemporary furnishings, including plush sofas and loveseats, would offer a relaxing and inviting atmosphere for socializing. The welcoming atmosphere, engaging associates, modern Asian cuisine, and unique drinks would entice guests to visit often.

Problems with the staff started occurring almost immediately. Several of the wait staff were having significant problems dealing with each other, and their testiness was wearing on Jennie. On the day before their opening, Jennie decided that one of the wait staff (Jim) would be let go. Jim was not the only problem; Sarah was also troublesome. However, Jennie thought the removal of Jim and an admonishment to Sarah would solve the problem. Jennie and Doug both felt that this was probably a blessing in disguise. They needed to send an early message to their employees about collegiality, and this gave them that opportunity.

EXERCISE 1

1. Do you think letting Jim go would have a negative impact on the other employees?

2. What would be the impact of letting Jim go but not Sarah?

3. What could the owners have done to prevent such problems?

4. What are the potential legal implications that the owners should be worried about at this stage?

5. Do you think Sarah's behavior will change?

Human resource management includes the hiring, inspiring, and managing of personnel, which is one of toughest and yet most important functions for a new firm to develop. For example, hiring personnel that are consistent with your business strategy and style is critical to business success, since without them it is unlikely that you will be able to implement your strategy. Similarly, managing the firm's personnel so that you increase their skill development allows the firm to develop a key resource. This type of resource is one that other firms cannot easily copy and one that may in turn lead to better firm performance.[1] The business of simply meeting the basic legal requirements of your human resource function can be daunting—yet is insufficient for the firm to be successful. This chapter will explore the rich set of issues, both legal and nonlegal, that a start-up business must consider.

LO 10.1 What Is Human Resources?

Human resources has been defined in economics as the quantity and quality of human effort directed toward producing goods and services. What this means to a small business owner is far more than simply having the right number of people with the right skills for a particular job. As Philo discovered in the example on page 198, you can hire someone with the perfect skill set and still have problems. An organization is fundamentally its own small society which exists within a community or city. Why one person works at one particular company or another is often because of the quality of the society which the small business represents. The establishment of this small society requires a number of deliberate actions by the business founder.

The elements that this chapter will explore include these: hiring employees (job descriptions, job advertisements, discrimination, job interviews, testing, job offers); retaining employees (compensation and benefit systems, wages and hours requirements, performance reviews); and dealing with difficult employees (probation, firing). After dealing with these issues, the chapter will also examine several other issues specifically relevant to dealing with family in a business.

human resources

As defined in economics, the quantity and quality of human effort directed toward producing goods and services.

LO 10.2 Hiring Employees

To visualize how important hiring is to a small firm, compare the impact of one person in a large organization to that of one person in a small organization. If a large organization has 1,000 employees, one problem employee represents only 0.1 percent of its workforce. In a small firm with five employees, one employee causing problems represents 20 percent of the workforce. An unhappy person not working at full capacity will result in the small business person's spending an inordinate amount of time dealing with the problems caused by the troublesome employee. Thus, a poor employee has a triple impact on the small firm: (1) the owner's time is lost; (2) the organization does not fully benefit from the employee; and (3) the problems may bleed over to other employees. Where larger firms can absorb the resulting difficulties due to their built-in slack (excess resources), a small firm can be devastated by a bad hiring decision. The process of finding and hiring new employees is critical and should involve a series of deliberate steps.

Job Description

A **job description** does as it sounds: It describes the job that is to be filled. In a small business, this document is not meant to be a formal, highly structured document as it might be in a large corporation.[2] Nonetheless, we highly recommend that all positions that are hired into the business have a written job description. Too often small business people say they know what they want in an employee but never write

job description

Document that describes the job that is to be filled.

it down. The reason is probably multifold, including a lack of time, an unclear picture of the new position, or a desire to remain flexible for the right individual. However, the process of generating a job description will assist the founder immensely as he carefully considers the skills, background, and ability of a potential new hire. All too often, the small business person who fails to develop a job description ends up hiring someone because he "likes" the person.

Taking the time to write down those skills and capabilities will go a long way toward ensuring that all dimensions of the job are considered. For example, today the operation of a computer and the ability to do word processing is widespread. However, if you do not ask the job applicant if she has those skills, you may be unpleasantly surprised after hiring the person. You may even need to be more specific than simply saying you want those general skills. For example, you may need someone who can work particularly fast at typing or enter data into and use an Excel spreadsheet. However, the skills that the average person may have in these areas may not reach the level you need or work for the specific software program you possess. You will need to determine what skills are critical at the stage of hiring and those that you are willing to help develop after you hire someone.

In a similar vein, there is information you need to share with the potential employee. For example, if you require uniforms, will they be provided or are they an employee's responsibility? This kind of information may be seen by the founder as a small matter, but it may be enough to impact whether or not an employee will be happy in the job. Imagine the impact if an employee arrived on the first day only to be told that he was responsible for bringing in his own tools. When making a hiring decision, the new business person needs to consider whether there are skills not required today, but which may be needed in the near future. Putting the job description in writing helps in this process by ensuring that all the elements of the job are considered, as well as forcing the business owner to consider changes as the firm grows. A brief example is shown below:

Job Title:	Furniture Refinisher
Salary:	$26,500–$32,400 per year
Benefits:	Medical for employee is provided at no cost to the employee. Medical for family is provided whereby the employee pays a premium equal to the difference between the family-policy premium and the employee-only premium.
Vacation:	Two weeks of vacation will be earned after 6 months of employment.
Sick Days:	The individual will accrue 1 sick day for every 2 months of employment.
Description:	This individual will be responsible for evaluating, repairing, and refinishing a variety of office furniture, including desks, cabinets, file cabinets, bookcases, and chairs.
Skills:	Skills needed in woodworking, metal fabrication, upholstery, as well as general carpentry skills. Having completed a carpenter apprenticeship program is a plus.

Job Advertising

Once the small business owners have generated the job description, they need to try to attract the largest pool of applicants possible for the job. While word of mouth is a means to advertise for a job, we suggest that it is but one of many possible methods for attracting a wider audience. There are a variety of ways to advertise and a large number of organizations that can help promote information on your job opening at little or no cost. These include

- College placement offices
- Trade associations
- Employment agencies

Similarly, if the business is in a very visible location, then a sign can be posted outside the office.

A more expensive means to locate potential employees is a traditional help wanted ad, placed either in a newspaper or via an Internet employment site. These advertisements vary widely in cost and ability to reach the audience that you desire. Information from the advertising location on readership/viewership, statistics on reply rates, and rates charged are all important pieces of information for the small business person seeking to place an advertisement.

Finally, for very unique skill requirements, there are companies that do an extremely good job recruiting and placing people. These companies traditionally charge the company seeking to hire the employee, and that fee can range from a set fee to a significant percentage of the placed employee's first-year salary. As you can see, this can be very expensive, so the new business needs to clearly think through the benefits of casting a more professional net.

In writing the advertisement for the new hire, the small business person should keep it concise and oriented toward the basic information needed for a potential applicant to evaluate his qualifications for the position. However, there are thousands of generic advertisements placed every week that look identical to one another. You will want your advertisement to be distinct enough to stand apart so it will draw the attention of potential applicants. If possible, your ad should communicate the culture of the firm and your desire to have the right person join your organization. The advertisement should also express excitement about the business. Overall, remember to write the ad to sell the job and the business honestly to the potential employee. Even though many people who read the advertisement may decide that they are not qualified, you would like them to walk away with a positive view of the business from their reading of the advertisement.

The advertisement should ask applicants to submit a resume and a short list of references. Virtually all potential candidates will have resumes unless they are applying for the jobs at the very lowest skill levels. A deadline should be established for applying in order to fairly evaluate the applicants in comparison to each other. A typical wording might state, "The application deadline is January 15, 201X or until the position is filled." This allows a comparison across candidates after January 15th, but also allows for the possibility that no one will meet all of your requirements by the deadline.

EXERCISE 2

1. What jobs will be necessary in your new business during the first year?
2. Briefly outline the skills needed to handle each job.
3. Based on your cash flow statements, how much do you expect to invest in salaries/benefits during the first year?

---

discrimination

In the workplace, hiring, dismissal, level of pay, or promotions based on race, color, gender, religious beliefs, or national origin of the employee. Such actions are prohibited by federal and state laws.

Discrimination It is important in designing the advertisement that the firm be nondiscriminatory. Title VII of the Civil Rights Act prohibits **discrimination** in hiring, dismissal, level of pay, or promotions on the basis of race, color, gender, religious beliefs, or national origin. This law currently applies to all firms with more than 15 employees. However, there are also state laws that may apply to firms with fewer than 15 employees, plus other federal laws that put the small business person at risk even if the firm has fewer than 15 employees. Therefore, the small business should avoid any discrimination or even the appearance of discrimination. The adherence to a nondiscrimination posture takes effort by the small business.[3]

The small business should write job descriptions and advertisements in a nondiscriminatory manner. Terms like "salesman," "handyman," "young," or "counter girl" should be avoided. Antidiscrimination laws do not require that you hire any one particular person; however, you must give everyone an equal opportunity to be considered. The wide advertising of a job and the establishment of a job description will help the small business person establish that he acted in a nondiscriminatory manner. If you advertise widely, you have not prevented anyone from applying. The job description helps to ensure that all individuals are judged on the same basis.

Supreme Court rulings have played a huge part in how human relations function in modern business.

EXERCISE 3

1. Write an ad for a position in your new business.
2. Have your fellow classmates evaluate it for effectiveness and proper language.

Interview

Regardless of whether the candidate has or does not have a resume, you should ask each one to fill out an application for employment. It is important to establish set criteria for every applicant and to have the ability to track exactly who applied for each position. There are a variety of generic forms available at any office supply store or via any one of several software packages. We believe that at a minimum, the following information should be obtained in the application/interview process:

- Name, address, telephone numbers (home, cell), e-mail address (if applicable)
- Other addresses for the past three years
- Social security number (SSN)
- Driver's license number and state of issue
- Work history
- Date available for work
- Position for which the candidate is applying

- How the candidate heard about the job
- Education and training
- Professional organization memberships
- Any record of conviction and, if so, details of that conviction
- If not a U.S. citizen, the appropriate documentation authorizing the candidate to work. (Note that sometimes very good people will come and apply for a job and ask you to sponsor them. This typically requires several thousand dollars, which the applicant may be willing to pay. You as a business owner will have to be willing to take the time to act as a sponsor. You will also have to verify that this job requires some unique set of skills that only this person has.)
- References

Once the candidate pool has been set, the founder must winnow the candidate list down to a group to be interviewed. We recommend that you sit with the applications and the job description at one set time period, so that a direct comparison of the applications and job needs can be completed. Those candidates who do not have the minimum requirements for the position should be rejected immediately. Those who closely match your job description should be the ones where you focus your next effort. Those that appear to be the best fit in that group should be considered for an interview.

During the interview process (whether it is in person or on the phone), it is important that the small business person not discriminate against any given individual. There is a short list of topics that should not be asked about in any interview. You should not ask questions about, nor can you consider in the hiring decision, any of the following:

- Age
- Race
- Disability
- Gender
- National origin
- Religion or creed

Note that you can ask about prior convictions, but may not ask about the candidate's arrest record. An arrest is not the same as a conviction. In summary, the discussion during the interview should be based on the needs of the job.

The interviewer should also use the interview to provide a realistic preview of the job and the company to the interviewee. You should not overpromise what the job will be or the relevant job security present in the firm. Too often firms try to sell the employee on the job by over-promising what the job is or underselling the expectations the firm has of the employee. Instead, you should provide a valid and realistic per-spective that promotes the firm but also sets appropriate expectations for the potential employee.

Although it is a tedious process, the founder needs to check as many ref-erences as possible. However, the small business owner should balance the checking of references with the nature of the job. If the job requires very low skills, then perhaps the need for references might be a bit less impor-tant. However, if the job is more central to the organization and has higher required skill levels, then the importance of the references increases. The small business person should also closely check references if the employee might be in a position to put either the business or its customers at risk. Thus, someone mowing lawns for you in a lawn mowing business might require only a simple employment check. In contrast, a new plumber, who will have access to clients' homes, and must be covered under your liability policies, requires a more rigorous background check. The references proposed by the interviewee and any others that the founder believes would have knowledge of the person should be contacted. If the job requires driving, as it does for many salespeople, then the small business person should inform the job candidate that he will be checking the candidate's driving records. In order to make these contacts and receive information, the person hiring must have signed permission from the candidate.

The interview process and the checking of references is a time-consuming process. It is for this reason that the screening of resumes or applications prior to beginning this course of action is important. However, the small business person does not want to shortchange the interview and reference process. As a result, should you still be unsure about which candidate to hire after an initial interview and background check, then a second round of interviews should be employed.

Some organizations go even further in making sure that the person is right for the firm and the firm is right for the person. For example, several organizations that we have worked with over the years require the candidates to spend a full day at the company. During the day the applicant will work with other members of the team, have lunch with the other workers, and get to see and be seen in the day-to-day environment. An evaluation by the employees of the company and the candidate at the end of the day provides the needed feedback to management prior to a hire decision. The small business person should keep continuous records of all advertisements that have been run, who responded, and the criteria for the job. If there are ever questions and/or if discrimination is charged, this type of record keeping will be quite helpful in defending your actions.

Testing

Ultimately, the small business owner should choose the employee that best meets her needs. Testing can be a part of that decision process, and testing comes in many forms and in response to many concerns. Some business owners wish to assure a drug-free workplace, and the founder has the right to insist on testing.[4] In fact, some states, such as Florida, offer a reduction in the rates of workers' compensation insurance if the business has a drug-free workplace program. This can be encouraged by requiring all new employees to submit to a drug test as well as requiring all employees to periodically submit to random drug testing. Most small businesses choose not to have drug testing, and they face risks in conducting such tests. The privacy rights of employees can come into conflict with the desire to have a drug-free workplace. Small business people are encouraged to consult a local lawyer before beginning such programs.

Another level of testing consists of testing candidates on the basic requirements of a position. For example, we know of one business that requires all of its potential employees to pass a 10-question, multiple-choice basic mathematics test to be eligible for an interview. The founder's explanation for this is that every employee is handling cash, and basic mathematics is a fundamental need of the organization.

A number of companies extend this testing to include personality testing or work behavior testing. All of this is perfectly acceptable if a direct link between performance on the test and the skill set necessary for success on the job is made.

The Offer

Once you have selected your top candidate, an offer needs to be extended. We suggest that all of the details of the offer be developed prior to any conversation with the candidate. Consideration should be given to the possibility that the candidate might wish to negotiate the deal. You should decide upon your negotiation position and how much you are willing to offer for this particular candidate. While this is primarily an art, we do recommend that once an offer is made, you allow the candidate the opportunity to accept the offer or return to you very quickly with a counter position (establish the amount of time that the offer will remain in effect before you withdraw it and offer the position to another candidate). At that point, you can make whatever concessions you feel are appropriate and then respond to the candidate. Once an offer is agreed upon between the parties, it should be put in writing by the founder, signed, and sent to the candidate. Only when the candidate returns a signed original of the offer letter should you consider the position closed. We don't wish to be too formal with this process, but we have watched many small business people be frustrated by employees who thought their agreement differed from that actually offered by the firm.

LO 10.3 Retaining Employees

Once you have actually hired each new employee, you'll want to retain those employees that perform well. The process described above takes a lot of time and effort. If it is done poorly and you don't retain the employee, then this process can simply be a waste of valuable time and money, not to mention the loss of productivity as each new employee has to be brought up to an acceptable level of performance. Therefore, the small firm needs to retain those employees that add value. The key issues here are the compensation and benefits offered as well as the method and means of reviewing performance.

Compensation

The compensation system chosen by the firm is the aspect that is often highest in the minds of employees. In building the compensation system, the small

Compensation is going to be a hot topic among employees, which makes equitable treatment in an employer's best interest. Are there ever instances in which paying two employees a different amount for the same job and experience might be a good idea?

business person needs to maintain a fair and equitable system for all employees, both now and as the firm progresses into the future. Salary and benefits may appear to be a private matter between you and your employees: however, history would suggest that all information quickly becomes public knowledge among fellow employees.

Equity theory is helpful to understand how to avoid problems with compensation. This theory argues that we all judge how we are treated relative to how we see others being treated. Thus, employees have a powerful need to feel that their compensation given their level/performance is equitable relative to that of other employees in their firm or other individuals in similar situations. As a result, all employees need a clear rationale for how their compensation stacks up against that of others in the organization. Employees can accept that someone who has been in the organization longer has a better overall package; however, they would have difficulty accepting it if they were hired at the same time as another employee and did the same job but received less pay. The owner might have a reason for that difference, but the presence of the difference would be difficult for the employee to understand.

Due to the level of complication within the workforce of most large firms, these firms require a systematic program that evaluates comparable employees both in the region and around the country. This systematic review of the employees will often include the following: (1) how they performed relative to their objectives; (2) plans for future employee growth through experience and training; (3) defined objectives for the next year; and (4) pay raise being awarded.

A small business needs a significantly less developed system. The small business founder should decide on a basic form of compensation. The options might include the following:

- Hourly wage
- Salary
- Commission
- Hybrid/profit-sharing system

An **hourly wage** is simply the amount paid per hour for work performed. A **salary** is similarly straightforward, as it is a set amount of money for a given time period. A **commission** is involved when the small business owner pays an individual a percentage of sales, and is typically associated with the compensation of sales representatives.

A commission compensation system can be abused and may be a source of frustration for employees and the small business owner. The abuse of the system can occur when a salesperson is so focused on his commission that he fails to watch for the overall good of the firm. For example, a commission can be based on sales made, and those sales could involve financing instead of immediate payment. A difficulty might occur with a particular salesperson who books a large number of clients who are financially weak and who later default. The salesperson got the commission, but the firm is stuck with a bad account.

Another potential for frustration with commissions comes when the firm either does, or does not, change the commission program to reflect the growth of the firm. To illustrate, when the company is young, the first salesperson may be paid a commission of 20 percent on sales. As the firm expands and hires more salespeople, the business

---

equity theory

The theory that we all judge how we are treated relative to how we see others being treated.

hourly wage

The amount paid per hour for work performed.

salary

A set amount of compensation for a given time period.

commission

Payment by the small business owner of some percentage of sales, typically associated with the compensation of sales representatives.

would suffer if the owner attempted to continue paying a 20 percent commission. At this stage the firm is more established, with customers contacting the firm directly. Yet, the founder would have difficulty telling the new salespeople that he would be making less per sale than the existing salesperson. Similarly, the founder would have difficulty in cutting the existing salesperson's commission. Therefore, when you set the first salesperson's commission, realize that you may be establishing the standard for a long time in the organization. Any change will be viewed by those already in place as a negative.

The small business person can also build a **hybrid compensation system,** where a sales commission can be paid in addition to a basic salary. **Profit sharing** is another example of a hybrid system. The firm may set some relatively low level of salary but offer to share a percentage of the profits at the end of the year or some other period of time with the employees. A **bonus** system is similar to profit sharing; a bonus is offered to the employees based on their performance. Typically, bonus systems are not as well defined as profit sharing; instead, the level of reward is left to the discretion of the small business owner. The time period for which such profit sharing or bonuses are given should be relevant to the individuals in the firm and within the realities and constraints of the business. It is important that the small business person provide bonuses in a timely manner. A small business owner may visualize a year as a relevant time frame, whereas workers may be looking for monthly or quarterly feedback on their performance through a bonus. It is very useful for the small business person to consider the industry standards in developing her compensation system. Those in your industry who have developed a compensation system that works have the potential to provide information not only on the level of total compensation but also on how to structure it.

Legal Issues with Pay The **Fair Labor Standards Act (FLSA)** establishes a minimum wage for workers. Virtually all workers (other than workers on small farms and administrative employees) are covered by the act. This law requires that employees be paid a minimum wage, which in 2009 was $7.25 per hour. However, states may have higher minimum wages. For example, in 2009 the minimum wage in California was $8.00 per hour. It is even possible for local governments to pass their own minimum wage requirements as long as they exceed the federal requirement. Many major cities have what they call "living wages"; a living wage is an index wage that requires the minimum wage to be at least what someone who works 40 hours a week needs to stay out of poverty. As a result, in 2009 the minimum wage in San Francisco was $9.36 per hour. If your business is covered by the FLSA, it is also covered by the Equal Pay Act, which requires that an employer not discriminate in pay to men and women who do the same job.

The FLSA requires that all nonexempt employees who work over 40 hours a week be paid at the rate of time and half. Compensatory time is not typically allowed from one pay period to the next. Therefore, if the pay period is only one week and you have employees work overtime this week, then you must pay the overtime rate for those hours. You cannot give them time off next week as compensation If, however, the pay period is two weeks, then time off in one week can be used as compensation for

hybrid compensation system
A compensation system where there is a salary along with commission.

profit sharing
An example of a hybrid compensation system. The firm may set some relatively low level of salary but offer to share a percentage of the profits at the end of the year or some other period of time with the employees.

bonus
Similar to profit sharing, a reward offered to the employees based on their performance. Typically, bonus systems are not as well defined as profit sharing; instead, the level of reward is left to the discretion of the small business owner.

Fair Labor Standards Act (FLSA)
The act that established a minimum wage for workers.

time worked in the previous week. Thus, the firm needs to be very clear on its time frame for issues like pay. Another legal issue related to pay is child labor. The government closely regulates the use of children under age 16. The small business owner would be well advised to seek out legal advice if he plans to employ children, even his own, in the business if they are younger than 16 years of age.

Benefits

There are a wide variety of benefits that any business can choose to offer. For example, benefits can include the following:

- Paid vacations
- 401(k) plan
- Paid holidays
- Medical care
- Retirement plans
- Sick leave
- Life insurance

The package of benefits the firm chooses to offer can have as much impact on the success of the small business's human resource efforts as the compensation offered.[5]

Some benefits represent costs to the small business, but are relatively easy for the small business to provide. For example, a two-week vacation after an individual has worked at a firm for a year can be provided by most firms. There is an expense since you are paying an employee that is not working; however, calculating when the benefit is due and managing the process is relatively easy. The same may be said of paid holidays and sick days; the sick days build up over time as the employee is working with the small business.

Benefits that are more difficult to effectively manage include medical care and retirement plans. Medical care is one of the most expensive costs for any business, and yet it is also one of the most desired benefits by employees. On average, private businesses spend in excess of $4,000 per person per year providing health care for their employees.[6] However, the plans most small businesses provide are not the full-coverage plans provided by large businesses. Large businesses are paying in excess of $9,000 per person per year providing for health care costs.[7] The impact of such costs to the small business compared to the large business cannot be overestimated. One of the biggest differences in the cost of auto plants for the large American auto manufacturers like General Motors versus those from Japan, like Toyota, who have plants in the United States is health insurance. The Japanese-owned plants' pay is equivalent to that of GM, but the Japanese auto plants are all new, and have hired young, healthy workers. The American auto plants are staffed by older workers, a trend that only gets more severe with every layoff, since workers with seniority get laid off last. The result is that the health benefits cost GM far more than they cost Toyota. Health insurance can be a competitive disadvantage when U.S. companies have to compete against companies from countries where health care is provided by the government.

For the small business, the cost of health insurance per employee will be more than that for a large firm. Large firms have the advantage of

You were part of a two-person team that was assigned to interview candidates for a new sales position. The new employee will be on the road five days a week and will need to be able work with a wide variety of people. The main client companies that the salesperson will have to work with are filled with former military officers.

During the interview your partner starts asking a series of questions that make both you and the candidate very uncomfortable. After the first interview you talk to your partner about the questions that he asked. They included these: (1) Are you married? (2) Do you own a car? (3) When did you graduate from high school? (4) Do you have any small children at home? (5) What church do you attend on Sundays?

Your partner explains that knowing these answers will really improve the chances of choosing the right candidate and will make it more likely that you will keep that person. He tells you that if the candidate is bothered by the questions, then he or she doesn't have to answer, and that will tell you all you need to know.

1. What should you do? Is there any justification for asking these questions?

2. What if the candidate doesn't mind answering the questions?

3. What if the candidate does mind answering the questions—how should you respond?

spreading losses across a large number of people, whereas the small business can be dramatically impacted by a single significant claim. To illustrate, out of 100,000 employees you may expect 23 heart bypass operations and can budget for that with insurance. In a small firm, you may have only 10 employees—but what if one employee needs a bypass? The insurance company has likely not charged you enough to cover the costs of the bypass, no matter what it has charged you in the past. The result is that the small firm is a much greater risk than the large firm. This leads to higher deductibles, user copayments, and out-of-pocket costs for employees of a small business. The small business person will need to investigate the costs and packages offered by a variety of insurance companies. The sources for such insurance can be located through other small businesses in the area, the chamber of commerce, national trade associations, and the Internet. The small business person would be well served to investigate and compare various medical programs closely before choosing one.

While traditional retirement plans have fallen out of favor, some types of personal retirement plans have become quite popular. Referred to generally as 401(k) and Roth 401(k) programs, they are usually offered by an employer so that employees can contribute to their retirement on a tax-free basis. Most small firms do not provide any matching, while many larger firms offer matching funds for these accounts.

Performance Reviews

No matter what the size of an organization is, performance reviews should be a part of the management system.[8] In a **performance review,** the small business owner reviews the employee's goals and outcomes on those goals over some given period. Workers are motivated by more than salary. The formal conversation with a worker who is doing a good job, showing that her work is appreciated, is another form of compensation. If the worker is not performing as expected, then the employer

performance review
Review by the small business owner of the employees' goals and outcomes on those goals over some given period.

should also be very clear about that fact. While we recommend that all performance reviews be done in writing, we do not suggest that a complex form need be utilized. Providing effective feedback can be handled in a number of ways but should cover each of the areas of the employee's responsibility.

During this feedback, the founder is well advised to provide praise where it is warranted and detail any deficiencies and areas that need to be developed. As will be discussed in the next section, it is critical that the employee know exactly how his performance is compared to expectations. Too often small business people do not want the confrontation, so they will give only positive feedback, but then later fire the person. The result is a surprised employee who may seek legal representation to get compensation for unfairly being fired. As will be discussed in the next section of this chapter, if you have not provided accurate performance reviews, the individual may win if the parties do go to court.

Central to being able to do any review is the setting of goals for the employee. The setting of such goals allows the small business person to judge how well the employee is performing. These goals should be realistic, tied to the performance of the company, based upon some measurable outcome, and reset periodically. Again, the time frame for these goals should be one that is relevant for the employee. Thus, for some jobs it may be weekly or biweekly, a time period that relates to the pay period. For most jobs, the relevant time frame will be quarterly or perhaps longer.

LO 10.4 Probation and Firing Employees

Despite your best efforts, you will at some point hire the wrong person. At times you may find it necessary to fire that person. As a small business owner you have the right to hire and fire employees. However, you still must have legitimate, well-documented reasons for the firing. If you do not, you are opening yourself up to a lawsuit by the dismissed employee. Furthermore, you should provide all employees (short of their having done something illegal) the opportunity to rectify their performance.

Thus, you must develop a paper trail regarding all employees and must be particularly diligent in your efforts to assist a poorly performing employee. Recall that in discussing reviews, we argued that an employer needs to be honest about an employee's performance and document those times when she is not performing as desired. This can form part of your paper trail. You specify over time what is expected of the employee and then document how she is or is not performing to expectations. Firing someone for poor performance which has been documented over a time and in which you have offered a means to correct the problem will go a long way toward providing a defense in any legal proceeding and a proper justification for the employee. If there are concerns about firing an employee, the small business owner should not hesitate to contact a lawyer for advice.

When hiring an employee, a small business person typically does not consider issues like a noncompete agreement or a secrecy agreement (one designed to protect the competitive advantage of the business).

While struggling employees are not a highlight of business ownership, they can impact your bottom line.

rodriquez family auto repair shop

The Rodriquez family was full of family members who had skills related not only to automobiles, but also to the running of a small business. Alex had planned to run the business virtually as a solo operation, but rapidly found that he needed all types of help. He and his sister had always been close. She was within a month of earning a degree in accounting from a national career school and wanted to work with her brother. As a result Alex planned for her to run the front counter, have customer interaction, and maintain all of the books, which included keeping track of every item that came into and out of the business. Unfortunately, Alex had no idea how much he should pay her or how he would interact with her in the business.

Alex and his sister sat down together at a local coffee shop one morning to talk about her coming on board. He desperately needed someone. Even before the business was formally opened, he was struggling to keep track of his expenses, with so many vendors to work with. He knew it would only get worse when he actually opened for business and there were customers to take care of. Therefore, he asked her how much she wanted to make and what she thought would be reasonable. She told him that she was willing to take a minimal salary and virtually no benefits if she could participate in the profits of the business. She suggested that if she really did her job well, then the whole company would do well. Alex liked the idea of sharing the business's fortunes with his family, since they were so central to his life and to starting the business. He also liked the fact that she would be taking very little from the business unless it did very well. Thus, Alex and his sister decided that she would start the next day and that she would work whenever she wasn't in class. They established a set of company milestones, which, if achieved, would lead to her taking home 15 percent of the profits of the business. However, she would not have an ownership stake.

The relationship between Alex and his sister worked very well. With her help, Alex was able to push the business toward opening more aggressively. He wanted to hire at least one more part-time mechanic. Alex's expertise was in brakes and air conditioning systems. However, he needed someone to be able to help out on bread-and-butter issues like oil changes, safety inspections, and changing of belts. He knew that these tended to be lower-skill jobs that generated considerable revenue in an auto shop. Alex wanted the person to be part time so he would not have to pay benefits, as he was just starting the business. Alex knew he could call his father and his uncle to help him out if he needed it, but he also wanted to have someone who was more permanent.

When Alex shared his plans with his father, Alex's dad suggested that he consider hiring a cousin who was very good with cars, but had been in some legal trouble. His personality was a bit rough and while he was talented, he did not seem very motivated to Alex. This suggestion proved very troubling. While he was open to hiring family, as shown by hiring his sister, he was not sure if he should hire his cousin. Alex would have over $100,000 worth of tools in his shop. While he could not imagine his cousin stealing from him, he was not sure of his cousin's friends. In addition, he was not sure how the cousin's background would effect his being able to be bonded. Finally, how could he ever fire his cousin if he did not work out?

On the other hand, he was also not sure how his uncle would respond if he did not hire the cousin. His uncle had been very helpful to Alex in his efforts to open the business. While his father did not say so, he was almost sure his father had made the suggestion because his uncle had suggested it to him.

However, when you dismiss an employee these issues may become critical. If you are a restaurant owner and have several secret recipes that are central to your success, then you do not want a disgruntled kitchen worker to post that information on the Internet. Therefore, at the initial hiring, you can limit later problems if you consider having your employees sign the appropriate documents. These documents are available via many software packages and are relatively easy to understand.

EXERCISE 5

1. What would you do in terms of hiring the cousin if you were Alex?
2. What alternatives would you suggest in staffing?

LO 10.5 Other Issues

There are a series of issues related to employees that all small business people must be concerned about, although not all companies may be directly impacted by each in the same way.

Workers' Compensation **Workers' compensation** laws are designed so that employees who are disabled or injured while on the job are provided with some type of compensation. Workers' compensation insurance is regulated by each state, with some states running their own insurance funds, while others use private firms. The rates of the insurance can differ widely in the various states, depending upon the regulations and generosity of the state legislature. However, the rates for individual firms within that state are fairly standard and are generally based on the industry and size of the firm. The payments are typically given to the employee if he qualifies, whether or not the small business owner was at fault for the injury from an unsafe workplace. However, the payments to the employee are limited to partial wage replacement and medical bills. The employee cannot receive workers' compensation for pain and suffering. The employee usually cannot sue the small business owner for his injury if he accepts workers' compensation payments.

The Occupational Safety and Health Administration (OSHA) The Occupational Safety and Health Administration (**OSHA**) is charged with protecting the health of workers. OSHA has attempted to shape its regulations to be more lenient toward small business. For example, firms with fewer than 10 employees do not have the record-keeping regulations that apply to larger businesses. Additionally, any fines are lower for small businesses with fewer than 25 employees than they are for large businesses. Effectively, OSHA will not impact many new small businesses, such as small retailers. However, other small businesses, such as manufacturing firms, need to pay specific attention to OSHA requirements regardless of their size. We would advise a small business owner to consult with industry associations and your local chamber of commerce to judge the potential impact on your firm. If the impact looks to be significant, then a visit with your attorney is merited.

Unemployment Compensation Every state has an **unemployment compensation** law which was put into place in order to provide financial assistance for some period of time to those people who lose their jobs through no fault of their own. Unemployment compensation pays to the former employee some set amount of money for a given period after she loses her job. During the time she receives these payments, she is required to look for a job. The small business person is required to pay an unemployment tax to help fund this system. That tax will vary by state depending on the unemployment benefits that state provides, as well as the experience rating (the history of unemployment) of the company.

The Americans with Disabilities Act (ADA) The Americans with Disabilities Act (ADA) generally covers those firms with 15 or more employees and provides that each and every business must provide unfettered access to all disabled people. This means at a minimum that ramps or elevators and Braille signs must be provided in the business. The small business may also be required to offer special accommodation to employees who need physical adaptations to work at the firm. Some states and cities have additional requirements beyond the ADA that may impact the small business in this regard.

LO 10.6 Family Business

A special category of human resource management applies in family businesses. A family business is one that is generally run by and for a particular family. Human resources in such businesses are still critical, but since family members make up many of the significant employees in the company, everything becomes more delicate.[9] The combination of father, mother, uncles, aunts, and children all in the business has impacts well beyond the standard HR practice. As you can recall from the Rodriquez Family Auto Repair discussion on page 211, the introduction of family brings new issues into the business that must be considered. One difference that arises in such businesses is that hiring does not always occur in the manner described earlier in this chapter. Instead, the family member is simply hired. You should recognize that this does not eliminate issues of discrimination if the firm is large; placement of family members because they are family members into positions in a large business can still result in charges of discrimination. The key issue in discrimination is that everyone is not given a fair chance at a job.

Managing family members can be difficult, as these individuals know all of the "hot buttons" that make a fellow family member angry. However, there is no effective way to fire or truly discipline the person without causing major ruptures in the family structure. The result is that family businesses and the human resources in them have more in common with family counseling than they do with the legalistic methods described in the earlier part of this chapter.

One especially tricky human resource issue that occurs in family business is succession. The business may have been founded by the father or mother. He or she is ready to retire and has a son and daughter in the business. Who in the next generation becomes the leader of the business? Too often the parent will put off the tough choices. The parent dies and a battle results in the family. To avoid this situation, the parent needs to choose a successor and prepare that person for the position by ensuring that he or she has all the contacts and understanding necessary to be successful. If the parent then decides to leave the business early, that parent needs to step back and let the son or daughter lead the business as he or she sees fit. Firms struggle to survive with two leaders of the business. The fact that the other child is not selected can result in difficulties in the family. Again, part of the means to overcome these difficulties is to work with professionals who act almost as family counselors to help the family see the rationales for the choices and how to deal with them positively.

summary

This chapter examined the wide range of issues involved in the human resources aspects of hiring, rewarding, and compensating employees. Many legal issues are involved in this arena, which explains why there are books devoted exclusively to the topic. We have endeavored to develop a basic checklist for the new small business person to utilize in the process of developing the firm's human resource requirements.

The chapter examined a number of complex issues related to human resources and the hiring process, including the following:

1. Hiring
2. Job descriptions
3. Job advertising
4. Discrimination
5. Interviewing
6. Testing
7. Making an offer

The chapter also examined the means by which companies retain employees, including these:

1. Compensation
2. Legal issues
3. Benefits
5. Performance reviews

Human resources is intimately tied to keeping businesses within the legal structures that affect all companies. These include the following:

1. Workers' compensation
2. OSHA standards
3. Unemployment compensation
4. ADA—the Americans with Disabilities Act

The chapter finished with a short discussion about how human resource actions are changed by being in a family business.

key terms

bonus 207

commission 206

discrimination 202

equity theory 206

Fair Labor Standards Act (FLSA) 207

hourly wage 206

human resources 199

hybrid compensation system 207

job description 199

OSHA 212

performance review 209

profit sharing 207

salary 206

unemployment compensation 212

workers' compensation 212

review questions

1. What means would you suggest to improve the process of hiring the right people for a new business?
2. What elements should a good job description contain?
3. What are the various ways to advertise a job opening?
4. What means would you suggest to help avoid job discrimination?
5. What techniques improve the interviewing process?
6. How can testing be used to improve the hiring decision?
7. What is the best method for making an offer to a candidate?
8. How does compensation impact the ability to retain an employee?

9. What legal issues are related to the retaining and firing of employees?
10. What benefits might be offered to new employees?
11. How are performance reviews related to employee retention?
12. Describe the impact that OSHA has on a new restaurant operation.
13. How does ADA affect retail organizations?
14. What is the impact on hiring decisions when the business is family owned and run?

individual exercises

Develop a human resource plan for your new business that consists of the following items:

1. Pay scale plan
2. Benefit plan
3. Advertising plan
4. Interviewing and hiring plan

group exercises

Rewrite the following poorly worded job descriptions.

1. JOB TITLE: Coffee Room Lady
She has to do everything to keep the coffee room running smoothly: ordering and stocking merchandise, as well as collecting money and controlling credit. She is told what to do by verbal instructions from the supervisor. If she has any problems she tells him about it and he tells her what to do.

One of the things she does is to order the merchandise from various vendors. When it arrives she puts it on the shelves for the employees. When they buy the stuff she collects the money or IOUs using a calculator or paper and pencil. Every day she has to clean the coffee room. This includes the coffeepot.

2. JOB TITLE: Break Room Attendant
Perform duties to order and stock merchandise, maintain cash and credit control, and clean break room. Work from instructions. Buy merchandise from vendors. Stock merchandise for purchase by employees. Maintain bookwork for cash and credit transactions. Clean break room and equipment daily. Notify supervisor of problems. Use cleaning equipment, coffeepot, calculator, paper, and pencil. Follow safety rules and keep work area in a clean and orderly condition. Perform other related duties as assigned.

everyday edisons class discussion

Go to www.everydayedisons.com/randyBill.html and read about Randy and Bill.
1. As you look at Randy and Bill, what type of person should they hire as their first employee?
2. If you had to write a job description for that person, what would it include?

Mike Poole and Brett Ross—Old Town Auto Works

Old Town Auto Works is a story about trust, doing the right things, and the success that can bring to a business. Mike Poole and Brett Ross own Old Town Auto Works, but this was not their first business venture together. Both men met back when they were teenagers attending a career school in auto mechanics in the early 1980s. They joined one of the largest franchise chain auto repair businesses in the United States after graduation. Over the next few years both men worked extremely hard at their jobs, learning their craft. In addition, the company sent them to a number of training programs in various parts of the business. They would tell you that many of the lessons about how to run their own business came from that first business experience. In addition to learning what they did want in a business, they also learned what they did not want in a business. The large chain focused on constant up-selling to the customer, forcing the customers into services they really didn't need.

Both men left the company within a year to work for a local service station that was part of a bigger oil company in the area. They learned a lot at the business, but really disliked the approach that the service station manager used. His business model was similar to that of the large franchise. He liked to bill each client for as much as possible and often for work that was not necessary. After several years, Mike and Brent left to work at different auto-related businesses. They kept in touch and talked about how they would like to open their own business. This desire to own their own business was partially spurred by frustration, as they commonly each worked 80 hours a week and were not getting ahead.

In 1989 the owner of the Shell stores in the area approached Mike and Brett to see if they were interested in buying a dying Shell station in another part of the town. The previous owner had been running the place as an absentee owner. The employees had been stealing equipment and supplies from the business and there were virtually no customers left at the operation. Mike and Brett bought the business, fired all of the employees, and set out to make it the type of business they wanted to run. They were going to be hands-on owners who worked in the shop every day. They wanted to work with good mechanics that did the right things for the customers. One outcome of this decision was to have no commissioned people in their operation. Operating on commission drives mechanics to find high-value activities to do on a car, since they get a percentage of the charge. In their business, everyone would be salaried, and most important, they wanted to have fun while they worked. It was getting the job done, working together, and enjoying the people you worked with that was most crucial to them. Setting out how you want the business to run is one of the most crucial steps in having a business that you like.

There was virtually no business at first. They slowly developed a client base built on their principles and not on advertising. They were well known in the mechanics trade in the area, which led to word-of-mouth business for them. Once a customer used their services, he rarely left for another shop. Over the next 11 years, they grew their business into one of the biggest Shell stations on the East Coast of the United States. Since they leased the building, they worked to convince the oil company to add another building to their operation so that they could service more cars, but were frustrated that the rent on the place went up relentlessly. Eventually they found that the rent they were paying would be more than enough to buy their own place.

We've often said that luck is where perspiration and preparation meet. Mike and Brett were looking for a location that they could buy, they had the clientele that was loyal to them, they had the resources to do what needed to be done, and they knew what type of operation they wanted to have for their own business.

A parts distributor talked to Brett one day about one of his other customers who owned a garage that he was looking to sell. The business had an eight-bay shop in front and a three-bay shop out back that was leased.

Brett and Mike talked with the garage owner about buying the place. Over the next year, the owner moved back and forth on whether he would sell the business. Finally he decided to sell the operation to Mike and Brett. The next few months were spent paving the parking lot; getting signage; filling out forms and licenses; obtaining a working capital loan; and mostly cleaning, cleaning, and cleaning a shop that had not been truly cleaned in years. Old Town Auto Works opened for business in 2000.

Mike and Brett's operation originally started as a partnership, and then both men moved it to a Subchapter C corporation for protection. Today they employ six full-time auto mechanics who are all salaried. The shop is open Monday through Friday only. Both men have families and feel that it is important to have a life, not just a business. During the week, the shop is a beehive of activity where every customer is known by name and the friendly mood in the shop is transferred to the customer interaction. They simply take care of their customers. They talk about what could be done and what needs to be done. They scour the area for better parts and are well known as a place that other mechanics can call upon for help with difficult problems.

Mike and Brett have a few great pieces of advice for new business owners, although they want to argue about whether they are really businessmen!

1. You've got to have fun in your business or it will eat you alive.

2. Take a practical business management class if you can. Mike and Brett arrive at 5:30 every morning to pore over the records of the business, pay all the bills, match parts to projects, and keep the cash moving.

3. Only buy what you really need. Salesmen will show up trying to sell you anything and everything. Do your own research and really think about the *needs* of the business.

4. Remain loyal to your suppliers. Mike and Brett have been with the same uniform company for 20 years, and the same parts supplier that worked with them when they started is still their primary (not only, but primary) supplier.

5. Information is your biggest advantage in business today. Mike and Brett subscribe to multiple database services. Every car is unique in its design and the permutations are innumerable. Data is king.

learning outcomes

After studying this chapter, you will be able to

11.1 Discuss the basics of a marketing plan.

11.2 Explain how to develop a pricing model.

11.3 Differentiate between the various types of promotion available to a new business.

11.4 Identify the methods for sales management.

Marketing

ZHEN COSMETICS

Susan and Jane Yee were shopping one day when Jane Yee decided to get a makeover at a department store. She ended up spending $200 on cosmetics. Unfortunately, when she went outside into the sun, she and her sister quickly realized that the cosmetics did not produce a very becoming result. This had been a typical problem for the six Yee sisters as they grew up in Columbus, Ohio. The skin coloring of the Chinese sisters was not suited to the nature of most cosmetics.

This experience triggered the idea for Zhen Cosmetics, which would be targeted to Asian women. The sisters developed the cosmetics through trial and error. Once the products were developed, they then sought to market the products. The sisters decided to sell their creations through mail-order catalogs. They used $20,000 to produce 50,000 catalogs. The sisters saved money by using friends as models. They used another $10,000 for a toll-free (1-800) phone number and lines to take the orders, while spending approximately $10,000 on inventory. The requests for catalogs were minimal until they started running advertisements announcing the availability of the catalogs in magazines targeting Asian women. The costs for these advertisements were not high, since they served small, very targeted audiences.

Their success led them to contracts with Nordstrom and other retailers, which led in turn to a well-developed Web page and some significant press coverage. They have been featured in *Fortune, Vogue, People,* and *Ladies' Home Journal* magazines. It was getting to their targeted group of customers that triggered the Yee sisters' ability to be successful.

M. Berss, "The Zhen uine Article," *Forbes* 155, no. 12 (1995), pp. 104–6; H. Chaplin, "Making Up a Market," *Fortune Small Business* 10, no. 1 (2000), p. 90–94.; H. C. Fisk, "Face Value," *Entrepreneur* 24, no. 5 (1996), pp. 220–28; J. Fowler and M. Nelson, "True Colors," *People* 54, no. 4 (2000), pp. 95–97; J. M. Rosenberg, "Cosmetics Line Designed for Asian Women," *Marketing News* 30, no. 22 (1996), pp. 15–18.

1. Do you think that Philo's original target market should still be its target market?
2. What forms of marketing/advertising should Philo create to generate greater customer knowledge about the firm with its target audience?
3. Out of all of the marketing outlets available, which will be the most productive for Philo given its product? Why?
4. How would you evaluate the television ad expenditure? Is it a good value for Philo?

At this point in the process of building a small business, the founders should have developed a unique product or service to offer, and established its business operations so that it is physically able to offer that product or service to the public. However, if the public does not know about the product or service, regardless of how much effort has been put into the small business to date, all of that prior work will accomplish very little. The old axiom "if you build it they will come" works fine in the movies, but the reality of business is that you must do quite a bit to make potential customers aware of your business. People are creatures of habit and in order to get some form of change in their behavior, we must stir the target customers to action.[1] Thus, a new business must aggressively seek to make its target customers aware that they have a product or service that offers a solution to a problem of those customers. A central part of this is that the small business needs to build a credible case as to why individuals need to use their product/service because it is better, cheaper, higher quality, or reparable, or has some other characteristic that other existing products/services do not offer.

To illustrate the critical nature of marketing for any firm, let's revisit Philo Asian Grille.

LO 11.1 Marketing Plan

Creating the business and the means to operate it is a necessary but not sufficient condition for business success. An underlying theme throughout this book is that planning and preparation are critical to the success of a small business. Plans may change, but rather than shifting direction with every change that may appear, a business that has a plan will be able to evaluate its past actions, changes in the environment, and what changes need to occur in the future. The same is true of marketing. There is little to manage, record, or evaluate without customers. Therefore, to be successful the small business also needs a plan for its marketing effort. Then when faced with changes, the firm can adapt that plan rather than beginning anew with each small problem faced.

marketing plan

The plan developed by the small business to specify who the customers are and how they will be attracted to the company.

The **marketing plan** is developed by the business to specify who the best customers are and how they might be attracted to the company. Developing a marketing plan can be a complex undertaking. Furthermore, marketing is a complete discipline whose level of complexity can be daunting. There are many consulting companies and business courses available to aid you in developing your marketing plan. As the new business grows, it may be advantageous to employ an outside firm to help focus its marketing efforts. However, hiring experts or consulting firms will cost you resources at a time when it would seem that the business could least afford the expenditure. Because such expenses can be very high in some cases, they can be hard to justify when you have limited cash despite the additional knowledge gained.

The events for the bank had gone well and the founders felt that the setup of the restaurant and where they had located the business had worked out well. Now it was time to actually open the restaurant and begin operations. To promote the restaurant for the opening the founders developed and faxed flyers to all businesses in the downtown area. Overall, the founders of Philo felt they had a competitive advantage since their restaurant was a clever idea that was unique, they had a great location, and they felt good about the staff they had hired.

After less than a month of being open, their lunch and dinner business had not developed as quickly as they had expected when they wrote their business plan. Interestingly, the success of the bank catering job had led to six other catering events. Some of those events were held at the restaurant and some were catered at other locations. Unfortunately, these catering opportunities often came with prices that were much lower than the owners would have liked. These opportunities also came with a problem not accounted for in the business plan. The catering business required clients to pay 50 percent of the fee up front while the remainder was billed to the clients after the event. These companies were taking anywhere from 30 to 45 days to pay their bills and Philo was being put into a real cash crunch. The founders suspected that some of the individuals hiring them for catering sensed the financial difficulties facing the firm and were being very aggressive in their demands for pricing.

Philo was faced with a setting where the buyers they had expected, individual lunch and dinner customers, had not materialized. Instead, catering customers who were negotiating much tougher prices had turned out to be the growth area of the business. As they considered their situation, they also recognized that the more they shut the restaurant for special events, the less likely they would be to develop that steady clientele of individuals who typically paid their bills immediately.

What the owners soon realized was that the knowledge of their business by individual consumers in the area was limited. The flyers they had faxed were not very useful. They heard from some people that that type of material was seen as spam and typically thrown away. As a result, the founders decided that they needed to build some significant awareness of the restaurant, and they needed to do it sooner rather than later.

The founders initially decided to advertise on television, since it seemed to be a great way to reach a large audience. They called each of the local affiliate stations to discuss the development and airing of a commercial. The general pitch each station made included the stations agreeing to develop the commercial for free if the founders bought a minimum of 60 thirty-second "spots" during the following 3 months at a total cost of $25,000. The owners of Philo hoped to build awareness of the business and yet didn't know if this was the best use of their limited cash. Beyond that, it seemed that not only was television expensive, but the customers they were seeking to reach did not include everyone in the city. They really believed that their perfect customers were those who lived and worked in the downtown area. That said, the founders had noticed how many of their customers seemed to be older and complaining about Philo's lack of valet service. The result of these issues was that the founders just weren't as sure of their target market for the restaurant as they had been when they built their business plan.

The information garnered in the process of researching and evaluating the market that you are operating within will return substantial benefits to the owners.

The focus of this chapter is the establishment of a workable marketing plan that can be developed by any entrepreneur. This plan should, at a minimum, include identifying your market, specifying the ideal and general target customer, determining a pricing policy that is in line with the strategy of the firm, developing promotion, determining sales management procedures, and finally, forecasting sales. After developing each of these areas for a marketing plan, we will spend some time discussing unique distribution channels.

Identifying Your Market

In Chapter 4 we outlined a means for the small business person to identify her target market and identify the "industry" in which she will be competing. This was done in the context of developing the idea for the business. The small business now needs to use that information as a foundation to develop a practical and actionable plan for attracting those customers.

An initial point needs to be made about the marketing effort for a small business. These marketing efforts need to be as clearly stated as the business's mission statement.[2] The use of such a mission/strategy statement helps to ensure that the firm is focused and will not seek to be all things to all people. The same focused approach needs to be used by the small business to market the firm's products to those customers that are most likely to buy its products at the price desired. As appealing as it may sound, a small business person is not trying to get every person in the city to his business in the hope that they all buy the company's product or service. Instead, the small business person is trying to reach those individuals most likely to actually buy from the business.

You will recall from our prior discussions that customers will travel only a given distance to buy from a business. This distance grows shorter as the number of competitors in the area increases. Therefore, a sandwich shop, hair stylist, dry cleaner, or similar business could reasonably expect to have large numbers of competitors and should expect customers to drive only a very short distance to shop at their location.

Geography and marketing can work hand in hand for business success.

If you market to too broad an area, the costs can be financially draining. A newspaper advertisement in a paper that serves a large city has virtually no targeting to specific consumers—it is a shotgun trying to hit a small target for the entrepreneur. A small business would simply hope that someone who had a need for its product/service would happen to see the advertisement, live close by, and hopefully respond to the advertisement. An analogy would be hoping to win the lottery.

Therefore, recall from Chapter 4 the exercise where we asked you to develop a reasonable geographic estimate of the radius your small business might draw customers from. As we stated in that earlier chapter, if you open a sandwich shop in the downtown area of a city, the shop most likely competes with other sandwich/fast food shops in a one- to two-mile radius, and perhaps less, if walking is the primary means of transportation for downtown lunching workers. There are limits to how far someone will travel for a sandwich. Drawing a practical radius around your potential new business location will help the business target the customers that are most likely to patronize your business. Philo faced this exact situation. The founders thought about using television, even though it was expensive and the message would be delivered to a much broader audience than what the restaurant was hoping to reach. Their main target was in the downtown area, a radius of about a mile and half around the restaurant location.

In considering the geographic area, the small business person should also consider how he will reach the potential customers in the area. Every contact outside his market area is really wasted money. There is a wide variety of potential marketing activities that can be pursued, including flyers, sponsoring events within the area, and affiliating with complementary businesses. As you look to define your geographic area, there will be several methods that fit naturally with part of your geographic area, but which may not be consistent with another geographic region. Thus, the small business must target the right geographic area and do so with the right marketing tool to be successful.

To illustrate, consider a small business that plans on using direct mail to contact potential customers. You may find that a given zip code covers 85 percent of the market you planned to target. The other 15 percent of your target geographic area is spilt between two other zip codes. The cost of addressing those two zip codes, due to the smaller size and special attention, may exceed the addressing costs for the other 85 percent of your market. Therefore, the reasonable thing to do at this stage would be to limit your target market to the one zip code. Defining a geographic market served should be a more complex analysis than simply drawing a circle around your potential business. The drawing of a circle is only a start. Building on that, the entrepreneur should make a reasonable estimate of what she can do with the least resources to reach the most people as efficiently as possible. Once the geographic area is defined, then the small business owner should remember that the money invested in her marketing effort should be primarily, if not exclusively, aimed at her target market area.

Target Customer

Once the geographic area is defined, the small business person needs to define the particular segment of the market that he is seeking to serve. For example, if the small business person is establishing a children's consignment and resale store, it is not likely that parents who send their kids to an exclusive private school in the area will shop there. While the private schools may ask you to advertise in the programs for their school events, spending your scarce dollars advertising in that venue would be a wasted effort if you expected these parents to buy there (although seeking their clothes to sell might be useful).

As part of the basic market/customer identification performed in Chapter 4, you have identified broad customer groups that the new business would serve. Now your operational marketing plan needs to go deeper and specifically identify potential customers. Most small businesses have restricted resources, and this is one of the things that differentiate a small business from a large business. It is this lack of funds that pushes the small firm to direct all of its marketing resources toward reaching the ideal customer. Therefore, once the small business person has identified the target market, she needs to identify the specific customers who meet those criteria in the market area chosen.[3]

To illustrate, consider a new athletic club that was opening in an upper-income area of a large city. Most gyms in the region charged $100 to $150 per month for someone to belong to the club. That represents a cost of $1200 to $1800 per year, not including any initial membership fees. An individual would need a reasonable income to support that expense. The owners of the gym also felt that the distance that individuals would drive to a gym was slightly farther than the distance they would drive to a sandwich shop. A brief survey by the founders of members enrolled at a friend's gym in a nearby city found that most customers drove approximately two and a half miles or less.

The owners drew a circle of two and a half miles around their location and found that a relatively high population lived in the area. However, this region of the city had a mixture of individual homes and apartments. The newer apartments typically had their own small gyms. Additionally, many of the older apartment complexes were relatively inexpensive and populated by individuals that worked service jobs in the restaurants and retail outlets in the area. The result was that the owners came to realize that their perfect customers were the individuals that lived in the houses in the area. This realization helped the owners target their customers very specifically. Those individuals they needed to reach were homeowners in their area who had a high enough income to join the gym. and renters who did not have the service already in their apartment complexes. Advertising could now be targeted using real estate records. The methods used could be direct mail or phone calls (to those not on the national do-not-call list).

This is not to suggest that the gym would turn away potential customers who did not meet their ideal profile. There might be some customers who joined the gym because they heard about it from another source. There might be others who would join with a friend. However, these customers would not be a direct result of the firm's marketing, so the cost of obtaining those customers would be much lower.

Once the target population is identified, the small business should try to answer questions such as these: (1) How many of these individuals exist within your market area? (2) What percentage of these individuals do you believe is reasonable for you to attract as customers? (3) What is the percentage in the general population of people that belong to a gym? (4) Do these numbers match your cash flow projections? (5) What do you need to change if they do not?

EXERCISE 2

1. Identify your ideal customer. Describe in short bullet points what characteristics this customer has that makes your product/service attractive.
2. What is the geographic range of your business?

LO 11.2 Pricing

Pricing of your product or service is a critical consideration for the small business. One approach is to value your products for what you believe they are worth to the market. Most small businesses charge a premium for their products or services. However, the higher the profit appears to be, the faster competitors will challenge the small business.

One method for a small business with specific products that are comparable to other products in the market is a cost-plus pricing method, where the firm determines its cost and then adds onto that cost some level of profit it determines to be appropriate. This method can be difficult to implement effectively.[4] Recall the difficulty that Philo had (discussed in Chapter 9) estimating the cost of catering the bank function.

The method requires that the small business initially determine what the total cost is for a particular product. This break-even point is referred to as the **pricing floor,** since the small business person will not want to price a product at a loss. In calculating the floor cost of your product, you will need to include your estimated cost of marketing and an administrative overhead allocation. The cost of your estimated marketing might change as you developed your marketing plan. As a result, you would need to go through the pricing process several times as you refined the marketing plan.

Occasionally, the small business owner may choose to have a product that is referred to as a **loss leader.** In other words, a small business may sell something at a non-operating loss (that is, the price only accounts for the actual cost of the product) to simply get customers to patronize the business. Our advice is that the small business owner not employ loss leaders until the business has developed some substantial momentum. The small business owner needs to get the firm on solid ground before employing such actions, which take considerable skill and have high risk associated with them. A loss leader can become quite a burden if customers buy the leader without buying the other services/products of the company.

In determining the cost of a product/service, we also suggest that the small business owner avoid the time-consuming nature of making detailed calculations for every product, especially if there is a wide product selection. Instead, the small business owner should place products in reasonable categories that balance the need for detailed pricing, as compared to managing an ever-expanding database of information. For example, if Philo has five beers on its menu, rather than treating them separately, the firm may wish to combine them into one category. Philo has limited personnel, and the need to manage a database of hundreds of products may be too demanding on the firm's time. The major airlines are large enough to have the resources and the technological ability to manage a system where every person on the plane may pay a different price, depending on when the ticket was bought, and on predicted occupancy of the plane when it takes off. As a small business person, you will not have that level of sophistication, nor is it necessary for an effective pricing policy. Therefore, having a data system that generates information that is useful and manageable should be the focus.

Information on the costs of the business is the foundation for determining **cost-plus pricing,** with the small business person adding the percentage profit she desires to that cost. Small business can seek a profit of 10 percent, 15 percent, 20 percent, 25 percent, or 100 percent or more on product categories. Part of the desired profit margin will be determined by how competitors price their products and how much overhead the business has. There will be a comparison effect as consumers evaluate different firms' products and make decisions based on an internal cost/benefit calculation. For example, you may have a small retail clothing store. Your prices may be higher than those at a large mall store, but your personalized service may be evaluated by consumers to be worth that premium. Alternatively, you may be able to charge a premium if you have an image that consumers believe to be valuable. If another clothing store opens up down the street and has clothing lines similar to yours that are priced at 15 percent less, then your business

pricing floor
The break-even point, or the lowest amount that can be charged for a product or service while still making a minimal profit.

loss leader
A product or service that is sold at a non-operating loss (that is, the price only accounts for the actual cost of the product) to simply get customers in the store.

cost-plus pricing
Pricing in which the small business person initially determines her cost structure and then determines what profit margin she desires and adds that to the cost.

might have some difficulty. Significant deviation between your prices and those of your competitors will have to be justified internally and will have to have merit with customers. The small business person needs to keep abreast of his competitors and their pricing to be able to make such judgments.

Pricing a service is a bit more complex. With a product, you have a potential price floor based on costs, whereas a service like counseling, financial advising, or interior decorating has only time as the base operational cost. There will still be overhead expenses (rent, utilities, etc.); however, the principal value inputs are your education and experience, which are difficult to establish as a cost. In the case of services, we encourage the entrepreneur to more closely examine the pricing of competitors. These prices can be critical information in determining how to value your service. We would suggest that you do not underestimate the value of experience. A consultant with extensive experience delivering expert testimony in courts will be able to charge far more than a consultant just starting out.

The small business person providing a service should also recognize that pricing is a valuable tool to balance customer flow with the time he has available. There are price-sensitive customers who will make decisions based solely upon price; therefore, for those customers, as the price goes down customer flow goes up, and vice versa. Small business people who have been in business for awhile may find they have too many low-margin customers and cannot provide the level of service they would like to provide. Thus, as their customer base increases, they might need to raise prices to limit the customers coming in at an unprofitable level so that they can serve them and profit from their business adequately.

In establishing pricing, there are several caveats that the small business person should remember. Typically, a small business starting out will need to offer an even greater value for the money charged in order to build a customer base. Once the business has developed a positive reputation, the value offered to the consumer can be changed to provide a bit more financial benefit to the company. Recall that individual consumers are generally unwilling to change the suppliers of their goods and services. As the business grows, the small business person can shift from a cost-plus type of pricing to one that is based more upon what the market will allow.

A second caveat applies to the actual price charged. Small increments of money should be avoided regardless of the exact percentage of margin desired. Thus, rather than charge $1.01 for a low-cost item, a more attractive pricing would be $0.99. The two cents' difference makes a reasonably large difference in appeal to consumers. Similarly, when prices are over $1,000, the small business person should avoid using cents in the price.

Finally, the small business owner will have to determine if she wants to offer a quantity discount. Much of this decision is based on the nature of the business which the small business person establishes. For example, a retailer typically does not sell in large enough quantity to be concerned with such issues.

EXERCISE 3

1. How will you price your product/service? Why?
2. What do your competitors charge? Why should your price vary from that industry standard?

LO 11.3 Promotion

Although it is only one part of marketing, people often think of marketing as the promotion of the product or service. **Promotion** is the means by which we make our product or service known to potential customers. The most readily seen versions of such promotion are the visual advertisements seen in a newspaper, viewed on the Internet, heard on a radio station, or seen on television. However, there are many means of promoting the business and each has varying costs and impacts. Promotion must be targeted to the market and customer groups within the industry, as we discussed earlier in this chapter. Furthermore, you will want your promotional efforts to reach the specific target consumers in the most efficient manner possible.

While most promotional efforts involve some type of financial commitment, there are some promotions that are strictly financial arrangements in which you pay for some outputs, such as radio advertisements. These are referred to as **pure promotions.** There are other promotions that cost something but also have an element of community support, and are referred to as **mixed-model promotions.** Lastly, there are promotions that have a very limited financial cost but have a time commitment requirement from someone in the firm; these are referred to as **virtually free promotions.** We will briefly discuss each of these ways to promote the business.

Pure Promotions

This category encompasses the majority of promotional efforts targeted by the firm. Any form of advertising that is purely designed to promote the products/services of the company falls into this category. This type includes use of signs, flyers, Web pages, newspapers, radio, trade shows, and television. Each of these will be reviewed briefly.

Signs. An oft-overlooked means of advertising the company comes in the form of a sign on the building or on the street, and on the letterhead/checks/business cards of the firm. A catchy name, a well-designed logo, and some substantial efforts to get the logo/name out can pay significant benefits in recognition and impression management. For most customers, there are myriad businesses with which they can spend their money. Why a customer spends that money with your business is at least partially a result of what that customer thinks of your business when that purchase decision comes about. Most sign firms will be willing to aid you in the development of whatever signage you purchase, although the quality of that advice may vary widely. The key thing to remember as you design your signage is that "simple but distinctive" is the goal.

Flyers. As we mentioned earlier in this chapter, if you can target a very specific geographic area and perhaps identify a likely customer profile, then using something as simple as flyers might be very effective. They can be delivered directly to the customer's business or home, or posted at appropriately visible spots. Flyers can be changed frequently, printed cheaply, and delivered with low-cost labor. Unfortunately, these very characteristics mean that they have a smaller impact upon customers.

---

promotion
The means by which a small business advances its product or service.

pure promotions
Promotions that are strictly financial arrangements in which you pay for some outputs, such as radio advertisements.

mixed-model promotions
Promotions that cost something but also have an element of community support.

virtually free promotions
Promotions that have very limited financial cost, but have time commitment requirements from individuals in the firm.

Web Page. A relatively recent need for virtually all companies is the availability of an effective Web page. While a Web presence was considered a truly unorthodox competitive advantage just 10 short years ago, today it is an expectation. Customers look to Web pages for basic corporate information, information about products and services, and the ability to purchase online. The sophistication of your Web page should be dependent upon the goals of your organization; but particularly for a small business that sells a unique product with a wider target market, this may be one of the primary means to reach clients that live outside your region. The first step, acquiring a domain name, is now an easy process available from a number of third-party providers on the Web. The second and third steps include purchasing time on a server (almost always a service provided by the same acquisition provider, as well as a number of Web design firms) and having a company design a Web page for your business. For any Web design beyond the most basic, we suggest that you have a professional develop your Web presence.

Newspapers. A standard method for promoting your business is through a newspaper advertisement. This process involves two steps: One is designing the ad and the second is placing it in the newspaper. Your local paper will work with you on both parts, or you can hire an advertising agency to design and place the ad for you. Either method is effective; however, newspaper advertisements mean that you will be paying for "views" by many individuals who will never be your customers. This a broad-based "shotgun" type of advertising. It should also be recognized that in many large cities there are specialized newspapers that may be better suited to your business. Philo was able to take advantage of a newspaper designed specifically for downtown businesses. It was smaller and dealt with local downtown news. An alternative outlet would have been the local business press. Both of these would have been much cheaper for Philo than the television approach they initially considered, and more targeted to their desired customers than both television and the city newspaper.

Radio and Television. As with newspapers, a radio/television advertisement can be designed and aired by the station, or you can employ an advertising agency to develop and place an ad. While there may be only one major newspaper in a market, it is likely that you will have a number of radio and television stations reaching your target group. This fact encourages us to recommend the use of an advertising agency whose loyalty is to you and which will place the ads regardless of the desires of a particular station. Radio and television advertisements are qualitatively more difficult and financially more draining than the other approaches. A radio or television advertisement must be designed to make your points, not upset anyone, and be sufficiently creative to draw customers to your business.

Trade shows. Trade shows are events established around a particular theme where individuals are allowed to set up booths in order to promote their goods or services. In an industry such as toy manufacturing, there is an annual trade show (as well as numerous regional shows) in which all toy manufacturers display their products to sell to retailers. Similarly, for services, there are often trade shows in which a small business

How far would you go to sell a product or service? How far would you expect someone to go for you as the small business owner in selling a product?

Consider a salesman that worked for a small business. In order for the salesman to earn his bonus he needed to sell another $36,000 worth of product this month—and it was the last day of the month. He was the only income earner for the family, so they depended on his income, and they had come to depend on his bonus to pay some of the bills. The salesman had heard of other salesmen in the industry that would work with clients so that they would book a sale in one month and just take delivery later, in the next month. Another salesperson in the company would regularly book phantom sales in one month if she were sure the company would actually make the purchase early the next month.

1. If you were the salesman, would you book a sale in this manner?
2. If you were the owner, how would you respond to the salesman if you found that he or she was actually doing this?
3. Why would each of these parties perhaps see this situation differently?
4. Could this lead to broader ethical concerns in a firm?

person may wish to participate. If you have a wedding planning service, you will likely want to participate in bridal shows that happen in a number of cities. Trade shows can be expensive to participate in. However, a small business can successfully participate by strategically focusing its efforts and ensuring that pre–trade show promotion makes potential customers aware of the presence of the small firm at the trade show.[5]

Mixed Promotions/Community Support

There are a number of opportunities to promote your business and help out the community in a way that targets your customer base. Schools are in constant need of sponsors. Angling your sponsorship to those activities that will provide maximum exposure to your potential client base is an effective and relatively inexpensive means of keeping your name in front of them. Depending upon the business, sponsoring sports activities, clubs in the school, events (dances and fundraising activities), etc., allows you to put your stamp on positive activities and hopefully reach the parents/children in your target customer group. For example, if you have a sports store in a city suburb, then sponsoring sports teams in the immediate area will allow you to be viewed as the official outfitter of those teams. The members of those sports teams, their families, and their friends will more than likely buy what they need from you in the future because of that relationship.

A second group of mixed promotions/community support are churches within your target area. Church groups look for sponsors to help in various activities for the community or for their youth. Carefully targeted efforts can help the new small business reach an audience that is not normally as targetable.

Virtually Free Promotion

Virtually free promotions are also widely referred to as **bootstrap marketing,** since they require little capital. There are many opportunities to speak with groups about your business or even a specific area of

bootstrap marketing
Marketing efforts that require little capital.

expertise. To illustrate, the individuals that started the athletic club we discussed earlier in this chapter sought out speaking opportunities to groups in their area. The age of the typical Lions, Optimist, or Kiwanis Club member was within the range of the target market for the club. Additionally, those individuals that have time to commit to such organizations typically have sufficient income to belong to a health club. Therefore, the owners actively sought out opportunities to talk about health programs and how to start exercising to a variety of groups. To arrange such talks they contacted leaders of the groups and offered their services, particularly at the beginning of a new year, since many people start off each year with fresh resolutions about their weight. Incidentally, that is when gyms have their greatest increase in membership.

There are speaking opportunities with schools, clubs, and religious groups throughout the year. If the group is relevant to your small business, you should take advantage of talking to it. The presentation should be more generic than a simple promotion for your business. For example, an owner of garden supply store may visit with a club like the Optimists about what flowers to plant in the spring or how to maintain lawns. After you make these presentations. it will hopefully be your business that the consumer considers when she seeks out a business in your field. There are other free opportunities that the small business owner should seek out—for example, if an opening arises with the local news to comment on current events. There are also many local morning talk shows for which you could put together something interesting for a show spot. For example, if you have a restaurant, then you may be able to prepare a favorite dish on the local morning show.

In any case, it is important to remember that no single advertisement will be sufficient for the business. The attention of your target market is pulled in many different directions. It can take numerous "impressions" for an individual consumer to take notice of your firm or product.[6] When the firm develops its promotional program, it is important that a systematic effort take place that will commit the time and effort needed to be sure that the firm obtains the recognition of the consumers.

EXERCISE 4

1. Think of the promotional activities that are relevant in the area where you live.
2. Which of these would be most economical for a small business?

LO 11.4 Sales Management

sales management

The methods employed to, and individuals who build and maintan relationships with customers.

Sales management refers to the individuals who build and maintain relationships with customers, as well as to the methods and means by which they do this. To a certain extent everyone in an organization is involved in sales; however, sales management refers to how that whole sales process is managed. Issues that need to be considered include the following:

1. How many contact points will the business have with each customer?
2. How will each customer be greeted?
3. What is the process for managing a customer once an order has been placed?
4. What look will the sales force present?

Alex had everything ready for the grand opening of his business, and he knew that he needed to get publicity about the new business out to the community. He first looked for as many free methods to publicize the business as he could. He started by making a few needed repairs on the church vans owned by the churches of the priest and minister that sat on his board of advisors. He knew both people would make a nice announcement about the repairs and point out his new business. They were both strongly tied to a community-wide effort of building local businesses.

Alex contacted a high-school classmate of his sister. She ran an early Sunday morning talk show on a local radio that focused on their neighborhood. It was a public service to the community. To be honest, on Sunday morning the number of listeners was probably not very high. However, Alex thought that if he could get on the show and talk about weatherizing your car for the coming summer as well as a new law related to automobiles, some exposure had to be better than none at all.

He then stopped by to see the editor of a paper that served the local Hispanic community. Alex lived in a major city that had several very large specialized newspapers for different communities. For those papers, one more auto repair shop was not of much interest. On the other hand, this newspaper served a small area and had more local news. He stopped in to see the editor, since he wanted to know about local advertising costs for an ad and he hoped to get a small story about the opening of his shop. As is often the case, the newspaper seemed very interested in running a story about the new business, especially if Alex would buy some advertisement space.

As Alex thought about running the ad, he realized that the newspaper covered a much larger area than he saw as his target market, but the cost seemed reasonable. Alex knew full-page advertisements in a newspaper like *The Wall Street Journal* could cost over $200,000, while a similar advertisement in the *Los Angeles Times* would cost over $70,000. He was gleeful to find out that a full-page advertisement in the local weekly paper cost less than $2,000. Alex knew he would not run a full-page advertisement. Instead he would run smaller advertisements. The newspaper had four columns (there can be four to six columns on a newspaper page, and the length is typically 21 inches). Thus, a quarter-page advertisement would be 21 column inches (4 times 21 divided by 4) and would cost $500. He thought that for the first four months, he would run the advertisement once each month.

Beyond these choices, Alex was not sure what other advertising he should consider.

1. What do you think of Alex's choice to advertise in the local newspaper?

2. What other things could Alex do for advertisement that would be relatively cheap?

---

5. What controls are in place to ensure the quality of the product delivery?

6. How much information will be collected on each customer?

7. What will the business do with the information collected?

Designing and maintaining a sales management system is certainly part art and part tedious coding; however, a consistent approach and image that is designed around your mission statement will pay off tremendously as your business develops. The process starts with the hiring of a sales force.* One of the real keys to small business success is the

---

* The role of the sales force considered here in Chapter 11 and the role of human resources considered in Chapter 10 illustrate an issue that the authors have highlighted several times. The chapters here present the material in a sequential manner, but many of the issues that the small business owner must decide occur simultaneously. The small business person cannot know whom to hire for the sales force until she knows how she wants to market the product or service. Therefore, while the two issues are separated here, it is actually difficult to makes such splits easily.

development of a relationship with the customer. A popular television show (*Cheers*) was set in a bar and every time one of the regulars came into the bar, the employees in the bar would loudly greet him. That is the level of recognition that many customers desire from a small business, whether they are being provided a haircut, buying clothes, or being advised on their investments. Indeed, one of the reasons for patronizing a small business could well be this expectation for exceptional recognition of loyal customers.

Beyond that level of recognition, returning customers are looking for an understanding of their needs, not just a fixation upon making a sale. A client of ours loves good wine and while he could go to any of a dozen stores that sell a wide selection of wine, he chooses a business run by a small group of wine enthusiasts. Every time he walks into the store, they greet him and make suggestions to him based upon their personal knowledge of his tastes. If he chooses a wine, even an expensive wine, that they believe he will not enjoy, they are quick to point this out to him and try to steer him to wines that he will enjoy. They are not fixed on the label, the price, or the fact that they have 30 cases of another wine back in storage. Relationship management is a process and a practice.

Forecasting Sales

Estimating sales without any history is an act of guesswork that is dependent upon the founder's ability to narrowly focus a customer group as well as to attract that customer group to purchase. There are many ways to estimate sales, all of which should be modified as real sales data become available. The two methods we will examine are market potential and customer demand.

Market potential methods take a macro look at the market and estimate potential sales for the firm based upon the number of potential consumers in the target area. This data is then modified by a likely percentage of those potential consumers that will be attracted to the specific business. This can be estimated by looking at the direct competitors in the area or looking at close competitors in another, similar area. As we pointed out in Chapter 4, your direct knowledge of the market and your competitors will be essential to your sales forecast. To illustrate, the founders of the gym we have been discussing believed that their customer base would exist within a two and a half mile radius of the business and that those customers would own houses. Data from the census bureau and the local government helped identify the number of homes that met the criteria. The individuals starting the gym estimated there were one and a half potential consumers per house and limited their analysis to those individuals who had full-time employment. The result was a potential population of almost 50,000 customers in their geographic area of interest.

The small business start-up owners must then estimate what percentage of their total market potential might use a business in a given area. For some companies, there will be industry information from industry associations. However, even without this it is relatively easy to estimate. For example, several of the fitness Web sites estimate the number of people who are members of a gym. Armed with that information and a quick search to find out how many gyms there are in the United States, our founders estimated the size of their likely customer base. They then talked to a gym owner in another state to find out how long it took that gym to ramp up to its current level of customer traffic. They made a logical estimate of monthly growth and then modified it as customers actually signed up for memberships.

The second method is customer demand. This method takes a micro look at the market and estimates how many customers the business can handle given its location, staffing, etc. The founder then estimates how many individuals it will take to break even, make X profit, etc. For example, one business made the following estimate:

1. The business had parking for no more than six cars at one time.

2. It was estimated that each customer would be in the storefront for an average of 30 minutes (2/3 of time browsing—20 minutes; 1/3 of time purchasing—10 minutes).

3. Staffing meant that most of the time they could handle only four customers actually making a purchase.

4. The average sale was expected to be $850.

5. It was estimated that during a typical day, only twice per day would the storefront be full of customers.

With this information, the business was able to establish a sales forecast and staff the business appropriately. They owners modified their forecasts based upon the experience of the firm once it was actually in business.

Distribution Channels

The prior discussion focused on small businesses which establish a fixed location and serve customers from that location in retail or wholesale. However, there are other methods of distributing your products/ services. These methods do not require as extensive an understanding of geographic location, since, for example, they may be selling an industrial product that has the potential for a nationwide distribution or they involve situations, such as Internet services or sales, where there is no limit due to geography. These methods include the following:

1. Independent sales agents.

2. A contract sales force.

3. Web pages.

4. Mail-order catalogs.

Each of these will be discussed in turn.

Independent Sales Agents. **Independent representatives** can be used to sell industrial products.[7] The independent distributor is the representative for a variety of products for a number of companies in a given domain. The independent representative agrees to sell/distribute each of the products for a percentage of the sales price. The percentage that the representative will receive depends on the demand for the product and how much effort the manufacturer wishes that representative to invest in promoting its product. A small business starting out needs to carefully negotiate the price paid to such representatives. Clearly, these representatives will promote those products for which they make the most money. Securing the right representatives for the right price can be crucial to achieving success when using this distribution channel.

independent representatives

Representatives for a variety of products for a number of companies in a given domain who try to sell those products.

For example, a new small medical device company that we worked with for some time used distributors to sell its product. These distributors already had the necessary relationships with specific doctors, and these relationships are critical in the sales of any new medical product. Some doctors will actually allow representatives from certain sales agents into the operating room to help demonstrate the use of a new product. For this to occur, the distributor has to have salespeople with the proper training and relationships with the doctors. In this setting, choosing the right independent distributor was probably more critical than any other hire in the firm.

Contract Sales Force. A second distribution channel is a **contract sales force.** Contract sales companies provide independent salespeople with a wide variety of experiences and contacts on a contract basis. Thus, you can hire a sales force for your firm for a given period of time. While it is a relatively expensive means of jump-starting sales, it can be the difference between success and failure. We worked with a company whose entire business plan was dependent upon quickly locking up venues in long-term contracts. Then, armed with those contracts, the company could market its service to potential clients. The process envisioned in the plan required more than 20 experienced salespeople for a period of nine months. After that time, all sales could be handled by four inside salespeople who were to be hired during this process. A contract firm provided more than 80 resumes, from which the founders selected 21 salespeople to initiate the business.

Web Pages. A third rapidly growing distribution channel is the Internet.[8] Internet-based marketing employs the Web in much the same way that a fixed-site store uses its physical location as an advantage. The Web page displays the products, provides means to ask questions about those products, and in many cases allows the customer to buy the products. The list of Web page capabilities and its uses for marketing is expanding daily. Such sites can be used by businesses which focus purely on Internet sales or by those that use it as a supplement to the other marketing efforts of the firms. Web-based businesses rely upon the designs of their Web pages to present the information about the products and their benefits. Thus, Web page design is a crucial part of the company process. However, it is important to remember that the Web page is there to sell products, not to show off some technical prowess in Web page design.

To illustrate, consider the wonderful graphics and animations that are capable of being included in a business Web site. These graphics take time to load, but many people still use a phone modem at home and do not have high-speed Internet access. As a result, it can take a long time for complex graphics to load. If you walked into a local store and no one sought to help you in five minutes, you would likely leave the store with plans to never return. That time frame is compressed when it comes to navigating a Web site, as customer patience is very short. Similarly, in designing the Web site, the small business person should ensure that she does not design a site that works only with a particular browser type. The site must be usable, with the minimum number of clicks necessary for the client to achieve what he wishes to achieve.

contract sales force
Independent salespeople with a wide variety of experiences and contacts, provided by a company on a contract basis.

Sales and marketing depend on each other for success.

Individuals will not roll endlessly through a series of screens to reach what they desire. Lastly, the content of the Web page must be timely. Time and effort must be dedicated to maintaining the Web page so that the information is accurate. A Web page is not something that can be created and forgotten.

The classic example that individuals can look to for a Web-based business that started small, although it is now large, is Amazon.com. The firm's Web site is accessible and easy to use. The site not only provides information but also allows customers to browse, purchase, pay for, and arrange shipping for any of hundreds of thousands of products.

Developing a system to the level of an Amazon.com is prohibitively expensive for a new business. Every firm needs to determine if the Web will be its only outlet or if it will use the Web to supplement the fixed-location business. Web sales reach well beyond any physical boundaries and generally reach low-cost customers for the business. However, the business must offer very unique items that cannot be easily obtained elsewhere for there to be sufficient demand to warrant the time and effort involved with the mixed model. The end result may be that the time and effort to develop the Web page correctly may be more than the small business is willing to invest. If this is the case, the small business should still consider a basic Web page that provides information and directs customers to call to place their order. Such a site is relatively easy to prepare and maintain. The level of complexity increases dramatically as the business attempts to increase the capability to include the ability to order and pay for products.

Mail-Order Catalogs. The last type of distribution method is mail-order catalogs. Many businesses do not have a fixed retail location but instead reach customers through the mail. These individuals will mail a catalog to customers at their homes. The catalogs will display a consistent set of products and provide a means to order those products—typically over the phone. A professional company can be hired to receive those calls and send the orders to your business. The mailing out of the goods themselves is typically not difficult, unless it is at a time such as Christmas, where time sensitivity is critical and the standard delivery systems are overloaded.

As could be predicted, identifying the customers to mail the catalog to is a critical part of the process. A small firm cannot afford to mail a catalog to every person in the country. Thus, understanding and targeting your customer once again becomes critical. One useful means to do this is to buy a mailing list from a group which may have an interest in products that you wish to sell. For example, if you wished to establish a mail-order business for historical guns such as flintlock rifles, you could seek to buy the mailing list of the National Rifle Association. Similarly, if you wished to sell environmentally sound cosmetics, you could seek to buy the mailing list of the Sierra Club and send the catalog to women on the mailing list.

One difficulty in running a mail order/catalog business is the need to be able to handle credit card sales and returns. Credit card fraud has been particularly troublesome for this industry, and transaction fees need to be accounted for in the pricing of products.

summary

Marketing is a critical function in the small business. Too often the small business focuses strictly on the technological aspects of the product produced and not the customers.[9] To be successful, the small business must know the customers that would be ideal targets for its product/service. It is clear as we examine this chapter that marketing of the product and the strategy of the firm share a great similarity. The small business must utilize its developed mission/strategy to narrowly target the perfect customers. If the small business does not understand these issues, it is easy to spend the firm's scarce resources in a manner that produces no tangible benefit.

key terms

bootstrap marketing 229
contract sales force 234
cost-plus pricing 225
independent representatives 233
loss leader 225
marketing plan 220

mixed-model promotions 227
pricing floor 225
promotion 227
pure promotions 227
sales management 230
virtually free promotions 227

review questions

1. Describe the basics of a marketing plan.
2. What advice would you provide to a potential new business owner about establishing a marketing plan?
3. What are some of the ways that you can identify competitors in your market area?
4. What elements are necessary for a target customer profile?
5. How is a target customer profile used in the operation of a new business?
6. What are the means by which products/services may be priced?
7. How can a new business leverage free promotions?
8. What promotions might a new business use and why?
9. In what context might independent sales agents be utilized?
10. How is a contract sales force used in new businesses?
11. Explain how the Web is used by businesses for advertising.
12. How might you use mail-order catalogs to create sales for your business?

individual exercises

1. What channels do you intend to use to market your product/service?
2. What are the costs for each?
3. Develop an overall marketing plan that encompasses a defined customer/target area, the methods of promotion, the pricing, and the distribution channels.

group exercises

Throughout history, well-known companies have lowered prices to increase sales. History suggests that this technique simply reduces profitability and leads to a decline in the overall business. The business then has a harder time justifying its place in the market. Customers generally perceive that a lowered price equates to lowered quality. First individually and then in your group, answer the following questions:

1. Can you think of examples of products that would suffer if they lowered their prices?
2. Why can some businesses easily lower prices and gain customers while others cannot?
3. Can you think of any products or services where lowering prices could result in enough increase in sales to justify the lower prices?

everyday edisons class discussion

Go to www.everydayedisons.com/stan.html to read about Stan.

1. How would Stan be able to market this tool on his own?
2. Does a great idea make a great product?
3. Does a great product make a great business?

Craig McCliment—Southern Accent Interiors

Craig McCliment has been painting rooms and hanging wallpaper for his entire adult life. Along the way, he has experienced virtually every variation of business formation likely to be seen by a small business person. Craig has owned Southern Accent Interiors for the past 25 years. The primary business includes painting, basic carpentry, and wallpaper removal and installation for high-end homeowners. He generally avoids commercial businesses as they don't really appreciate his high-touch, perfectionist approach to his craft. Instead, commercial accounts want the fastest, cheapest painting method to complete the job.

Craig graduated from high school in 1977 and went to work for his older brother in Baltimore, MD. His brother had a business doing painting and wallpaper work for commercial businesses, primarily hotels. Craig had no experience in either and apprenticed with his brother, whom Craig describes as a natural talent in the "art" of the business. Less than a year later Craig's brother moved the business to Asheville, NC so that he and his family could live in the mountains and enjoy a more organic lifestyle. Craig moved with his brother and they restarted the business in Asheville. Within a very short period of time, one of Craig's other brothers joined the business and all three began leading crews on different jobs in the area.

The business grew via word of mouth, but Craig started to chafe under the direction of his older brothers. He had developed the skills needed in the business and really believed that he should be on his own. Craig's competitive advantage over many in the trade is that he is truly a perfectionist. He wants the job to be done

extremely well. That often means that the walls and ceilings need a lot of work prior to the application of the paint or wallpaper. The commercial businesses don't appreciate that level of detail and many homeowners just want the cheapest price they can get. There is no shortage of people who can do the basics; Craig felt that the sweet spot in the industry would be working for customers who would appreciate and pay for his attention to detail.

After two years in Asheville, Craig left his brother's operation and moved to Winston-Salem, NC to start up a new business with a friend of his. This move allowed Craig to start his business while not directly competing against his brother. The new business was called Accent Interiors. Craig and his partner prepared a list of references from their prior years, had business cards developed for the new business, and then visited every interior decorator, wallpaper store, and paint store in the area. They left cards, talked with the owners, and pitched their ability. The business picked up quickly, but once again Craig really struggled with a partner in the business. Differences in work approach and on what constituted quality work kept creeping into the business. Despite these differences, their business grew to the point where they need to hire a number of work crews to do the work and they would manage the process in order to ensure the quality efforts. Craig had been doing painting and wallpapering for six years and had learned a valuable lesson about what he wanted in a business. He liked to do the work himself, he liked to control the entire process, and he did not like managing a lot of employees.

In 1983 he broke off from his partner, letting him keep the Accent Interiors business, and he formed a sole proprietorship with the name Southern Accent Interiors. He approached the business start-up in the same manner as before by visiting all the same stores, but this time really targeting his high-quality, personal approach to the effort. His pricing was higher, but so was his quality. His business developed quickly, and this time it was mostly custom repainting of expensive homes. He never advertised, instead relying on word of mouth. His high-end clients passed his name along to friends of theirs and his name made it to the circles in the local country clubs.

Over the years, Craig has hired dozens of workers to help with seasonal demand. He feels that hiring people for his business is relatively simple. He advertises in the local newspaper, but more often than not he simply goes to the paint stores in the area and asks for names of folks looking for work. Most of his employees apprentice on the job with Craig as their mentor. He hires everyone on a contingent basis and looks for those that have a precise approach to their work, are dedicated workers, show up on time, and are willing to learn. Some employees last a day and others have lasted six years. His long-term dedicated employees have become competitors over the years as Craig has ended up training his competition.

When asked for the advice he would provide potential entrepreneurs he suggested the following:

1. Don't get into partnerships. He really likes to control his own operation and says that finding a partner who acts and thinks like you do is very difficult. He partnered with his brothers and with a friend, but found that coordinating the work between them all while assuring that the business ran as it should was very difficult.

2. The customer is king. Craig's business is a very personal service. He performs the decorating that his clients envision in their most personal spaces. He advises entrepreneurs to listen, listen, and listen some more; have a lot of patience and do the work that they want done. Too many contractors try to tell the customer what they need; his business is based upon being able to picture what the customer wants it to look like when the project is done.

3. Quality control is the key to success. Craig believes that the toughest critic should be the owner of the business. Don't let anything slide. If he has a customer who doesn't like what was done, Craig simply re-does the project regardless of the costs. His business is completely word of mouth and he wants a 100 percent satisfied customer base.

Financial Analysis

learning outcomes

After studying this chapter, you will be able to

12.1 Describe the importance of solid financial foundation in small business.

12.2 Discuss techniques for measuring performance.

12.3 Explain ratio analysis.

12.4 Explain deviation analysis.

12.5 Explain sensitivity analysis.

12.6 Describe the use of short surveys in business.

12.7 Analyze the importance of having a measurement focus.

VaVaVroomonline.com

As Bank of America was getting ready to take over LaSalle Bank, the executives from La Salle had some big decisions to make about what they would do in the future. For Denise L. Maple, 39, it was a no-brainer: Take a buyout, from Bank of America which was being offered to reduce the staff at the acquired bank and hit the open road on her new, dual-sport motorcycle. The former vice president for corporate development also became an entrepreneur, investing $31,000 in VaVaVroomonline.com, a Chicago start-up that sells hoodies and snug, multicolored riding tops she helped design, alongside accessories and apparel of other brands.

While motorcycle sales overall have declined, the number of female buyers has increased 20 percent since 2003. "I saw a need in the market," Maple explains. "When I started riding five years ago, there was almost no motorcycle gear in women's sizes, let alone with style." Racer Café in St. Charles, Ilinois, was the first of 14 Chicago-area stores to retail her T-shirts. Maple is expanding into more sizes and aims to hit $300,000 in sales in 2008. This is one easy rider.

With the new business up and running, the focus of the firm shifts from developmental activities to day-to-day operations. In starting a successful business, good initial development is important, but perhaps as important are the efforts of the business as it grows. Once in operation, the business exists within the competitive marketplace and is subject to competitive attack, customer response to the product offering, supplier problems, inventory management issues, collections issues, etc. No operating business ever matches the proposed business exactly. The reality of operations and the ability to adjust to those realities is the key to managing a successful business. Adjusting requires an in-depth analysis of the firm's progress. To illustrate, let's revisit Philo Asian Grille.

LO 12.1 Financial Foundation

The evaluation of a firm starts with the mission of the organization and is (as was pointed out in Chapter 4) always relative to the industry in which the firm competes. The key measures of the firm should focus on the key aspects with which the firm hopes to build its competitive advantage. For example, if the mission of the organization was to be a low-cost operation, then rigorous control of expenses would be the focus. This would suggest that very little money would be spent in such activities as research and development, or new product introductions. The firm's outcomes would be measured at intervals that were relevant to the business, which, in the case of evaluating cost savings, might mean measuring such items very frequently, perhaps even daily. To illustrate, consider a restaurant that plans to have broccoli as a side dish this week and receives its order of fresh broccoli on Monday. Unfortunately the sales of broccoli during the week are significantly less than expected. If the firm accurately monitors its broccoli supply, it can determine that it needs to offer broccoli soup as an option on Thursday and Friday. Hopefully this will result in a significant reduction in the waste of the broccoli. (The development of potato skins as a snack food that appears at so many restaurants is a direct result of the way the baked potatoes from the prior day were used to prevent wastage.) Poor monitoring of the situation will result in waste for the business and the same mistake being made week after week.

In this chapter we will examine the development of the various metrics (measures) that should be used to evaluate the business. These analytical techniques are easily available and readily understandable by any business owner.

LO 12.2 Measuring the Firm

There is virtually an unlimited number of items upon which you could perform an analysis of your business, its activities, and its performance. However, taking the time to do this analysis means time away from the running of the business, and we therefore like to limit the

Philo had been in business for almost six months when the founders realized that they needed major revisions in the kitchen. They had bought used equipment when they opened the restaurant. However, the equipment they had bought was designed for a much smaller operation and was not very efficient for the volume that Philo was experiencing. The restaurant was growing with more customers and more catering opportunities, so the founders decided to re-equip the kitchen. This time, rather than buying used equipment, the founders decided that they would buy new equipment to take advantage of warranties and the efficiencies that the new equipment offered. Just as in buying a new car versus a used one, some of the bias toward buying new was as much psychological as practical. The founders felt like they were going to be in business to stay and wanted others in the industry to see a top-flight kitchen. They also believed that this would help to secure some of their employees who might prefer to work in this environment.

Through a well-known businessman and personal friend, the founders arranged to meet with the national sales representative from the leading supplier of commercial ovens and ranges. They identified approximately $50,000 worth of equipment they thought would work best in their business. However, rather than closing the deal that night, the saleswoman seemed almost hesitant. The next day the personal friend of the founders and the saleswoman came to see the founders.

The friend began to question the owners as to whether they could really afford the equipment at that stage of the restaurant's development. He asked pointed questions about their true returns and whether this included the cost of capital. What was the depreciation on their existing equipment? What was the nature of the financing they would rely on for new equipment? When this friend asked the owners to think about whether they truly were profitable, they realized that they had performed no real analysis of the business to date. They had customers coming into the restaurant and their checking account had maintained a nice balance; they were making payroll every month; they had money to make the payments on their loans; and they felt that things were good. Unfortunately, they didn't really know how much profit they were making, nor did they really know if the business could continue to expand. The reason that the mutual friend had come to ask these hard questions was that the salesperson had told him she had seen the scenario many times. A new restaurant starts to do particularly well and the founders decide to splurge on something new for the kitchen. However, too often the owners of the restaurants are not making as much money as they believed, and the new equipment contributes to the restaurant's failing. As a salesperson, she felt she could not say she would not sell them the equipment, but had asked their mutual friend to visit with them to ensure they knew the implications of making such a large purchase on credit.

The questions asked helped the founders of Philo realize that the time had come for them to start doing some serious analysis of their business in order to determine how they could proceed.

analysis to those areas that are critical to the business's ability to make economic rents, or to make a premium in excess of the opportunity costs. Company analysis should proceed from the general and move toward the specific. In that light, we review four classic analysis techniques prior to our discussion of designing and monitoring the core metrics for a particular organization. These four classic techniques are as follows:

1. Ratio analysis
2. Deviation analysis
3. Sensitivity analysis
4. Short surveys

Figure 12.1
Balance Sheet

BALANCE SHEET

	12/31/2008	12/31/2009	Difference
Assets			
Current Assets			
Cash	$ 50,000	$ 61,000	$ 11,000
Acct Receivable	$ 12,400	$ 16,700	$ 4,300
Inventory	$ 29,000	$ 31,000	$ 2,000
Total Current Assets	$ 91,400	$108,700	$ 17,300
Fixed Assets			
Land	$100,000	$100,000	$ 0
Buildings	$150,000	$150,000	$ 0
(Accumulated Depreciation)	($ 15,000)	($ 30,000)	($ 15,000)
Office Equipment	$ 75,000	$ 82,000	$ 7,000
Machinery	$ 45,000	$ 45,000	$ 0
(Accumulated Depreciation)	($ 3,500)	($ 7,000)	($ 3,500)
Total Fixed Assets	$ 351,500	$340,000	($ 11,500)
Total Assets	$453,000	$430,000	($23,000)
Liabilities			
Current Liabilities			
Accounts Payable	$ 35,000	$ 42,000	$ 7,000
Notes Payable (less than a year)	$ 4,500	$ 7,000	$ 2,500
Accrued Payroll	$ 15,000	$ 23,000	$ 8,000
Total Current Liabilities	$ 54,500	$ 72,000	$ 17,500
Long-Term Liabilities			
Mortgage	$200,000	$192,000	($ 8,000)
Bank Loan	$ 35,000	$ 30,000	($ 5,000)
Total Long-Term Liability	$235,000	$222,000	($ 13,000)
Owner's Equity	$163,500	$136,000	($27,500)
Total Liabilities/Owner's Equity	$453,000	$430,000	($23,000)

Before examining these four techniques of analysis, students should quickly review the sample balance sheet in Figure 12.1 and the income statement in Figure 12.2. This data will be employed to illustrate the analytical methods.

Figure 12.2
Income Statement

INCOME STATEMENT

Receipts:		2008	2009
	Sales	$ 178,790	$ 241,650
	Less Returns	$ 4,000	$ 7,000
	COGS	$ 54,700	$ 67,662
	Gross Profit	**$120,090**	**$166,988**
Expenses			
	Salaries	$ 28,000	$ 37,000
	Travel	$ 6,545	$ 7,650
	Car Leases	$ 6,000	$ 6,000
	Rent	$ 3,150	$ 3,600
	Payroll Taxes	$ 1,720	$ 2,450
	Insurance	$ 1,450	$ 1,800
	Fuel/Maint.	$ 1,412	$ 1,733
	Benefits	$ 2,100	$ 3,600
	Advertising	$ 1,896	$ 3,000
	Utilities	$ 1,104	$ 1,946
	Misc.	$ 1,528	$ 1,255
Total Expenses		**$ 55,208**	**$ 70,034**
Operating Income		**$ 64,882**	**$ 96,954**
Interest		$ 11,975	$ 13,800
Taxes		$ 14,274	$ 22,299
Profit After Taxes		**$ 38,633**	**$ 60,855**

LO 12.3 Ratio Analysis

Ratio analysis is a tool for the small business person to use to examine the overall health of the organization.[1] Ratios by themselves are of little value. Instead the ratios for any given firm need to be evaluated in comparison to other similar organizations, an industry average, or simply the previous month's or year's performance. There are four basic categories of performance ratios which we will discuss: liquidity, activity, leverage, and profitability (Figure 12.3). We will first provide the means by which these ratios are calculated and then provide some insights that each brings to the business owner.

ratio analysis

A series of ratios along four areas of company performance (liquidity, activity, leverage, profitability) that provides a picture of the health of the company.

Figure 12.3
Commonly Used Ratios

Liquidity Ratios

Current
$$\frac{CurrentAssets}{CurrentLiabilities}$$

Quick (or Acid Test)
$$\frac{CurrentAssets - Inventory}{CurrentLiabilities}$$

Activity Ratios

Inventory Turnover
$$\frac{CostofGoodsSold}{Inventory}$$

Accounts Receivable Turnover
$$\frac{CreditSales}{AccountsReceivable}$$

Total/Fixed Asset Turnover
$$\frac{NetSales}{FixedAssets}$$

Leverage Ratios

Debt to Equity
$$\frac{TotalLiablities}{TotalAssets - TotalLiabilities}$$

Debt to Assets
$$\frac{TotalLiablities}{TotalAssets}$$

Times Interest Earned
$$\frac{OperatingIncome}{Interset}$$

Profitability Ratios

Gross Profit Margin
$$\frac{GrossProfit}{NetSales}$$

Operating Profit Margin (or EBIT)
$$\frac{OperatingIncome}{NetSales}$$

Net Profit Margin
$$\frac{NetProfit}{Netsales}$$

ROA (return on assets)
$$\frac{NetProfit}{TotalAssets}$$

ROE (return on equity)
$$\frac{NetProfit}{Equity}$$

Liquidity Ratios

liquidity ratios

Ratios that measure the short-term ability of the firm to meet its obligations.

Liquidity ratios measure the short-term ability of the firm to meet its obligations. These obligations would include debt or accounts payable that must be paid by the business in the near term.[2] Financing institutions generally require that liquidity ratios be kept within certain ranges. If the business drops below the lower bounds of its liquidity level, then the bank may limit the line of credit to the firm or require a higher interest rate on the debt, as the risk position of the firm will have increased. Even for companies that appear to be growing well and have good prospects,

---

EXERCISE 2

1. Using the information from the income and balance sheet provided to you, calculate each of the ratios in Figure 12.3 and fill in the chart provided in the figure for 2009.

the ability to meet the short-term obligations of the firm is a significant concern. There are two specific types of liquidity ratios that are of interest: current ratio and acid ratio.

Current Ratio: Current Assets divided by Current Liabilities. The current ratio measures those assets that can be quickly turned into cash and used to pay for immediate liabilities. In general, this is the cash balance of the firm plus inventory divided by all short-term liabilities.

Quick (Acid) Ratio: Current Assets minus Inventory divided by Current Liabilities. The quick ratio removes the ability to sell inventory and examines the pure cash position relative to the current liabilities. The term used here is "quick ratio," but it is also sometimes referred to as an "acid test."

Calculating Liquidity Ratios Using the balance sheet (Figure 12.1), let's take a look at these two calculations. Look for the lines labeled Current Assets, Current Liabilities, and Inventory. Following the formula for 2008 and 2009 yields the following:

Current Ratio	2008	$62,400/$54,400 = 1.147
	2009	$77,700/$72,000 = 1.079
Quick Ratio (or Acid Test)	2008	$62,400-$29,000/$54,400 = .61
	2009	$77,700-$31,000/$72,000 = .65

Interpreting these items relative to each other, you can see that this business has held relatively constant over these two years in its ability to meet its short-term obligations. The current ratio is just over 1.0, which tells us that the company has just enough money to meet all of its short-term obligations. The quick ratio tells us that the firm has slightly improved its ability to pay cash for its short-term liabilities. However, the firm relies extensively on inventory to pay its current liabilities. That is not a concern in and of itself, but it can be problematic if the inventory in this industry becomes dated quickly. Therefore, it would be useful to evaluate the firm's ratios against the ratios for the industry (if available). An important issue in ratio analysis is ensuring that you are comparing apples to apples. However, often the ratios you may find are based on Fortune 500 firms, and these will have little or no relevance to a small business. We suggest for comparison purposes that a small business use sources such as the data published by the Risk Management Association (formerly Robert Morris Associates). This alliance of community banks gathers data from the portfolios of all of its member firms and then provides typical ratios by industry. The firms in the database are generally smaller than those in most other generic data sources. This database must be purchased; however, most public libraries subscribe to either the hard copy or the CD version of the data. For our example firm, the data show that the quick ratio is very consistent with the industry averages.

Activity Ratios

activity ratios

Ratios that measure the efficiency with which you are handling the resources of the business.

Activity ratios measure the efficiency with which you are handling the resources of the business. They are particularly helpful as the business develops, since you will be able to compare from month to month (or more often if you wish). There are three specific ratios in which we are interested.

Inventory Turnover: Cost of Goods Sold divided by Inventory. Cost of Goods Sold is the direct costs involved with a product. As this inventory turnover rises, the firm is getting closer to a just-in-time system. There are pros and cons to operating in a just-in-time system, and in some cases, the reality of the industry means that this is not a reasonable approach. Generally an inventory turnover ratio that is better than the industry average or one that is improving each month means that the firm is operating more efficiently.

Account Receivable Turnover: Credit Sales divided by Accounts Receivable. This metric examines how fast the company turns credit sales into cash. The faster the firm is able to turn credit sales into cash, the better the cash flow position of the firm is. Credit sales should also be aged into categories based on how long it has been since the sale. Unfortunately, this is necessary because the older the debt is, the less likely it is that you will be paid. Almost all debt 30 days and under is considered highly likely to be paid. After 90 days past due, however, only a small percentage of the debt will be realistically recovered. We will discuss this topic more when we examine collections at the end of this chapter.

Total/Fixed Asset Turnover: Net Sales divided by Fixed Assets or Net Sales divided by Total Assets. Small businesses will likely use one of these numbers more often than the other. The difference principally turns on whether or not the business has large amounts of fixed assets. For example, a small manufacturer will want to focus on the productivity of its fixed assets. It is how efficient the business is in using those fixed assets that determines how competitive the firm is in the marketplace. In contrast, a retail store will be more interested in total assets. Such a firm has limited fixed assets but does have extensive inventory. In either case, the founder is attempting to examine the ability to generate sales from the assets employed by the organization. As this number increases, the firm is being more efficient. New businesses should try to minimize the amount of both fixed and total assets in order to conserve cash.

Calculating Activity Ratios To calculate activity ratios requires information from both the balance sheet and the income statement. For example, the inventory turnover ratio derives the numerator (cost of goods sold) from the income statement, while the denominator (inventory) comes from the balance sheet. Using the numbers provided in Figures 12.1 and 12.2, we calculate the following activity ratios.

| Inventory Turnover | 2008 | $54,700/$29,000 = 1.88 |
| | 2009 | $67,662/$31,000 = 2.18 |

Accounts Receivable Turnover	2008	$178,790/$12,400 = 14.42
Total Asset Turnover	2009	$241,650/$16,700 = 14.47
	2008	$178,790/$453,000 = .39
	2009	$241,650/$430,000 = .56
Fixed Asset Turnover	2008	$178,790/$351,500 = .51
	2009	$241,650/$340,000 = .71

To interpret these numbers (in the absence of industry comparisons), the small business person should focus on the relative change. Such a comparison would tell the business that the inventory turnover rate has gone up in 2009. The business then would want to determine the cause for this greater efficiency. The firm could have been very inefficient in 2008 and may be just now gaining the experience necessary to gain the efficiencies of more mature firms. However, another reason might be that the firm has discovered some activity or method that provides the firm a level of efficiency greater than those of its competitors. If this is the case, the business will want to identify that source of competitive advantage and nurture it. Therefore, the business will likely want to have industry information on industry turnover. The evidence from the RMA suggests that the business is more efficient than its peer group in that region of the country.

The other ratios changed little over the time period and appear consistent with those of other similar firms in that region of the country. Therefore, the small business probably does not want to focus its attention on those issues.

EXERCISE 3

1. Using the pro forma statements that you developed for your business (as discussed in Chapter 6), calculate each of the liquidity and activity ratios for your business.
2. How do these compare with the industry averages?
3. If this causes you to reexamine your forecasts, explain why.

Leverage Ratios

Leverage ratios are used to examine the relative level of indebtedness of the small business. Specifically, all creditors (whether they are suppliers of goods or banks with outstanding loans) want to ensure that the small business has the ability to generate sufficient funds to pay the supplier or repay the loans. High levels of debt are dangerous when the economy turns down, as we have all seen these past few years. There are three ratios that are commonly used to evaluate the relative level of indebtedness of a business.

leverage ratios
Ratios that are used to examine the relative level of indebtedness of the small business.

Debt-to-Equity: Total Liabilities divided by Total Assets minus Total Liabilities. The denominator of this equation (Total Assets minus Total Liabilities) is effectively the owner's equity. This ratio provides the information on the portion of the business owned by the lenders and that portion owned by the founder(s).

Debt-to-Assets: Total Liabilities divided by Total Assets. A slight variation of the debt-to-equity ratio, this measures the percentage of the assets of the firm that are actually owned by the creditors.

Times Interest Earned: Operating Income divided by Interest. This figure estimates the number of times that the firm could repay the current interest owed on its debts. The higher this number is, the more capable the firm is of servicing its debt load.

Calculating Leverage Ratios The information for most of the leverage ratios will come from Figure 12.1, the balance sheet. However, calculating times interest earned will require information from both the balance sheet and Figure 2, the income statement. Using the data for our firm we can generate the following data.

Debt-to-Equity Ratio	2008	$289,500/$163,500 = 1.77
	2009	$294,000/$136,000 = 2.16
Debt-to-Assets Ratio	2008	$289,500/$453,000 = .64
	2009	$294,000/$430,000 = .68
Times Interest Earned	2008	$64,882/$11,975 = 5.42
	2009	$96,954/$13,800 = 7.02

In calculating these ratios, what appears is a pattern with a significant change in the debt-to-equity ratio between 2008 and 2009. Similarly, the times interest earned appears to have undergone a significant shift that year. These areas should attract the businessperson's immediate interest. The businessperson would want to compare these numbers to the industry to identify if this was an industry-wide pattern. In the case of times interest earned, the industry-wide numbers are very similar to what our sample firm experienced. The reason for this was the overall drop in interest rate costs in the United States during that time. The increase in debt-to-equity is more troubling. The industry averages are closer to 1.15 than they are to 2.16. Even more disturbing is that the increase in debt-to-equity ratio appears to be due to lower equity in the firm. This raises a troubling picture. It appears that the business is slowly eating away the equity position of the firm. In other words, more is being taken out of the firm than is being put back into it. This may be the result of a negative net cash flow or something as simple as the founders' drawing more off in salary than the business can support. The result is not an immediate failure of the business but a slow spiral downward that ultimately results in failure. In a normal business that has achieved a break-even position, we would expect the equity position of the business to increase over time, not decrease. Therefore, the small business person should flag this result and question what type of long-term pattern of performance is being established.

Profitability Ratios

Although profitability is the focus of much of the business press, it should be recognized as an outcome of the business's other activities. Thus, profitability is a result of effectively managing the assets and cash flow of the firm, not the activity of focus itself. **Profitability ratios** examine the performance of the firm and its ability to make economic returns over and above its costs. There are five profitability ratios that generate the greatest attention.

profitability ratios

Ratios that examine the performance of the firm and its ability to make economic rents over and above its costs.

> **Gross Profit Margin:** Gross Profit divided by Net Sales. This ratio is used to determine the overall profit that is obtained from all sales during the period being evaluated. Gross profit is a category created by taking the total net sales of the firm and subtracting

returned merchandise as well as the direct cost of the goods sold. This is the most basic of the profitability measures.

Operating Profit Margin: Operating Income divided by Net Sales. A finer-grained measure, this looks at the gross profit minus all of the operating expenses. This figure is also known as Earnings before Interest and Taxes (EBIT) and represents the operating efficiency of the organization.

Net Profit Margin: Net Profit divided by Net Sales. Net profit is the bottom line calculation from the income statement. This figure presents a picture of the relative margin earned after all obligations and expenses are considered.

Return on Assets (ROA): Net Profit divided by Total Assets. This is one of the two overall calculations that are standards in almost any industry. This ratio examines the ability of the firm to return an overall profit compared to the amount of assets that the firm has invested into the effort.

Return on Equity (ROE): Net Profit divided by Equity (Total Assets minus Total Liabilities). This ratio is used to provide all investors with an evaluation of how much each dollar of their investment is generating in profit.

Calculating Profitability Ratios The calculations for the first three profitability ratios come from Figure 12.2, the income statement. The last two ratios combine information from both Figure 12.1—the balance sheet—and Figure 12.2, the income statement. Using the information from our sample firm, the following calculations are generated.

Gross Profit Margin	2008	$120,090/178,790 = .67
	2009	$166,988/241,650 = .69
Operating Profit Margin	2008	$64,882/178,790 = .36
	2009	$96,954/241,650 = .40
Net Profit Margin	2008	$38,633/178,790 = .22
	2009	$60,855/241,650 = .25
Return on Assets	2008	$38,633/453,000 = .085
	2009	$60,855/430,000 = .141
Return on Equity	2008	$38,633/163,500 = .24
	2009	$60,855/136,000 = .45

The profitability ratios present a firm that appears to be improving in all aspects. All of its margins increased nicely year after year. Its ability to make a profit on the assets and owners' equity provided improved nicely. This was partially due to a reduction in the value of the asset base and partially due to a very pleasant increase in sales without an equivalent increase in expenses. However, it was also due to a serious erosion of owners' equity in the business. While it is nice to efficiently use the equity, we would normally look for owners' equity to increase as sales were growing. This needs to be looked into and given serious consideration by the founders.

Even though businesses vary, the core concepts involved in healthy financial endeavor are universal. What are some of the similarities and differences between the financials for a restaurant versus a clothing store?

Summary of Ratios

The ratios provided on page 251 can be valuable tools to the firm. All of the statements necessary to calculate these ratios are standard with any accounting package that you might choose. In fact, most of these accounting packages will automatically calculate these ratios. As a small business owner, you will likely choose only one or two of the ratios in each category (liquidity, activity, leverage, and performance, or profitability) to use for examining the company, since you can be buried in data if you do not. It is important to understand the broad indicators of the different types of ratios to be able to pick them intelligently. Establishing a good data collection system (as outlined in Chapter 9) is necessary for any of this analysis to be useful or effective for the entrepreneur. Finally, it is important in analyzing ratios that the small business person remember that it is only through the comparison of those ratios over time or compared to some other firm or group of firms that the ratios can be interpreted. The ratios by themselves are interesting but do not provide much insight.

LO 12.4 Deviation Analysis

deviation analysis

A chart tracking various performance measures from one time period to the next.

A second analysis method that is valuable for examining the firm, its activities, and its performance is a **deviation analysis.** This type of analysis is simply a chart tracking various performance measures from one time period to the next (month to month or year to year). The deviation chart has two additional columns, one showing the actual change and the other showing a percentage change. A deviation chart should be maintained for all important metrics. These might include several of the ratios listed above as well as other metrics that the organization deems to be important. An example is shown in Figure 12.4.

Notice that whether a particular item is good or bad for a company depends upon the direction desired by the small business person. As you can see, the drop in current ratio from 2009 to 2010 is a negative event, while the drop in number of complaints, during this period, from 27 to 21 is a positive event. A deviation analysis allows the entrepreneur to quickly evaluate the performance of the organization on those items that she considers most important to the success of the firm.

ITEM	2009	2010	ACTUAL DIFFERENCE	% DIFFERENCE
Current Ratio	1.147	1.079	−0.068	**−5.90%**
Inventory Turnover	1.88	2.18	0.2	**10.60**
Gross Profit Margin	0.67	0.69	0.02	**2.90**
Net Profit Margin	0.22	0.25	0.03	**13.60**
# of Complaints	27	21	6	**22.20**
Hours of Operation/Week	42	56	14	**33.30**
# of Employees	2	7	5	**250**
# Who Say We Are Their First Choice	47	117	70	**148.90**

Figure 12.4
Deviation Analysis

While this particular example shows only data from one year to the next, significantly greater insight would be gained by comparing data on more frequent intervals. The resulting picture of the firm's trends is always more revealing about how the company is performing. The business is encouraged to develop a chart using shorter time periods so that the patterns and deviations can be observed and used in the analysis of the business. As a result, we suggest that this chart be maintained at least monthly. Most businesses have some type of seasonality that could be significant for ordering, staffing, advertising, etc. In addition, an annual chart should also be prepared that allows comparison across the years as the firm matures.

In this particular example we also included several metrics that went beyond the basic financial ratios. As will be discussed shortly, we believe that measuring the performance of a business goes well beyond the financial aspects. The success of the company in pursuing its strategy should be a part of the analysis maintained by all companies.

EXERCISE 4

1. Prepare a deviation analysis for your business using your financial forecasts.
2. What unique items might you include in your deviation analysis that go beyond the basic ratios?

LO 12.5 Sensitivity Analysis

A third method of examining the ability of the organization to handle changes in the future is for the firm to perform a **sensitivity analysis.**[3] This type of analysis involves taking the current cash flow statement, income statement, or balance sheet and making projections based upon a dramatic increase in sales, a dramatic decrease in sales, or the business's undergoing a major change. This method of examination allows the small business person to look at how sensitive the business is to various factors. In the example on pages 255–257, we use a cash flow statement to contemplate the impact of a dramatic sales increase or decrease. If the firm experiences a sudden 50 percent increase or decrease in sales, what will the impact be on the overall organization? In the case of

sensitivity analysis

A chart utilizing current cash flow statement, income statement, or balance sheet in order to create a pro forma projection based upon a dramatic increase in sales, a dramatic decrease in sales, or the complication of a major change in the business.

Alex had been in business for several months. He felt that the business was doing pretty well, although he really only knew that he was busy all the time. His sister was proving to be very valuable to him. During the first week of business, she saw Alex simply placing in a shoebox receipts and invoices that he planned to review at the end of the day. Unfortunately, he missed a few days and they started to pile up. She convinced him to set up and use a computer-based system. The system was not complex and relied on a relatively cheap standardized PC from a local retail chain. He would enter the invoice and receipts as the transaction happened so there was a complete tracking of his work.

At the end of the second month, Alex's sister had printed out the totals of a few basic items for the month, such as total sales, revenue received, receivables, total expenses, the amount actually paid out on bills, and what was still owed on bills. Alex was very happy to be able to see the numbers but really did not know how to analyze them. Then his sister started a basic tracking and ratio performance chart for him like the one below:

	Month 1	Month 2	Change
Current Ratio	1.147	1.079	−0.068
Gross Profit Margin	0.65	0.70	0.02
Net Profit Margin	0.20	0.26	0.03

This triggered a conversation with his sister and his family about how the business was doing and what these numbers really meant.

1. What do these numbers mean for Alex's business?

2. What would you need to be able to analyze these numbers?

3. Using data that you can obtain on the Internet about auto repair businesses, compare Alex's business performance for the first two months.

4. If Alex opened in June and these numbers reflect June and July, how might that impact your analysis?

an increase, how many new staff must be hired to accommodate these sales? What might the impact be upon travel or insurance? First we list the projected cash flow statement for the firm (Figure 12.5) and then we provide one with a 50 percent increase (Figure 12.6) and another with a 50 percent decrease in sales (Figure 12.7).

Under the rapid increase in sales scenario, the firm is hurt during its first two years, but then recovers for an extraordinary third year. The firm will need more funding if this scenario occurs and should have a plan for handling such situations. Under the decrease in sales projection, not only is the firm not making any positive net cash flows, but the net cash flow number is actually increasingly negative. For the firm to miss its projections by this amount would be devastating for the future of the business. Sensitivity analysis provides the businessperson an opportunity to test out assumptions and view the potential impact of those assumptions prior to committing any new resources.

LO 12.6 The Short Survey

The fourth and final means to analyze the business, its activities, and its performance is the survey. The prior three methods examined (ratios, deviation, sensitivity) focused on financial data. As has been mentioned several other times in this text, the new businessperson should also recognize that there are nonfinancial methods of analysis that can

Figure 12.5
Cash Flow—Projected

Receipts:	YEAR 1	YEAR 2	YEAR 3
Sales	$ 25,000	$325,000	$675,000
Consulting	$ 20,000	$ 20,000	$ 60,000
Total Receipts	$ 45,000	$345,000	$735,000
Disbursements:			
Salaries	$ 45,000	$ 95,000	$210,000
Travel	$ 4,050	$ 31,050	$ 66,150
Car Leases	$ 4,000	$ 6,000	$ 7,500
Rent	$ 900	$ 6,900	$ 14,700
Payroll Taxes	$ 2,700	$ 5,700	$ 12,600
Insurance	$ 5,500	$ 6,000	$ 7,500
Fuel/Maint.	$ 960	$ 4,500	$ 8,000
Executive Comp	$ 64,000	$ 72,000	$ 78,000
Benefits	$ 13,500	$ 28,500	$ 63,000
Advertising	$ 2,000	$ 26,000	$ 54,000
Supplies	$ 225	$ 1,725	$ 3,675
Utilities	$ 3,150	$ 24,150	$ 51,450
Misc.	$ 900	$ 6,900	$ 14,700
Total Disbursements	$ 146,885	$ 314,425	$ 591,275
Beginning Balance	$ 0	$ 98,115	$ 128,690
Equity Investment	$200,000		
Net Cash Flow	($ 101,885)	$ 30,575	$ 143,725
Ending Balance	$ 98,115	$ 128,690	$ 272,415

be useful to the entrepreneur. So much of what we would like to know about our customers, suppliers, and employees is contextual information that is not easily categorized and is subject to interpretation. This is the ideal reasoning for using a survey to gather information. While survey methodology is virtually a science unto itself, we believe that anyone can develop an effective survey with just a little care.

Short surveys can be given to any party to a transaction with your business and provide you with the opportunity to evaluate your company's performance on dimensions that may lead to financial success. If there is a very large set of customers, the small business person may choose to sample every third customer. This is a type of random sample and the expectation is that this subset of the total customers (presuming that the sample is sufficiently large) will in fact reflect all customers (within a small margin of error). Alternatively, a small business person may choose to try to survey all of his customers.

In either case there will be some bias in your survey, since only those individuals who wish to fill out the survey will do so. Therefore, the information from the survey can be useful, but judgment is still

Figure 12.6
Cash Flow—50%
Increase in Sales

Receipts:	YEAR 1	YEAR 2	YEAR 3
Sales	$ 37,500	$487,500	$1,012,500
Consulting	$ 30,000	$ 30,000	$ 90,000
Total Receipts	$ 67,500	$ 517,500	$1,102,500
Disbursements:			
Salaries	$ 90,000	$190,000	$ 420,000
Travel	$ 6,075	$ 46,575	$ 99,225
Car Leases	$ 8,000	$ 12,000	$ 15,000
Rent	$ 1,350	$ 10,350	$ 22,050
Payroll Taxes	$ 5,400	$ 11,400	$ 25,200
Insurance	$ 7,500	$ 8,500	$ 10,000
Fuel/Maint.	$ 2,200	$ 6,000	$ 10,200
Executive Comp	$ 64,000	$ 72,000	$ 78,000
Benefits	$ 27,000	$ 57,000	$ 126,000
Advertising	$ 3,000	$ 39,000	$ 81,000
Supplies	$ 338	$ 2,588	$ 5,513
Utilities	$ 4,725	$ 36,225	$ 77,175
Misc.	$ 1,350	$ 10,350	$ 22,050
Total Disbursements	$ 220,938	$ 501,988	$ 991,413
Beginning Balance	$ 0	$ 46,563	$ 62,075
Equity Investment	$200,000		
Net Cash Flow	($ 153,438)	$ 15,513	$ 111,088
Ending Balance	$ 46,563	$ 62,075	$ 173,163

required to interpret the results. The questions on the survey should be designed to answer questions directly related to the mission/strategy of the company. Some examples of questions for a high-end manufacturer are as follows:

1. How do you rate our prices:

Better than most		Same		Higher than most
1	2	3	4	5

2. Is the quality of our product:

Better than most		Same		Higher than most
1	2	3	4	5

3. The nature of our service is:

Better than most		Same		Higher than most
1	2	3	4	5

Receipts:	YEAR 1	YEAR 2	YEAR 3
Sales	$ 12,500	$162,500	$337,500
Consulting	$ 10,000	$ 10,000	$ 30,000
Total Receipts	$ 22,500	$172,500	$367,500
Disbursements:			
Salaries	$ 45,000	$ 95,000	$210,000
Travel	$ 2,025	$ 15,525	$ 33,075
Car Leases	$ 4,000	$ 6,000	$ 7,500
Rent	$ 450	$ 3,450	$ 7,350
Payroll Taxes	$ 2,700	$ 5,700	$ 12,600
Insurance	$ 5,500	$ 6,000	$ 7,500
Fuel/Maint.	$ 480	$ 4,500	$ 8,000
Executive Comp	$ 64,000	$ 72,000	$ 78,000
Benefits	$ 13,500	$ 28,500	$ 63,000
Advertising	$ 1,000	$ 13,000	$ 27,000
Supplies	$ 113	$ 863	$ 1,838
Utilities	$ 1,575	$ 12,075	$ 25,725
Misc.	$ 450	$ 3,450	$ 7,350
Total Disbursements	$ 140,793	$266,063	$488,938
Beginning Balance	$ 0	$ 81,708	($ 11,855)
Equity Investment	$200,000		
Net Cash Flow	($ 118,293)	($ 93,563)	($ 121,438)
Ending Balance	$ 81,708	($ 11,855)	($ 133,293)

Figure 12.7
Cash Flow—50%
Decrease in Sales

This particular sample firm wants to be competitive in most regards, but given its goals, wants to be better than competitors on both service and quality. Ideally each survey will have several questions that look at various aspects of the same issue. We would want to see some consistency in the pattern of answers within the survey as well as between surveys.

Survey data can be tabulated and examined with some fairly simple statistical techniques, such as percentages. Therefore, a fact as simple as "only 55 percent of your customers indicated that your service is better than the service of your competitors" would be a trouble signal for a firm where service was presumed to be a key competitive advantage. However, with just a slight increase in sophistication in the analysis techniques, quite a bit more can be learned from the data. Cross tabulation of related items and simple regressions can form a picture of the organization that leads it beyond its competitors. Both of these are available in virtually every spreadsheet package, and while the level of statistical sophistication can get quite complex, the basics are relatively easy to use and comprehend. A cross tabulation displays the distribution of two or more variables in columns. Thus you could see, for example, how your drinks matched your entrees in a restaurant.

	meat dish	salad only
Wine	35%	25%
Beer	40%	15%
Coffee	5%	60%

A regression is a more complex analysis and concerns how well points of information fit along a line. The results allow you to see how different variables explain the differences for a given measure, such as profits.

LO 12.7 Measurement Focus

This understanding of your key competitive advantages and the ability to develop measurements that ensure you are fulfilling your strategic goals is worth greater focus. Remember from Chapter 5 that there are two aspects to any business, the standard and the extraordinary. The standard parts of a business are those that must be done just to be considered a part of that particular industry, while the extraordinary represents those areas where the business really tries to differentiate itself. A business needs to do the standard and they need to do it well, but only as well as the rest of the industry. Thus, the standard parts of the business should be managed in the simplest way possible, with very little extra analysis. As long as the firm is performing as well as the rest of the industry, then sufficient effort has been placed in these areas.

A very simple example illustrates just how easy it is to overinvest in the standard. An owner of a bus tour company said he was contemplating getting a postage machine. The natural question to ask the owner when advising him was how many pieces of mail went out in a day. Putting stamps on more than about 10 pieces a day easily justifies a postage machine, if for no other reason than the savings in time spent purchasing stamps, maintaining a supply, and putting stamps on envelopes. This company was sending out between 170 and 225 pieces of mail a day. This is a standard activity for a company and no matter how much time or effort is spent, no customer will pay you extra for a stamp versus a postal imprint. We felt that this was an easy, standard decision that should take virtually no time away from the core of the business. That said, the founder decided to make a project out of this decision. He invited three companies to meet with him and demonstrate their machines. He analyzed the amount of time it took to place stamps on the envelopes (about 20 minutes a day) and added in the time for traveling to and from the post office (another 20 minutes or so a week). After all the analysis, the company decided to get a postage machine. The owner wanted to track the success of the decision by having the person who ran the envelopes through the

In the process of doing an analysis of your business as well as those of your competitors, you realize that the data for one of your competitor firms are quite unusual. Despite the fact that its customer count is very low and its suppliers deliver less than one-fourth of the goods supplied to you and the other retailers, this one operation is reporting sales to the government that far exceed your own. During several conversations at a local business social club meeting, you are told by several businesspeople that you should steer clear of that business because they are laundering money.

1. Do you have an obligation to tell the authorities?

2. The business that you suspect is a major advertiser in the local media and is always putting down the competition. You'd like to see the firm out of business. Does this confuse your ethical obligation?

machine record the amount of time it took each day and to include the time it took to periodically recharge the machine. This type of analysis is of no value to the ultimate success of an organization. Not only did it waste the time of the people involved, but it also meant that they were not doing their core jobs during this time. Unfortunately, it is very easy to become consumed with the minutiae of analyzing a business and fail to focus on those operations that are most critical for the customer.[4]

The focus should be on those areas that provide competitive advantage to the firm. In the example of the bus tour agency, there was no competitive advantage to be gained from either a stamp or an imprint. This firm made large segments of its income from arranging annual foliage bus tours for senior citizens to look at the changing colors of the leaves in the mid-Atlantic states. Therefore, measuring the efficiency of the buses employed, the advertising dollars spent reaching that population, the experience on each tour, and the time spent to secure each account would be much more critical. Concentrating the analysis efforts on those areas that are extraordinary puts the founder's focus on those areas that can create a differentiation for the business compared to those of the competitors.

summary

Small businesses have very few slack resources relative to their larger competitors. The result is that a large firm can make a series of mistakes and still maintain a going concern. With a much tighter margin of error, a small business should actively monitor its performance relative both to itself and to its competitors. This chapter provided a series of relatively quick, easily maintained techniques for developing and maintaining an effective picture of the company.

key terms

review questions

1. What are the four means to evaluate the firm, its activities, and its performance?
2. What do liquidity ratios seek to measure? What are the major types of liquidity ratios?
3. Why are industry averages important to the interpretation of ratios?
4. What do activity ratios seems to measure? What are the major types of activity ratios?
5. What do leverage ratios seek to measure? What are the major types of liquidity ratios?
6. What do performance ratios seek to measure? What are the major types of performance ratios?
7. List two performance measures and explain their significance.
8. How is a deviation analysis used by a business?
9. How is a sensitivity analysis used to protect a business?

individual exercises

1. Examine the mission statement for your new business. What metrics could you design to examine your success at achieving the mission?
2. Using your library's resources, examine the Risk Management Association records to determine an appropriate industry set of business financial metrics.
3. Using your pro forma statements developed in earlier chapters, compare your proposed financial ratios to those from the industry standards.
4. What changes do you need to make in your forecasts?

group exercises

Go to the Internet and pick one of the following large firms: IBM, Yum Brands (parent of Pizza Hut), or Home Depot. Conduct a ratio analysis for this firm using at least six key ratios. Ensure that you find comparable ratios for its industry. Have the other members of the group do the same company. Compare your findings.

1. Which ratios did you pick and why?
2. What was the financial performance for this firm in 2008?
3. Predict what you believe the financial performance of the company will be based on the pattern of performance in 2008 and before.
4. What was the actual performance of the firm last year?

everyday edisons class discussion

Go to www.everydayedisons.com/russBrent.htm and read about Brent and Russ.

1. Brent and Russ had a spectacular idea and yet had no ability to produce the product. What ways would you suggest that they approach this issue?
2. How would you recommend they analyze the "life" of the product?

Karen Taylor—Taylor Cuisine Café & Catering, Inc.

Karen Taylor grew up working in her family's restaurant business in Westchester, New York, getting to know every aspect of running a restaurant. At one time or another, she did everything from cooking and washing the dishes to running the register. Despite this background or because of it, she chose not to take over the business when her father was getting ready to retire. She had graduated from Franklin Pierce University (New Hampshire) with a degree in business management and was ready to tackle the corporate world. For the next 20 years she worked for a variety of companies, including Bell South in Atlanta, Georgia. As an account executive at Bell South, she loved her job, but found during the last couple of years that her passion had shifted from telecommunications to food.

Over the years she had hosted numerous events at her home. She constantly had guests ask her about catering their events. This success, her background in food preparation, and her growing interest encouraged her to pursue this area. She started a part-time catering business and began working on a volunteer basis at The Cook's Warehouse. The Cook's Warehouse is the award-winning culinary store and teaching school in Atlanta where celebrity chefs regularly offer their expertise. She found herself really enjoying her time associated with food more and more, which led her to think more about opening a restaurant.

Karen's parents had retired to the beach community of Southport, North Carolina, and her father kept talking to

her about the lack of a good breakfast and lunch places in the area. Karen started considering a move to the area and opening a place, but wasn't sure where she might locate it.

A restaurant on the main street in Southport had been a poorly run Chinese restaurant for some time when it was purchased by two Vietnamese sisters. The sisters renovated the location and put in brand-new, state-of-the-art kitchen appliances. The two had a very different approach to running the business, and the result was that the business was run very intermittently. Sometimes it was open on a particular day and sometimes it wasn't. Karen visited the restaurant for lunch one day less than six months after the Vietnamese restaurant had opened. The sisters showed her the whole place and asked her if she wanted it. Karen talked it over with her parents and they financed her start-up. Taylor Cuisine Café & Catering was about to become a reality.

Taylor Cuisine Café and Catering was to be a breakfast and lunch place. However, she wanted to open something that had a unique position in the market. Over the next few months she talked with a wide range of people about the market and about what people wanted to eat. She ended up focusing on southern cuisine because that was really desired, but it would be with a twist because she wanted to make the offering special. These included such items as "Taylor Made Onion Rings" that would be served with her own special aioli sauce and "Fried Green Tomatoes" that would be seasoned with red pepper sauce and crumbled goat cheese.

Karen began by marketing her place through traditional Yellow Pages advertising, the Web, and word of mouth. She had always thought that running a business in a small town would be easy from a marketing perspective. Surely everyone would know you were there in very short order. Unfortunately, that was not the case. People are still coming into the restaurant, which has now been open for four years, surprised that it exists. Still, Karen believes that several types of marketing have really made the difference over the past few years.

The first is her new porch, which extends out from the front of the building between her main restaurant and the road. People spot the porch immediately and Karen says that it has paid for itself many times over. A second visibility approach is her volunteer work. Karen is on the board of directors at both the Chamber of Commerce and the Boys and Girls Club. She also belongs to the local chapter of the American Culinary Foundation. The third area is her very creative use of free media and the local media outlets' desire to fill broadcasts with some fun stuff. She changed her menu during the primaries and again near the election in 2008 with candidate-named creations that brought out the television stations. She always opens during the big Fourth of July celebrations and the media uses her restaurant as a broadcast point that is in touch with the community. She also uses some traditional advertising, including printed ads that are placed in every room of the local Hampton Inn hotel.

Catering makes up about 15 percent of her business, and she has very recently begun exploring opening for dinner. She started opening on Friday nights and has now expanded the dinnertime opening to Thursday through Saturday.

She has some great advice for new entrepreneurs to consider:

1. Don't go into business solely for the money. Making money is hard and running a business is hard. You need to go into a business because you have a passion for it. The money will come, but only after a lot of hard work.

2. Know your business inside and out. The key to success is the ability to do everything that a business requires and to understand everything that has to be done.

3. Take advantage of free advertising. As mentioned earlier, Karen and her employees look for creative ways to be in front of the press.

4. Beware of taxes. She says that one of her biggest surprises has been the amount of taxes that are assessed to the business. In Southport, they count every item in her business for assessing her tax bill. This includes every piece of silverware.

Karen says that she looks forward to coming to work every single day and that is worth a lot!

chapter

13

learning outcomes

After studying this chapter, you will be able to:

13.1 Explain the need for developing an exit/harvest plan and ideal timing for that plan.

13.2 Outline the steps for selling a business.

13.3 Discuss the concept of turnaround as it applies to a decline in business.

13.4 Recognize the implications and issues involved in closing a business.

Exit/Harvest/Turnaround

TEALUXE

Bruce Fernie opened Tealuxe in 1997 in downtown Boston to bring "Tea for All" to the masses in the same way that Starbucks brought specialty coffee to the world. Carrying more than 100 types of tea, he opened storefronts in trendy, urban, college campus areas. Tea is not the same business as coffee in the United States. While tea is the "second most popular beverage in the world after water" (Sloane, 2001), it is not very popular as a daily drink in the United States. Starbucks provided a premium product that a majority of Americans already drank on a daily basis: coffee. However, it was not clear that there was a demand for a wide range of teas beyond those Starbucks also offered.

Tealuxe stores were attractive and nicely placed, and some were doing a significant business. Unfortunately, Bruce Fernie had no interest in actively managing the storefronts, or for that matter, the operational side of the business. He considered himself a big-vision person and did not enjoy the daily operations. With no consistency in operational management, the company made numerous missteps. For example, he once opened a storefront in the New York City Atrium at a rental rate that all but guaranteed failure. He closed that operation within six months.

Having to repeatedly put expansion plans on hold kept distracting the management from the business of running the stores. In July 2001, Tealuxe cut back to four stores from seven and filed for Chapter 11 bankruptcy. "Chairman and Co-Founder Bruce Fernie, who himself expressed no interest in running the business day to day, blames the management that was hired to implement his ideas and the abysmal real estate deals and store-level control they implemented."

Businesses fail for many reasons, but for a small business, a hands-on approach and a complete understanding of the competitive advantage model for the business is essential to survival.

Source: J. Sloane, "Bruce Fernie Wants to Do for Tea What Howard Schultz Did for Coffee . . . Is He Kidding?", *Fortune Small Business* 11, no. 3 (April 2001); J. Sloane, "Tealuxe Puts Its Plans on Ice," *Fortune Small Business* 11, no. 8 (October 2001).

Eventually there will come a time when the founder(s) need to, or want to, exit their business. This decision may be based on a variety of factors. One may be that the business has done very well and the founder(s) have decided to cash out of the venture. On paper the founder(s) may appear to be very wealthy, but if all of the assets are in the business, then the individuals are not very liquid and are subject to rapid changes in wealth as the value of the business changes. Selling the business turns some of the hard-developed value into cash. The ability to turn some or all of the business value into cash at some point allows the business owners a real flexibility of choice as they go forward.

Alternatively, it may be that things have not gone well and the founder(s) need to either turn the venture around or close down the business. There is a wide set of issues that must be addressed in all of these cases, including such issues as a plan for paying off the investors, establishing the value of the business, attracting buyers, negotiating a sale, meeting all of the legal requirements for the sale, and consummating the deal. These issues can become even more complex if you have to look at turning a business around that has started badly. While difficult, the ability to turn a business around is a valuable skill, as markets can change dramatically and quickly. This chapter will explore these areas. To illustrate these issues, let's examine some of the concerns that Philo has had to deal with in this regard.

Using this method, the founders estimated the value of the business today as approximately $130,000. Using either method suggested, the offer looked generous. Both of the founders were quite young and could pursue other opportunities after making some nice money on this one deal. Neither felt bound to the company; they just wanted to make good long-term decisions for themselves and their families. The founders decided to ponder the issue and to check into some other sources to determine a fair value for their business.

EXERCISE 1

1. What do you think is a fair value for this firm?
2. Assuming that a fair value can be calculated, should the founders sell the firm at this point? Why or why not?
3. What does your answer to question 2 say about your risk propensity?

LO 13.1 Exit/Harvest

The small business owner benefits from considering several dimensions of what is required to sell the business, both at the founding and when she begins the selling process.

Why Consider Exit/Harvest Now

It may appear odd to consider the topic of exit and harvest while you are only beginning the process of getting the new business up and running. However, this early stage is the best time to develop a well-defined exit plan before personalities clash. A business is an investment of both time and money. Developing a practical exit plan will help validate the business idea and provide some peace of mind to the family and the investors. The key starting point for any decision to exit or harvest the firm is the true valuation of the firm. Developing an accurate valuation at, or just prior to, founding helps

1. Provide insight for the founders as to the amount of capital and labor that they should invest in the effort.

2. The business obtain loans (either direct or working capital) by demonstrating the value of the firm to potential creditors.

Although the founders of Philo had never even considered selling their business, they were caught completely off guard when one of the suppliers that they had been talking with about providing a new source of fresh food approached them about buying the entire operation. In the surprise call, the company president let the founders know that he would buy them out right now for $400,000, and furthermore, he wanted the founders to stay on with the business. The buyer would provide the founders a guaranteed two-year management contract at $90,000 per year per person, plus 15 percent of the yearly profits. The supplier president presented this deal to the founders of Philo claiming that the total package was approximately $800,000 (assuming that profits grew respectably), which he claimed was the value of the business right now. The resulting conversation amongst the two founders focused upon three critical issues. First, should they even consider selling the business at this point? Second, if they did consider selling, what would be a reasonable price for the business? Third, what were their personal long-term goals, and did this offer get them closer to those goals?

In order to consider these questions, the founders had to figure out how much the business was worth. For advice, they approached a friend who had worked in mergers and acquisitions (M&A) as a consultant to manufacturers, and he suggested that the real value of a business was simply the market value of the assets of the firm plus a premium (which he referred to as goodwill) which represented the future value of the firm. He suggested that many M&A deals pay a 20 percent premium above the market value of an established public business. Using this calculation, the founders estimated that the business was worth $180,000 ($150,000 in equity capital and equipment plus 20 percent). However, this number did not seem to account for the potential of the business, and in any case, was substantially less than the dealer had offered.

The founders contacted two members of their board of advisors and asked for their advice. They quickly discounted the suggestion of the M&A friend as not applicable to small business. They told the founders to forecast net cash flow for the next five years (five years was chosen as a reasonable return period) and then discount that number back to the present time using a reasonable discount rate for risky newer ventures (say, 20 percent). So, the founders estimated net cash flow for the next five years as follows:

Year 1 ($94,296)	5-Year Total Earnings $322,159
Year 2 $15,075	Discount Rate @ 20% 2.488
Year 3 $102,305	322,159/2.488 = $129,485
Year 4 $132,066	
Year 5 $167,009	

3. Convince outside equity investors of the potential long-term returns associated with the harvesting of the business.

4. The owners field potential offers to buy out the business (a relatively common occurrence in the life of a small business).

5. Benchmark the growth of the firm by establishing a true starting point.

Why Consider Exit/Harvest Later

Having at least laid some initial groundwork will help the small business person if he later decides to exit the business. As discussed in Chapter 2, the small business entrepreneur must determine what he is in business to accomplish. If the business is very successful but no longer interesting or enjoyable, it is probably a good time to exit. A small business takes too much time and personal commitment to be something that is not enjoyable. Similarly, there may be other opportunities available. The small business person may not have time to run the existing business and pursue these new opportunities at the same time, so it becomes necessary to exit the first business. Alternatively, the founder may sense that the while the business is strong now, the future does not hold the same potential for similar success.

One example was a small business person we knew who set up a number of sports shoe stores. Several years after founding, the owner began to realize that there were major chains entering the market, which was leading to market saturation in his area. He would have to completely reset the strategy of the business in order to compete in the future. This individual decided to harvest the venture and sell it to someone else. He reaped the value of the business that he had grown without having to go through the painful process of resetting the strategic position of the firm.

LO 13.2 Steps in Selling a Business

When a business owner decides to sell or harvest the business, there is a series of steps that need to occur. The first is to develop some sense of the true value of the business. The second is to prepare the business to be sold. The last step is the negotiation and actual selling of the business.

Valuation

There are several standard valuation models and rules of thumb for established, publicly traded businesses. For example, public companies have an established market capitalization that is technically the value of the business as it exists at the present time. Following the standard on Wall Street, this market capitalization already accounts for future earnings and all future prospects of the business that are known today. If you wished to acquire one of these organizations, the general assumption would be that the market capitalization is the floor from which all negotiations begin. Calculating the premium that will be offered above the market capitalization is more a matter of art than one of science.* Issues such as how much cash will be paid versus stock transferred and the future investment in the newly combined organization are a matter of negotiation, not to mention the overwhelming concern regarding what will happen to the executives of the acquired firm. These issues are substantially different when we consider the valuation and acquisition of a privately held venture.

Virtually all small businesses are private firms that do not report their earnings to the public. In addition, small businesses often adjust their annual company "earnings" with the payment of large year-end bonuses to the founders in order to limit the profit and therefore the taxes on the business. The small business may also have creative company **perquisites** ("perks") for the owners in order to minimize the tax owed by the organization. The owners of a small business may also have other individual personal expenses paid for by the firm. The result is that the firm pays fewer taxes, but the firm also may appear to be worth less than it really is worth.

For example, a firm such as Philo that is owned by two individuals allows the founders to use "profits" for the benefit of the firm as well as themselves in a perfectly legal and ethical manner. If sales were

perquisites

Benefits paid for by the company. Examples include vacations, vehicles, loans, gifts, financial contributions to retirement plans, etc.

---

* There are a number of other quick methods for calculating a purchase price, including a multiple of sales, discounted future earnings, discounted projected free cash flow, etc. We provide all of this by way of comparison.

particularly good in one year, the founders may decide to provide luxury cars as a perk for themselves. This expense dramatically reduces the "profit" of the venture, whereas the reality is that the business is quite profitable. Similar expenses also occur in public companies (as we have seen quite vividly during the past year); however, they are required to disclose such items in an audited annual report, whereas a small business venture rarely goes to the expense of having audited financial records. Thus, it should be clear that different methods of valuation are needed when considering the purchase of a private company.

There are a large number of unique systems used for the valuation of a private business. Most accounting groups and many private companies provide business valuation services. We would suggest that you work with these organizations when you are really ready to sell the business. They will use commonly accepted practices to refine the value of the ongoing business. However, in general, we encourage the small business person to utilize only a few of the most common methods to get a rough estimate of the value of her business as the business begins and grows. Valuing a business is as much art as it is science. Ultimately, the true "value" of the business is the amount of money that a willing seller and a willing buyer agree upon for the sale of the business. Thus, you want to be well prepared for the range of prices that may be offered and understand why you might agree or not agree with those prices. An investor, lender, or potential purchaser may take issue with several of the assumptions in your projections, or might want to reduce the numbers more severely than the founders believe is realistic. In order to maximize the selling price of the firm, the founders must intimately understand the numbers to be able to discuss such issues intelligently with those individuals. These methods include: (1) discounted future net cash flow; (2) price/earnings valuation; (3) asset-based valuation; (4) capitalization of earnings valuation, and (5) market estimation valuation.

Discounted Future Net Cash Flow By far the most widely accepted method of valuation, and the most insightful, involves some form of discounting the estimated future net cash flows of the business. As you might recall from Chapter 6, cash flow tracks the actual cash inflows and outflows of the business. For estimation purposes, a potential buyer can subtract any perks that have affected the net cash position of the venture. The detail available in a well-designed cash flow statement and the understanding that it is not profit, but free cash flow, that is the key to entrepreneurial success makes this the ideal document to use in the valuation of a business.

The cash flow method of valuation requires that the net cash flow of the business be projected for some period of time into the future. Our experience has suggested that estimating cash flows five years into the future and adding a salvage value for the firm is a good ballpark floor valuation for a small business. The information for this example appears in Figure 13.1.

In this example, the net cash flow for each year is as follows:

Year 1 ($101,885)

Year 2 $30,575

Year 3 $143,725

Year 4 $161,000

Year 5 $446,100

Receipts:	YEAR 1	YEAR 2	YEAR 3	YEAR 4	YEAR 5	TOTALS
Sales	$ 25,000	$325,000	$ 675,000	$ 880,000	$1,560,000	$3,465,000
Consulting	$ 20,000	$ 20,000	$ 60,000	$ 80,000	$ 100,000	$ 280,000
Total Receipts	$ 45,000	$345,000	$ 735,000	$ 960,000	$1,660,000	$3,745,000
Disbursements:						
Salaries	$ 45,000	$ 95,000	$ 210,000	$ 305,000	$ 450,000	$ 1,105,000
Travel	$ 4,050	$ 31,050	$ 66,150	$ 86,400	$ 149,400	$ 337,050
Car Leases	$ 4,000	$ 6,000	$ 7,500	$ 11,000	$ 13,800	$ 42,300
Rent	$ 900	$ 6,900	$ 14,700	$ 19,200	$ 33,200	$ 74,900
Payroll Taxes	$ 2,700	$ 5,700	$ 12,600	$ 18,300	$ 27,000	$ 66,300
Insurance	$ 5,500	$ 6,000	$ 7,500	$ 9,000	$ 13,000	$ 41,000
Fuel/Maint.	$ 960	$ 4,500	$ 8,000	$ 13,000	$ 21,000	$ 47,460
Executive Comp	$ 64,000	$ 72,000	$ 78,000	$ 84,000	$ 89,000	$ 387,000
Benefits	$ 13,500	$ 28,500	$ 63,000	$ 91,500	$ 135,000	$ 331,500
Advertising	$ 2,000	$ 26,000	$ 54,000	$ 70,400	$ 124,800	$ 277,200
Supplies	$ 225	$ 1,725	$ 3,675	$ 4,800	$ 8,300	$ 18,725
Utilities	$ 3,150	$ 24,150	$ 51,450	$ 67,200	$ 116,200	$ 262,150
Misc.	$ 900	$ 6,900	$ 14,700	$ 19,200	$ 33,200	$ 74,900
Total Disbursements	$ 146,885	$ 314,425	$ 591,275	$ 799,000	$ 1,213,900	$3,065,485
Beginning Balance	$ 0	$ 98,115	$ 128,690	$ 272,415	$ 433,415	
Equity Investment	$200,000					
Net Cash Flow	**($101,885)**	**$ 30,575**	**$143,725**	**$161,000**	**$ 446,100**	**$ 679,515**
Ending Balance	$ 98,115	$ 128,690	$ 272,415	$ 433,415	$ 879,515	$ 1,812,150

Figure 13.1
Example Cash-Flow Statement

Those most interested in a good estimation of firm value (potential buyers, lenders, equity investors, and founders) will recognize that these numbers are simply estimates that are based upon a set of assumptions. In order to understand and accept the cash flow predictions, it is important that each interested party accept the underlying assumptions. Therefore, a critical addition to any business plan, and certainly a necessity for any valuation analysis, is a complete set of assumptions used by the founders. An example from a group of entrepreneurs that were proposing a specialty transport company in the spring of 2009 appears in Figures 13.2 and 13.3. This company would transport people to sports events related to local colleges. The business would start focused on a single school and ultimately expand to other schools. The plan was to sell alcohol and limited food on the bus.

Discounting the Cash Flow The example above illustrates that to understand a cash flow statement, a small business person needs to have an in-depth knowledge of the assumptions that went into the statement.

Figure 13.2
**General Cash Flow
Assumptions for
Specialty Bus Company**

- Liquor sales are not included in the cash flow statement and are determined on a per trip basis, depending on how much alcohol the group orders. We will charge a 10 percent markup rate for each order.

- We applied an 8 percent payroll tax to salaries.

- Championship games for football are not accounted for in the cash flow statement. There will be a price markup which will be determined based on factors such as how big and how important the game is, who they are playing, etc.

- We assume that the men's and women's basketball teams play a total of 6 out of 12 possible games in the tournament.

- We are assuming that the base school makes it to a bowl game.

- Pricing on the competitive map is based on football season rates.

- We plan to fill the buses during various alumni events during the summer. The base school currently has five major events on its annual calendar. We assume we can fill all four buses for each event because of their high importance. This is accounted for in the cash flow statement. We assume there will be other events we can cater to, whether through alumni associations or directly through the base school. We did not account for these numbers on the cash flow statement because estimating how many events we will book and how big each will be is difficult at this point, but we will stay in close contact with the school and alumni groups and work on making reservations. We are confident our summer sales will be higher.

- Gas costs were based on an assumption that the price is $1.60 per gallon for diesel fuel. According to Energy Information Administration, this has been the average price for the last two years in the Midwest region.

- We assume there will be no significant economic recessions within the next five years.

- We have researched laws pertaining to continuous operation for a commercial driver and will assure that all itineraries are planned accordingly.

Given the nature of predictions and assumptions in general, there is a need for these values to be discounted by some rate that not only represents the return expected by an investor, but also accounts for the riskiness of the venture. We have seen discount rates range from a ridiculously low 10 percent to an almost absurd 90 percent. However, a rule of thumb for new small businesses being operated by owner/managers is to use 30 percent as a discount factor. This should not only account for a generous annualized rate of return but also build in a reasonable factor for risk. While we are in favor of simplicity in these calculations, we recognize that some interested parties prefer to separate return from risk. There are a variety of sophisticated financial models available to those who wish to be more precise in their analysis.

Using this rule of thumb, the entrepreneur should take the net cash flow figure generated for each year and discount that cash flow back to today's dollars. The discount rate remains the same, while the factor increases as you move farther away from today. Thus, in year 2 the discount rate is squared (1.3 * 1.3), in year 3 it is cubed (1.3 * 1.3 * 1.3), etc. To illustrate with our previous example, we calculate the present value of the net cash flow on page 272.

Figure 13.3

**Example of
Specific Cash Flow
Assumptions**

- Sales tax for each state and the surrounding municipality is 7 percent, applicable to the rental price.
- Income will be consistent throughout all of the centers in the different states. This is because we have hand-picked each school and have taken great efforts to make sure that they are all similar in population, athletic activity, demographic makeup, and geographic locations.
- Maintenance overhaul will occur in the first quarter for each bus at a cost of $1,000 per bus.
- All acquisitions and expansions will be financed internally; there will be no need for second- and third-round financing.
- Salaries are set at $30,000 for each officer, with an increase to $35,000 in year 3.
- Insurance is a once-a-year payment, including $10,000 for base coverage with each additional bus adding $1,000 plus tax, stamping, and processing fees.
- Waste removal is billed by volume plus service fees, estimating $75 to $100 per visit.
- Credit card charges account for 30 percent of all sales with a processing fee of 2.1 percent.
- Transportation costs are associated with moving buses within the state, either to their home stations or to meet customers.
- Accounting/legal fees will occur periodically throughout the year, with a concentration of accounting fees during tax season and legal fees during periods of expansion/acquisition.
- Fees/permits include registration costs, inspection fees, and other associated costs with each bus, as well as the costs of providing CDL licenses and training to officers at the inception of the company.

Illustration of Present Value of the Net Cash Flow Using the information in Figure 13.1 and assuming a 30 percent discount rate, we can calculate the present value of the net cash flows as follows:

$$(101,885)/1.3 + 30,575/1.3^2 + 143,725/1.3^3 + 161,000/1.3^4$$
$$+ 446,100/1.3^5 = PV(NCF)$$

$$(101,885)/1.3 + 30,575/1.69 + 143,725/2.19 + 161,000/2.85$$
$$+ 446,100/3.71 = PV(NCF)$$

$$(78,373) + 18,091 + 65,959 + 56,372 + 120,145 = \mathbf{\$182,194}$$

Without accounting for the sale price of the business, this calculation would suggest that the current value of the business is approximately $180,000.

Price/Earnings Valuation Another method of estimating the value of a business is to use the industry **price/earnings (P/E) ratio.** This is a relatively straightforward system that utilizes the industry in which the start-up operates. The founder should locate the P/E ratio for public companies in the same industry via the many sources of this information (the Internet, *The Wall Street Journal,* the library, etc.). That average should be multiplied by the net cash flow for year 5 and discounted back as a potential sales price in year 6 of the venture. Therefore, use 1 + the discount rate raised to the 6th power. In our example that would be 1.3^6 (4.826).

price/earnings (P/E) ratio

A value derived from public companies that divides the current earnings per share into the price per share.

Illustration of P/E Ratio Valuation This example illustrates how to calculate your P/E ratio valuation:

P/E for Industry	10 (obtained from industry sources)
Net Cash Flow for Year 5	$446,100
Discount Rate	30%
Sale/Residual Value	446,100 * 10 = $4,460,000
	$4,460,000/1.3^6$ = Discounted Sales Price
	4,460,000/4.826 = $ 924,005

Utilizing these calculations, we would suggest that the value of the firm today would be the addition of the present value of the future cash flows plus the discounted sales price of the firm. For this example, that would be the following:

Discounted Cash Flow + Discounted Sales Price = Current Value

$182,194 $924,005   = **$1,106,199**

There are two other relatively popular methods for valuing a business: asset-based valuation and earnings valuation.

Asset-Based Valuation **Asset valuation** involves accounting for all of the hard assets of the organization: buildings (if owned), equipment (if owned), furniture, cash, and marketable securities held in the name of the company, as well as (in most cases) the value of any signed and executable contracts. Once all of the assets of the organization are tallied, the value of the business is typically calculated by taking that total number and adding an acquisition, or goodwill, value to it. This acquisition/goodwill value is determined by examining similar companies that have been acquired, or more often by simply looking at the percentage premium being offered in general on all new public acquisitions. If the business were performing poorly, there would be virtually no goodwill value. Asset valuation is typically the lowest business valuation number that you will calculate, unless you are an asset-intensive business.

asset valuation
A method of business valuation that simply totals all of the hard assets of the organization and adds in a goodwill value.

Illustration of Asset Valuation Following is an illustration of asset valuation:

Building (Market Value minus Mortgage)			=	$108,755
Equipment				
	1)	1 Grill	=	$ 8,450
	2)	3 Cook Counters	=	$ 950
	3)	2 Fryers	=	$ 1,300
	4)	1 Walk-in Freezer	=	$ 1,850
	5)	3 Refrigerators	=	$ 4,600
	6)	2 Computers/Accessories	=	$ 1,300
	7)	Various Cooking Utensils	=	$ 3,904
	8)	Bar Equipment	=	$ 3,700
				$ 26,054

Furniture

1)	41 (2-top) Tables	=	$ 10,900
2)	17 (4-top) Tables	=	$ 6,050
3)	6 (6-top) Tables	=	$ 2,800
4)	197 Chairs	=	$ 13,902
5)	4 Counters	=	$ 980
6)	1 Complete Bar	=	$ 3,700
			$ 38,332
	Cash/Marketable Securities	=	$ 26,800
	Total Asset Value	=	$199,941

Total Asset Value * Acquisition Premium = Value of the Business

$199,941 * 4.3 = $859, 746

In this particular instance, a quick analysis of the industry revealed that an average asset acquisition premium for this particular industry was running at approximately 4.3 times assets. Therefore, the business as it currently stands (via this method) would be worth approximately $860,000. This method tends to depress the true future value of a growing business, so some investors/lenders will factor in a growth premium to "bulk up" the total valuation. "Art" intrudes once again.

Capitalization of Earnings Valuation Very similiar to asset valuation, **capitalization of earnings valuation** is performed by taking the earnings (net profit) of the organization; subtracting or adding any unusual items that the lender/investor feels are not customary, normal, or usual items; and dividing that figure by a capitalization rate. The capitalization rate is determined (rather loosely) by the nature of business, including longevity, business risk, consistency of earning, quality of management, and general economic conditions.

Illustration of Capitalization of Earnings Valuation This illustrates capitalization of earnings valuation using our example firm:

Net Profit (Earnings) of the Company	=	$32,900
Capitalization rate	=	.2

$ 32,900/.2 = $ 164,500

Utilizing this system involves much more than simply accepting a final net profit figure. As was stated in Chapter 6, the net profit of a small business is an easily manipulated figure that is wholly dependent upon the needs/desires of the founders. Therefore, lenders/investors adjust this figure to account for the individual actions of the founders. Would-be buyers readjust the net profit of the company to account for these nuances of small business and then apply a capitalization rate that is a combination of the buyers' risk propensity and the current situation in the business acquisition marketplace.

Market Estimation Valuation A valuation via **market estimation** is by far the simplest of the techniques. Fundamentally, it involves taking the earnings (or projected earnings) of the small business and multiplying that figure by the market premium of companies in their industry.

capitalization of earnings valuation

A method of valuation achieved by taking the earnings (net profit) of the organization; subtracting or adding any unusual items that the lender/investor feels are not customary, normal, or usual items; and dividing that figure by a capitalization rate.

market estimation

A method of business valuation that involves taking the earnings of the small business and multiplying that figure by the market premium of companies in its industry.

A popular method is to take the EBITDA (earnings before interest, taxes, depreciation, and amortization), reworking the figure based upon an analysis of the cash flow statement, and multiplying the remaining figure by a market multiple. An examination of the NASDAQ or NYSE provides a group of companies in virtually every industry classification. Taking the group as a whole or attempting to find companies that are similar to your business yields an estimated market premium that can be used to calculate the value of the business. Once again, lenders/investors will attempt to adjust the earnings of the organization to reflect a more balanced picture.

Market Estimation Illustration The following illustrates market estimation valuation using our sample firm:

Net Profit (Earnings) of the Company   = $32,900

Industry Multiple   =   13

$32,900 * 13 = $427,700

Valuation Overview As can be seen, there are wide variations in the potential valuations of this business, from several hundred thousand dollars to 1.5 million dollars. Every company has unique features that provide it some type of competitive advantage. In Chapter 5, we developed a strong argument for the development of a sustainable competitive advantage that enabled the new business to gain true economic rents relative to the competition. These "art" characteristics of an organization are important considerations in the valuation of a business and should be part of the equation when determining the true value of your business.

Preparing the Business for Sale

When the determination has been made to sell the business, the small business person must begin a process that is somewhat akin to selling her home. There is a need for the small business person to make sure the business looks its best in order to obtain the highest premium possible.

One of the key issues for the survival of the business after the sale is the change in leadership that will occur. Consider for a moment a small business we knew that sold equipment to research laboratories. The founder of the business had all the key contacts for the business. When he first tried to sell the business, there were very few individuals interested in the firm. This was despite the firm's having received the Outstanding Small Business of the Year award from the local government the prior year. The key problem was that there was little value in the business beyond the founder himself. Buyers bought the company's products because of the founder's reputation and his unique ability to install the products. Potential buyers did not want to buy a firm whose contacts and relationships walked out the door when the founder sold the business. This story

EXERCISE 2

1. Using your projected cash flow statement, develop a business valuation for your proposed company. This will mean forecasting cash flow five years into the future.

2. Use your annual net cash flow as an estimate of earnings. Use the earnings valuation method and the market valuation method to estimate the value of your organization five years from now. Assume that the P/E for your industry is 7 and the acquisition premium is (P/E ratio plus 3).

3. Using the same cash flow statement, estimate your total assets and compute an asset-based valuation for the business.

4. Looking at the range of figures that you have just developed, explain why one particular figure is more representative of the value of the business.

raises important questions for any seller. How will the business run after the founder leaves? How do you transfer the founder's contacts/reputation to the new owners? There should be a transition plan in place for this transfer in order for any purchase to be viable.

This difficulty is compounded by the reality that most small businesses run a very tight operation where every individual has specific functions and there is little slack available for cross-training. The company founder might handle all of the marketing/sales for the organization. This may include meeting clients, handling contract negotiations, and being the point person for each customer, while the company has another individual handle all of the operational details. Replacing this personal contact person would require that the founder begin to incorporate others in the handling of customers and/or include a new individual to join him in the process of client meetings. All of this requires a significant investment in the future without obvious payoffs in the present. Most small business people find this quite difficult. These and other types of human resource issues unique to a small business were covered in Chapter 10.

The firm also needs to examine its operations to ensure that the procedures of the business are codified and simplified for easy handover to a new owner. It is a reality in small business that the operational procedures develop as the business grows. The effort to put these procedures in writing will go a long way toward making for a more seamless transition. Another operational issue is the accounting of the firm. A system where the founder keeps the books herself is perfectly acceptable and perhaps even desirable when starting up and running the small business. However, a potential buyer wants to assure himself of the accuracy of the financial information. Our advice for ventures considering a sale is to contract with a CPA firm to have it do the following:

1. Audit last year's financial statements.
2. Put all of the statements into a standardized format.
3. Develop procedures for the accounting of all activities.
4. Provide an audit of this year's financial statements and render an accounting opinion.

This effort provides a level of legitimacy to the business and assures the buyer of the accuracy of the financial statements of the organization.

Maintaining an estimate of the value of a business as it grows and develops is the responsibility of the business owner. However, the small business owner should obtain a professional valuation of the business before attempting to actually sell the business. The valuation may turn out to be much less than the owner feels that the firm is worth, and therefore there would be little need to pursue the attempt to sell the firm.

The methods that will be used by the professional valuation experts will likely be very similar to those detailed earlier in this chapter. The businessperson would be well served to conduct her own estimate and then compare that to what the professional advises. The small business person should actively challenge the analysis and discuss it with the valuation professional. The knowledge that the small business person develops regarding the valuation of the business will help her as she negotiates the sale of the business.

In the process of preparing his firm to be sold, one entrepreneur sought to make the business look as attractive as possible to prospective buyers. He had the opportunity to make a large sale right before the business would be inspected. However, the entrepreneur was well aware that the buyer was in bankruptcy proceedings and that he might or might not actually be paid. On the other hand, the price being offered was quite high. He also had a large manufacturing equipment base that could be made to look better with some minor cleaning.

The maintenance records were sketchy at best, so the value of the equipment might lie in its appearance.

1. What are the entrepreneur's legal requirements in presenting the business to a buyer?
2. Do the ethical requirements differ? Isn't it simply "buyer beware"?
3. How do you as a business owner make sure that the firm looks attractive to purchase but at the same time provide realistic information?

Another important aspect in preparing the business for sale is the recording of all the informal practices of the organization. Policies and procedures develop in the life of a new venture. When to order certain supplies, what time to begin closing each day, the process of closing each day, the methods for dealing with customers, payment practices, human resource benefits and policies, etc., must all be codified. Anyone wishing to purchase a whole company will want all of these practices to be in writing for ease of analysis and for the understanding that this provides for the inner working of the business.

The small business founders also need to plan for the type of sale that will maximize their returns. The best method to actually exit the firm will very much depend upon the type of business. Businesses that have moved well beyond the founder's personality will be simpler to sell than those that are intimately tied to the active participation of the founder. While there are literally thousands of possible ways to construct a sales agreement, it might take some careful forethought and years of preparation work to make the business valuable to an outside investor.

One of the authors recently worked with an established accounting business where the two founders were both in their early 70s and looking to exit the business, but really wanted a continuing revenue stream. One of the founder's sons was also an accountant who wanted to take over the company. Unfortunately, neither partner felt that he had the ability to carry on the work of the business in a managing role. Therefore the two partners began to ponder how they would sell the firm. In the accounting business, as in many other companies, relationships are critical to the success of the business. Rather than a quick sale that would lead to the founders' leaving the firm immediately, they envisioned an opportunity where they would leave gradually. They also had a specialized customer base that consisted primarily of hospitals. Hospital audits are usually completed on a schedule that differs from that of traditional corporate audits, which could allow a larger accounting business to rationalize its accounting work flow. At a conference during the prior year, a larger firm had expressed an interest in an association

Specialization within a business, like hospital auditing, can make the process of selling a business more complicated. What are some things to consider?

with the firm. The two partners approached the head of the larger firm and worked out a deal that included the following:

1. A small up-front cash payment.
2. A five-year management agreement with the two founding partners.
3. A gradual handover to executives from the larger firm.
4. An annuity payment to the founders for 10 years, based upon bookings.

The result was a smooth sale of the business in which both the acquiring and the acquired firm's owners were pleased with the results.

Actually Seeking to Sell the Business

Once the decision has been made to sell the business to an outside party, then there are a number of choices available to the small business person. The most common would be to sell the business intact to a third party with the aid of a broker, lawyer, etc. A second very common option is to sell the business to a competitor or a larger business interested in your location, your position in the market, your product, etc. A third option is to divest portions of the business that will maximize the value of the business. It is not uncommon for the total value of the firm to be higher if the business is split into separate entities. A fourth option, which is rarely used but certainly the option most idealized by the business press, is an **initial public offering (IPO).** The reality is that only a very small fraction of start-up businesses that end up being very high growth actually seek to conduct an IPO. In fact, for the small business person, an IPO may not be the most profitable means to exit the business. Given the rarity of this type of event, we only mention IPOs.

Not surprisingly, actually putting a business up for sale is a bit more art than it is science. The process of getting the word out that a business is for sale can occur through a variety of avenues:

1. Hiring a business broker who will market the business for a percentage of the sale price.
2. Contacting competitors or businesses that have expressed an interest in your business.
3. Letting your accountant and your lawyer know that you are interested in selling your business. Individuals in both of these professions have numerous business contacts and may be aware of individuals seeking to buy a business.
4. Contacting your suppliers and perhaps (if appropriate) your significant clients to let them know about your interest in selling the business.

Negotiation Strategies

While it may be obvious to state this, negotiating a sale is the art of trying to reach an agreed price between a willing buyer and a willing seller. Thus, a sale is based in the needs/wants of both parties. For example, if the buyer has other similar businesses in the city and the acquisition of your firm will provide coverage in the final section of the city where they currently are not located or will provide the buyer

initial public offering (IPO)

The initial listing of a firm as a public entity in the public equities market.

Alex had not been in business six months before his former boss at the auto parts store approached him early one morning with a question that shocked Alex. Would Alex be interested in selling the business and continuing to run it as the manager? His former boss was impressed by the setup that Alex had achieved and by the rapid increase in his business. Alex had hired four new mechanics, only one of whom was related to him. His sister had graduated from the career school she attended and was doing a magnificent job not only with the books, but handling the whole front-desk operation. Many customers would stay in the shop while their car was being worked on because they enjoyed talking with his sister. She had an amazing ability to carry on a conversation while completing her work as fast as the work came in.

Flabbergasted at the offer, Alex asked him how much he thought the business was worth. His former boss told him that he didn't know right then, but he knew a good operation when he saw one. He wanted to have a chance to go over the books and he asked Alex to think about a few things in the meantime. How much did he think the business was worth? Would he want to maintain an ownership interest in the business? How long might he be willing to commit to running the business if his former boss purchased it from him? Would he sign a noncompete agreement, and if so, how long did Alex think was reasonable?

Alex quickly got his bearings and told his former boss that before he could see any of the books or even say anything about this, Alex wanted some time to think and he needed to talk with his family, who had an ownership interest in the place. Alex told him that he would get back with him within a week.

1. What would you recommend that Alex do during the next week? Why?

2. The business is so new, why should Alex even consider an offer at this point in time?

3. What would you advise him to do to determine the value of the business right now?

an outlet in the fastest-growing part of the city, then perhaps a higher price will be offered. Similarly, if the buyer is only interested in the business if he can get a bargain, he might try to pay less. The small business person should not believe there is some absolute price that the buyer will not go above or below. Negotiating to sell the business is a process that the small business person must actively engage in if she is to be successful.

Negotiation is a completely separate field of study, and texts exist for understanding the nuances and techniques that are available. Several important points to keep in mind regarding the negotiation of a sale include the following:

1. Use a professional mediator for anything but the most basic level of discussions. Your lawyer can play this role provided he has the experience. As we discussed in Chapter 7 (on the legal aspects of the small business), you will want all issues to be clear and specific. Do not make assumptions. Your lawyer can make sure that what you think the contract says is what actually ends up in writing.

2. Know the buyer. Ask for as much information about the company that is making an inquiry as they ask from you, or more. If they agree to pay you over a period of years but they default after a year, the result may be that you have a failed business returned to

you, with only part of the former value of the firm having actually been paid to you.

3. **Retain your own advisors.** It is very tempting to save money at this point and allow the buyer to provide the services; however, you are well served by having your own independent advisors.

4. **Recognize that there are a myriad of options for selling the business.** You may sell the company as a whole or you can break up the business for maximum value. For example, you can sell the equipment to one company, the location to another, the name to yet another, etc. The goal upon exit is to maximize your own value.

5. **Get cash for the firm.** Frequently buyers may want to combine your firm with their firm to create a new business. As a result, they will offer you part cash and part stock in the new venture. If you take stock in the new venture, you are dependent upon their success and your liquidity is often reduced.

6. **Look to the details.** For example, frequently new owners want a noncompete agreement from you once you sell. This will prevent you from directly competing with the new owners for X number of years. However, if your buyout is not substantial, how will you make a living? Be sure you know all the details and ramifications of the negotiations.

LO 13.3 Turnaround

Another related issue that faces small businesses is turning around a firm that is in a decline. It is possible that you have developed a solid business that prospered for a number of years. However, after some time and for a variety of factors, both internal and external to the firm, the business starts a period of decline. The effort to reverse that decline is referred to as **turnaround.**

It is very difficult to successfully turn around a small business once it starts into a decline. The fact that the small business has limited slack* or excess resources results in the small business's having a very small leeway to respond to a decline. This is in contrast to large firms with massive resources which the firms can rely on for years in the face of poor performance.

The firm must first seek to retrench. This activity is analogous to medical situations where doctors must quickly seek to stabilize the patient before they can do more substantive actions. If they do not stabilize the patient first, the patient might die and there will be no value in trying other activities. For a small business, such retrenchment efforts focus on the firm's gaining control of its cash flow quickly, regardless of the impact to the long-term effort. This can be accomplished by bringing in accounts receivable more quickly, delaying the payment of accounts payable, renegotiating with suppliers so that supplies do not have to be

turnaround

The effort to reverse the decline of a business.

Remodeling is just one way to help turnaround. What are some other options?

---

* "Slack" in this case is the time available per individual that is not dedicated to day-to-day work. It includes most time spent in meetings, as well as time spent reading the newspaper, talking in the hallways, getting coffee, taking smoking breaks, answering personal e-mail, making personal calls, etc.

paid for in cash, eliminating staff, and working with employees to cut costs. Once the bleeding of cash flow has been slowed, the firm can move on to more substantive actions.

While it is obvious that a huge environmental shift in the economy can cause a serious decline in virtually all businesses, the root internal causes of decline are usually based in either operating or strategic problems. To place it in straightforward terms, operating problems relate to either not selling enough of the product or not being sufficiently efficient in producing the product. Strategic problems are most often related to poor positioning choices. Strategic problems often include diversifying into unrelated domains and not being able to successfully manage the business.

Unfortunately, businesspeople tend to focus on the easiest problems to solve first. These are most often simply symptoms that take significant time to correct and yield very little in overall business results. Therefore, we advise businesspeople to pick the one key reason that the business is suffering. Identify it as either operating or strategic and dedicate the resources of the firm to solving that one immediately.

If it is an operating problem, then the solution should be an operating solution. These solutions include increasing marketing or marketing effectiveness to sell more products if the problem is that sales are down. Alternatively, if the problem is production inefficiency, then the focus should be oriented toward reengineering, simplifying, and measuring. Recall that we discussed quality management in Chapter 8. This is most often the focus of operating solutions and is certainly one of the best places to start the effort to turn around the business.

Strategic solutions rely on exiting those poor strategic choices that have been made over the years. We watched a wonderfully successful firm that installed in-ground pools diversify into backyard furniture and toys (such as swing sets). The business had solid positive cash flow and was looking to find a positive outlet for all the cash it was generating. Within a year the owners realized that not only were they losing money on their new business, but they were also installing fewer swimming pools because their corporate officers were distracted by trying to get the new business up and running. They quickly exited the non–pool installation businesses and redoubled their efforts on their core operations. It took almost two years to return the firm to the point where it had been before the foray into the seemingly related business. Recall that we discussed in Chapter 2 the need for small business people to evaluate the skills they personally possess before going into a business. In this situation, the small business owners may be quite good at managing a pool installation business, but that does not mean that they will be successful with businesses that appear on the surface to be related. The key to success is not seeking to learn the backyard furniture business (one that involves a wide inventory with no need for installation), but instead, focusing exclusively on the pool installation business. When bad strategic choices are made, exit them quickly.

The business press suggests for a large, established business that the CEO of the organization and its top management team be changed in a turnaround situation. The argument suggests that these individuals have paradigms, or ways they view the world, that created the decline in the first place. It is therefore supposed to be difficult for such individuals to see the problems and be creative in developing solutions to solve those problems. Small businesses do not have this option. We have found few small business founders that are looking to fire themselves. Therefore, it is necessary that the small business person in a decline situation actively seek creative solutions. While not easy to do, this means that they must question themselves and others to a much greater extent than they have done before.[1] A well-developed board of advisors, which we have discussed previously, can be a critical aid in this regard. A board of advisors that will provide honest and insightful advice that challenges the small business person can be very helpful in viewing new ways to compete and new ways to overcome the problems faced by the firm.

LO 13.4 Closing the Business

It is unfortunate, but bankruptcy may need to be filed by the small business owner if the turnaround effort does not succeed quickly enough. The processes/procedures for bankruptcy are arduous and have lasting impact upon the founder(s), and yet there are circumstances where this is the only viable route. There are several types of bankruptcy that can be filed.[2]

Chapter 11 bankruptcy allows the firm to be reorganized. When you file a Chapter 11 bankruptcy, the firm receives immediate protection against all lawsuits and other efforts to collect from the firm. At this stage the firm has 90 days to propose a reorganization plan. This plan needs to show how the business will pay off its past-due debts and stay current with its other debts. The company's banker and other creditors will commonly refer to your account as a "workout." They will be willing to meet with you and seek a resolution regarding the money that is owed to them. Most creditors will be willing to take less than their full payment with the hope that the strength of the firm will return in the future and they will then be in a position to receive more of their debt repayment. If they do not work with the failing small business, they face the potential of the business simply liquidating and the lender only receiving a small percentage of the proceeds from the sale of the assets. This reduction in the amount of money that the creditors ultimately accept is referred to as a "haircut."

If the firm's debts are less than $2 million, there is a fast-track version of Chapter 11 that gives creditors far less control than in a larger organization Chapter 11 filing. The fast-track plan must show how back taxes will be brought current over a five-year period. It must also show how those creditors who have pledged collateral behind their debt will be brought current. The unsecured creditors are those who do not have collateral pledged behind their debt, and their debt is the lowest priority. It is generally not necessary to show how unsecured creditors will be paid in this type of Chapter 11 reorganization. During the reorganization process it is possible to terminate leases, contracts, and union agreements that are too burdensome. The bankruptcy judge has the ability to force creditors to accept a plan for reorganization if it appears equitable and fair but the creditors are still unwilling to accept it.

Unfortunately, there are instances where the business must simply be closed. In this case, a Chapter 7 bankruptcy is invoked. In these cases, selling the business consists of selling the "assets" of the business. The assets of the organization include all of the physical assets (equipment, signs, furniture, fixtures, etc.) as well as any valuable intangibles, such as the corporate name or patents held. The process is similar to that of selling the business, but the owner can add a liquidator to the scenario, as well as the possibility of an auction, as a quick means to clear out of the business.

Two other types of bankruptcy are Chapter 12, used by family farming businesses, and Chapter 13, which is used by sole proprietorships. In each of these cases, the individual files for bankruptcy and includes the firm in her personal assets and liabilities. Chapter 13 is intended for small firms with limited debts and assets. The effect of a Chapter 13 filing is similar to that of a Chapter 11. However, since it is for a smaller firm, the process is even easier. For example, the time to approval is typically quicker and no creditor committee is required.

A final point to be made regarding the turnaround or closing of a business is the protection of personal assets. As was discussed in Chapter 7 (on legal matters), the form of business chosen has many impacts upon the operation of the business as well as the ending of the business. One of those is the extent to which the individuals involved in founding a firm are personally liable for its debts. Incorporating a business (using the Subchapter S, Subchapter C, or LLC forms that were discussed in Chapter 7) goes a long way toward providing limited liability to the small business owner. However, many entrepreneurs personally guarantee loans that are made to the company. Doing this negates the limited liability nature of a corporation and exposes the entrepreneur to a major loss of personal assets. While no one starts a business with the intent of failure, the reality is that many do fail. Effectively preparing for that possibility at the beginning of the venture can be a great blessing in the event that the business does not develop as the founder(s) had hoped.

summary

This chapter focused on the exit, harvest, turnaround, and closing of the small business. These are tough but important issues that should be considered when designing a new business. What should be clear is that these activities are as much art as science. Even something that appears as straightforward as business valuation is actually a process that leads to a set of results as opposed to a unique answer. The small business person who chooses to pursue starting a new venture is well advised to develop a plan for harvesting a business as well as handling situations that might require a major turnaround or closure.

key terms

review questions

1. Why would an entrepreneur seek to exit a business?
2. How can an entrepreneur be a millionaire on paper yet have no money in the bank?
3. What are the steps in valuing a business?
4. Explain the difference in the following valuation methods.
   a. Present value discounted cash flow.
   b. Price/earnings ratio.
   c. Asset value.
   d. Capitalization of earnings.
   e. Market estimation.
5. What steps should a business owner go through to prepare the business to be sold?
6. What four options does a business owner have to sell the business?
7. Which of these is the least likely to be pursued by the business owner?
8. What are six things a business owner should keep in mind as he enters negotiations to sell a business?
9. What is a turnaround?
10. What are the different types of bankruptcy and when are they each appropriate?

individual exercises

1. Develop a harvest plan for your planned business. Have several fellow classmates review the plan for completeness.
2. What are the two or three things that you would want most out of a sale/succession negotiation?
3. Imagine a worst-case scenario. Explain how you have protected your personal assets.

group exercises

Form into groups in the class. Go to your favorite search engine and put in the term "small business for sale" and your city name.
1. What Web site did you identify with firms for sale in your area?
2. How many firms are listed?
3. Pick one business. What is the asking price for that business?
4. What is the basis for that asking price? Can you see one method that they appeared to utilize from the types of valuation methods discussed in this chapter?
5. Tell your group about your evaluation of the business that is for sale and whether you think it is a good business opportunity or not.

everyday edisons class discussion

Go to www.everydayedisons.com/frank.html and read about Franklin.

1. Franklin's idea was quite simple. Do you believe it can actually make money?

2. What advice would you provide to Franklin about his idea?

Cliff Silverman—Karajen Corporation

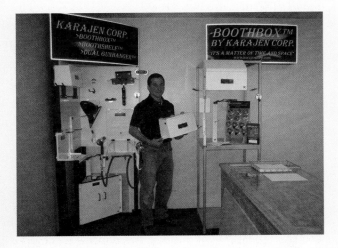

Cliff Silverman is always looking for ways to make life better and easier. He found a way to apply his problem-solving and inventive skills to a very specific industry that he knew intimately: developing products that would make life easier for people who paint cars for a living. Cliff started his own business, Karajen Corporation, in 2004 outside of Chicago, and now has a business that has more than 20 unique items. All of these are intended to be used by auto and industrial painters to speed up the process of painting cars, trucks, and other related items.

The focus on auto and industrial painters was a natural fit for Cliff. After graduating high school, Cliff earned a degree in auto body repair and painting at an automotive tech school. He went to work for various body shops painting cars. After about four years of painting cars, Cliff decided he wanted to try something new, and knew that he didn't want to paint cars for the rest of his life. He enrolled at his local community college to earn an associate's degree in business administration and then continued his education by transferring to Northern Illinois University, earning his bachelor's degree in marketing. While at NIU, he worked part time as a bus driver at the university and worked at a body shop in the summers and long breaks to pay some of his living expenses.

After graduating, he was offered a job as the manager of the body shop where he was the painter. He chose not to do that since he wanted something different. He sent his resume to various companies and then interviewed with a large paint company that manufactured automotive paint and sold its products directly to body shops. Cliff saw this as a great fit since he understood the industry

and painters' needs. He stayed with this company for 10 years in a variety of roles, starting as a sales rep and working his way up to sales manager for two different company-owned branches.

He learned sales by trial and error. He visited shops to sell them paint and to provide technical support and service, and often ended up being their consultant. He was good at problem solving, made customers feel special, and most important, was successful at retaining existing, and adding new, customers in highly competitive markets. This ability to keep customers and to help them improve their work processes was a key reason that he was personally so successful. It was during this time in his life that he realized some of his own ideas might have potential to be developed into products that could form the basis of a business.

A spray booth is standard equipment in the 50,000 firms that do auto and industrial painting in the UNITED STATES The booth needs to be a sealed and clean environment. When the painter is painting the car, nothing else is usually in the spray booth. The regulations prohibit anything in a paint booth that might collect pockets of dust and overspray, and the fire codes can be very strict in certain areas. If a painter needs an item during the painting process (which is a very common occurrence), then that painter must leave the "clean room," get what is needed, and then return to the paint booth—tracking in dust and outside contaminants. Otherwise, the painter must ask someone else to get what he needs and wait for the person to return. That process is slow and the risk of contamination is high. Cliff's idea was for a specialized cabinet that could be kept in the spray booth. It would hold everything that a painter might need during the process of painting a car and would include a place to set spray guns, air hoses, and other paint equipment. The cabinet would hang on brackets—set away from the paint booth wall to allow free air flow—and be removable for cleaning.

Cliff was working on this idea when he was offered a job by an Italian manufacturer of paint mixing equipment that wanted to reenter the U.S. market. Cliff accepted the job as the company's sole U.S. market researcher. His job included visiting major paint manufacturers and auto body repair shops in his effort to find a market for the products proposed by the Italian firm. After a year, he concluded that there was little opportunity for the Italian company in the United States. The Italian company offered him another position, but he had already decided that it was time for him to take the plunge and start a business, making accessories for the auto body painter.

He named the business Karajen Corporation after his three little girls (Kayla, Rachel, and Jenna). He had a slew of new product ideas, but decided to start with the "BoothBox"—the corner-mounted paint booth cabinet. During his spare time at night and on weekends while working for the Italian company, he had made a more serious set of drawings and developed a wooden prototype version of the BoothBox. He hooked up with a prototype designer who had the ability to make a more refined prototype out of foam board. He and Cliff made a number of modifications to the original design. Once it was complete, Cliff took the prototype to a metal fabrication shop owned by a friend of a friend.

The result was a metal cabinet that was attractive, functional, and powder coated and hung securely on its brackets. Through the process of designing the product, Cliff had found sources for all of the associated materials needed to complete the product. He had 10 cabinets built and took them to body shops to sell. They loved the cabinets. Cliff would haul the big metal cabinet into the paint booth and found that he could sell the cabinet about 7 out of every 10 times. One painter told Cliff, "My BoothBox cabinet was the best thing the boss has ever bought me, and I've been here 20 years!"

Cliff quickly sold his first batch of 10 cabinets and had the metal fabrication shop make 50 more. Cliff realized that he would need to keep creating new products, since the BoothBox was a one-time sale item. While he was spectacular at selling the cabinets, he really needed to get a set of distributors to sell the cabinets so he could focus on designing new products. He tried to work with each distributor who picked up his product. He would convince the distributor to buy a number of cabinets and then Cliff would work with its salespeople to help sell them. Almost every time he went with the salespeople, they would sell out of the cabinets. Unfortunately, he found that as soon as he left the process to them, sales would drop off quickly.

The cabinets are big and they are heavy to carry around (to show customers), and it took a bit of skill, and some courage, to drill holes and mount them into a customer's $50,000 to $150,000 spray booth. To overcome this barrier he devised a new cabinet—a smaller version of his original that was less expensive and was magnetic. The magnetic capabilities meant that the cabinet did not have to hang just in the corners. Now, the salesperson could walk into the paint booth and slap the cabinet up on the wall with no brackets to install. Cliff saw new success with this product but still had some price objections, so he developed a smaller and less expensive version of that one, too, which helped to add new sales and to further enhance his line offering. Constantly thinking about what would make life better for the painter, Cliff designed a whole series of products, including unique magnetic spray gun hangers, magnetic shelves, tape belt clips, mirror hangers, magnetic hooks, airbrush hangers, and other related items. Karajen has become a comprehensive supplier of accessories for body shops and other outfits that specialize in industrial painting, specialty/custom painting, and airbrushing, and has also devised a product niche for a well-known national hardware chain, which is beginning to show sales growth. Karajen can be found at www.karajencorp.com.

Cliff has taken his experience in the auto painting business and merged that with his talent in sales and finding solutions where others see only problems. He has used that experience, and his confidence, to form a business.

learning outcomes

After studying this chapter, you will be able to

14.1 Describe the elements of franchising.

14.2 Explain the process for buying a franchise.

14.3 Discuss the process for buying an existing business.

Franchising and Purchasing an Existing Business

BIG LEAGUE TOURS

Glenn Dunlap grew up a Cincinnati Reds fan in Summitville, Indiana, but when the marketing consultant looked for vacation packages to visit all 30 Major League Baseball stadiums, all he found were of the overcrowded "bus and ticket" variety. So Dunlap wrote a business plan, put up a slick Web site and $10,000, and started Big League Tours. By the start of the 2006 season, Big League Tours was booking deluxe trips to famous ballparks, including meet-and-greets with former players, close-in seats, private-bus travel, meals, and four-star lodging. A sample four-day excursion? For $2,325 a person, a Red Sox game in Boston (including a Fenway Park tour and time with former pitcher Bill "Spaceman" Lee); the National Baseball Hall of Fame in Cooperstown, New York; and one of the final games in the old Yankee Stadium. Dunlap, 39, runs the business on nights and weekends after his day job in Indianapolis, with the help of one full-time employee. Revenue rose more than 300 percent in 2008, after a 400 percent increase in 2007, and the company is "close to profitable."

Source: "America's Most Promising Startups: Deluxe Tours for Baseball Fans, Big League Tours." Reprinted from September 30, 2008 issue of *BusinessWeek* by special permission. Copyright © 2008 by The McGraw-Hill Companies, Inc.

From his initial interaction with the founders of Philo, William Lang knew several things about himself: (1) he worked hard, (2) he had an entrepreneurial orientation that allowed him to take risks, and (3) he also knew that while he was willing to take risks, he needed to take calculated risks. Additionally, he knew that organization was not one of his strong assets. In fact, he really needed some discipline to be imposed upon his activities for him to be successful. It was these observations that led him to seek another path to entrepreneurship. The path that seemed to take advantage of his strengths and yet compensate for his shortcomings was to find a franchise operation in an area where he had some skill. The opportunity for success is much higher with a franchise than with an untested start-up, if for no other reason than that the business model has been tested and refined prior to your acquisition of the franchise. In addition there is some level of support (which varies considerably) from the business that sells the franchise. Thus, franchising seemed to offer a calculated risk he could tolerate. He also knew that franchises typically came with operational systems already in place. These preexisting operational systems would help him to overcome his shortcomings in organization.

However, the realization that a franchise might offer the best opportunity for him was just the first step in his business start-up process. Which franchise should one choose? An initial investigation found that there were thousands of franchisors, with wide variations in the availability, price, resource requirements, level of support, and success rate of those various franchises. William knew that he wanted to be in a service industry with lots of customer contact, and while his experience in sales was deep, it was not very broad (he had been with the same company since he graduated high school 10 years earlier).

Therefore, he began looking for holes in the services provided by businesses in the city in which he lived. In this effort two specific opportunities came to light. The first was in fast food; specifically, there was no sandwich shop in his part of town. There were hamburger locations, pizza restaurants, sit-down restaurants, and ethnic restaurants, but there were no sandwich shops. The second opportunity seemed to be with companies that provided oil changes and other related auto services. William lived in a fast-growing section of town. There were several large car dealerships on the interstate, and there were individual mechanics. Somehow the quick oil change operations, which also did a few other basic services, such as changing windshield wipers, were not located in his section of town. His assessment was that the car dealerships required appointments, tended to operate quite slowly, and were expensive, while the individual car mechanic operations tended to be located in shops that were perpetually cluttered with vehicles, relatively dirty, and not particularly inviting to businesspeople, people taking their kids to various events, or those intimidated by automobiles. Therefore, William felt that there was a strong opportunity for both types of franchises.

William next looked into the specific firms in these two industries that offered franchising in his area. His initial investigation of the oil-changing types of franchises found that they were relatively expensive. For example, he found that an express oil change franchise cost between $300,000 and $450,000; it included not only start-up aid but also strong support once the venture was started, which was attractive. However, this was far more than he could afford even if he mortgaged all of his personal assets. A quick examination of several other companies confirmed that this was not an uncommon amount of money for this type of business. Therefore, he ruled this idea out and began to focus on sandwich shops.

In his initial screening, he found that the cost of a variety of franchised sandwich shops was dramatically less. The cost could be as low as $50,000 and rarely would exceed $250,000. However, the range of services offered by the franchisor to the franchisee also varied greatly. He began a more detailed examination of the franchises available. Ultimately, there were three franchises that interested him the most. Each of these had an initial cost of approximately $150,000, had very strong operational plans, and had well-developed support services. For example, each of these franchises helped the franchisee locate the franchise in the best location available and had managers on staff that worked on-site during the pre-start-up and start-up phases of the business. Furthermore, although it would be a stretch financially, he and his wife felt that they could put together sufficient funds to begin this type of operation.

After initial conversations with each of the three potential franchisors, William contacted several franchisees from each of the franchisors. He picked the franchisees himself by looking in phone books in different cities. The sample he selected may not have been ideal since it was not a random selection, but it avoided using the franchisors' lists, which he figured might be one-sided. Interestingly, even in his limited sample he found that franchisees for two of the companies had significant complaints about support and value for their dollar. Only one franchisor

(continued)

had no franchisees that were unhappy. Looking at the success statistics (profit levels, sales growth, number of franchisees that go out of business, and increasing sales price of franchisees wishing to sell), William found that this one franchisor ranked the highest among the three franchisors. This franchisor offered a relatively unique concept for a sandwich operation, utilizing a wrap that was somewhat like a tortilla. Furthermore, the franchisor used a seven-mile radius as its competitive density, meaning that no other franchisee of that particular business would be allowed to open a shop within seven miles of William's. Thus, the strategy of the firm, its product, and its operations all seemed to be a good fit with William's skills and needs, and with the opportunity that William saw in the area. He proceeded to start negotiations to buy a franchise from this franchisor.

Introduction

This book has focused principally on the process of starting a new small business from scratch. Two other common options exist for individuals interested in starting their own businesses. The first is purchasing a franchise. The other is purchasing an existing business. Both of these activities have opportunities and drawbacks in comparison to starting a new business and we will examine these, beginning with the opportunities and drawbacks with franchising.

To illustrate the range of issues of interest in a franchise operation, let's revisit one of the original individuals who considered starting the firm we know as Philo. You will recall that originally there were three individuals that got together to investigate the potential of starting a firm. However, one of the potential partners, William Lang, ultimately did not join the other two partners in Philo; the compatibility of the partners as well as timing was not right for him to be part of the business. However, after watching the success of his friends in Philo, he decided to revisit the idea of starting a business. One type of business he had begun to investigate was the franchise.

LO 14.1 Basics of Franchising

The purchase of a well-honed, thoughtfully positioned franchise can dramatically decrease the downside risk inherent in the process of starting a business. Franchising can be viewed as the new business entrepreneur's creation of a business from a well-established formula. Thus, the franchise is essentially a prepackaged business, where there are policies, procedures, and buying patterns in place prior to beginning operations.

The **franchisor** is the firm that originates the idea for the business and develops the operational methods. The entrepreneur is the franchisee. The **franchisee** pays a fee to obtain a franchise from the franchisor. This fee entitles the franchisee the right to open a branch of the business in a given area, use the franchisor's name, and operate a

EXERCISE 1

1. Are there questions and concerns where William Lang should have focused his investigation but did not?
2. Do you feel that in entering the negotiations, William will be an attractive candidate as a franchisee for the franchisor? Why or why not?

franchisor

The firm that originates the idea for the business and develops the operational methods, then sells them to franchisees.

franchisee

The entrepreneur that buys the franchise from the franchisor.

franchise agreement

The basic contract generated by the franchisor for all franchisees; it usually contains clauses requiring the purchase of supplies, the displaying of marketing material, and the payment of fees that are based upon the sales of the branch operation.

business within the guidelines of the agreement. The franchisee also receives operational advice on how to run the business and typically some level of marketing support to promote the firm. Responsibility for the business location, establishment of the business, and build-out is the franchisee's and must usually be fulfilled in accordance with the specifications of the franchisor.

The franchisor, in turn, establishes minimum standards regarding the operation of the business. For example, the **franchise agreement** is the basic contract generated by the franchisor for all franchisees and it usually contains clauses requiring the purchase of supplies, the displaying of marketing material, and the payment of fees that are based upon the sales of the branch operation. The requirements, however, may be more extensive. For example, McDonald's requires that its franchisees clean not only their own property but also the block around their franchise unit.

The International Franchise Association estimates that in the year 2005, franchises made up almost one million establishments in the United States, providing almost eleven million jobs. The range of franchises you use every day would likely surprise you. For example, most hotels, most restaurants, and many daily service providers are simply locally owned franchise operations.

In part, the reason franchising is so widespread is that the franchisor can offer a standard, well-known product, that is produced by a consistent, well-tested process. The group purchasing power for supplies, supported with specific regional and perhaps more generic brand-building national advertising, furthers the success of the franchise. The franchisor will also continue research and development on the products and processes that a small single business simply could not afford to pursue. This all occurs with the entrepreneur spending less of her resources than if she had had to found such a firm by herself. The franchisor benefits by enabling a rapid expansion while minimizing the funds invested in that expansion.[1]

The success of franchising is dependent upon the hard work of the franchisee and the value added by the franchisor.[2] You will recall that we discussed agency theory in Chapter 2. There are factors that mitigate alignment of goals between a manager and an owner. In a franchise operation, businesspeople work for themselves, not for some large corporation, and as a result, all the decisions that the small business person makes are to maximize the value of his own business. The success of franchising is also a result of the fact that the franchisee will act in ways to maximize the profit of the business where a corporate employee might not do so, a prediction consistent with agency theory.[3]

The franchisor makes money in a variety of ways, including these: (1) selling the franchise to the franchisee; (2) selling supplies to the franchisee; (3) collecting a percentage of sales; and (4) in some cases, providing company-specific training courses/materials. For example, a very successful franchisor like Sonic, which sells hamburgers and related items using a drive-in format in over 30 states, charges a fee to obtain a franchise, but the significant income

Going into business with a Sonic franchise, for instance, allows you the freedom of ownership while also providing built-in support. How might ownership differ for franchisees versus traditional business owners?

comes from royalties and being able to sell the franchisee items that range from Sonic-labeled hamburger wrappers to the peppermints that come with the food. The franchisor typically argues that it can obtain the supplies cheaper through its bulk buying; plus, it wants to ensure that the output continues to be a consistently high-quality, name-enhancing experience, since it is sold under the Sonic brand. A franchisee that has inconsistent quality, service, etc., not only hurts her own business, but impacts the brand image of all franchisees.

The continuing revenue stream to the franchisor from royalties and selling of inputs to the franchisee is a more important revenue source than the initial fees for selling the franchise. Thus, the franchisor and the franchisee are successful by helping each other. The franchisor makes money when the franchisee stays in business, needs lots of inputs, and pays continuing royalties. On the other hand, the franchisee is successful if the franchisor puts a program in place for all of the franchisees to be successful, such as high-quality marketing, good site selection, high-quality products, and continuous research into both product/process development and brand management.

LO 14.2 Buying a Franchise

As we have emphasized throughout this text, the entrepreneur that is best prepared will be the most likely to succeed, whether his focus is starting a business from scratch, buying a franchise, or purchasing an existing business. Thus, many of the issues in choosing a franchise are similar to the issues already examined in this text.

General Franchise Questions

Some issues can be viewed as broad, generic issues rather than issues specific to that particular franchisor. These general issues include the following:

1. The potential franchisee should carefully evaluate her individual interests and skills to determine a potential fit with running a franchise and to identify an industry or multiple industries in which she wishes to attempt to purchase a franchise.

2. When determining the industry to enter, each potential franchisee should examine that industry, the potential competitors in the industry, and his position relative to other new franchisees that are entering the industry.

3. The potential franchisee should carefully examine the competitive strength of various franchises in the industry. For instance, what are their various sustainable competitive advantages in the market?

4. The individual looking to buy a franchise should identify a franchisor that is the best potential match for him or her in terms of support, history, expansion plans, etc.

5. The person considering a franchise should examine that franchisor as though the potential franchisee were buying the whole business. This includes contacting other franchisees to discuss their experience as well as comparing the franchisor to other franchise opportunities.

Specific Franchise Questions

Each franchisor will have a different package it will try to sell a franchisee. The franchisee needs to examine the exact package that is offered and balance the cost and the benefits offered. The issues to consider in examining which franchise to purchase include these: what a franchise includes; franchisor and franchisee obligations, as stipulated in the United Franchise Offering Circular (UFOC); and steps in the process of obtaining a franchise.

Each of the issues to consider in purchasing a specific franchise will be examined in turn.

What Does a Franchise Include? There is an extraordinary range of support that can be provided by a franchisor to the franchisee. This ranges from simply buying into a name and general plan for operation to what almost amounts to a full partner living your business with you. There is no universal standard regarding what is provided by a franchisor; instead, as in any market system, different franchisors offer distinct sets of supports at varying prices. The entrepreneur must choose which package of benefits he wishes to pursue, and at what price. The discussion below lists some of the issues that a new businessperson buying a franchise should consider to ensure the franchise has the right mix of supports and costs for him.

Both the franchisor and the franchisee have an alignment of interest in their mutual desire to produce a quality product and successfully expand the business. However, they can have honest disagreements about what is best for the organization. Franchisors make decisions based upon what is best for the total business; franchisees want to have the ability to cater to their local market. Thus, can you as a local franchisee of a sandwich shop in Texas add hot peppers to the standard sandwich—or if you are in Wisconsin, can you add sauerkraut to the same sandwich? The franchisor may want uniformity and thus consistency, but the franchisee will want the flexibility to meet local needs. The individual buying a franchise needs to examine if the franchise will have the level of flexibility she feels is necessary for success.

When you purchase a franchise, you typically are buying some consistent items, although the specifics of what you are buying in each individual case should be examined. These include the right to

1. An established name, branded products, and service.
2. Operate under that name for a period of time. The time period is usually some standard such as 5, 10, or 20 years.
3. A single store or the right to have multiple units.[4]
4. A commitment from the franchisor to limit the number of franchises within a specific radius of the new franchise. This is one of the most important issues involved in the purchase. One of the key competitive advantages is having the name-brand operation without having to compete against fellow franchisees. In the best situations, franchisees work with each other in local geographic areas.

The franchisor typically provides both the operational systems and the monitoring techniques to run the business in a manner that matches the rest of the organization. The specificity of this operational information varies widely from franchisor to franchisor. You will recall from Chapter 8 that an in-depth understanding of operations is necessary to be successful in a small business. Although most of the operational management systems will have been designed by the experience of the franchisor, the franchisee must intimately understand both why and how these systems work. To illustrate, if you purchase a franchise for a shop that makes photocopies, the franchisor will have established procedures for the design of the internal layout of the shop, plus the look and feel of the physical storefront. It will have established processes for virtually every type of service that could be requested by a customer. If you do not have at least a minimal understanding of copy shops, it will be difficult to judge the operating system the franchisor is providing. Buying a franchise does not eliminate the need for the small business person to have a deep understanding of the business. If you do not have that understanding you cannot judge the quality of the operational support provided by the franchisor.

True understanding of those processes comes from experience. In many cases, potential franchisees are required to work in an established operation of the business for some period of time prior to their being allowed to purchase a franchise. This time period allows the potential franchisee the opportunity to learn the business from the ground up, learning the procedures not from a manual, but from experience with an established operation. This fact is particularly important since some franchisors have very specific limits on how many changes you can make to their operational systems. The franchisor wants a franchisee in Oklahoma City, Oklahoma, and another in Utica, New York, to operate in essentially the same manner in order to develop and preserve the brand. A careful examination of the amount of regional/local customization available can be an important part of the business acquisition process.

There are a number of specific support areas that the potential franchisee should use to evaluate the franchisor's operations:

1. Accounting Support. As part of the operational aspects of the business, the franchisor will often provide an accounting system that is custom tailored to the dual needs of the franchisor and the franchisee.

2. Marketing Support. This is a broad area that encompasses such things as brochures, signs, logos, television advertisements, newspaper advertisements, sales techniques, and internal business design. The quality, quantity, and overall value of each of these items can vary widely from franchisor to franchisor. There are also some significant downside risks to this apparent positive. First of all, advertising support comes at a price. Most franchisors charge each franchisee a fee that becomes part of a larger common advertising budget. The franchisor develops the advertising and buys the spots/spaces in the newspapers. Doing this centrally allows for volume discounts as well as expertise in ad development/placement. Second, if you are the only franchisee in Colorado while most of the other franchisees are in Minnesota, Iowa, and Wisconsin, you are likely to see a smaller relative share of the advertising budget being targeted to your area. What are the franchisor's development plans for Colorado?

3. Training. Franchisors offer a variety of training opportunities for the new franchisee and his employees. These include classroom training, training at other locations, having an experienced manager work at your location for a period of time, or, as we have

mentioned, working at a current establishment. The more that is offered as part of the franchise fee the better it is for the franchisee. In addition, the availability of continued training opportunities should be an important criterion to help ensure franchisee success.

4. **Real Estate Services.** Some franchisors operate a large and profitable real estate brokering service. Others offer a more basic site selection service, or nothing at all. The assistance in real estate selection, acquisition, building construction, etc., can be invaluable if done professionally.

5. **Other Services.** Human resources support to develop performance management programs; quality control methods; forecasting; and purchasing of equipment are all very valuable services that act as guidelines rather than mandates in deciding on a franchise.

As this discussion indicates, there is a wide range of potential activities that the franchisor may provide to the franchisee. The range of those activities, the quality of those activities, and the cost should be judged by the small business entrepreneur.

Government Requirements for the Franchisor/Franchisee Relationship The principal governing mechanism of the franchisor/franchisee relationship is the **Uniform Franchise Offering Circular (UFOC).** As with many business domains, at one time there were excessive abuses in the industry. Individuals thinking they were buying a franchise that gave them an opportunity for success found that they had paid for what amounted to little more than a name, which often had a terrible reputation. The result was the passage of the UFOC, which specifies what information must be provided to the franchisee prior to her investment.

This document must be provided to the franchisee early in the process of her buying a franchise. In effect, the UFOC is a franchisor disclosure document with 23 specified items:

1. **The Franchisor, Its Predecessors and Affiliates.** Full disclosure on any predecessors to the current business and other businesses affiliated with the business must be disclosed.

2. **Business Experience.** The background of the principals must be detailed. Issues such as how long they have been in the business and their experience in the industry must also be detailed. You want to make sure those running the franchisor have experience in the industry.

3. **Litigation.** Any pending litigation must be noted. Such litigation can destroy the value of your franchise if it concerns issues such as who developed the idea for the product and your franchisor loses.

4. **Bankruptcy.** Any prior or current filings by firm or key management must be disclosed.

5. **Initial Franchise Fee.** Under items 5 and 6, the franchisor must disclose all fees that are charged.

6. **Other Fees.** The "other fees" category is an area that entrepreneurs should clearly understand. The cost of the initial purchase

---

EXERCISE 2

1. Rather than starting a business from scratch, you have decided to look into franchises. What industry and what franchise opportunities might you consider?
2. What special skills do you bring to the franchise?
3. What market conditions exist that suggest to you that this franchise might be successful?

Uniform Franchise Offering Circular (UFOC)

The principal governing mechanism of the franchisor/franchisee.

of the franchise may appear low, but if there are extensive fees that the franchisor can charge the franchisee for services that are offered, the value of the franchise may be very different than initially thought. The supports provided may appear to be desirable; however, there may be separate costs for those supports that are independent of the initiation fee to buy the franchise.

7. **Initial Investment.** This is more than the initial fee paid by the franchisee; it includes a reasonable estimate of the total investment needed to begin operations.

8. **Restrictions on Sources of Products and Services.** This is one of the critical parts of the document, where franchisor sourcing is detailed. The potential franchisee needs to be clear about what must be purchased directly from the franchisor and what may be sourced independently.

9. **Franchisee's Obligations.** Specific obligations must be listed. For example, the franchisor may require that the product be produced by certain equipment and that equipment be replaced on a certain time schedule. These restrictions can extend into domains that the small business person may not initially consider to be the purview of the franchisor. Thus, once again questions such as what flexibility the small business entrepreneur will have in operating the franchise need to be examined. For example, upon opening, you as the franchisee may be happy with some balloons, having the local mayor cut a ribbon, and a story that goes into the local paper. But the franchisor may have an extensive program that it requires of all new franchise openings. The franchisee may be required to fund these activities through various fees, whether or not he agrees with the program.

10. **Financing.** Many franchisors make significant financing available to potential franchisees. The financing available and terms are outlined in this section of the document.

11. **Franchisor's Obligations.** In this section, all of the ancillary services are detailed. As outlined above, this may include site selection, training, placing experienced managers on-site for a period of time, etc.

12. **Territory.** This section details the amount of exclusivity your franchise will have relative to other operations of the franchisor.

13. **Trademarks.** Items 13 and 14 detail the exact status of all trademarks, patents, copyrights, and trade secrets that are part of the business.

14. **Patents, Copyrights and Proprietary Information.**

15. **Obligation to Participate in the Actual Operation of the Franchise Business.** The franchisee can be required to take an active role in the daily management of the business, as opposed to simply hiring managers.

16. **Restrictions on What the Franchisee May Sell.** This section lists limits placed on the franchisee by the franchisor. The franchisor may put extensive restrictions on the franchisee as to what she can do with the product and its production.

17. **Renewal, Termination, Transfer, and Dispute Resolution.** The exact method of dispute resolution is detailed, along with which party will have the financial responsibility.

18. **Public Figures.** This details any public figures or celebrities involved in the business and what they are paid.

19. **Earnings Claims.** This section contains a description along with some specific detail regarding the financial performance of typical franchisees.

20. **List of Outlets.**

21. **Financial Statements.**

22. **Contracts.** This section contains sample contracts you will be asked to sign later.

23. **Receipt.** You will be asked to sign a page to acknowledge that you received this information.

The small business person is well served to study the document carefully to understand all of the details of the business arrangement. It is a long document, and should be read through several times and reviewed with an attorney prior to agreeing to the stipulations. A clear understanding of the document now will prevent significant problems in the future.

Franchise Process The founding of a franchise is quite similar in form and method to creating a new business from scratch. A significant upfront cash payment is necessary and the ability to leave the venture if the entrepreneur does not enjoy the business is severely limited. Similarly, an assessment of the skills of the individual should be a mandatory beginning of any new business investigation. If the individual has no skills in styling hair and he buys a hairstyling franchise, the odds of success are not particularly good, regardless of what supports are present in the franchise.

Depending upon the franchisor for market analysis is a poor move under any circumstances. The market must also be thoroughly and independently understood by the potential franchisee. As we pointed out earlier, sometimes there is a very good reason that no similar businesses are in a particular area. We knew an individual who was searching out a franchise to buy. She hit upon the idea of buying a franchise that supplies temporary employees to local businesses. Unfortunately, all of the local businesses (and there were only a few) used only full-time employees. The market for temporary workers was severely constrained. We would also caution against purchasing a franchise that is part of a fad. Pet rocks and Pogs were a lot of fun for a while, but owning a pet rock or Pog franchise was a disaster for the franchisees. Those fads died as quickly as they were born, but the franchise agreements lasted anywhere from 5 to 20 years. It does little good to invest money in a franchise that will see demand for the product disappear quickly. In the case of a fad, we have very simple advice. Get in, make as much money as you can as an independent, and GET OUT!

The International Franchise Association is a good source for quickly locating potential franchisor firms; its Web page can be found at www.franchise.org. Each of the franchisor firms typically has a Web page where you can request information from that firm. They will gladly send you a packet of information that details the firm's operations, its business, and the costs of the franchise. At this stage, there will be a very short application form that the entrepreneur must fill out. With this information the franchisor will call the entrepreneur and have a phone interview to ensure that the individual is at least a potential match for the firm. The small business person needs to note that it is a mutual selection process. The franchisee can select among one of the 10,000 or more franchise opportunities. The franchisor also gets to decide to whom it will sell a franchise. Given the geographic restrictions imposed by many franchisors and encouraged by the franchisees, it is in the best interest of the franchisor to pursue only the most motivated, best capitalized, and most skilled individuals. A poorly performing or disruptive franchisee detracts from the overall operation as well as taking time and effort of the franchisor away from the business of growing the brand. Because of this, it is simply easier to make sure that there is a match between the two parties from the beginning.

Once the potential franchisee has been vetted (a credit and personal background check has been completed), the entrepreneur will be sent the complete UFOC and asked to fill out a more complete application. A series of meetings ensues between the franchisor and other franchisees in the area, between the franchisor and the potential franchisee, and between the potential franchisee and the other franchisees in the area. The ability to meet other franchisees is critical in the evaluation process. While the UFOC does not require that specific information on profitability of individual franchises be provided, it is quite simple to back into such information by calculating the total profits of the group and then dividing by the total number of franchises. Unfortunately, there may be a bimodal distribution, with some great performers and some that perform poorly. The ability to interact with franchisees in your geographic area, with similar profiles to what you can expect from your operation, helps provide great insights into the reality of the franchise life. You will gain tremendous insights from these individuals regarding their relationship with the franchisor. The relationship between franchisor and franchisee is somewhat like a marriage; they are both dependent on each other for success. If the relationship is an unhappy one, there can be nothing quite as miserable. Existing franchisees can also provide you insight regarding the value of the franchisor's staff. Many of the services that the franchisor provides are dependent upon the quality of the people providing the service. Marketing advice is a qualitative area that can be either very helpful or of limited value, depending on who is developing and delivering the research.

Assuming that both parties are pleased with their findings, negotiating the deal is the next step. While the franchise fee tends to be set in stone, most franchisors are willing to negotiate on a wide range of items. For example, if there are few franchises in an area, the franchisor may be willing to finance a greater portion of the start-up expenses, provide additional marketing support, or even pick up some of the initial expenses of a franchise in order to get a foothold in a new geographic area. Similarly, if you have had prior success in business and the franchisor is new, it might negotiate a completely different deal with you in order to get started with a self-sufficient operator. Also, very high-profile individuals frequently can negotiate unique deals. For example, in a region of the country where there is a professional athletic team, high-profile players on that team often obtain preferential opportunities. This allows the franchisor to publicize that that person is one of its

Over the past few weeks you have been reviewing the franchise agreement for a new concept in flower design and delivery. You have met with several current franchisees and talked with the franchisor on more than a few occasions. You have had the opportunity to see them in operation and to look at the books. After all this effort, you have concluded that you don't need the franchisor to run a business like this one. You've decided to open up your own flower design and delivery shop and plan to run it virtually the exact same way as is done by the franchisees.

You have made a significant effort to make some of the operations different, but you also like most of what you saw. What you didn't like was the $44,000 in up-front fees, the $28,000 in training costs, and the fact that you would have to pay the franchisor 8 percent of sales.

1. Do you have any ethical obligations to the original franchisor?
2. No one is required to buy a franchise; therefore, isn't their opening all the books simply their means of trying to make a sale?
3. Does a firm have any obligation other than to make money?

franchisees. The small business person should explore what aspects of the contract are negotiable by making a list of wants and desires.

Some areas that such negotiations should explore include up-front capital requirements, financing arrangements, and continuing fees. Does the ability exist to purchase other franchises or build out the existing franchise? The time frame of the franchise (5, 10, 20 years) may be negotiable, as well as a first right to renew your franchise. An important consideration is not only the territory of the initial franchise, but also first rights on adjacent or fast-growing territories. Some franchisors will have performance quotas to maintain the franchise; if yours does, ask what those quotas are and what percentage of franchisees meet the quota. If you fail at those quotas, or some other aspects of the franchise, can you negotiate the remedies to solve that problem? Does the franchisor require a personal guarantee? The personal guarantee is something many successful entrepreneurs seek to avoid, since it places their personal assets at risk. Are there operational constraints that you feel would put you at a disadvantage relative to your competition that you wish to have the franchisor waive? The small business person is well served to take the time to work with a lawyer and develop a solid contract that meets the needs of the franchisor and still gives the franchisee the best opportunity for success.

EXERCISE 3

1. What specific concerns do you have regarding a potential franchise?
2. Put together a list of three items that you must have in place prior to accepting a contract to purchase a franchise.
3. Do you believe that franchises are more or less risky as compared to beginning a new business from scratch?

LO 14.3 Buying an Existing Business

We covered the process of obtaining a franchise first because this process is well defined and well regulated, and there is a wealth of information available to anyone who would like assistance. Another very popular means of going into business for oneself is the purchase of an existing business. To illustrate the concept and some of the

jack nash and hollywood nights

Like the issues that arise for Alex working for Rodriguez Family Auto Repair, Jack Nash has circumstances unique to working at a franchise business.

Jack Nash had always wanted to go into business for himself. He had a good job working for an engineering firm, but he felt that his prospects for rising any further in the organization were limited. He was increasingly concerned with the strategic direction that the firm was pursuing and felt that the advice of long-time employees was being routinely ignored. This feeling had only grown stronger since he had noticed his good friend Doug was doing so well at Philo and seemed so happy.

Every Friday Jack and his family rented movies and watched them together. Jack loved movies and felt the development of the DVD rated as one of the greatest inventions of all time. While Jack was in the store on one particular Friday evening, the owner told Jack he was going to sell the business. Both of his children now lived in Oregon and he wanted to move to be closer to them. In the discussion that followed, Jack and the owner talked about many things, and Jack worked into the conversation an inquiry as to the price the owner wanted for the business. It was $210,000.

At home over the weekend Jack began to look at his finances and talk with his wife about the business. Jack looked at his savings of about $50,000 and realized it was not enough. He then calculated he could close the IRAs he had set up for retirement and take that money as well. After all the taxes and penalties were subtracted, that would yield an additional $65,000. At church that Sunday, he visited with a friend who worked at a bank and felt reasonably comfortable that if he signed a personal guarantee, he could borrow the rest of the money.

At this stage Jack approached the owner of Hollywood Nights and indicated his strong interest in buying the business. The owner of the business seemed almost eager to sell and negotiations progressed quickly.

difficulties in buying an existing business, consider another friend of the Philo founders, Jack Nash.

How to Buy

Similar to a franchise, an existing business has the benefit of having an established set of processes; although unlike a franchise, a continuing business has an established cash flow which you are purchasing. As such, the operation has a higher likelihood of success when compared to starting a business from scratch, and yet as the Hollywood Nights case illustrates, that does not mean that buying a business does not take as much planning and thought as starting a business from scratch. There are still significant risks involved in buying a business.[5]

Since a business you may buy is an ongoing entity, there is a greater premium attached to the business than if you started it from scratch. The primary exception to this is if you buy a troubled business at a discount. You will need to quickly restructure that business. Turnaround is a special topic and requires very specific skills for you to be able to act quickly to reverse that decline.[6] Our typical advice to small business owners is to not attempt such activities unless they have specific skills and a plan to turnaround a business that is in significant decline.

EXERCISE 4

1. Jack Nash was not trained in business. What are the types of business questions he should have been asking the owner of Hollywood Nights as he entered into negotiations for the purchase of the building?

2. What types of information should Jack have tried to get on his own about the business or the industry before buying the firm?

3. What would be the danger signals to Jack that this might not be the right business for him?

For the purchase of a reasonably stable or healthy firm, all of the same processes that have been discussed in this text should be the foundation of your effort. Therefore, you first need to understand your own skills and abilities and the nature of the current market. Assuming that you have completed all of the preliminary analysis effort, there are still several unique aspects to purchasing an existing business. These include (1) locating a business to purchase; (2) developing a plan for the business; (3) negotiating a deal to acquire exactly what you want from the operation; and (4) organizing the process of change within the organization.

business brokers

Businesses that specialize in selling businesses.

Locating a Business to Purchase Locating a business for sale is a job that takes lots of patience and effort. There are **business brokers** in virtually every city in the United States that specialize in selling businesses. Additionally, businesses are listed for sale in newspapers, in local magazines, and on Web sites. All of these are fine places to start your search process; however, we recommend several other means for finding a business that meets your needs:

1. Attorney and CPA firms may have clients who have expressed their desire to sell their business. Contacting local firms and asking about businesses they might know that are for sale usually yields some interesting possibilities.

2. Our personal favorite is to identify a particular business that you believe is not maximizing its opportunity, one to which you believe you could bring unique skills/advantages that could propel the business. We recommend that you put together a short letter to the owner indicating your interest in the business and follow that up with a request to take the owner to lunch to discuss the opportunity. Most (if not all) owners of an ongoing business are willing to listen to an offer to buy their business.

3. The trade association for an industry usually maintains a listing of all member companies and is a wealth of information regarding the status of various organizations within the industry.

4. The local Small Business Administration Office and/or the Small Business Development Center in your area has significant contact with businesspeople and both are geared toward supporting and encouraging the growth of small business.

5. Another favorite of ours is to look at the bankruptcy filings in your local community. Many companies file for bankruptcy due to lack of financial resources or poor management practices. The opportunity to contact these individuals and buy the operation before the bankruptcy procedure is completed can be the source of a business at a bargain price. However, remember that this effort would be a turnaround project that would require unique skills and abilities.

Plan of Operation Once you have located a business for sale, but prior to beginning the negotiations to purchase the business, you as the potential small business person should develop a plan of operation for the business. The cost of the business should include any premium for its current performance. What will you do differently from what is currently being done? If you are paying a premium for a business but have no plans to change the business operations, then how do you hope to achieve success?

Will you bring a new mission to the business? Will you position the firm or its product differently? Do you have some unique talent, etc., that will make the business that you are considering buying a success, or make it more successful? An understanding of what you have to offer and what the current business is missing will provide the basis for your negotiations. What is important to the current owner may or may not be important to the potential owner, given the new direction for the company. Adding value to a business is a critical step in the process of deciding to purchase a business. We would recommend that the entrepreneur take the same approach as was outlined in Chapter 5 to develop a new mission for the organization. What are the resource-based advantages of the new organization under the new leadership?

Having developed a new plan for the business, the potential small business person is prepared to negotiate the deal. In Chapter 13 we outlined procedures that a seller should use to put his business in the best position for sale, as well as negotiation strategies. We would recommend that a potential buyer do the same and demand this from any seller.

Finally, there is the complex issue of organizing the process of change from the former business to the new business. While there are a number of ways in which this can be accomplished, the tasks are relatively the same. We must point out that there is a lot of nuance and "art" in the handling of these processes. Once negotiations are complete and all contracts are signed, there will be a transition period that should be spelled out in the contract for sale. During that transition time period, there are a number of tasks that should be completed. The new owner should

1. Meet and discuss the transition with every member of the current staff. If there is a layoff plan, then that should be enacted immediately.

2. Spend significant time being visible in the new operation, talking with employees, making suggestions, and doing some of the more menial work.

3. Make all significant changes in one day so as to alleviate any lingering concerns by the employees.

4. Implement new metrics and standards as soon as possible.

5. Ask the former owner(s) not to be at the business for several weeks while the transition is taking place. Loyalties and work processes get confused when the former owner is around every day.

6. If appropriate for the type of business that has been purchased, send out a letter/e-mail to every customer/supplier informing each one of the ownership change. Ideally this letter is signed by both the former owner and the new owner.

summary

This chapter examined two common methods for becoming a small business person. Both techniques fundamentally rely upon all of the same analysis/development techniques that have been developed in this text. Franchises are a well-developed and expansively available method for starting a business. There are more than 10,000 franchisors in the United States and franchises are rapidly expanding in many parts of the world.[7] Franchise operations run the gamut from those that are fully developed complete partners in business to ones that are little more than a name. Franchises significantly improve the chance of survival for a small business, but do not eliminate the potential for failure.[8] We reviewed the UFOC as well as those areas that are unique to a franchise operation. We finished the chapter with a discussion of the unique considerations involved in buying an existing business.

key terms

business brokers 302
franchise agreement 292
franchisee 291

franchisor 291
Uniform Franchise Offering
Circular (UFOC) 296

review questions

1. How does a franchise work?
2. How do the franchisee and the franchisor differ?
3. What is the benefit of buying a franchise versus starting your own business? Are there any drawbacks?
4. What are the questions a person should ask herself before she starts a franchise?
5. What is typically included in a franchise?
6. What is the UFOC? What are its major provisions?
7. Why would someone buy an existing business?
8. How do you locate a business that you would like to purchase?
9. Once you actually buy the business, how do you make sure that you are successful?

individual exercises

1. Starting with the Independent Franchise Association Web page, www.franchise.org, put together a plan for purchasing a franchise.
2. For the industry that you chose in exercise 2 of this chapter, how many franchise opportunities exist?
3. What resources exist to help you in your effort to acquire a franchise?

group exercises

1. Form small groups in the class. As a class, pick one industry, such as retail restaurants. Have every team then select a franchise to buy in that industry independently.

   a. What is the range of franchises picked?

   b. What is the range of costs and services offered?

   c. Why did each team pick the franchise that it did? List your top five reasons for picking that franchise.

   d. Each team should make a five-minute presentation on the franchise it picked as if it were selling the idea to an investor.

   e. Then vote as a class for the best franchise idea.

everyday edisons class discussion

Go to www.everydayedisons.com/jennifer.html and read about Jennifer.

1. What do you think about the potential for Jennifer's product idea?

2. What would be the best way for her to "cash in" on the product?

Jennie & Gary Grassia, Trifork Enterprises, LLC

Gary and Jennie Grassia have been together for 16 years. During that time they have built both a family and a business. For many years, Jennie's parents owned a franchise called "Little Gym" that provided athletic activity and developmental education for young children. Jennie and Gary started working at the gym in high school and college, respectively, eventually becoming managers of the two facilities in the franchise, and then partners. In the fall of 2008 the opportunity to start a new franchise by themselves became available: Simply Fondue.

Simply Fondue is a restaurant franchise operation that is based on fondue cooking. A fondue restaurant is one where the raw food is cooked at the table by the customer. The food arrives at the table cut into bite-sized segments and is then cooked to taste by the customers using long forks. Fondue is generally thought of by Americans as dipping food in cheese and chocolate—which is certainly part of the experience. However, "fondue" comes from a French word "to melt." So in addition to the cheese and chocolate fondue, there is also hot oil or broth which can be used to cook a variety of items, including beef, chicken, shrimp, and mushrooms. The restaurant has a real competitive advantage in comparison to other restaurant operations because it does not require a large kitchen staff to cook the food; only preparation is needed. For this particular Simply Fondue's market, the typical ticket for an individual plate at the restaurant will average approximately $45. Thus, the restaurant is typically thought of as a high-quality (because you can see your food cooked), higher-priced meal experience.

The Grassias had become familiar with the Simply Fondue franchise 12 years before by frequenting a nearby Simply Fondue. They had known for a while they wanted to start another business, so they had been doing a wide-range examination of different types of franchises available. They were drawn to the restaurant business, since there always seemed to be demand and there were many well-established franchisors. They were drawn to fondue franchises, since it seemed like a unique niche, but one with growing demand. There are two major franchise chains that offer such food. Gary visited with both major franchise groups, but the leadership of the Simply Fondue franchise operation really impressed him. He was convinced that this would be the most supportive franchisor. One critical key issue that became clear for Gary and Jennie when they were involved with the child development franchise was the importance of strong support by the franchisor. Franchisors promise support in return for the monthly royalty payments that the franchisee must pay. However, the follow-through and willingness to help the franchisee succeed is often less than promised. Thus, one of the key issues that Gary focused on when making his evaluation of the two franchise systems was which one was actually going to be the most helpful to them. He found that the total costs of the franchise purchased from either group would be the same, and the nature of what was promised was largely the same. Thus, the judgment of which franchise to buy would be based on which one of the franchisors would actually follow through on what it promised.

They began to look at locations for a restaurant in the large southwestern city in which they lived. However, by early 2008 they realized that the corporate franchisor was also looking to open a corporate store in their city. In fact, the franchisor had already begun lease negotiations to open a store in a very popular downtown area. Using the contacts that he had developed in his research on the businesses, Gary contacted the president of the franchisor company. During the next few conversations it became clear that the franchisor president wanted either a company, or privately owned, franchise in this downtown location, but it was too good a location to not have something in place soon. Grassias were able to arrange to buy the franchise and take over the lease negotiations. The funding for the purchase of the franchise, the preparation of the restaurant, and other initial costs came from a Small Business Administration loan.

The preparation of the site took longer than expected: nine months. The space had been a storage location prior to their purchase and lacked everything needed for the restaurant. However, they did not have to pay rent during the construction phase, so even though it took a long time, it was not nearly as costly as it might have been. In most retail operations, the key ingredient for success is often said to be location, location, location, but the Grassia's experience highlights the fact that while that is true, another variable is the cost of that location. Their location is much cheaper than many in the same downtown area because although they have a street-front entrance, their restaurant is actually downstairs in a basement.

The restaurant is open and is performing ahead of schedule in terms of profitability. The lessons learned by the couple during their first year of operation have been numerous. The couple originally thought that the fact that individuals cooked their own meals would limit the number of complaints that occurred. They found out that this was not the case. They've received complaints from customers about getting too much service from wait staff as they fill the water glasses too often, and complaints that the salads that go with the meals are too large. Overall, they have learned that no matter what the restaurant concept is, people can and will complain about everything. The days have been long for the Grassias even though the restaurant is only open for dinner. The cooking of food through fondue is a long process and is not designed for the quick turnaround necessary at lunch. The couple decided that the restaurant would be open until 2:00 a.m. to increase the sales of drinks. This strategic choice was the result of the fact that almost all other restaurants in the downtown area close between 10:00 p.m. and midnight. The goal was to become the place that the other wait staff in the area would come to after work for a relaxing time. It has proven to be a wise strategic decision.

The managing of a business as a couple introduces its own unique challenges. The couple work together and enjoy it. However, with three small school-age children at home, they have to divide work differently in the restaurant business than they did at the child development center. The days are very long for Gary, as he is doing the hands-on management of the facility. Jennie focuses solely on the financials and accounting systems for the organization. In many ways, the transition to this division of labor has been harder for her, since she is used to being a hands-on manager with Gary in their prior business. The key to the success of their business together is trust. It is also recognizing that their business is like their marriage in that there is lots of compromise. Thus, as they make strategic decisions, they must each be willing to compromise.

Their goals are to open another Simply Fondue restaurant. They would like to have three restaurants—one for each of their three children.

The Grassias have learned many things from their experience:

1. Work with people. It does not pay in the long run to yell and make unreasonable demands. For example, the contractor took longer than expected to complete the finish-out on the restaurant. However, if they had yelled and screamed at the workers, they might have gotten the work done a bit sooner but would have been likely to not care as much about the quality.

2. Keep lines of communication open with your partner and those you have to deal with on a regular basis, such as lenders, leaseholder, etc. They all want you to be successful since that is how they get paid. These relationships are mutually beneficial and a solid relationship is the key to their success.

3. Run your franchise in the manner that the franchisors suggest. Why pay for a franchise if you are not going to do what they suggest? They have systems that are proven. Take full advantage of that. Beyond that, if you do not do as they suggest and something goes wrong, you cannot go back to the franchisors for support.

Building a Business Plan

Developing a business plan is the logical outcome of preparing to launch a new business. There are as many formats for a business plan as there are people to design one. Nevertheless, we would like to suggest that most business plans have some elements in common. The list below is a comprehensive list of potential elements in a business plan, so we would not expect every plan to incorporate all of these elements. The entrepreneur must exercise considerable discretion to determine which elements are important to her particular business plan. For example, if she is developing a new restaurant then the plan will deal extensively with operational issues since these will be particularly critical to its success. On the other hand, if she is planning a new book store, the business plan will focus more extensively on the marketing as an especially critical factor of success.

We will briefly describe the major areas in a business plan and highlight particularly critical elements that small business entrepreneurs should include in their plans. Then we will present a plan that was developed by undergraduate students while they were taking a course using this text. It is not an example of a "perfect plan"; rather, it is an example of what might be reasonably accomplished in a single semester. After each major section of the plan, we will discuss the positives and negatives as well as provide references to the appropriate chapters.

Key Parts of the Business Plan

Executive Summary

- Brief Description of the Company
- Mission Statement/Value Proposition
- The Product and/or Services Being Offerred
- Competitive Advantages
- Brief Financial Forecast
- Management Team
- Current Advisors
- Financing Requirements and Return Expected

You can conceive of this particularly critical section of the plan as the "hook" that encourages the reader to examine the entire plan. The executive summary is very useful in ensuring that you, the small business person, remain focused in your analysis. If you cannot briefly explain your complete business concept in one to two pages, then you have not thoughtfully and thoroughly analyzed the potential business. You should be clear about how you will provide value to the customers, what the value proposition is for the business, what your competitive advantage is, and how your background has prepared you for this business.

History and Position of the Business to Date

- The Company's Mission
- Company History from Business Conception to This Point
- Management Team and Key Personnel
- Business Structure

This is the section of a business plan which many entrepreneurs choose not to include. If you have created other businesses and your new business is somehow dependent on those businesses for success, then such information is important. However, for most small businesses the issues highlighted here simply provide context to potential investors, clients, and/or suppliers.

Market Research

- Target Markets
- Geographic Area within Which the Business Will Operate
- Competitive Environment and Opportunity Space
- Competitor Analysis
- Position of the Firm
- Market Description
- The Desired Customer
- Market Growth Opportunities

Market research codifies and describes the specific market space that you hope your new business will occupy. The preparation of this section helps assure that there is indeed a group of customers available for your business and that the business will be in a position to acquire these customers.

Business Strategy

- Mission of the Small Business
- Strategy
- Value Proposition
- Evaluation of Competitive Advantage
- Length of Time before Imitation
- Comparison to Substitutes

You need to specify how the firm will compete in its targeted market. The firm's strategy details not only how you expect it to compete, but it also begins the process of exploring the expected outcomes of that strategy and the potential dangers to the firm from its competitors. The issue of imitation is a continuing one for all organizations as they try to achieve and maintain what is unorthodox about their businesses.

Marketing Plan

- Target Customer
- Sales Forecast
- Pricing
- Methods of Promotion
- Promotion Scheduling and Placement

The marketing plan specifies how your firm will reach the target customer. Particularly critical here is the specification of the customers and the details of how you actually will price and promote the product to those customers. One of the most difficult areas for any new business is how to actually reach the customers in a way that they will want to buy your product/service. Getting customers to change to your firm from another is very hard to accomplish.

Operations

- Location
- Accounting Systems
- Quality Control
- Build Out
- Hours of Operation
- Processes
- Equipment
- Staffing Schedule
- Critical Path Analysis to Start the Business

Operations include the details about how you will operate your small business, and these details will differ widely depending on the type of business you are launching. If it is a small manufacturing business, then the operations section most likely will be central to your plan. For example, your equipment may be part of the competitive advantage of your manufacturing firm and as such you will want to spend considerable time on that aspect of the business. On the other hand, if your new business is a restaurant then the equipment is typically generic and not a major factor in the firm's success, so your business plan will minimize its discussion. The location of your restaurant would be an important element of its success, however, so you should elaborate on that aspect of your business.

Financial Analysis

- Cash Flow Projections and Analysis
- Ratio Analysis
- Break-Even Analysis
- Expected Gross and Operating Margins

As explained in Chapters 6, 9, and 12 of the text, financial analysis is a major concern for all new small businesses. This section in your plan will focus on a discussion of the various financial concerns related to the startup and running of your business. Tables with your actual data should appear as support for this discussion at the end of your plan.

Risk Analysis

- Discussion of Systems Risks and Controls
- Discussion of Business Risks and Controls

There are risks in every business. You do not need to spend extensive effort detailing your risks but you want to acknowledge them. For example, we mentioned that young people starting a business may not have extensive prior experience in business. In this section you may wish to acknowledge those risks and what actions you are taking to ensure the success of the business. For example, if you have obtained a board of advisors consisting of successful business people who will work with you to reduce your risk, then this is an important point to illustrate.

Funds and Their Use

- Funds Required and Timing
- Use of Funds
- Funding Sources
- Valuation
- Distribution of Control

Ultimately you will need money from others and/or will need to be clear about how you will spend the money if you are self funding the business. Therefore, your business plan needs to specify those numbers. The greater the detail provided, the more help the plan will provide you in establishing benchmarks that can be evaluated to judge your new firm's progress.

Summary

Next is the sample business plan we mentioned earlier. As you read the plan, remember that we have noted both positives and negatives. As with all plans there are items that need additional research as well as items that are simply not researchable. Small business people need to gather as much information as they can and present that information as clearly and concisely as possible. While there is always other information that they would like to include, ultimately all potential entrepreneurs must make decisions with less than complete information.

A particular concern that we remark on in several places in this plan is the need for a greater description regarding particular points. Recall this is an actual student business plan that was created in a 15-week course. Our suggestions are intended to improve the students' final product prior to it being used for financing, as a pitch for a potential customer, or as a means of attracting a supplier.

Also note that many of the sections of this plan do not match the exact order of our key areas list at the start of this appendix. A business plan is not a formula within which the entrepreneur can plug various pieces of information. Instead it is a document that should be read easily and be very understandable. The information should appear where it ultimately makes the most sense as well as where it best supports the entrepreneur's arguments about the new business.

GameDay Bus, LLC

AUTHOR NOTE

The GameDay Bus company was the business creation of a student group in Dr. Chuck Bamford's undergraduate entrepreneurship class. Although generally well developed, the plan has flaws and is not intended as a perfect example of a small business plan. Instead it is an effective vehicle for discussing the issues developed in this text and for demonstrating their application in a full-blown plan. The format, detail, and approach are expressed quite well. The authors wish to thank the students responsible for this plan: Kellen Vaughn, Nathan Winston, Casey Walterscheid, Aaron Ewert, and Connie Zeender.

CONFIDENTIAL BUSINESS PLAN

DRAFT

April 2009

This business plan is the property of GameDay Bus, LLC. This copy is to be used for evaluation purposes only and the information contained herein is not to be disclosed to any party without the expressed written consent of GameDay Bus, LLC.

This is not an offering

Table of Contents

GameDay Bus
Est. 2009

"More room for comfort, more room for team spirit."

Executive Summary

GameDay Bus, LLC will provide transportation to athletic and alumni events for University of Tennessee (UT) alumni chapters in the central Tennessee area. The founders have personal relationships with Volunteer alumni in Nashville, Memphis, and Knoxville chapters and will be prepared for the football season of 2009.

GameDay Bus has differentiated itself from its competitors in a variety of ways. The business will target alumni chapters initially in Tennessee to provide transportation to any athletic and school events. The double-decker buses will be personalized with Tennessee traditions and painted orange and white to make sure the true Tennessee fan arrives in Volunteer style. The buses will literally be a college sports bar on wheels, with alcoholic beverages, comfortable leather couches, and satellite television.

The focus of the business will be for athletic events. However during off-season periods our buses will be more charter bus oriented yet focused on alumni and campus events. For example, our buses can also be utilized for events such as NASCAR at Bristol Motor Speedway, UT new student orientations, reunions, campus events, and other general alumni events.

GameDay Bus expects at end of year five to be valued at $24 million. This valuation is a product of an average P/E ratio within our industry of 23.4 and our estimated net income after taxes in year 5 of $1,025,649.84. GameDay Bus is seeking $805,000 to begin operation in return for 40% of ownership. With numerous surrounding university campuses, growth and expansion are very promising for GameDay Bus. If sales meet expectations, harvest will remain after year 5 but expansion will unfold in years 3 and 4. These expansions will be financed completely internally without mezzanine level investing required.

The officers of the company will aid in the sales and promotion of the buses throughout the state at local events. Through these promotions, we will secure clients who wish to use our services. Many of the customers will hire us for their 1 day trips to and from a football game, while others will take advantage of our ability to accommodate multi-state, multi-day trips for away games.

Market and Company Concept

There are many charter companies within the Tennessee area, but GameDay Bus is the only service completely devoted to the University of Tennessee sporting events. Our goal is to make game day traveling as much a part of the excitement as it can be. In catering our services to Tennessee alumni groups, we are allowing the die-hard fans an opportunity to travel in luxury while enjoying safe pre-game partying with friends.

The company will be located in Nashville, Tennessee, due to the city's central location between Memphis and Knoxville and the convenience of Interstate Highway 70. GameDay Bus will run double-decker buses (imported from England) during the football season and for selected men's and women's basketball games. In addition to the athletic seasons GameDay Bus will continue to serve alumni groups for select university/alumni events in the months of May, June, July, and August.

There will be four double-decker buses to start that will be stripped of the bench seating, and converted into a spacious, luxurious lounge setting decorated inside and out with a Tennessee Volunteer theme. Each bus will have a unique exterior custom paint job using the Volunteer colors. The inside of the bus will feature a bar and a restroom on the lower level along with a lounge area and satellite television to

AUTHOR NOTE

As a succinct explanation of the business and the competitive reason for its existence, the executive summary is a critical part of any business plan. The founders should be able to explain their vision for the business in a few short sentences. We suggest that all executive summaries have the following: (1) the name of the company and a short explanation of its sustainable competitive advantage; (2) a listing of the personnel who are founding the business and relevant parts of their background to the business; (3) the value proposition; (4) how much money the founders are seeking (and how much equity they look to exchange for that money); and (5) The value of the business.

This business is asking for a considerably higher amount of money than many small businesses. However, regardless of the amount needed, the business should be able to explain why it is needed and how that investment will be successfully utilized. In this case it would help to expand on the background of the founders in the summary only if it is a competitive advantage for the small business. The difficulty in a class setting is that many young people do not have enough business experience to make their background a benefit. In that case the founders may specifically acknowledge their youth and stress issues such as advisors or partners that they have obtained to help ensure the profitable operation of the business.

watch the other games. The upstairs will also feature satellite television and a very spacious lounge area.

There will be enough seats on the bus for everyone at maximum occupancy to have a seat, which adheres to Tennessee state laws.

Alcohol will be provided for an extra charge, and the bar will be stocked according to the customers' orders by the time they get on the bus. Customers will help themselves to the service bar during the trip and take any leftover alcohol after the end of the trip. There are no alcohol licenses required for this type of service.

Industry Analysis

GameDay Bus's industry is the transportation/motor coach business, with a specialty in transportation to sporting events. This industry is currently occupied with companies that offer transportation services on board motor coaches to and from destinations requested by the occupants. The industry ranges from standard charter buses with bench type seating, to converted motor coaches with lounge atmospheres. The standard charter bus companies charge either per hour, or per mile, depending on which rate is the highest. Aside from the base cost of the trip, most companies require additional charges for fuel, driver salary and accommodation (if necessary for overnight trips), and bus cleaning costs. The converted entertainment coaches typically charge per day, and the cost per trip is around $80 per person per day. These companies usually provide services for large corporations, weddings, parties, shuttle services, inter-state travel, corporate outings, and special pre-determined tours.

The average multi-day tour expenditure by passengers on a coach is $1,000 to $2,000 per day (38- to 55-seat coaches). 10.3 million people took multi-day tours; 12.7 million took one-day tours in 1995. The group tour industry generated $10 billion in direct expenditures in North America in 1995. The tour industry generates $887 million in local and state government revenues. As far as safety is concerned coaches are driven by professional, fully qualified and tested drivers. Coaches are required to pass federal safety and inspection criteria. Interstate motor carriers must have operating authority issued by the Federal Highway Administration. Insurance liability of $5 million is required of interstate passenger carriers. Most highway fatalities (64%) occurred in automobiles.

GameDay Bus's specific role in this industry is unique, and its services are without direct competition. We provide luxury shuttle and transportation service to people who are traveling to sporting events where the University of Tennessee athletes are playing. We have carved out a niche market in the industry where we specifically target a school and provide a more relaxed, comfortable, and party atmosphere to our clients who are traveling to the home games in Knoxville or wherever their Volunteers are playing.

AUTHOR NOTE

After establishing a simple description in the executive summary, this plan now presents an expanded description of the company concept. As noted previously, small business people need to tailor their plans to their own needs. The unique nature of this business merits providing greater detail regarding the business concept.

This section also represents part of the students' efforts at market research. This part of the business plan is not as detailed as would be desirable. The students do provide information about where they will operate and why. However, specific information like the number of alumni, number of alumni events, other events that might benefit from use of the bus, and the number of participants for each event would be very helpful. The absence of this market information is one of the major shortcomings of this plan. It should be noted that issues such as removing alcohol at the end of the trip and not needing licenses is perhaps unique to their understanding of Tennessee law. It is incumbent upon the founders to ensure that specific regulations that impact a business are carefully and clearly listed in a plan.

Competitor List

Anchor Bus Charters

Big Bidness

Cumberland Tours

David Hemphill Coach Co.

Flair Tours

Gaylord Opryland Resort &
Convention Center—Catering

Gigtours—Majestic Coach

Gray Line Tours—Nashville

Grey Line Country & Western
Tours

Lifeline Tours And Charters

Love That Tours Incorporated

Majestic Coach Inc.

Nitetrain Coach Co Inc.

Phoenix Touring Services

Queen City Bus Line Inc.

Shockey Tours Inc.

Southeastern Motor Coach Inc.

Transport J L Rangel

Transportes Regiomontanos

Greene Coach Charter & Tours

Coach USA

Rocky Top Tours

Stage Coach VIP Inc.

USA Charter

Phantom Coaches

Music City Coach

Agape Charter & Commuter Service

Waytogo Coach Inc.

Travel One Charter & Tour Inc.

Orion Charter Tours

Pyramid Coach Company

All Points USA

Competitive Map

	ORTHODOX			UNORTHODOX
	# OF PASSENGERS	***COST PER CUSTOMER**	**# OF BUSES**	
USA Charter	47	$25	+10,000	Top of the line buses; nationwide company with tremendous economies of scale. Can charge low prices.
Greene Coach Charter	47-57	$20	9	13 drivers with a total of 172 years of experience. Long standing operation in Tennessee.
US Luxury Limo	25	$80	Unavailable	Offers luxurious travel with limo, and bus options.
GameDay	50	$90	4	School specific double decker buses with ultimate pre-game party experience.

*Cost per customer is based on a 180 mile run from Nashville to Knoxville.

AUTHOR NOTE

A competitive map is one of the more dramatic means with which to summarize your competitive advantages relative to others in the industry. This chart only shows a few characteristics and does not seem to play to GameDay's most important advantages. We would suggest expanding the chart to include those areas where GameDay will differentiate itself from its competitors.

Competitive Environment

The main entry barrier into the market of luxury alumni GameDay Bus is the capital investment required. Each bus will cost $110,000 to purchase and finish out at the level needed. The buses will have to be maintained as well as fueled for every trip to minimize any possible problems while en route. Insurance will be another large cost associated with operations. The expenditures will exceed revenues for the first few months as in most new ventures.

In addition to the investment needed, the other entry barriers include relatively similar substitutes such as limousines and normal charter buses. The limousines have the finish out that will be sought by most of our potential clients, but they lack the desired space and ability to handle large groups. Charter buses, while having the transportation level needed, are much less luxurious and spacious. The focal point in this sector is differentiation.

Strategy

GameDay Bus competes with a differentiation strategy not by offering the lowest cost product, but by offering a unique combination of a charter bus coupled with the luxuriousness of a limousine service. The tailor-made feel of each location to the school colors and insignia of the universities and alumni organizations we work with. Our focus is on servicing the middle- to upper-class alumni groups interested in using the mode of transportation that holds the aura of being both highly visible and highly exclusive. We offer a premium service at a premium price.

We have chosen to focus initially on alumni groups at the University of Tennessee in part due to the strong commitment to the university and its various activities by alumni. Also, game schedules and alumni organizational events are ongoing all year round. This provides the opportunity to maximize bus usage as opposed to becoming a more public service dependent on booking by random groups within a community wanting the transportation to any number of venues. Focusing on the alumni groups allows us to tailor our buses with school colors and school logos to make the experience that much more distinctive. In the future, GameDay can expand this concept to other universities.

Advertising for the service since it focuses on alumni at the University of Tennessee allows the business to also be much more focused due to the fact that the large majority of potential customers can be reached through the use of a very small number of marketing avenues.

Mission Statement

GameDay Bus: Providing the safe, reliable, and luxurious party environment for game day transportation.

Competitive Advantage

GameDay Bus is providing a service with a competitive advantage over other chauffeur companies for several reasons. Our company is unique in that we provide a comfortable and spacious atmosphere in a classic

AUTHOR NOTE

An analysis of the entry/exit barriers provides some information on the amount of time/money it would take for a competitor to compete directly with the business being proposed.

AUTHOR NOTE

Note that in this section the students have discussed issues such as the customer and advertising, which do not appear in the list of strategy concerns at the front of this appendix. In this business plan these points make natural contributions to the discussion of strategy. This is another example of the need to tailor your plan in a logical manner. Do not blindly follow a set of topics from a book or Web site and plug in words. You are trying to convince the reader of the value of the idea. You need to construct sections that support what you are trying to say.

AUTHOR NOTE

The students' mission statement meets the basic criteria laid out in Chapter 5. Their statement here is separated out. However, the statement may appear more effectively as part of the strategy section or even earlier in the plan. You must determine where it best fits in your plan. An issue with a stand-alone mission statement is that without some descriptive material this section does not add to the flow of the paper.

AUTHOR NOTE

The plan lays out the firm's competitive advantage as well as the lead time needed by potential competitors to imitate the business. However, the students do not make a strong case regarding the lead time nor about their own ability to lock up the University of Tennessee as a customer. It is also worth noting that the definition of the industry seems to change here in their plan. Previously the plan discussed various forms of charter and transportation industries while here they talk of the chauffeur industry. Each of these terms has slightly different meanings and implies different competitors. The students should clearly and concisely define the industry they are entering and use that term throughout the plan. The use of consistent terms helps readers follow a plan.

AUTHOR NOTE

Note that the students' plan has used many visual aids in the development of the idea. This is a valuable contribution. Even if you are self funding a business, you will likely need to show your plan to suppliers and customers. Visual aids that help illustrate ideas, charts that summarize data, or pictures that make the document more interesting are all useful in making the plan more realistic and visually descriptive.

AUTHOR NOTE

The value proposition is developed, but it needs significant additional research. A chart showing the value provided in a trip would be a great addition here. There also needs to be an analysis comparing the proposed operation against each of the other means by which individuals can be transported to a game.

double-decker bus, providing the groups desired alcoholic beverages at a mini bar. We also have a lounging area set up with leather couches and satellite television in order to make their experience more enjoyable. Our purpose is to provide a transportation service where our passengers almost forget that they are in a bus. We want their travel experience to be just as enjoyable as the actual destination.

It is somewhat difficult to find double-deckers for sale in the United States and that is why our team outsourced supplying buses to KGM Charters, a small company that not only provides double-deckers, but also makes any appropriate conversions that we may need. If competitors decide to replicate our idea, it will take them at least a year to find a company that sells double-deckers, and make any necessary conversions. By then, our company will have established a more binding relationship with alumni groups for colleges than they can catch up with, and our brand name will be well established and easily recognized among our customers, thus, making our proposal durable.

GameDay Bus's service is relatively non-substitutable, simply because no other bus or limousine company offers this much space, comfort, and luxury to groups for up to 50 people. For this reason, we provide value and can charge a premium price for our services.

Value Proposition

The price for our service will vary based on the trip length and duration but will fall on the higher end relative to competitors. For example, a trip from Knoxville, Tennessee to Athens, Georgia for a football game would cost approximately $82 (round trip) per person for Greyhound charter. An airplane ticket for a similar distance would run around $215 (round trip). The comfort level on either of these options would be significantly less than what is available from GameDay Bus. A typical spot on the bus for a trip of this nature would cost the guest around $250. This price includes seating on the bus as well as refreshments along the way.

The main elements of GameDay Bus's offering that separate it from the competition and provide significant economic rents are:

- Luxury and spaciousness afforded on the bus that are not available in smaller vehicles such as SUV limousines.
- Unique experience of riding with other alumni in *the* GameDay Bus conspicuously adorned in school colors/logo.
- Unique experience of riding in a double-decker bus.

Target Customer Group

GameDay's target customer group includes males or females who are alumni of the University of Tennessee and who live in Nashville, Memphis, or the outskirts of these cities. They will usually be a member of the local chapter of the Alumni association and a true University of Tennessee fan. The target will include those who travel to most home, and some away, games no matter what the cost or the performance of the team.

He will usually drive but would love the opportunity to travel on a GameDay brand bus to party and cheer on the Volunteers the whole way there and back.

Perfect Customer

The perfect customer is a 45-year-old male who is an alumnus of the University of Tennessee. He will be a season ticket holder to football, men's basketball, and women's basketball games. He will be a member of the Nashville alumni chapter, and hold his social endeavors in high regard. Most importantly this person is a Volunteer sports fanatic, and lives for the next sporting event.

Location

The location of the business will be on the outskirts of Nashville, Tennessee. It will be a one-acre site. The land includes city water, electricity, and excellent roads. The leasing price is $1,500 a month. It has a mobile home that will be used as our office. We will set up an 800 number so that our customers can contact us easily and at no long distance charge. We will start off with using one computer to keep track of sales and other important company information. GameDay will take orders over the phone and record it in a computer database. The firm will accept Visa, MasterCard, and check. We will have at least one person by the phone at all times during business hours and set up an answering service when we are closed. Each of our team members will be equipped with cellular phones and in close contact with each other at all times. In addition, all members will be available to do marketing at the games and be on-call for any emergency that might arise. Our business hours are 9:00am–5:00pm on Monday through Friday.

Bus Description and Acquisition

GameDay Bus will initially purchase four double-decker buses from KGM Charters, a California-based Internet development and multimedia marketing company.

AUTHOR NOTE

Here the students are beginning to address the marketing plan of the firm. In preparing the strategy segment, it made sense for them to separate the strategy section from the value proposition. However, separating the different elements of marketing results in several very short sections that are redundant when read. Instead, the students would be better served to combine Target Customer and Perfect Customer into a single marketing section.

AUTHOR NOTE

While somewhat interesting and potentially valuable, this section of the plan needs to outline **why** this is the perfect customer. What are the demographics that encourage this group of individuals to value this business operation? This level of detail with information such as the age of the customer leads us to believe they have more data collected than they are demonstrating here.

AUTHOR NOTE

The location chosen is appropriate for the business proposed, but the reasoning is a bit weak. Planning the operational aspects of the business is best kept within the operations section of the plan. Additionally, as discussed in Chapter 7, regulation of a business can be critical to its success. Thus, if you were establishing this business you would need to obtain information on issues such as zoning at this site and potential environmental issues.

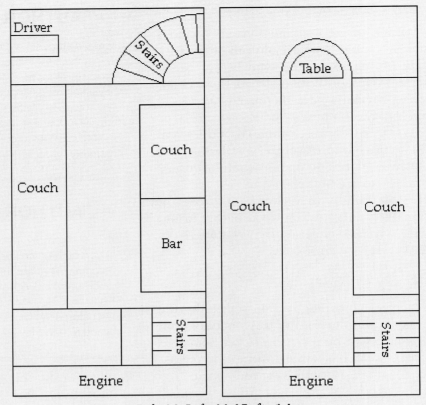

30 ft X 8 ft X 13 ft 6 in

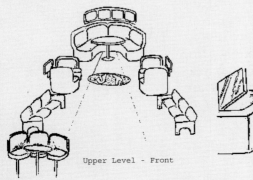

Upper Level - Front

Lower Level - Front

GameDay will order a Leyland Atlantean bus with complete conversions on the interior, painted exterior, and a new P/A system installed. Each bus has a storage compartment behind the stairwell sufficient for overnight trips where customers have bags. We will receive a package of hard to find spare parts with the purchase of each bus. This model costs $30,000. KGM Charters will also perform the conversions and add a bar, restrooms, lighting, carpeting, etc. The price for this project is quoted at about $70,000. In addition, we will install one 27-inch television set in each bus for about $2,700 each, and purchase a satellite package for $3,500. In addition, we will have a DVD player and 10-disc CD player with surround sound speakers for $2,200. Our estimate is that the total cost for each bus will be around $110,000.

Processes

GameDay Bus will attain all of the necessary components of a business. As mentioned earlier, a Web site will be created by members of the executive team. The Web site will be used for informational and contact purposes and established as another avenue of business generation. Each of the founders will be afforded a title appropriate to their job description from Chief Executive Officer on down.

Uniforms will be implemented for all personnel interacting with guests on the bus. The uniform will consist of a buttoned polo-style shirt with the GameDay Bus logo as well as khaki pants, or drivers will be able to wear University of Tennessee jerseys with their favorite player's number on the back. All male employees must be clean shaven and all female employees must have their hair restrained. GameDay Bus strives to maintain a professional, yet relaxed atmosphere to provide the guest with the most enjoyable experience possible while on board the bus. We want our guests to have a great time regardless of whether or not their team wins.

A bank account will be established complete with business sized company checks complete with the GameDay Bus logo.

GameDay will start off by paying the executive team, Business Development Director, and Marketing Director, $30,000 a year. This salary will increase every couple of years depending on the success of the company. Since the marketing director and secretary are the same person, we will not pay an additional salary; however, in future years we will pay on a per hour basis and at the current market rate according to where we expand. The average rate in Nashville, Tennessee, is $15 an hour. Bus drivers will also be paid on a per hour basis and at current market rate: $15 an hour. Benefits include health care, dental care, and one week paid vacation. Benefits will be 33% of salary.

AUTHOR NOTE

This is a relatively weak start to an important section of the plan—operations. More detail is needed on the actual plan for internal operations. Customer service is critical in this industry and will be particularly important for this firm given its strategy. Therefore, the students should address how the firm will get the quality of people it wants and how its internal operations will be structured.

Production Flow

The basic production flow of GameDay Bus is straightforward. First, the customer will contact GameDay Bus via phone, fax, or e-mail to book an event. At the time of booking, a 25% deposit will be made to hold the reservation via credit card which the customer must sign off on. This deposit fee can be refunded as long as the reservation is not cancelled within 72 hours of the event departure. A contact person able to authorize final processing of the sale will be on board the trip to sign off once the run has been completed.

On the day of the event, the buses will arrive at the designated departure location approximately 30 minutes before the planned departure. During travel, customers will have access to satellite television, lavatories, and a mini-bar. Stops along the way should only be in an emergency. Exceptions to this guideline include any long distance travel where the bus must stop to refuel.

For sporting events, the buses will depart with the intention of arriving no less than 1½ hours before the start of the game to prevent any delays from occurring that would cause the participants to arrive after kickoff, tip-off, etc. Most sporting arenas offer a bus drop-off location or unloading zone relatively close to the entrance. The time buffer is in place to make sure that the customer always is able to get to the game on time regardless of the drop-off point. For all other events, the bus will run on times determined by the guest at the time of booking.

After releasing all passengers at the event, the bus driver will make a fuel run and do some minor cleaning and maintenance on the bus in preparation for the ride back.

In the event of an overnight event, although none have been scheduled in the first fiscal year, the customer will plan the complete itinerary for the trip and be responsible for all housing arrangements including acceptable lodging provisions for the bus driver. GameDay Bus assumes no responsibility for lodging, food, or any other miscellaneous issues besides transportation.

Once all passengers have left the bus, the contact person will sign off on documents presented by the driver. The bus will then be returned back to the lot to be fueled and cleaned before the next run. Customer feedback forms will also be presented to the customer at the time of arrival so as to get accurate comments at the time of the service.

In the event of bus failure or any unforeseen delay, cooperative agreements will be established with other charter bus companies within reasonable distances along the route. The bus driver will be provided with a Nextel walkie-talkie phone and a complete list of phone numbers and contact information for these organizations. In addition, contact information for bus wrecker services will be included in the event that the bus is unable to return to the storage lot.

AUTHOR NOTE

There are many questions embedded in the production flow discussion which are left unanswered. There is no information on how the customer will "sign off," why the money would be refunded with a 72-hour cancellation, how GameDay would collect money from delinquent customers, or exactly how the firm would collect the money and from whom. The process should be described in a simple step-by-step manner.

Critical Path Chart

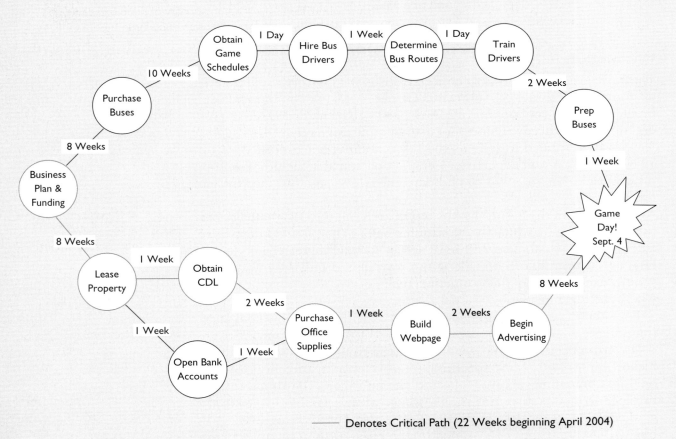

——— Denotes Critical Path (22 Weeks beginning April 2004)

Sales Forecast

In determining the sales forecast for Game-Day Bus, we have examined the University of Tennessee's Alumni Association. The alumni at the University of Tennessee hold the utmost pride to their school and their team. Founded more than 165 years ago, the University of Tennessee National Alumni Association continues to grow and strengthen its support of UT in all facets. UT has over 300,000 Alumni Association members nationwide. All students with over 24 hours at the University of Tennessee become honorary members free of charge. Other than Tennessee, the remaining bulk of alumni live in Georgia, Florida, or North Carolina. Alumni chapters are spread throughout Tennessee with principle chapters being in Davidson County, Memphis, and Knoxville.

During football season, we will target the fanatical Volunteer fans from Nashville and Memphis chapters. This will be our busiest season as we transport the avid fan to watch his alma mater play. Last year Tennessee had an attendance of over 735,000 fans. This was an average of 105,000 per game. This ranked 3rd among all NCAA Division I schools. During the spring, our focus will move from the football field to the court. Basketball games also bring a large following from traveling fans. Last year attendance was 233,400 for UT men's basketball, an average of 13,730 fans per game. Women's basketball in Tennessee is also a religious following for many. On average there were almost 13,000 fans per game. Once we establish ourselves as Tennessee alumni supporters and our bus becomes commonplace at each athletic outing, we will be utilized throughout the year with other various events. Alumni calendars are literally filled with activities on a weekly basis throughout the year.

Over 150,000 Volunteer alumni live in the state of Tennessee. Alumni members are the highest percentage of season ticket holders. Many are living in two of Tennessee's most populous cities—Memphis and Nashville. These two cities are home to two of UT's biggest Alumni Chapters. Out of the large target market of alumni members in Memphis and Nashville, we will aim to book seats for 180 people per game. Football season will be our busiest time period. For this reason we will be prepared to enter the market before the fall 2009 Volunteer football season. Table 1 shows the season ticket holders in Nashville and Memphis as well as customers. Customers are defined as those individuals who purchase tickets but are not listed as season ticket holders. With the data provided by the University of Tennessee's marketing director for student athletics,

AUTHOR NOTE

This is certainly not a classic critical path chart; however, it is effective in presenting the information. It is very useful to your reader to be able to visualize what is needed to start your business and where you may encounter problems getting started.

AUTHOR NOTE

Some of the information on the size of University of Tennessee alumni market would have been helpful at the front of the plan. The danger is that the readers lose interest before they reach this point of the plan.

Table I

	SEASON TICKET HOLDERS	OTHER CUSTOMERS	TOTAL
Nashville	3,000	3,000	6,000
Memphis	500	600	1,100
Total	3,500	3,600	7,100

we can see the total number of travelers from Memphis and Nashville to UT games. This being said, we have determined that we only have to focus our efforts to attain 2% of these individuals.

Marketing

The most effective method of marketing is word of mouth. Before any print ads are created, we will travel to various alumni organizational events to inform them of the new service being offered. We will also meet with organizational heads to book trips and hopefully broker partnerships with them. In addition to the alumni groups, visits and calls will also be made to various sports and administration departments around the campus. Making some of the higher positioned administrators such as the chancellor and athletic director aware of the company's presence, could provide some great opportunities to get recommended to prominent alumni groups. Since most of our business will be funneled through school organizations and activities, this form of guerilla marketing should prove highly effective in the long run.

Concerning paid advertisement, we will publish print ads in periodicals such as the *Tennessee Alumnus*, the *Torchbearer*, and various game day programs available at university sporting events. These magazines and programs can reach a very large number of potential customers that fall into our pool. The advertisements will be submitted for publishing two months in advance in order to adhere to the publishing schedules and assure that the advertisements will reach the target market in an appropriate time frame. We also hope to get ads in the alumni newsletters as well. Prices for the various publications are listed below.

Torchbearer Newsletter

Full Page	Back Cover	Half Page
$3,700	$3,500	$3,700

Gameday Programs

	Color		Black & White	
	Full Page	2/3 Page	Full Page	2/3 Page
Football	$4,275	$3,190	$2,980	$1,800
Men's Basketball	$3,780	$2,835	$2,645	$1,990
Women's Basketball	$2,230	$1,680	$1,610	$1,205
Combination	$9,255	$6,935	$6,515	$4,890

A Web presence will also be established to provide customers with company information, pictures of the fleet, pricing information, contact information, and other miscellaneous items. The site will also provide an electronic form for customers to submit their contact information and comments on the service and on interested events. To save cost, the Web site will be built in-house under the domain name www.gamedaybus. com. Some of the top management have experience in site design and

Web hosting; therefore, the added expenditures of outsourcing to a consulting firm are unnecessary.

GameDay Bus is also considering sponsorship for various events and organizations around the school such as providing charity prizes and sign placement in game arenas. Flyer distribution at these same events will also be implemented. Hopefully, having conspicuous placement will prompt potential business related to these school events.

The last form, and possibly the second-most effective step, will be parking one of the buses around events attended heavily by alumni groups. Buses in use serve as a great marketing tool in themselves, but having one of these unique vehicles in frequent view should stir some curiosity into the service.

AUTHOR NOTE

This is nice start to the marketing section of the plan.

Financial Analysis

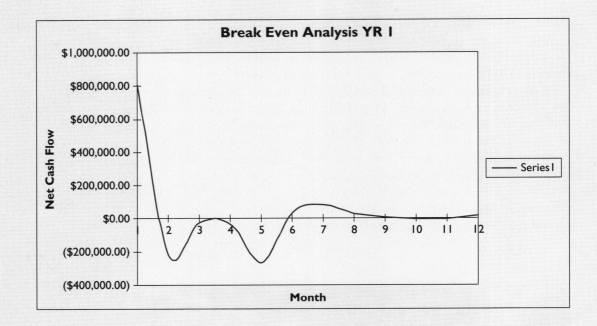

Break Even Analysis YR 1

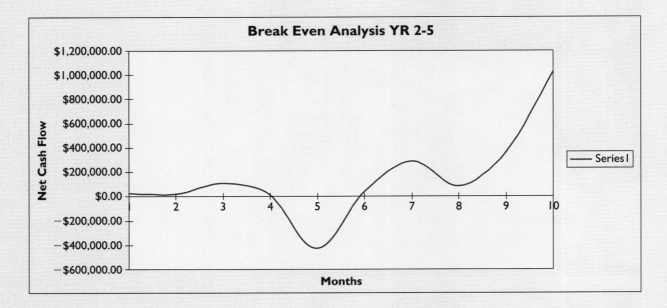

Break Even Analysis YR 2-5

AUTHOR NOTE

Charts are a good way to summarize information so your reader can access it quickly. The students were correct to place the supporting information for these charts in the back of the plan

AUTHOR NOTE

Greater detail on the use of funds raised would be helpful.

The details supporting these charts appear at the end of this document.

Funds Needed

The equity structure of the company will consist of a total of 10,000 shares valued at $201.25 each. The total investment of $805,000 we are seeking will yield a distribution of 4,000 shares or effectively 40% ownership in the business. The remaining 6,000 shares (60% ownership) will be divided evenly among the founding entrepreneurial team.

Management Team

- CEO—Kellen Vaughn
- CFO—Nathan Winston
- COO—Casey Walterscheid
- Director of Business Development—Aaron Ewert
- Director of Marketing—Connie Zeender

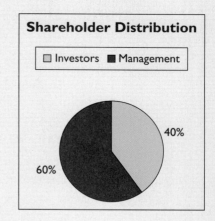

Financial Projection Supports

Pricing Structure

TRIP	TRAVEL TIME	GAME TIME	RATE	# OF BUSES	# OF TRIPS	TOTAL
Nashville-----Knoxville	5	6	$375.00	2	3	$ 24,750.00
Memphis----Knoxville	12	6	$375.00	2	3	$ 40,500.00
Sept. Total						**$ 65,250.00**
Memphis----Knoxville	12	6	$375.00	2	2	$ 27,000.00
Nashville-----Knoxville	5	6	$375.00	2	2	$ 16,500.00
Memphis----Athens	16.5	6	$375.00	2	1	$ 16,875.00
Nashville----Athens	10.5	6	$375.00	2	1	$ 12,375.00
Memphis---Oxford	3	6	$375.00	2	1	$ 6,750.00
Nashville---Oxford	9	6	$375.00	2	1	$ 11,250.00
Memphis---Columbia, SC	21	6	$375.00	2	1	$ 20,250.00
Nashville---Columbia, SC	14.5	6	$375.00	2	1	$ 15,375.00
Oct. Total	91.5	48				**$126,375.00**
Memphis----Knoxville	12	6	$375.00	2	2	$ 27,000.00
Nashville-----Knoxville	5	6	$375.00	2	2	$ 16,500.00
Memphis----Nashville	5	6	$375.00	4	1	$ 16,500.00
Nov. Total	22	18				**$ 60,000.00**
Memphis----Knoxville Bball	12	4	$200.00	2	2	$ 12,800.00
Nashville----Knoxville Bball	5	4	$200.00	2	2	$ 7,200.00
Nashville----? Bowl Game	10	8	$375.00	2	1	$ 13,500.00
Knoxville----? Bowl Game	12	8	$375.00	2	1	$ 15,000.00
Dec. Total	39	24				**$ 48,500.00**
Nashville--Knoxville Men Bball/W Bball	5	4	$225.00	4	1	$ 8,100.00
Nashville--Knoxville Men Bball	5	4	$225.00	1	1	$ 2,025.00
Nashville--Knoxville Men Bball	5	4	$225.00	2	1	$ 4,050.00
Nashville--Knoxville Men Bball	5	4	$225.00	1	1	$ 2,025.00
Nashville--Knoxville Men Bball	5	4	$225.00	4	1	$ 8,100.00
Jan. Total	25	20				**$ 24,300.00**

Continued

TRIP	TRAVEL TIME	GAME TIME	RATE	# OF BUSES	# OF TRIPS	TOTAL
Nashville--Knoxville Men Bball	5	4	$225.00	2	1	$ 4,050.00
Nashville--Knoxville Men Bball	5	4	$225.00	1	1	$ 2,025.00
Nashville--Knoxville Men Bball	5	4	$225.00	1	1	$ 2,025.00
Nashville--Knoxville Men Bball	5	4	$225.00	2	1	$ 4,050.00
						$ 12,150.00
Nashville--Knoxville Women Bball	5	4	$225.00	2	1	$ 4,050.00
Nashville--Knoxville Women Bball	5	4	$225.00	1	1	$ 2,025.00
Nashville--Knoxville Women Bball	5	4	$225.00	1	1	$ 2,025.00
Nashville--Knoxville Women Bball	5	4	$225.00	1	1	$ 2,025.00
Nashville--Knoxville Women Bball	5	4	$225.00	2	1	$ 4,050.00
						$ 14,175.00
Feb. Total	45	36				$ 26,325.00
Men Bball SEC Tournament	9	30	$200.00	2	1	$ 15,600.00
Women Bball SEC Tournament	9	30	$200.00	2	1	$ 15,600.00
NCAA Tournament	3	30	$200.00	2	1	$ 13,200.00
	21	90				$ 44,400.00

AUTHOR NOTE

Here we removed the short biographies of each person for privacy reasons. A brief listing of the management team is quite sufficient for most plans. In some cases, though, entire resumes are attached to the end of a plan. Since the backgrounds of the entrepreneurs here is not a key competitive advantage, they have not highlighted their experience. Clearly, if these individuals had 25 years of experience in the industry or some special connection to the University of Tennessee Alumni Association, their backgrounds would be stressed to a much greater degree and much earlier.

Financial Projections—Additional Income

In the first two quarters of the fiscal year, GameDay Bus will be devoted to many different possible events and trips. While five of these six months are during the off-season for targeted sports, they are prime traveling months. The time will be spent taking reservations for any trips that are requested, while maintaining service to the University of Tennessee, and its alumni group functions. Below is a list of possible business opportunities for the respective months:

- Conventions/Seminars and Trade Shows
- Alumni Group Parties and Promotional Events
- UT Promotional Events
- Family Reunions and Outings
- Concerts
- Fraternity and Sorority Events
- Casino Trips
- Corporate Outings
- UT Orientations

- UT Community Service Events
- UT Summer Recruitment/Road Show
- Executive Travel
- Any Event Where GameDay Bus Is Needed
- NASCAR at Bristol Motor Speedway

Financial Projections—General Assumptions

- Liquor sales are not included in the cash flow statement and are determined on a per trip basis, depending on how much alcohol the group orders. We will charge a 10% mark-up rate for each order.
- We applied an 8% payroll tax to salaries.
- SEC championship games for football are not accounted for in the cash flow statement. There will be a price mark-up which will be determined based on factors such as how big and how important the game is, who they are playing, etc.
- We assume that the men and women basketball teams play a total of 6 out of 12 possible games in the SEC tournament.
- We are assuming Tennessee makes it to a bowl game.
- GameDay pricing on the competitive map is based on football season rates.
- We plan to fill the buses during various alumni events during the summer. Tennessee currently has five major events dated. We assume we can fill all four buses for each event because of their high importance. This is accounted for in the cash flow statement. We assume there will be other events we can cater to, whether through alumni associations or directly through the University of Tennessee. We did not account for these profits on the cash flow because estimating how many events we will book and how big each will be is difficult at this point, but we will stay in close contact with the school and alumni groups and work on making reservations. We are confident our summer sales will be higher.
- Gas costs were based on assuming the price is $2.60 per gallon for diesel fuel.
- We assume there will be no significant economic recessions within the next five years.
- We are aware of laws in Tennessee, Georgia, and Florida pertaining to continuous operation for a commercial driver and will assure that all itineraries are planned accordingly.

AUTHOR NOTE

The students have chosen to not focus on the risks present in their plan, which is acceptable. There is actually considerable debate whether such risks should be presented in a business plan. This is a topic about which individuals have different but equally strong opinions. Some individuals like to state such risks within their plans; others prefer not to state them but will discuss them with you in person.

AUTHOR NOTE

Normally charts such as this with extensive detail should be placed as appendixes at the end of the plan. Focus on discussing the implications of such information in the plan itself and leave the detail for the end of the plan. The impact on the reader is the most important criteria.

Cash Flow Assumptions

- Sales tax for each state and surrounding municipality is 7%, applicable to the rental price.

- Income will be consistent throughout all of the centers in the different states. This is because we have hand-picked each university and taken great effort to make sure that they are all similar in population, athletic activity, demographic make-up, and geographic locations.

- Maintenance overhaul will occur in the 1st quarter for each bus at a cost of $1,000.00 per bus.

- All acquisitions and expansions will be financed internally; there will be no need for 2nd and 3rd round financing.

- Salaries are set at $30,000 for each officer, with an increase to $35,000 in year 3.

- Insurance is a once a year payment, including $10,000 for base coverage with each additional bus adding $1,000 plus tax, stamping and processing fees.

- Waste removal is billed by volume plus service fees, estimating $75–$100 per visit.

- Credit card charges account for 30% of all sales with a processing fee of 2.1%.

- Transportation costs are associated with moving buses within the state to either their home station or to meet customers.

- Accounting/Legal will occur periodically throughout the year, with a concentration of accounting fees during tax season and legal fees during periods of expansion/acquisition.

- Fees/Permits include registration costs, inspection fees, and other associated costs with each bus. Also, to provide CDL licenses and training to officers at the inception of the company.

activity ratios Ratios that measure the efficiency with which you are handling the resources of the business.

ADA Americans with Disabilities Act.

agency theory A managerial theory that argues that individuals act to maximize their own benefit. Thus, in settings where there is a split between ownership and control (most publicly traded corporations), the agents (managers) must be monitored, or they will act to maximize their own benefit, not necessarily that of those who own the firm (the shareholders).

anchor stores Major retail stores, such as department stores in a mall. They serve as the anchor for the retail establishment.

asset-based lending A loan provided for the purchase of a necessary asset for the business.

asset lease A form of lease tied to a particular asset used by a business to conserve cash and maintain the latest versions of whatever equipment is available.

asset valuation A method of business valuation that simply totals all of the hard assets of the organization and adds in a goodwill value.

balance sheet Summary of the assets and liabilities of the small business.

benchmarking Working with and learning from a company outside of your industry that has a particular skill that is potentially critical to your operation.

board of advisors Individuals outside the small business that advise the firm; formed at the discretion of the founders (regardless of the legal form chosen).

bonus A reward offered to the employees based on their performance; similar to profit sharing. Typically, bonus systems are not as well defined as profit sharing; instead, the level of reward is left more to the discretion of the small business owner.

bootstrap marketing Marketing efforts that require little capital.

bounded rationality Rational decision making that is constrained by the background and history of the person making the decision.

brainstorming A creative process whereby a group of individuals are brought together and asked to generate ideas with little or no effort made to evaluate the potential for each idea.

breakeven The point where revenue equals expenses.

break-even analysis Tool for the analysis of when the firm will reach breakeven.

break-even point The level where revenue coming into the firm is sufficient to cover expenses. When starting a business, it will take time for the business to reach this level.

budget Projection of all the costs that will be incurred by the organization over, say, the next year, and allocation of that expense evenly over the relevant time period.

business angels High-net-worth individuals that invest in businesses; a business angel does so not as a business, but as an individual.

business brokers Businesses that specialize in selling businesses.

cash flow Actual cash that flows into the firm minus cash that goes out of the firm.

capabilities Resources which combine to allow the firm to do things better than its competitors.

capitalization of earnings valuation A method of valuation achieved by taking the earnings (net profit) of the organization, subtracting out or adding back to it any unusual items that the lender or investor feels are not customary, normal, or usual items, and dividing that figure by a capitalization rate.

commission Some percentage of sales, paid by the small business owner and typically associated with the compensation of sales representatives.

competitive advantage Those things that your business does better than anyone else in your industry.

competitive map An organizational tool used to organize information about direct competitors on all points of competition.

contract An agreement between two parties to perform certain activities for some consideration.

contract sales force Independent salespeople with a wide variety of experiences and contacts, provided by companies on a contract basis.

copyright Ownership of creative materials the copyright holder has generated, such as books, magazines, advertising copy, music, artwork, or virtually any other creative product, whether published or unpublished.

cost-plus pricing The price of a product or service, obtained by the small business person's initial determination of the cost structure, followed by the owner's determination of the desired profit margin, and finally, the addition of that profit to the cost.

critical path chart Chart that demonstrates how the activities necessary to start the firm fit together and build on each other. This chart allows you to understand which activities can occur concurrently and which must already be in place before the next activity can occur.

credit card Card entitling the owner to use of revolving credit that is not tied to any particular asset, does not have a set repayment schedule, and is usually tied to a much higher relative interest rate.

current assets Assets such as cash or those assets that can easily be converted to Cash, such as accounts receivable and notes receivable.

current liabilities Liabilities or debts that the small business has to pay within one year. These include accounts payable, notes payable (such as bank notes), and accrued payroll.

debt A generic term to describe any type of non-equity funding tied to the business.

deviation analysis Analysis of the differences between the predicted and the actual performance.

discrimination Hiring, dismissal, level of pay, or promotions based on the basis of race, color, gender, religious beliefs, or national origin of the employee. Such actions are prohibited by federal and state laws.

draw A distribution of funds from the business. It is usually in the form of a cash dispersion in advance of salary, a bonus, an expected year-end distribution, etc.

economic rent Financial gains garnered from an asset or capability that are in excess of the ordinary returns in that particular industry.

economies of scale A condition that allows the long-run average cost to continue downward as production increases. It leads (in its most extreme case) to a condition where a single firm producing 100 percent of the production is the most efficient. In reality this condition is moderated by the ability of management to control the size.

Elasticity of demand Consumers' response to price changes. For example, as the price of luxury items increase the demand usually declines as these goods are not essential and their purchase can be delayed. This would be called elastic demand. However, items such as cancer drugs typically have inelastic demand as you will not stop using them as price increases.

equity Investment in the small business by the owners of the firm.

equity investment Funds received by the business in exchange for a percentage ownership of the business.

equity theory The theory that we all judge how we are treated relative to how we see others being treated.

exit barrier Barriers, such as investment in capital assets, that keep a firm from leaving that industry.

factoring The practice of selling Accounts Receivable at a discount to another company in order to receive immediate cash.

Fair Labor Standards Act (FSLA) The act that established a minimum wage for workers.

first mover advantage The phenomenon whereby the first firm to a market obtains the loyalty of the customers.

fixed assets Assets that have a physical presence; they include land, buildings, office equipment, machinery, and vehicles.

fixed costs Costs that must be paid no matter how many goods are sold, such as rent for the building.

float The difference between when the money goes out and when it comes in. For example, if you deposit a check today in payment for some good, typically you do not receive cash when you deposit it. Instead, there is a period of float before it is credited to your account.

followers: Firms that enter a market after the first mover.

Fortune 500 The list published annually by *Fortune* magazine listing the 500 largest corporations (by sales) in the United States. franchise agreement The basic contract generated by the franchisor for all franchisees; it usually contains clauses requiring the purchase of supplies, the displaying of marketing material, and the payment of fees that are based upon the sales of the branch operation.

fragmented markets Markets in which no one competitor has a substantial share of the market and the means of competition varies widely within the same market space.

franchisee The entrepreneur that buys the franchise from the franchisor.

franchisor The firm that originates the idea for the business and develops the operational methods, all of which are then sold to franchisees.

gap analysis A relatively simple process of systematically examining the difference between what was expected and what occurred. Thus, there is an examination as part of opportunity analysis of opportunities in the marketplace and the individual firm's ability to address those gaps with its accumulated skills, history, etc.

general partner In an LLP, the individual considered the manager of the firm, who, as such, has unlimited liability for any debts or judgments against the firm.

grants Special funds, neither equity or debt, designed to aid businesses in specific areas.

harvest plan A plan to exit the small business. Typically means the idea to sell the business to another firm or take it to an IPO.

hourly wage The amount paid per hour for work performed.

human resources Defined in economics as the quantity and quality of human effort directed toward producing goods and services.

hybrid compensation system A system employed by a small business where there is a salary along with the commission.

income statement Revenue of the firm minus expenses.

incubator Facilities that house new businesses, providing many critical services for these new businesses.

independent representatives Representative for a variety of products for a number of companies in that given domain who tries to sell those products.

industry Those direct competitors selling similar products/services within a specified geographic radius that is consistent with a customer's willingness to travel to purchase the product/service.

initial public offering (IPO) The initial listing of a firm as a public entity in the public equities market.

intangible assets Resources and capabilities in a business that are not physical but are just as critical to success, such as relationships with a key supplier.

job description Description of the duties involved in a job that is to be filled.

legitimacy The acknowledgment by key stakeholders, such as customers and suppliers, that you are a genuine business that will still be in operation next year.

leverage ratios Financial calculations used to examine the relative level of indebtedness of the small business.

liquidity ratios Financial calculations that measure the short-term ability of the firm to meet its obligations.

LLC A limited liability corporation.

LLP A limited liability partnership.

loan A contractual agreement whereby the firm receives some amount of money that must be repaid over a specified period of time at a specified interest rate.

long-term liabilities Liabilities that are owed by the business and are ultimately due more than a year from the current date. These include mortgages payable; owners' equity; and stockholders' equity, which is the investment by these individuals in the business.

loss leader A product sold by a business at a non-operating loss (that is, the price accounts for only the actual cost of the product) to simply get customers in the store.

market estimation A method of business valuation that involves taking the earnings of the small business and multiplying that figure by the market premium of companies in its industry.

marketing plan The plan developed by the small business to specify who the customers are and how they will be attracted to the company.

metric A measure to evaluate whether a person or firm is meeting its goals.

mission statement A brief statement that summarizes how and where the firm will compete.

mixed-model promotions Promotions that have a cost but also have an element of community support.

organizational slack Excess resources in an organization; typically found in large organizations rather than small businesses.

orthodox Term describing those areas of your business that are simply standard practice in the industry and area, and are necessary for you to be a player.

OSHA The Occupational Safety and Health Administration, which is charged with protecting the health of workers.

partnership A category of business formation that includes both general and limited types.

patent A claim of intellectual property that covers a specific innovation.

performance review A review by the small business owner of an employee's goals and the outcomes on those goals over some given time period.

perquisites Benefits paid for by the company. Examples include vacations, vehicles, loans, gifts, and financial contributions to retirement plans.

price/earnings (P/E) ratio A value derived from public companies that divides the current earnings per share into the price per share.

pricing floor The break-even point, or the lowest amount that can be charged.

profit and loss statement (P&L statement) A financial statement that summarizes the revenues, costs, and expenses incurred during a specific period of time.

profit sharing A firm's offer to share a percentage of the profits at the end of the year or some other period of time with the employees. This is used, for example, in a hybrid system, in which the firm may set some relatively low level for salary.

profitability ratios Financial calculations that evaluate the performance of the firm and its ability to make economic rents over and above its costs. promotion The means by which a small business advances its product or service.

pro forma Method by which a business owner estimates what the balance sheets and income statements will look like at some point in the future.

production chart A chart that provides a detailed understanding of a firm's production process.

pure promotions Promotions that are strictly a financial arrangement in which you pay for some output, such as a radio advertisement.

ratio analysis A series of ratios along four areas of company performance (liquidity, activity, leverage, profitability) that provides a picture of the health of the company.

resource-based analysis A methodology and theoretical approach that examines the functioning of the business in terms of whether a product/service simultaneously meets the criteria of being rare, durable, non-substitutable and valuable.

salary A set amount of compensation for a given time period.

sales management The method, means, and individuals that produce the relationship with the customer.

sensitivity analysis An examination of the best- and worst-case cash flow scenarios.

shrinkage The difference between what is sold and what was brought into the business.

Small Business Assistant Centers Centers funded by the Small Business Administration that advise individuals wishing to start new businesses.

sole proprietorship The simplest form of business organization, characterized by the fact that the person who owns the business and the business itself are treated as the same entity.

stakeholders Individuals or other organizations that impact the success of the business.

strategic alliances Firms joined together to form long-term, mutually complementary relationships.

strategy The broad approaches the small business will use to accomplish its mission.

strip shopping center A small retail center located typically along a major road. The center has only small businesses, and the center itself occupies only a small strip of land along the major street.

Subchapter C Corporation An organizational form that treats the firm as a unique entity responsible for its own taxes. There are no limitations to shareholder participation and the "owners" are protected beyond their equity investment.

Subchapter S Corporation An organizational form that treats the firm as an entity separate from the individuals. This allows the owner(s) to treat the income as they would if the firm were a sole proprietorship or a partnership. It has limitations in the number and type of shareholders.

substitute A product that performs a similar function or achieves the same result, but is not a precise imitation.

supplier credit Another form of non-equity funding that is available. Suppliers often will provide credit on both physical assets (refrigerators, molding equipment, etc.) and the actual supplies provided.

sustainable competitive advantage An advantage that others cannot immediately copy.

tangible assets Hard assets, such as equipment or a location.

threats to operational financing Specific threats to the new venture in financing its growth, including high development costs, rapid expansion plans, high inventory needs, and/or an entrepreneurial team with a low asset base.

threats to profit margin The threats created to the success of a new venture related to its ability to establish and maintain a high-margin product or service.

threats to sales generation schemes Threats created to a new venture regarding its opportunity to sell to many customers and to obtain repeat business.

time value of money The calculation of the value of your investment in time and money if you did not do the proposed venture, based on the realization that there are other uses of your investment dollars and your raw time.

trademark Claim of intellectual property that is associated with a specific business. This may be the name of the firm, a symbol representing the firm, or its products.

turnaround The effort to reverse the decline of a business.

unemployment compensation The provision of financial assistance for some period of time to those people who lose their jobs through no fault of their own; every state has a law providing such assistance.

Uniform Franchise Offering Circular (UFOC) The principal governing mechanism of the franchisor/franchisee relationship.

United States Small Business Administration (SBA; http://www.sba.gov) The agency officially organized in 1953 as a part of the Small Business Act of July 30, 1953, to "aid, counsel, assist and protect, insofar as is possible, the interests of small business concerns." It is a wealth of information and assistance at all levels of organizational development and management.

unorthodox Those areas of your business that are unique/unusual when compared to the standard practices of the industry, and that provide the opportunity for you to gain value over and above the ordinary returns in the industry.

variable costs Expenses that vary according to how many goods are sold or produced.

venture capital fund A fund that is organized to make significant equity investments in high-growth new ventures.

virtually free promotions Promotions that have a very limited financial cost but have a time commitment requirement from someone in the firm.

workers' compensation The provision by law of some type of compensation to employees who are disabled or injured while on the job.

Chapter 1

1. http://web.sba.gov/faqs/faqindex.cfm?areaid=24
2. Ibid.
3. CHI Research, "Small Firms and Technology: Acquisitions, Inventor Movements, and Technology Transfer," *Small Business Research Summary*, 2004. www.sba.gov/advo/research/rs233.pdf
4. R. Makaodok, "Interfirm Differences in Scale Economies and the Evolution of Market Share," *Strategic Management Journal* 20 (1999), pp. 935–52.
5. C. E. Bamford, T. J. Dean, and P. P. McDougall, "An Examination of the Impact of Initial Founding Conditions and Decisions upon the Performance of New Bank Start-Ups," *Journal of Business Venturing* 15, no. 3 (2000), pp. 253–77.
6. G. Rodriguez, "7 Methods in Choosing a Business," PowerHomeBiz.com, 2004. www.powerhomebiz.com/vol72/methods.htm
7. M. G. Blackford, *A History of Small Business in America* (New York: Twayne Publishers, 1991).
8. T. J. Stanley and W. D. Danko, *The Millionaire Next Door* (New York: Simon & Schuster, 1998).
9. Z. J. Acs, "Small Firms and Economic Growth," in *Small Business in the Modern Economy*, ed. P. H. Admiral (New York: Blackwell, 1996); A. Zacharakis, P. D. Reynolds, and W. D. Bygrave, "National Entrepreneurship Assessment: United States of America." (paper presented at Kauffman Center for Entrepreneurial Leadership. Kansas City, MO, 1999).
10. A. T. Kearney, "Call to Action for Illinois Small Business as the Future of Our Economy," *The Beacon for Entrepreneurs.* Chicagoland Chamber of Commerce, November 3, 2003. www.chicagolandec.org/TheBeacon
11. E. Watkins, "A Year of Opportunity," *Lodging Hospitality* 64, no. 16 (208), p. 4.
12. General Accounting Office, "Military Base Closures: Overview of Economic Recovery, Property Transfer, and Environmental Cleanup." Statement by Barry H. Homan, Director, Defense Capabilities and Management, 2001. www.gao.gov/new.items/d011054t.pdf
13. C. Smith, "Small Business Is Region's Driving Force," *Tribune-Review*, February 23, 2003. www.pittsburghlive.com/x/tribune-review/specialreports/enterprise2003/s_119101.html
14. I. M. Isidro, "Baby-Cakes.com: Turning a Hobby into Gold," PowerHomeBiz.com, 2004. www.powerhomebiz.com/OnlineSuccess/babycakes.htm
15. P. Engardio, "Commentary: A Way for Africa to Help Itself," *Business Week*, July 21, 2003. www.businessweek.com/magazine/content/03_29/b3842069_mz014.htm
16. www.cdc.gov/nchs/data/nehis/t1B3.pdf

Chapter 2

1. C. B. Schoonhoven and K. M. Eisenhardt, "Speeding Products to Market: Waiting Time to First Product Introduction in New Firms," *Administrative Science Quarterly* 35 (1990), pp. 177–208.
2. F. K. Pil and M. Holweg, "Exploring Scale: The Advantages of Thinking Small," MIT *Sloan Management Review* 44, no.2 (2003), pp. 33–40.
3. J. J. Chrisman, J. H. Chua, and R. A. Litz, "Comparing the Agency Costs of Family and Non-Family Firms: Conceptual Issues and Exploratory Evidence," *Entrepreneurship Theory & Practice* 28 (2004), pp. 335–55.
4. J. E. Grable and R. H. Lytton, "The Development of a Risk Assessment Instrument: A Follow Up Study," *Financial Services Review* 12 (2003), pp. 257–75.
5. C. Penttila, "Risky Business," *Entrepreneur* 36, no. 11 (2008), pp. 17–18.
6. J. Hopkins, "More Moms, Fewer Pops," *USA Today*, October 20, 2003, p. 3b.
7. R. D. Atkinson, "The Impact of the Defense Build-Down on State and Local Economies, *Economic Development Review* 10, no. 4 (Fall 1992), pp. 55–59.
8. H. M. Neck, G. D. Meyer, B. Cohen, and A. C. Corbett, "An Entrepreneurial System View of New Venture Creation," *Journal of Small Business Management* 42 (2004), pp. 190–209.
9. P. D. Hannon and P. Chaplin, "Are Incubators Good for Business? Understanding Incubator Practice—The Challenge for Policy," *Environment & Planning: Government & Policy* 21 (2003), pp. 861–82.
10. K. Jones and R. Tullous, "Behaviors of Pre-Venture Entrepreneurs and Perceptions of Their Financial Needs," *Journal of Small Business Management* 40 (2002), pp. 233–49.
11. H. H. Beam and T. A. Carey, "Could You Succeed in Small Business?" *Business Horizons* 32, no. 5 (1989), pp. 65–70.

Chapter 3

1. M. Maddock and R. Vitn, "Innovating During a Recession," *Business Week Online*, November 5, 2008, p. 13.
2. P. Croce, "Think Brighter," *Fortune Small Business* 15, no.9 (2005), p. 35.
3. K. H. Vesper, *New Venture Strategies*. (Englewood Cliffs, NJ: Prentice-Hall, 1990).
4. P. P. McDougall, J. G. Covin, R. B. Robinson, and L. Herron, "The Effects of Industry Growth and Strategic Breadth on New Venture Performance and Strategy Content," *Strategic Management Journal* 15 (1994), pp. 537–54; E. Romanelli "Environments and Strategies of Organization Start-up: Effects on Early Survival," *Administrative Science Quarterly* 34 (1989), pp. 369–87.
5. A. C. Cooper and F. J. Gimeno-Gascon, "Entrepreneurs, Processes of Founding, and New Firm Performance," in *The State of the Art of Entrepreneurship*, ed. D. L. Sexton and J. D. Kasarda (Boston, MA: PWS Kent, 1992), pp. 301–40; K. M. Eisenhardt and

C. B. Schoonhoven, "Organizational Growth: Linking Founding Team, Strategy, Environment, and Growth among U.S. Semiconductor Ventures, 1978–1988," *Administrative Science Science Quarterly* 35(1990), pp. 504–29.

Chapter 4

1. A. Ardichvili, R. Cardozo, and R. Sourav, "A Theory of Entrepreneurial Opportunity Identification and Development," *Journal of Business Venturing* 18, no.1 (2003), pp. 104–24.
2. F. Delmar, P. Davidson, W. Gartner, "Arriving at the High-Growth Firm," *Journal of Business Venturing* 18, no. 2 (2003), pp. 189–217.
3. http://www.sec.gov/info/edgar/siccodes.htm
4. N. Kumar, "The CEO's Marketing Manifesto," *Marketing Management* 17, no.6 (2008), pp. 24–29.
5. C. Comaford-Lynch, "The Power of Positioning," *Business Week Online*, June 3, 2008, p. 13.
6. G. Dess, "Consensus on Strategy Formulation and Organizational Performance: Competitors in a Fragmented Market," *Strategic Management Journal* 8, no. 3 (1987), pp. 259–79.
7. W. Bogner, H. Thomas, and J. McGee, "A Longitudinal Study of the Competitive Positions and Entry Paths of European Firms in the U.S. Pharmaceutical Market," *Strategic Management Journal* 17, no. 2 (1996), pp. 85–108.
8. M. Peteraf and M. Bergen, "Scanning Dynamic Competitive Landscapes: A Market-Based and Resource-Based Framework," *Strategic Management Journal* 24, no.10 (2003), pp. 1027–42.
9. D. Teece, G. Pisano, and A. Shuen, "Dynamic Capabilities and Strategic Management," *Strategic Management Journal* 18, no. 7 (1997), pp. 509–30.
10. M. Porter, *Competitive Advantage* (New York: Free Press, 1985).
11. J-C. Spender and R. Grant, "Knowledge and the Firm: Overview," *Strategic Management Journal* 17 (196), pp. 5–10.
12. S. A. Alvarez and L. W. Busenitz, "The Entrepreneurship of Resource-Based Theory," *Journal of Management* 27, no.6 (2001), pp. 755–75; J. B. Barney, "Firm Resources and Sustained Competitive Advantage," *Journal of Management* 17, no.1 (1991), pp. 99–120; R. M. Grant, "The Resource-Based Theory of Competitive Advantage: Implications for Strategy Formulation, *California Management Review* 33 (1991), pp. 114–35.; E. T. Penrose, *The theory of the growth of the firm* (New York: John Wiley & Sons, 1959); M. A. Peteraf, "The Cornerstones of Competitive Advantage: A Resource-Based View," *Strategic Management Journal* 14 (1993), pp. 179–91.

Chapter 5

1. http://circuitcity.com
2. K. M. Eisenhardt and D. M Sull, "Strategy as Simple Rules," *Harvard Business Review* (January2001), pp. 107–16.
3. B. Bartkus and M. Glassman, "Do Firms Practice What They Preach? The Relationship Between Mission Statements and Stakeholder Management," *Journal of Business Ethics* 83, no. 2 (2008), pp. 207–16.
4. R. Lussier, "A Nonfinancial Business Success Versus Failure Prediction Model for Your Firms," *Journal of Small Business Management* 33, no. 1 (1995), pp. 8–21.
5. T. Man, T. Lau, K. Chan, "The Competitiveness of Small and Medium Enterprises: A Conceptualization with Focus on Entrepreneurial Competencies," *Journal of Business Venturing* 17, no. 2 (2002), pp. 123–43.
6. T. Powell, "Organizational Alignment as Competitive Advantage," *Strategic Management Journal* 13, no. 2 (1992), pp. 119–35.
7. A. Davis and E. Olson, "Critical Competitive Strategy Issues Every Entrepreneur Should Consider Before Going into Business, *Business Horizons* 51, no. 3 (2008), pp. 211–21.
8. R. McNaughton, P. Osborne, B. Imrie, "Market-Oriented Value Creation in Service Firms," *European Journal of Marketing* 36, no. 9/10 (2002), pp. 990–1013.
9. I. Chaston, B. Badger, T. Mangles, and E. Sadler-Smith, "Relationship Marketing, Knowledge Management Systems and E-Commerce Operations in Small UK Accountancy Practices," *Journal of Marketing Management* 19, no.1/2 (2003), pp. 109–31.
10. R. Hall, "A Framework Linking Intangible Resources and Capabilities to Sustainable Competitive Advantage," *Strategic Management Journal* 14, no. 8 (1993), pp. 607–19.
11. M. Lieberman and D. Montgomery, "First-Mover (Dis)advantages: Retrospective and Link with the Resource-Based View," *Strategic Management Journal* 19, no. 12 (1998), pp. 1111–26.
12. D. Miller, "An Asymmetry-Based View of Advantage: Toward An Attainable Sustainability," *Strategic Management Journal* 24, no. 10 (2003), pp. 961–76.
13. M. Porter, *Competitive Advantage: Creating and Sustaining Superior Performance* (New York, NY: Free Press, 1985).
14. C. Christensen, "The Past and Future of Competitive Advantage," *MIT Sloan Management Review* 42, no. 2 (2001), pp. 105–10.

Chapter 6

1. J. Kelly and J. O'Connor, "Is Profit More Important than Cashflow?" *Management Accounting* 75, no.6 (1997), pp. 28–30.
2. D. Worrell, "Keeping Tabs on Cash Flow," *Entrepreneur* 37, no. 1 (2009), p. 32.
3. C. E. Chastain, S. Cianciolo, and A. Thomas, "Strategies in Cash Flow Management," *Business Horizons* 29, no.3 (1986), pp. 65–74.
4. R. Monk, "Why Small Businesses Fail," *CMA Management* 74, no.6 (2000), pp. 12–14.; L. R. Gaskill and H. E. Van Auken, "A Factor Analytic Study of the Perceived Causes of Small Business Failure," *Journal of Small Business Management* 31, no.4 (1993), pp. 18–32.
5. K. Klein, "How Small Business Owners Can Cope with the Crisis," *Business Week Online*, October 13, 2008, p. 14.
6. R. B. Lorance and R. V. Wendling, "Basic Techniques for Analyzing and Presentation of Cost Risk Analysis," *Cost Engineering* 43, no. 6 (2001), pp. 25–32.
7. J. M. Davis, "Project Feasibility Using Breakeven Point Analysis," *Appraisal Journal* 65, no. 1,(1998), pp. 41–47.
8. R. R. Crabb, "Cash Flow: A Quick and Easy Way to Learn Personal Finance," *Financial Services Review* 8, no. 4 (1999), pp. 269–83.

Chapter 7

1. W. R. Scott, *Institutions and Organizations* (Thousand Oaks, CA: Sage Publications, 1995a).
2. Q. Huang, R. M. Davidson, and J. Gu, "Impact of Personal and Cultural Factors on Knowledge Sharing in China," *Asia Pacific Journal of Management* 25 (2008), pp. 451–71.
3. C. S. Galbraith, "Divorce and the Financial Performance of Small Family Businesses: An Exploratory

Study," *Journal of Small Business Management* 41 (2003), pp. 296–310.

4. R. Lewis, "Why Incorporate a Small Business?" *National Public Accountant*, 39, no.11 (1994), p. 14.

5. L. Hodder, M.L. McAnally, and C. D. Weaver, "The Influence of Tax and Nontax Factors on Bank's Choice of Organizational Form," *Accounting Review* 78 (2003), pp. 297–326.

6. J. Freedman, "Limited Liability: Large Company Theory and Small Firms," *Modern Law Review* 63 (2000), pp. 317–55.

7. N. Upton, E. Teal, and J. Felan, "Strategic and Business Planning Practices of Fast Growth Family Firms," *Journal of Small Business Management* 39, no.1 (2001), pp. 60–74.

Chapter 8

1. A. Gunasekaran, L. Forker, and B. Kobu, "Improving Operations Performance in a Small Company: A Case Study," *International Journal of Operations & Production Management* 20, no. 3/4 (2000), pp. 316–36.

2. F. L. Levy, G. L. Thompson, and J. D. Weist, "The ABCs of the Critical Path Method" *Harvard Business Review* 41, no. 5, pp. 98–109.

3. K. Jensen and G. Pompelli, "Manufacturing Site Location Preference of Small Agribusiness Firms," *Journal of Small Business Management* 40 (2002), pp. 204–19.

4. D. A. Shepard and A. Zacharakis, "A New Venture's Cognitive Legitimacy: An Assessment by Customers," *Journal of Small Business Management* 41 (2003), pp. 148–68.

5. K. E. Papke-Shields, M. K. Malhotra, and V. Grover, "Strategic Manufacturing Planning Systems and Their Linkage to Planning System Success," *Decision Sciences* 33 (2002), pp. 1–30.

6. W. E. Deming, *Out of the Crisis*, (Cambridge, Mass.: Massachusetts Institute of Technology, 1992).

7. K. D. Brouther and G. Nakos, "SME Entry Mode Choice and Performance: A Transaction Cost Perspective," *Entrepreneurship Theory & Practice* 28 (2004), pp. 229–48; J. Liao and W. Gartner, "The Effects of Pre-Venture Plan Timing and Perceived Environmental Uncertainty on the Persistence of Emerging Firms," *Small Business Economics* 27 (2006), pp. 23–40.

8. S. R. Covey, A. R. Merrill, and R. R. Merrill, *First Things First* (New York: Simon & Schuster, 1994).

Chapter 9

1. R. A. Cole, L. G. Goldberg, and L.J. White, "Cookie Cutter vs. Character: The Micro Structure of Small Business Lending by Large and Small Banks," *Journal of Financial & Qualitative Analysis.* 39 (2004), pp. 227–52.

2. N. Wilson and B. Summers, "Trade Credit Terms Offered by Small Firms: Survey Evidence and Empirical Analysis," *Journal of Small Business Finance & Accounting* 29 (2002), pp. 317–52.

3. R. McGrath, "A Real Options Logic for Initiating Technology Positioning Investments," *Academy of Management Review* 22, no. 4 (1997), pp. 974–96.

4. D. De Clercq, V. H. Fried, O. Lehtonen, and H. J. Sapienza, "An Entrepreneur's Guide to the Venture Capital Galaxy," *Academy of Management Perspectives* 20, no.3 (2006), pp. 90–112.

5. Prowse, S. 1998. "Angel investors and the market for angel investments." *Journal of Banking & Finance* 22, pp. 785–83.

Chapter 10

1. J. C. Hayton, "Strategic Human Capital Management in SMEs: An Empirical Study of Entrepreneurial Performance," *Human Resource Management* 42 (203), pp. 375–92.

2. M. Carroll and M. Marchington, "Recruitment in Small Firms," *Employee Relations* 21 (1999), pp. 236–51.

3. R. Carlson, "The Small Firm Exemption and Single Employer Doctrine in Employment Discrimination Law," *St. John's Law Review* 80 (2006), pp. 1197–1273.

4. E. A. War, "Employee Drug Testing: Aalberts and Walker Revisited," *Journal of Small Business Management* 29 (1991), pp. 77–84.

5. S. H. Appelbaum and R. Kamal, "An Analysis of the Utilization and Effectiveness of Non-Financial Incentives in Small Business," *Journal of Management Development* 19 (2000), pp. 733–64.

6. www.bls.gov/news.release/ecec.nr0.htm

7. www.towersperrin.com/tp/showdctmdoc.jsp?url=Master_Brand_2/USA/Press_Releases/2008/20080924/2008_09_24b.htm&country=global

8. S. H. Appelbaum, S. H., & and R. Kamal, "An Analysis of the Utilization and Effectiveness of Non-Financial Incentives in Small Business," *Journal of Management Development* 19 (2000), pp. 733–64.

9. S. W. King and G/T. Solomon, "Issues in Growing a Family Business: A Strategic Human Resources Model," *Journal of Small Business Management* 39 (2001), pp. 3–14.

Chapter 11

1. R. Grewal, R. Mehta, and F. R. Kardes, "The Timing of Repeat Purchases of Consumer Durable Goods," *Journal of Marketing Research* 41(2004), pp. 101–16.

2. M. Gruber, "Research on Marketing in Emerging Firms: Key Issues and Open Questions," *Journal of Technology Management* 26 (2003), pp. 600–21.

3. T. McCollum, "High Tech Marketing Hits the Target," *Nation's Business* 85, no. 6 (1997), pp. 39–42.

4. T. Nagle and R. Holden, *The Strategy and Tactics of Pricing* (New York: Prentice Hall, 1995).

5. J. F. Tanner, "Leveling the Playing Field: Factors Influencing Trade Show Success for Small Firms," *Industrial Marketing Management* 31 (2002), pp. 229–40.

6. J. Gregan-Paxton, J. D. Hibbard, F. F. Brunel, and P. Azar, "So That Is What That Is: Examining the Impact of Analogy on Consumers' Knowledge Development for Really New Products," *Psychology & Marketing* 19 (2002), pp. 533–51.

7. K. Blois and S. Albers, "Sales Force Management," *Oxford Textbook of Marketing* (2000), pp. 292–318. Oxford University Press, Oxford, UK.

8. T. Chitura, S. Mupenhi, T. Dube, and J. Bolongkikit, "Barriers to Electronic Commerce Adoption in Small and Medium Enterprises: A Critical Review," *Journal of Internet Banking & Commerce* 13, no. 2 (2008), pp. 1–13.

9. D. Stokes, "Entrepreneurial Marketing: A Conceptualization from Qualitative Research," *Qualitative Market Research* 3, no. 1 (2000),pp. 47ff.

Chapter 12

1. P. Back, "Explaining Financial Difficulties Based on Previous Payment Behavior, Management Background Variables, and Financial Ratios," *European Accounting Review* 14 (2005), pp. 839–68.

2. W. N. Davidson III and D. Dutia, "Debt, Liquidity, and Profitability Problems in Small Firms," *Entrepreneurship Theory & Practice* 16 (1991), pp. 53–65.

3. C. M. Praag, "Business Survival and Success of Young Small Business Owners," *Small Business Economics* 21 (2003), pp. 1–17.

4. I. C. MacMillan and R. G. McGrath, "Discovering New Points of Differentiation," *Harvard Business Review* (July/August 1997), pp. 154–56

Chapter 13

1. R. Quinn, *Deep Change: Discovering the Leader Within* (San Francisco, CA: Jossey-Bass Publishers, 1996).
2. R. A. Anderson, I. Fox, and D. P. Twomey, *Business Law: Principles, Cases, Legal Environment* (Cincinatti, OH: South-Western Publishing, 1999).

Chapter 14

1. R. P. Dant and P. J. Kaufmann, "Structural and Strategic Dynamics in Franchising," *Journal of Retailing* 79 (2003), pp. 63–76.
2. M. Grunhagen and M. J. Dorsch, "Does the Franchisor Provide Value to the Franchisee? Past, Current, and Future Value Assessments of Two Franchisee Types," *Journal of Small Business Management* 41(2003), pp. 366–85.
3. J. G. Combs and D. J. Ketchen, Jr., "Why Do Firms Use Franchising as an Entrepreneurial Strategy? A Meta Analysis," *Journal of Management* 29 (2003), pp. 443–66.
4. J. E. L. Bercovitz, "The Option to Expand: The Use of Multi-Unit Opportunities to Support Self Enforcing Agreements in Franchise Relationships," *Academy of Management Proceedings* (2002), pp. Y1–Y7.
5. S. B. Kaufman, "Before You Buy, Be Careful," *Nation's Business* 84, no. 3 (1996), pp. 46–48.
6. R. D. Doyle and H. B. Desai, "Turnaround Strategies for Small Firms," *Journal of Small Business Management* 29, no. 3 (1991), pp. 33–43.
7. S. C. Michael, "Determinants of the Rate of Franchising among Nations," *Management International Review* 43 (2003), pp. 267–91.
8. S. R Holmberg and K. B. Morgan, "Franchise Turnover and Failure: New Research and Perspective," *Journal of Business Venturing* 18 (2003), pp. 403–19.

Chapter 1

Opener: © Ryan McVay/Getty Images; p. 3: © David A. Tietz/Editorial Image, LLC; p. 4: © Kevin Fleming/Corbis; p. 8: © Editorial Image, LLC/Alamy; p. 9: © Photodisc/Getty Images; p. 10: Courtesy of Baby Cakes, Inc.; p. 13: © Peter Macdiarmid/Getty; p. 14: © TRBfoto/Getty; p. 16: Courtesy of Everyday Edisons.

Chapter 2

Opener: © Form Advertising/Alamy; p. 19: Courtesy of Shea'la Finch and Jon Buonaccorsi; p. 20: © Digital Vision/Getty Images; p. 23: © Tim Boyle/Newsmakers/Getty; p. 24: © Ralph Crane/Time Life Pictures/Getty; p. 26 (left): © Barbara Penoyar/Getty; p. 26 (right): © Barbara Penoyar/Getty; p. 30: © Emma Lee/Life File/Getty Images; p. 34: © Royalty-Free/Corbis; p. 37: Courtesy of Charles Bamford.

Chapter 3

Opener: © Erica Simone Leeds; p. 41: AP Photo/The Herald, Dan Bates; p. 45: © Royalty-Free/Corbis; p. 46: © Big Cheese Photo/PunchStock; p. 50: © Rick Gomez/Corbis; p. 51 (left): © Randy Duchaine/Alamy; p. 51 (middle): © Getty Images/Digital Vision; p. 51 (right): © BananaStock/PunchStock; p. 55: The McGraw-Hill Companies, Inc./John Flournoy, photographer; p. 57 (left): © Randy Duchaine/Alamy; p. 57 (middle): © Getty Images/Digital Vision; p. 57 (right): © BananaStock/PunchStock; p. 60: Courtesy of Charles Bamford.

Chapter 4

Opener: © Andre Jenny/Alamy; p. 63: © David A. Tietz/Editorial Image, LLC;

p. 65: © Comstock/PunchStock; p. 68: © David R. Frazier Photolibrary, Inc./Alamy; p. 74: © Brand X Pictures/PunchStock; p. 80: Courtesy of Team Trident.

Chapter 5

Opener: © Andreas Karelias/Alamy; p. 83: © Comstock/Jupiter Images; p. 84: AP Photo/Chuck Burton; p. 91: © Ingram Publishing/Fotosearch; p. 93: © Laurent Hamels/Getty Images; p. 96 (left): © David A. Tietz/Editorial Image, LLC; p. 96 (right): © Royalty-Free/Corbis; p. 102: Courtesy of Dan Davis.

Chapter 6

Opener: © Brand X Pictures; p. 105: Courtesy of Graham Thompson; p. 108: © Stockdisc/PunchStock; p. 114: © Nick Koudis/Getty Images; p. 121: © TRBfoto/Getty Images; p. 126: © Comstock Images/Alamy.

Chapter 7

Opener: © Charles Smith/Corbis; p. 129: © D. Hurst/Alamy; p. 133: © BananaStock/Jupiterimages; p. 136: © MBI/Alamy; p. 137: © Royalty-Free/Corbis; p. 141: © Daniel Bosler/Stone/Getty; p. 143: © Stephen Chernin/Getty; p. 149: Courtesy of Shannon Shipp.

Chapter 8

Opener: © Jupiter Images/Brand X/Alamy; p. 153: © Studio 101/Alamy; p. 158: © BananaStock/JupiterImages; p. 160: © Len Holsborg/Alamy; p. 172: Courtesy of Keith Milburn.

Chapter 9

Opener: © Ei Katsumata/Alamy; p. 175: © David A. Tietz/Editorial Image, LLC; p. 180: © Comstock Images; p. 182: AP

Photo/M. Lakshman; p. 188: © Image Club; p. 194: © Don Farrall/Photodisc/Getty.

Chapter 10

Opener: © Comstock Images/Getty Images; p. 197: © Digital Vision/Getty Images; p. 202: © Hisham F. Ibrahim/Getty; p. 205: © Dex Image/Getty; p. 210: © Jamie Grill/Tetra Images/Getty; p. 216: Courtesy of Old Town Autoworks.

Chapter 11

Opener: AP Photo/Edgar R. Schoepal; p. 219: © Digital Vision/PunchStock; p. 222: © MBI/Alamy; p. 234: © Chris stock photography/Alamy; p. 238: Courtesy of Craig McClimint.

Chapter 12

Opener: © Stockbyte/Getty; p. 241: © Callie Lipkin; p. 247: © D. Hurst/Alamy; p. 252 (left): © BananaStock/PunchStock; p. 252 (right): © Inti St. Clair/Digital Vision/Getty; p. 258: AP Photo/Kathy Willens; p. 262: Courtesy of Taylor Cuisine.

Chapter 13

Opener: © Photodisc/Getty; p. 265: © Pixtal/SuperStock; p. 270: © John A. Rizzo/Getty; p. 277: © Brownstock Inc./Alamy; p. 280: © Brand X Pictures/PunchStock; p. 286: Courtesy of Cliff Silverman.

Chapter 14

Opener: © Michael Newman/PhotoEdit; p. 289: © Photodisc/Getty; p. 292: © Jonathan Larsen/Diadem Images/Alamy; p. 298: © Jules Frazier/Getty; p. 301: © Laurent Hamels/Getty; p. 306: Courtesy of Jennie and Gary Garissa.

index

Page numbers followed by n refer to notes.